CW01668776

Essential English Grammar

A self-study reference and practice book for elementary students of English

WITH ANSWERS

Raymond Murphy

SECOND EDITION

CAMBRIDGE
UNIVERSITY PRESS

Published in South Asia by

Cambridge University Press India Pvt. Ltd.
Cambridge House
4381/4, Ansari Road, Daryaganj
New Delhi 110 002
India

© Cambridge University Press

First South Asian Edition 1992
Tenth reprint 1997
Second edition 1998
First Sri Lankan edition 2005
Reprinted 2006, 2007, 2008, 2009, 2010, 2011 (twice), 2012

A catalogue record for this book is available from the British Library

This book is in copyright. Subject to statutory exception and to the provisions of relevant collective licensing agreements, no reproduction of any part may take place without the written permission from the publisher in advance.

Special reprint for Sri Lanka only, not to be sold elsewhere.

ISBN-13 978-81-7596-309-2 (Paperback)

(This book was previously published as "Essential Grammar in Use")

This edition of *"Raymond Murphy : Essential English Grammar"*, is published by arrangement with Cambridge University Press, The Edinburgh Building, Shaftesbury Road, Cambridge CB2 2RU, UK.

Published by Manas Saikia for Cambridge University Press India Pvt. Ltd. and printed and bound at Chennai Micro Print (P) Ltd., Export Division, 100% EOU, 130, Nelson Manickam Road, Aminjikarai, Chennai - 600 029 (India)

Contents

To the student (working without a teacher)

This is a grammar book for elementary students of English. There are 114 units in the book and each unit is about a different point of English grammar. There is a list of units at the beginning of the book *(Contents)*.

Do not study all the units in order from beginning to end. It is better to choose the units that you *need* to do. For example, if you have a problem with the present perfect (*I have been, he has done* etc.), use the *Index* (at the back of the book) to find the unit (or units) you need to study (Units 15–20 for the present perfect).

Each unit is two pages. The information is on the left-hand page and the exercises are on the right:

Information (left)

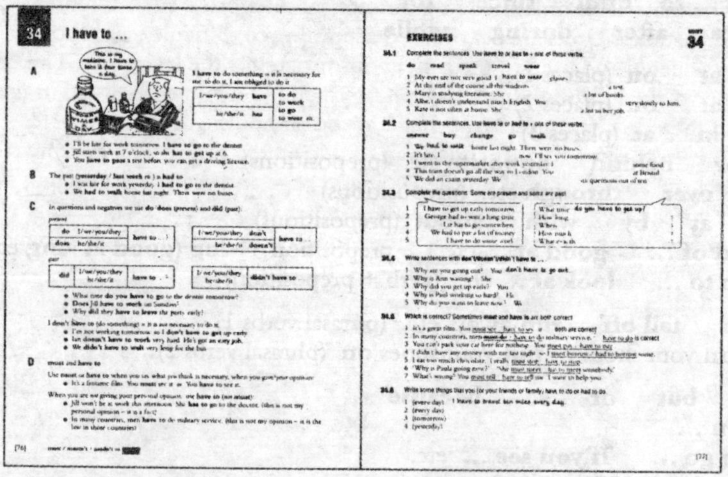
34 I have to ...

EXERCISES 34

Exercises (right)

You can use the book in this way:

1 Look in the *Contents* and/or *Index* to find the unit that you need.
2 Study the left-hand page (information).
3 Do the exercises on the right-hand page.
4 Use the *Key* to check your answers.
5 Study the left-hand page again if necessary.

Don't forget the seven *Appendices* at the back of the book (pages 239–247). These will give you information about active and passive forms, irregular verbs, short forms, spelling and phrasal verbs.

There are also *Additional exercises* at the back of the book (pages 248–264). There is a list of these exercises on page 248.

To the teacher

The most important features of this book are:

- It is a grammar book. It deals only with grammar and is not a general course book.
- It is a book for elementary learners. It does not cover areas of grammar which are not normally taught at elementary level.
- It combines reference and exercises in one volume.
- It can be used for self-study or as supplementary course material.

Organisation of the book

There are 114 units in the book, each one focusing on a particular area of grammar. The material is organised in grammatical categories, such as tenses, questions and articles. Units are *not* ordered according to difficulty, and should therefore be selected and used in the order appropriate for the learner(s). The book should *not* be worked through from beginning to end. The units are listed in the *Contents* and there is a comprehensive *Index* at the end of the book.

Each unit has the same format consisting of two facing pages. The grammar point is presented and explained on the left-hand page and the corresponding exercises are on the right. There are seven *Appendices* (pages 239–247) dealing with active and passive forms, irregular verbs, short forms (contractions), spelling and phrasal verbs. It might be useful for teachers to draw students' attention to these.

This new edition of ***Essential English Grammar*** also contains a set of *Additional exercises* (pages 248–264). These exercises provide 'mixed' practice bringing together grammar points from a number of different units (mainly those concerning verb forms). There are 33 exercises in this section and there is a full list on page 248.

Finally, there is a *Key* at the back of the book (pages 265–295) for students to check their answers. An edition without the Key is also available for teachers who would prefer their students to use this.

Level

The book is for elementary learners, i.e. learners with very little English, but I would not expect it to be used from the first day of a course for complete beginners. It is intended mainly for elementary students who are beyond the very earliest stages of a beginners' course. It could also be used by lower intermediate learners whose grammar is weaker than other aspects of their English or who have problems with particular areas of 'elementary' grammar.

The explanations are addressed to the elementary learner and are therefore as simple and as short as possible. The vocabulary used in the examples and exercises has also been restricted so that the book can be used at this level.

Using the book

The book can be used by students working alone (see *To the student*) or as supplementary course material. In either case the book can serve as an elementary grammar book.

When used as course material, the book can be used for immediate consolidation or for later revision or remedial work. It might be used by the whole class or by individual students needing extra help and practice.

In some cases it may be desirable to use the left-hand pages (presentation and explanation) in class, but it should be noted that these have been written for individual study and reference. In most cases, it would probably be better for the teacher to present the grammar point in his/her preferred way with the exercises being done for homework. The left-hand page is then available for later reference by the student.

Some teachers may prefer to keep the book for revision and remedial work. In this case, individual students or groups of students can be directed to the appropriate units for self-study and practice.

Changes from the first edition

The main changes from the first edition are:

- There are six new units:
  - Unit 16 present perfect + *just/already/yet*
  - Unit 22 passive (*is being done / has been done*)
  - Unit 25 *I used to* ...
  - Unit 56 *do* and *make*
  - Unit 57 *have*
  - Unit 112 *if I had* ... / *if we went*... etc.

  There is also a new appendix on active and passive forms *(Appendix 1)*.
- Some of the material has been revised and reorganised. For example, the content of Units 99-100 *(in/at/on)* in the new edition corresponds to Unit 94 and part of Unit 96 in the old edition.
- Some units have been redesigned, for example Unit 41 (originally 39) and Unit 54 (originally 52).
- Some of the units have been reordered and (after Unit 8) nearly all units have a different number from the original edition. A few units have been moved to different parts of the book. For example, Unit 50 (*work/working* etc.) was originally Unit 34.
- Many of the left-hand pages have been rewritten and many of the examples changed. In a few cases there are significant changes to the content, for example Unit 51 (originally 47), Unit 73 (originally 68) and Unit 82 (originally 77).
- Many of the original exercises have been modified or completely replaced with new exercises (for example, Units 4 and 5).
- There is a new section of *Additional exercises* at the back of the book (see *Organisation of the book* above).

Thanks

For their help in producing this new edition of ***Essential English Grammar***, I would like to thank Jeanne McCarten, Nóirín Burke, Liz Driscoll, Chris Hamilton-Emery, Geraldine Mark, Jane Walsh, Pam Murphy, Ruth Carim and Lelio Pallini.

Drawings by Richard Deverell, Richard Eckford, Sue Hillwood-Harris and Amanda MacPhail.
Book design by Peter Ducker MSTD.

UNIT 1

am/is/are

A

B

positive

I	**am**	(I'**m**)
he / she / it	**is**	(he'**s**) (she'**s**) (it'**s**)
we / you / they	**are**	(we'**re**) (you'**re**) (they'**re**)

negative

I	**am not**	(I'**m not**)		
he	**is not**	(he'**s not**	*or*	he **isn't**)
she	**is not**	(she'**s not**	*or*	she **isn't**)
it	**is not**	(it'**s not**	*or*	it **isn't**)
we	**are not**	(we'**re not**	*or*	we **aren't**)
you	**are not**	(you'**re not**	*or*	you **aren't**)
they	**are not**	(they'**re not**	*or*	they **aren't**)

- **I'm** cold. Can you close the window, please?
- **I'm** 32 years old. My sister **is** 29.
- My brother **is** very tall. He'**s** a policeman.
- John **is** afraid of dogs.
- It's ten o'clock. You'**re** late again.
- Ann and I **are** good friends.
- Your keys **are** on the table.

- **I'm** tired but **I'm not** hungry.
- Tom **isn't** interested in politics. He'**s** interested in music.
- Jane **isn't** at home at the moment. She's at work.
- Those people **aren't** English. They'**re** Australian.
- It'**s** sunny today but it **isn't** warm.

C

that'**s** = that **is** there'**s** = there **is** here'**s** = here **is**

- Thank you. That'**s** very kind of you.
- Look! There'**s** Chris.
- 'Here'**s** your key.' 'Thank you.'

am/is/are (questions) ⇒ UNIT 2 **there is/are** ⇒ UNIT 36 **a/an** ⇒ UNIT 64

EXERCISES

1.1 Write the short form (she's / we aren't etc.).

1 she is ...she's...
2 they are ....
3 it is not ....
4 that is ....
5 I am not ....
6 you are not ....

1.2 Put in am, is or are.

1 The weather ...is... nice today.
2 I .... not tired.
3 This bag .... heavy.
4 These bags .... heavy.
5 Look! There .... Carol.
6 My brother and I .... good tennis players.
7 Ann .... at home. Her children .... at school.
8 I .... a taxi driver. My sister .... a nurse.

1.3 Write full sentences. Use is/isn't/are/aren't.

1 (your shoes very dirty) Your shoes are very dirty.
2 (my brother a teacher) My ....
3 (this house not very big) ....
4 (the shops not open today) ....
5 (my keys in my bag) ....
6 (Jenny 18 years old) ....
7 (you not very tall) ....

1.4 Look at Lisa's sentences (Unit 1A). Now write sentences about yourself.

1 (name?) My ....
2 (from?) I ....
3 (age?) I ....
4 (job?) I ....
5 (married?) I ....
6 (favourite colour or colours?) My ....
7 (interested in...?) I ....

1.5 Write sentences for the pictures. Use: **afraid angry cold hot hungry ~~thirsty~~**

1 ...She's thirsty...
2 They ....
3 He ....
4 ....
5 ....
6 ....

1.6 Write true sentences, positive or negative. Use am / am not / is / isn't / are / aren't.

1 (I / interested in politics) I'm interested (OR I'm not interested) in politics.
2 (I / hungry) I ....
3 (it / warm today) It ....
4 (I / afraid of dogs) ....
5 (my hands / cold) ....
6 (Canada / a very big country) ....
7 (diamonds / cheap) ....
8 (I / interested in football) ....
9 (Rome / in Spain) ....

UNIT 2

am/is/are (questions)

A

positive	*question*
I **am**	**am** I?
he / she / it **is**	**is** he? / she? / it?
we / you / they **are**	**are** we? / you? / they

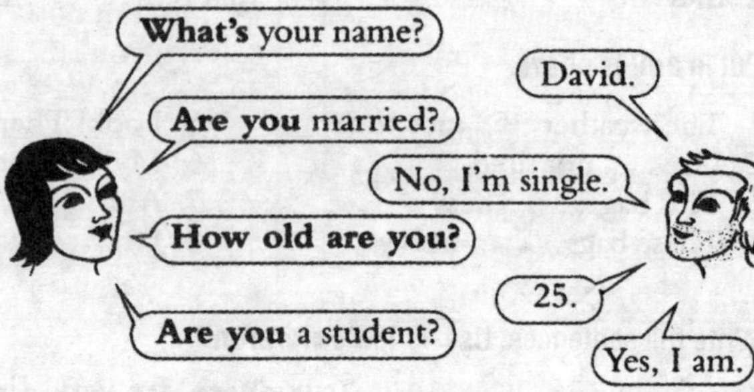

- 'Am I late?' 'No, **you're** on time.'
- '**Is your mother** at home?' 'No, **she's** out.'
- '**Are your parents** at home?' 'No, **they're** out.'
- '**Is it** cold in your room?' 'Yes, a little.'
- **Your shoes are** nice. **Are they** new?

We say:

- **Is she** at home? / **Is your mother** at home? (*not* 'Is at home your mother?')
- **Are they** new? / **Are your shoes** new? (*not* 'Are new your shoes?')

B

Where … ? / What … ? / Who … ? / How … ? / Why … ?

- **Where is** your mother? Is she at home?
- '**What colour is** your car?' 'It's red.'
- **How are** your parents? Are they well?
- '**How much are** these postcards?' 'Fifty pence.'
- '**Where are** you from?' 'Canada.'
- '**How old is** Joe?' 'He's 24.'
- **Why are** you angry?

what'**s** = what **is** who'**s** = who **is** how'**s** = how **is** where'**s** = where **is**

- **What's** the time?
- **Where's** Jill?
- **Who's** that man?
- **How's** your father?

C

short answers

Yes, I **am.**	No, I'm **not.**
Yes, he / she / it **is.**	No, he's / she's / it's **not.** *or* No, he / she / it **isn't.**
Yes, we / you / they **are.**	No, we're / you're / they're **not.** *or* No, we / you / they **aren't.**

- 'Are you tired?' 'Yes, **I am.**'
- 'Are you hungry?' 'No, **I'm not** but I'm thirsty.'
- '**Is your friend** English?' 'Yes, **he is.**'
- 'Are these **your keys?**' 'Yes, **they are.**'
- 'That's my seat. 'No, **it isn't.**'

am/is/are ⇒ UNIT 1 questions ⇒ UNIT 43 what/which/how ⇒ UNIT 46

EXERCISES

2.1 Find the right answers for the questions.

1 Where's the camera?	A London.	1 G
2 Is your car blue?	B No, I'm not.	2 ....
3 Is Linda from London?	C Yes, you are.	3 ....
4 Am I late?	D My sister.	4 ....
5 Where's Ann from?	E Black.	5 ....
6 What colour is your bag?	F No, it's black.	6 ....
7 Are you hungry?	G In your bag.	7 ....
8 How is George?	H No, she's American.	8 ....
9 Who's that woman?	I Very well.	9 ....

2.2 Make questions with these words. Use **is** or **are**.

1 (at home / your mother?) Is your mother at home?
2 (your parents / well?) Are your parents well?
3 (interesting / your job?) ....
4 (the shops / open today?) ....
5 (interested in sport / you?) ....
6 (near here / the post office?) ....
7 (at school / your children?) ....
8 (why / you / late?) ....

2.3 Complete the questions. Use **What... / Who... / Where... / How...**.

1 How are your parents? — They're very well.
2 .... the bus stop? — At the end of the street.
3 .... your children? — Five, six and ten.
4 .... these oranges? — £1.20 a kilo.
5 .... your favourite sport? — Skiing.
6 .... the man in this photograph? — That's my father.
7 .... your new shoes? — Black.

2.4 Write the questions. (Read the answers first.)

PAUL

1 (name?) What's your name? — Paul.
2 (married or single?) .... — I'm married.
3 (American?) .... — No, I'm Australian.
4 (how old?) .... — I'm 30.
5 (a teacher?) .... — No, I'm a lawyer.
6 (wife a lawyer?) .... — No, she's a designer.
7 (from?) .... — She's Italian.
8 (her name?) .... — Anna.
9 (how old?) .... — She's 27.

2.5 Write short answers (**Yes, I am. / No, he isn't.** etc.).

1 Are you married? No, I'm not.
2 Are you thirsty? ....
3 Is it cold today? ....
4 Are your hands cold? ....
5 Is it dark now? ....
6 Are you a teacher? ....

UNIT 3 I am doing (present continuous)

A

She**'s eating**.
She **isn't reading**.

It**'s raining**.
The sun **isn't shining**.

They**'re running**.
They **aren't walking**.

The present continuous is:
am/is/are + doing/eating/running/writ*ing* *etc.*

I	**am**	(not)	**-ing**	I**'m** work**ing**.
he / she / it	**is**	(not)	**-ing**	Chris **is** writ**ing** a letter. She **isn't** eat**ing**. (*or* She**'s not** eat**ing**.) The phone **is** ring**ing**.
we / you / they	**are**	(not)	**-ing**	We**'re** hav**ing** dinner. You**'re not** listen**ing** to me. (*or* You **aren't** ...) The children **are** do**ing** their homework.

B

am/is/are + -ing = something is happening *now:*

I'm working
she**'s** wear**ing** a hat
they**'re** play**ing** football
I**'m not** watch**ing** television

past ———— NOW ———— *future*

- Please be quiet. **I'm working**. (= I'm working now)
- Look at Sue! She**'s wearing** her new hat. (= she is wearing it now)
- The weather is nice at the moment. It**'s not raining**.
- 'Where are the children?' 'They**'re playing** in the park.'
- *(on the phone)* We**'re having** dinner now. Can you phone again later?
- You can turn off the television. **I'm not** watch**ing** it.

Spelling (⇒ Appendix 5):
come → com**ing** write → writ**ing** dance → danc**ing**
run → run**ning** sit → sit**ting** swim → swim**ming**
lie → l**ying**

am/is/are ⇒ UNIT 1 **are you doing?** (questions) ⇒ UNIT 4 **I am doing and I do** ⇒ UNIT 8
What are you doing tomorrow? ⇒ UNIT 26

EXERCISES

3.1 What are these people doing? Use these verbs to complete the sentences:

~~eat~~ **have** **lie** **play** **sit** **wait**

1 *She's eating* an apple.
2 He .... for a bus.
3 They .... football.
4 .... on the floor.
5 .... breakfast.
6 .... on the table.

3.2 Complete the sentences. Use one of these verbs:

build **cook** **go** **have** **stand** **stay** **swim** **~~work~~**

1 Please be quiet. I *'m working*.
2 'Where's John?' 'He's in the kitchen. He ....'
3 'You .... on my foot.' 'Oh, I'm sorry.'
4 Look! Somebody .... in the river.
5 We're here on holiday. We .... at the Central Hotel.
6 'Where's Ann?' 'She .... a shower.'
7 They .... a new theatre in the city centre at the moment.
8 I .... now. Goodbye.

3.3 Look at the picture. Write sentences about Jane. Use **She's -ing** or **She isn't -ing**.

1 (have dinner) *Jane isn't having dinner.*
2 (watch television) *She's watching television.*
3 (sit on the floor) She ....
4 (read a book) ....
5 (play the piano) ....
6 (laugh) ....
7 (wear a hat) ....
8 (write a letter) ....

3.4 What's happening at the moment? Write <u>true</u> sentences.

1 (I / wash / my hair) *I'm not washing my hair.*
2 (it / snow) *It's snowing. OR It isn't snowing.*
3 (I / sit / on a chair) ....
4 (I / eat) ....
5 (it / rain) ....
6 (I / learn / English) ....
7 (I / listen / to music) ....
8 (the sun / shine) ....
9 (I / wear / shoes) ....
10 (I / read / a newspaper) ....

UNIT 4

are you doing? (present continuous questions)

A

positive

I	**am**	do**ing**
he / she / it	**is**	work**ing** / go**ing** / stay**ing**
we / you / they	**are**	*etc.*

question

am	I	do**ing**?
is	he / she / it	work**ing**? / go**ing**? / stay**ing**?
are	we / you / they	*etc.*

- '**Are** you feel**ing** OK?' 'Yes, I'm fine, thank you.'
- '**Is** it rain**ing**?' 'Yes, take an umbrella.'
- Why **are** you wear**ing** a coat? It's not cold.
- 'What**'s** Paul do**ing**?' 'He**'s** read**ing** the newspaper.'
- 'What **are** the children do**ing**?' 'They**'re** watch**ing** television.'
- Look, there's Sally! Where**'s** she go**ing**?
- Who **are** you wait**ing** for? **Are** you wait**ing** for Sue?

B

Study the word order:

	is/are +	*subject* +	**-ing**	
	Is	he	**working** today?	
	Is	Paul	**working** today?	(*not* 'Is working Paul today?')
Where	**are**	they	**going**?	
Where	**are**	those people	**going**?	(*not* 'Where are going those people?')

C

short answers

Yes, I **am.**	No, I'm **not.**
Yes, he / she / it **is.**	No, he**'s** / she**'s** / it**'s** **not.** *or* No, he / she / it **isn't.**
Yes, we / you / they **are.**	No, we**'re** / you**'re** / they**'re** **not.** *or* No, we / you / they **aren't.**

- '**Are** you going now?' 'Yes, **I am.**'
- '**Is** Paul working today?' 'Yes, **he is.**'
- '**Is** it raining?' 'No, **it isn't.**'
- '**Are** your friends staying at a hotel?' 'No, **they aren't**. They're staying with me.'

EXERCISES

4.1 Look at the pictures and write the questions.

4.2 Look at the pictures and complete the questions. Use one of these:

cry eat go laugh look at ~~read~~

4.3 Write questions from these words. Use **is** or **are** and put the words in order.

1 (working / Paul / today?) *Is Paul working today?*
2 (what / doing / the children?) *What are the children doing?*
3 (you / listening / to me?) ....
4 (where / going / your friends?) ....
5 (your parents / television / watching?) ....
6 (what / cooking / Ann?) ....
7 (why / you / looking / at me?) ....
8 (coming / the bus?) ....

4.4 Write short answers (**Yes, I am. / No, he isn't.** etc.)

1 Are you watching TV? *No, I'm not.*
2 Are you wearing a watch? ....
3 Are you eating something? ....
4 Is it raining? ....
5 Are you sitting on the floor? ....
6 Are you feeling well? ....

UNIT 5

I do/work/like etc. (present simple)

A

They're looking at their books.
They **read** a lot.

He's eating an ice-cream.
He **likes** ice-cream.

They **read** / he **likes** / I **work** *etc.* = the *present simple:*

I/we/you/they	**read**	**like**	**work**	**live**	**watch**	**do**	**have**
he/she/it	reads	likes	works	lives	watch**es**	does	has

Remember:
he works / **she** lives / **it** rains *etc.*

- **I work** in a shop. **My brother works** in a bank. (*not* 'My brother work')
- **Linda lives** in London. **Her parents live** in Scotland.
- **It rains** a lot in winter.

I **have** → he/she/it **has**:

- **John has** a shower every day.

Spelling (⇒ Appendix 5):

-es after **-s** / **-sh** / **-ch**:	pass → pass**es**	finish → finish**es**	watch → watch**es**
-y → **-ies**:	study → stud**ies**	try → tr**ies**	
also:	do → do**es**	go → go**es**	

B

We use the present simple for things that are true in general, or for things that happen sometimes or all the time:

- I **like** big cities.
- The shops **open** at 9 o'clock and **close** at 5.30.
- Tim **works** very hard. He **starts** at 7.30 and **finishes** at 8 o'clock in the evening.
- The Earth **goes** round the Sun.
- We **do** a lot of different things in our free time.
- It **costs** a lot of money to stay at luxury hotels.

C

always/never/often/sometimes/usually + present simple

- Sue **always arrives** at work early. (*not* 'Sue arrives always')
- I **usually go** to work by car but sometimes I **walk**. (*not* 'I go usually')
- Julia **never eats** breakfast.
- Tom lives near us. We **often see** him.

I don't ... (negative) ⇒ UNIT 6 **Do you ... ?** (questions) ⇒ UNIT 7 **I am doing** and **I do** ⇒ UNIT 8
always/usually/often etc. (word order) ⇒ UNIT 93

EXERCISES

5.1 Write these verbs + **-s** or **-es**.

1 (read) she reads
2 (think) he ....
3 (fly) it ....
4 (dance) he ....
5 (have) she ....
6 (finish) it ....

5.2 Complete the sentences about the people in the pictures. Use these verbs:

eat go live ~~play~~ play sleep

1 He plays the piano.
2 They .... in a very big house.
3 .... a lot of fruit.
4 .... tennis.
5 .... to the cinema a lot.
6 .... eight hours a night.

5.3 Complete the sentences. Use these verbs:

boil close cost cost like like meet open ~~speak~~ teach wash

1 Margaret speaks four languages.
2 In Britain the banks usually .... at 9.30 in the morning.
3 The City Museum .... at 5 o'clock in the evening.
4 Tina is a teacher. She .... mathematics to young children.
5 My job is very interesting. I .... a lot of people.
6 Peter .... his hair twice a week.
7 Food is expensive. It .... a lot of money.
8 Shoes are expensive. They .... a lot of money.
9 Water .... at 100 degrees Celsius.
10 Julia and I are good friends. I .... her and she .... me.

5.4 Write sentences from these words. Put the verb in the right form (**arrive** or **arrives** etc.).

1 (always / early / Sue / arrive) Sue always arrives early.
2 (basketball / I / play / often) I ....
3 (work / Margaret / hard / usually) ....
4 (Jenny / always / nice clothes / wear) ....
5 (dinner / we / have / always / at 7.30) ....
6 (television / Tim / watch / never) ....
7 (like / chocolate / children / usually) ....
8 (Julia / parties / enjoy / always) ....

5.5 Write sentences about yourself. Use **always/never/often/sometimes/usually**.

1 (watch television) I never watch television. / I usually watch television in the evening. (etc.)
2 (read in bed) I ....
3 (get up before 7 o'clock) ....
4 (go to work/school by bus) ....
5 (drink coffee) ....

UNIT 6

I don't ... (present simple negative)

A

The present simple negative is **don't/doesn't** + *verb:*

She **doesn't drink** coffee.

He **doesn't like** his job.

positive

I we you they	**work like do have**
he she it	**works likes does has**

negative

I we you they	**do not (don't)**	work like do have
he she it	**does not (doesn't)**	

- I **drink** coffee but I **don't drink** tea.
- Sue **drinks tea** but she **doesn't drink** coffee.
- You **don't work** very hard.
- We **don't watch** television very often.
- The weather is usually nice. It **doesn't rain** very often.
- Gerry and Linda **don't know** many people.

B

Remember.

I/we/you/they **don't ...** • **I don't** like football.
he/she/it **doesn't ...** • **He doesn't** like football.

- **I don't** like Fred and **Fred doesn't** like me. (*not* 'Fred don't like')
- **My car doesn't** use much petrol. (*not* 'My car don't use')
- Sometimes he is late but **it doesn't** happen very often.

C

We use **don't/doesn't** + *infinitive* (don't **like** / doesn't **speak** / doesn't **do** *etc.*):

- I **don't like** washing the car. I **don't do** it very often.
- Sandra **speaks** Spanish but she **doesn't speak** Italian. (*not* 'doesn't speaks')
- Bill **doesn't do** his job very well. (*not* 'Bill doesn't his job')
- Paula **doesn't** usually **have** breakfast. (*not* 'doesn't ... has')

I do/work/like etc. (present simple) ⇒ UNIT 5 **Do you ... ?** (present simple questions) ⇒ UNIT 7

EXERCISES

6.1 Write the negative.

1 I play the piano very well. — I don't play the piano very well.
2 Jane plays the piano very well. — Jane ....
3 They know my phone number. — ....
4 We work very hard. — ....
5 He has a bath every day. — ....
6 You do the same thing every day. — ....

6.2 Study the information and write sentences with **like**.

	Bill and Rose	Carol	You
1 classical music?	yes	no	?
2 boxing?	no	yes	?
3 horror films?	yes	no	?

1 Bill and Rose like classical music.
Carol ....
I .... classical music.

2 Bill and Rose ....
Carol ....
I ....

3 ....
....
....

6.3 Write about yourself. Use: **I never ...** or **I often ...** or **I don't ... very often.**

1 (watch TV) — I don't watch TV very often. (OR I never... OR I often ...)
2 (go to the theatre) ....
3 (ride a bicycle) ....
4 (eat in restaurants) ....
5 (travel by train) ....

6.4 Complete the sentences. All of them are negative. Use **don't/doesn't** + one of these verbs:

cost **go** **know** **~~read~~** **see** **use** **wear**

1 I buy a newspaper every day but sometimes I don't read it.
2 Paul has a car but he .... it very often.
3 They like films but they .... to the cinema very often.
4 Amanda is married but she .... a ring.
5 I .... much about politics. I'm not interested in it.
6 It's not an expensive hotel. It .... much to stay there.
7 Brian lives near us but we .... him very often.

6.5 Put the verb into the correct form, positive or negative.

1 Margaret speaks four languages – English, French, German and Spanish. (speak)
2 I don't like my job. It's very boring. (like)
3 'Where's Martin?' 'I'm sorry. I ....' (know)
4 Sue is a very quiet person. She .... very much. (talk)
5 Jim .... a lot of tea. It's his favourite drink. (drink)
6 It's not true! I .... it! (believe)
7 That's a very beautiful picture. I .... it very much. (like)
8 Mark is a vegetarian. He .... meat. (eat)

UNIT 7

Do you ... ? (present simple questions)

A

We use **do/does** in present simple questions:

positive

I we you they	**work** **like** **do** **have**
he she it	works likes does has

question

do	I we you they	**work?** **like?** **do?** **have?**
does	he she it	

B

Study the word order:

do/does + *subject* + *infinitive*

	Do	you	**work**	in the evening?
	Do	your friends	**live**	near here?
	Does	Chris	**play**	tennis?
Where	**do**	your parents	**live?**	
How often	**do**	you	**wash**	your hair?
What	**does**	this word	**mean?**	
How much	**does**	it	**cost**	to fly to Rome?

Questions with **always/usually/often:**

	Do	you	**always**	**have**	breakfast?
	Does	Chris	**often**	**play**	tennis?
What	**do**	you	**usually**	**do**	at weekends?

What do you **do**? = What's your job?:

- '**What do** you **do**?' 'I work in a bank.'

C

Remember:

do I/we/you/they ...
does he/she/it ...

- **Do they** like music?
- **Does he** like music?

D

short answers

Yes,	I/we/you/they	**do.**
	he/she/it	**does.**

No,	I/we/you/they	**don't.**
	he/she/it	**doesn't.**

- '**Do you** play tennis?' 'No, **I don't**.'
- '**Do your parents** speak English?' 'Yes, **they do**.'
- '**Does George** work hard?' 'Yes, **he does**.'
- '**Does your sister** live in London.' 'No, **she doesn't**.'

I do/work/like etc. ⇒ UNIT 5 **I don't** ... (negative) ⇒ UNIT 6 questions ⇒ UNITS 43-46

EXERCISES

7.1 Write questions with **Do ...?** and **Does ...?**

1 I like chocolate. And you? ...Do you like chocolate?...
2 I play tennis. And you? .... you ....
3 Tom plays tennis. And Ann? .... Ann ....
4 You live near here. And your friends? ....
5 You speak English. And your brother? ....
6 I do exercises every morning. And you? ....
7 Sue often goes away. And Paul? ....
8 I want to be famous. And you? ....
9 You work hard. And Linda? ....

7.2 Write questions. Use the words in brackets (...) + **do/does**. Put the words in the right order.

1 (where / live / your parents?) ...Where do your parents live?...
2 (you / early / always / get up?) ...Do you always get up early?...
3 (how often / TV / you / watch?) ....
4 (you / want / what / for dinner?) ....
5 (like / you / football?) ....
6 (your brother / like / football?) ....
7 (what / you / do / in the evenings?) ....
8 (your sister / work / where?) ....
9 (to the cinema / often / you / go?) ....
10 (what / mean / this word?) ....
11 (often / snow / it / here?) ....
12 (go / usually / to bed / what time / you?) ....
13 (how much / to phone New York / it / cost?) ....
14 (you / for breakfast / have / usually / what?) ....

7.3 Complete the questions. Use these verbs:

~~do~~ do enjoy go like start teach work

1 What ...do you do...? — I work in a bookshop.
2 .... it? — It's OK.
3 What time .... in the morning? — At 9 o'clock.
4 .... on Saturdays? — Sometimes.
5 How .... to work? — Usually by bus.
6 And your husband. What ....? — He's a teacher.
7 What ....? — Science.
8 .... his job? — Yes, he loves it.

7.4 Write short answers (**Yes, he does. / No, I don't.** etc.).

1 Do you watch TV a lot? ...No, I don't. OR Yes, I do....
2 Do you live in a big city? ....
3 Do you often ride a bicycle? ....
4 Does it rain a lot where you live? ....
5 Do you play the piano? ....

UNIT 8

I am doing and I do (present continuous and present simple)

A

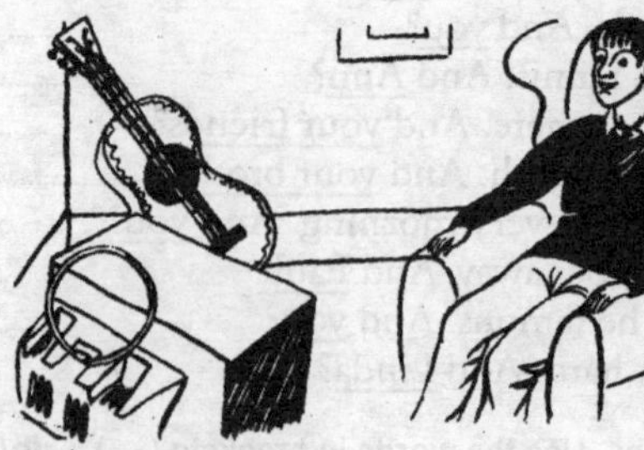

Jim is watching television.
He is *not* playing the guitar.

But Jim has a guitar.
He often plays it and he plays very well.

Jim **plays** the guitar
but he **is not playing** the guitar now.

Is he playing the guitar?	**No, he isn't.**	*(present continuous)*
Does he play the guitar?	**Yes, he does.**	*(present simple)*

B

Present continuous (**I am doing**) – now, at the time of speaking:

I'm doing

past ———— NOW ———— *future*

- Please be quiet. **I'm** work**ing**. (*not* 'I work')
- Tom **is** hav**ing** a shower at the moment. (*not* 'Tom has')
- Take an umbrella with you. **It's** rain**ing**.
- You can turn off the television. **I'm** not watch**ing** it.
- Why are you under the table? What **are** you do**ing**?

C

Present simple (**I do**) – in general, all the time or sometimes:

← **I do** →

past ———— NOW ———— *future*

- **I work** every day from 9 o'clock to 5.30.
- Tom **has** a shower every morning.
- It **rains** a lot in winter.
- **I don't watch** television very often.
- What **do** you usually **do** at the weekend?

D

We do *not* use these verbs in the present continuous (**I am -ing**):

like	**love**	**want**	**know**	**understand**	**remember**	**depend**
prefer	**hate**	**need**	**mean**	**believe**	**forget**	

Use the present simple only with these verbs (**I want / do you like?** etc.):

- I'm tired. I **want** to go home. (*not* 'I'm wanting')
- '**Do** you **know** that girl?' 'Yes, but I **don't remember** her name.'
- **I don't understand.** What **do** you **mean**?

present continuous ⇒ UNITS 3-4 present simple ⇒ UNITS 5-7 present for the future ⇒ UNIT 26

EXERCISES

8.1 Answer the questions about the pictures.

1 Does he take photographs? *Yes, he does.* Is he taking a photograph? *No, he isn't.*
What is he doing? *He's having a bath.*
2 Is she driving a bus? .... Does she drive a bus? ....
What is she doing? ....
3 Does he clean windows? .... Is he cleaning a window? ....
What is he doing? ....
4 Are they teaching? .... Do they teach? ....
What do they do? ....

8.2 Put in **am/is/are** or **do/don't/does/doesn't**.

1 Excuse me, *do* you speak English?
2 'Where's Ann?' 'I .... know.'
3 What's funny? Why .... you laughing?
4 'What .... your sister do?' 'She's a dentist.'
5 It .... raining. I .... want to go out in the rain.
6 'Where .... you come from?' 'Canada.'
7 How much .... it cost to phone Canada?
8 George is a good tennis player but he .... play very often.

8.3 Put the verb in the present continuous (**I am doing**) or the present simple (**I do**).

1 Excuse me. *Do you speak* (you/speak) English?
2 'Where's Tom?' '*He's having* (he/have) a shower.'
3 *I don't watch* (I/not/watch) television very often.
4 Listen! Somebody .... (sing).
5 Sandra is tired. .... (she/want) to go home now.
6 How often .... (you/read) a newspaper?
7 'Excuse me but .... (you/sit) in my place.' 'Oh, I'm sorry.'
8 I'm sorry, ... (I/not/understand). Can you speak more slowly?
9 It's late. .... (I/go) home now. ....
(you/come) with me?
10 What time .... (your father / finish) work in the evenings?
11 You can turn off the radio. .... (I/not/listen) to it.
12 'Where's Paul?' 'In the kitchen. .... (he/cook) something.'
13 Martin .... (not/usually/drive) to work. He
.... (usually/walk).
14 Sue .... (not/like) coffee. .... (she/prefer) tea.

UNIT 9

I have ... / I've got ...

A

You can say **I have** or **I've got**, **he has** or **he's got**:

I we you they	**have**	*OR*	I we you they	**have got**	(**I've got**) (we**'ve got**) (you**'ve got**) (they**'ve got**)
he she it	**has**	*OR*	he she it	**has got**	(he**'s got**) (she**'s got**) (it**'s got**)

- **I've got** blue eyes. (*or* I **have** blue eyes.)
- Tim **has got** two sisters. (*or* Tim **has** two sisters.)
- Our car **has got** four doors.
- Diane isn't feeling well. She**'s got** a headache. (she**'s** got = she **has** got)
- They like animals. **They've got** a horse, three dogs and six cats.

B

I haven't got / **have** you **got**? etc.

negative

I we you they	**have not** **(haven't)**	**got**
he she it	**has not** **(hasn't)**	

question

have	I we you they	**got?**
has	he she it	

short answers

Yes, No,	I we you they	**have.** **haven't.**
Yes, No,	he she it	**has.** **hasn't.**

- **I've got** a motor-bike but I **haven't got** a car.
- Mr and Mrs Harris **haven't got** any children.
- It's a nice house but it **hasn't got** a garden.
- '**Have** you **got** a camera?' 'No, I **haven't**.'
- 'What **have** you **got** in your bag?' 'Nothing. It's empty.'
- '**Has** Ann **got** a car?' 'Yes, she **has**.'
- What kind of car **has** she **got**?

C

I **don't have** / **do** you **have**? *etc.*

In negatives and questions you can also use **do/does** ... :

- They **don't have** any children. (= They **haven't got** any children.)
- It's a nice house but it **doesn't have** a garden. (= it **hasn't got** a garden)
- **Does** Ann **have** a car? (= **Has** Ann **got** a car?)
- How much money **do** you **have**? (= How much money **have** you **got**?)

had / didn't have (past) ⇒ UNITS 11-12 **have breakfast / have a shower** etc. ⇒ UNIT 57
some/any ⇒ UNIT 75

EXERCISES

9.1 Write the short form (**we've got / he hasn't got** etc.).

1 we have got *we've got* ....
3 they have got ....
5 it has got ....
2 he has got ....
4 she has not got ....
6 I have not got ....

9.2 Write questions.

1 (you / an umbrella?) *Have you got an umbrella?*
2 (you / a passport?) ....
3 (your father / a car?) ....
4 (Carol / many friends?) ....
5 (you / any brothers or sisters?) ....
6 (how much money / we?) ....
7 (what / kind of car / Julia?) ....

9.3 What has Tina got? What have you got? Look at the information and write sentences about Tina and yourself.

1 (a camera) *Tina has got a camera. I've got (OR I haven't got) a camera.*
2 (a bicycle) Tina ....
3 (long hair) ....
4 (brothers/sisters) ....
....

9.4 Put in **have got ('ve got)**, **has got ('s got)**, **haven't got** or **hasn't got**.

1 Sarah *hasn't got* a car. She goes everywhere by bicycle.
2 They like animals. They *'ve got* three dogs and two cats.
3 Charles isn't happy. He .... a lot of problems.
4 They don't read much. They .... many books.
5 'What's wrong?' 'I .... something in my eye.'
6 'Where's my pen?' 'I don't know. I .... it.'
7 Julia wants to go to the concert but she .... a ticket.

9.5 Complete the sentences. Use **have/has got** or **haven't/hasn't got** + one of these:

a lot of friends	four wheels	six legs	~~a headache~~	a toothache	a key	much time	~~a garden~~

1 I'm not feeling very well. I *'ve got a headache.*
2 It's a nice house but it *hasn't got a garden.*
3 Most cars ....
4 Everybody likes Tom. He ....
5 I'm going to the dentist this morning. I ....
6 He can't open the door. He ....
7 An insect ....
8 We must hurry. We ....

UNIT 10

was/were

A

Now Robert **is** at work.

At midnight last night he **wasn't** at work.

He **was** in bed.
He **was** asleep.

am/is (present) → **was** (past):

- I **am** tired. (now) — I **was** tired **last night**.
- Where **is** Ann? (now) — Where **was** Ann **yesterday**?
- The weather **is** good today. — The weather **was** good **last week**.

are (present) → **were** (past):

- You **are** late. (now) — You **were** late **yesterday**.
- They **aren't** here. (now) — They **weren't** here **last Sunday**.

B

positive

I he she it	**was**
we you they	**were**

negative

I he she it	**was not** **(wasn't)**
we you they	**were not** **(weren't)**

question

was	I? he? she? it?
were	we? you? they?

- Last year Rachel **was** 22, so she **is** 23 now.
- When I **was** a child, I **was** afraid of dogs.
- We **were** hungry after the journey but we **weren't** tired.
- The hotel **was** comfortable but it **wasn't** expensive.

- **Was** the weather good when you **were** on holiday?
- Those shoes are nice. **Were** they expensive?
- Why **were** you late this morning?

C

short answers

Yes,	I/he/she/it **was.**
	we/you/they **were.**

No,	I/he/she/it **wasn't.**
	we/you/they **weren't.**

- **'Were you** late?' 'No, **I wasn't.**'
- **'Was Ted** at work yesterday?' 'Yes, **he was.**'
- **'Were Sue and Steve** at the party?' 'No, **they weren't.**'

am/is/are ⇒ UNITS 1-2 **I was doing** ⇒ UNIT 13

EXERCISES

10.1 Look at the pictures. Where were these people at 3 o'clock yesterday afternoon?

1 *George was in bed.*
2 Carol and Jack ....
3 Sue ....
4 ....
5 ....
6 And you? I ....

10.2 Put in **am/is/are** (present) or **was/were** (past).

1 Last year she *was* 22, so she *is* 23 now.
2 Today the weather .... nice, but yesterday it .... very cold.
3 I .... hungry. Can I have something to eat?
4 I feel fine this morning but I .... very tired last night.
5 Where .... you at 11 o'clock last Friday morning?
6 Don't buy those shoes. They .... very expensive.
7 I like your new jacket. .... it expensive?
8 This time last year I .... in Paris.
9 'Where .... the children?' 'I don't know. They .... in the garden ten minutes ago.'

10.3 Put in **was/were** or **wasn't/weren't**.

1 We weren't happy with the hotel. Our room *was* very small and it *wasn't* very clean.
2 George .... at work last week because he .... ill. He's better now.
3 Yesterday .... a public holiday so the shops .... closed. They're open today.
4 '.......... Sue and Bill at the party?' 'Sue .... there but Bill ....'
5 'Where are my keys?' 'I don't know. They .... on the table but they're not there now.'
6 You .... at home last night. Where .... you?

10.4 Write the questions. Use the words in brackets (...) in the correct order + **was/were**.

1 (late / you / this morning / why?)
Why were you late this morning? → The traffic was bad.
2 (difficult / your exam?)
.... → No, it was easy.
3 (last week / where / Ann and Chris?)
.... → They were on holiday.
4 (your new camera / how much?)
.... → Sixty pounds.
5 (angry / you / yesterday / why?)
.... → Because you were late.
6 (nice / the weather / last week?)
.... → Yes, it was beautiful.

UNIT
11 worked/got/went etc. (past simple)

A

They **watch** television every evening.
(present simple)

They **watched** television yesterday evening.
(past simple)

watched is the *past simple:*

I/we/you/they he/she/it	watch**ed**

B

The past simple is often **-ed** *(regular verbs)*. For example:

work → work**ed**	clean → clean**ed**	start → start**ed**
stay → stay**ed**	arrive → arriv**ed**	dance → danc**ed**

- I clean my teeth every morning. This morning I clean**ed** my teeth.
- Terry work**ed** in a bank from 1986 to 1993.
- Yesterday it rain**ed** all morning. It stopp**ed** at lunchtime.
- We enjoy**ed** the party last night. We danc**ed** a lot and talk**ed** to a lot of people. The party finish**ed** at midnight.

Spelling (⇒ Appendix 5):
try → **tried** study → **studied** copy → **copied**
stop → sto**pped** plan → **planned**

C

Some verbs are *irregular* (= not regular). The past simple is *not* **-ed**. Here are some important irregular verbs (see also Appendix 2–3):

begin →	**began**	fall →	**fell**	leave →	**left**	sell →	**sold**
break	**broke**	find	**found**	lose	**lost**	sit	**sat**
bring	**brought**	fly	**flew**	make	**made**	sleep	**slept**
build	**built**	forget	**forgot**	meet	**met**	speak	**spoke**
buy	**bought**	get	**got**	pay	**paid**	stand	**stood**
catch	**caught**	give	**gave**	put	**put**	take	**took**
come	**came**	go	**went**	read	**read** /red/*	tell	**told**
do	**did**	have	**had**	ring	**rang**	think	**thought**
drink	**drank**	hear	**heard**	say	**said**	win	**won**
eat	**ate**	know	**knew**	see	**saw**	write	**wrote**

* *pronunciation*

- I usually get up early but this morning I **got** up at 9.30.
- We **did** a lot of work yesterday.
- Caroline **went** to the cinema three times last week.
- Jim **came** into the room, **took** off his coat and **sat** down.

was/were ⇒ UNIT 10 **I didn't** … / **Did you** … ? (negative and questions) ⇒ UNIT 12 **ago** ⇒ UNIT 19

EXERCISES

11.1 Complete the sentences. Use one of these verbs in the past simple:

~~clean~~ die enjoy finish happen open rain start stay want

1 I cleaned my teeth three times yesterday.
2 It was hot in the room, so I .... the window.
3 The concert .... at 7.30 and .... at 10 o'clock.
4 When I was a child, I .... to be a doctor.
5 The accident .... last Sunday afternoon.
6 It's a nice day today but yesterday it .... all day.
7 We .... our holiday last year. We .... at a very nice place.
8 Ann's grandfather .... when he was 90 years old.

11.2 Write the past simple of these verbs.

1 get got	4 pay	7 go	10 know ....
2 see	5 visit	8 think	11 put ....
3 play	6 buy	9 copy	12 speak ....

11.3 Read about Lisa's journey to Madrid. Put the verbs in the correct form.

Last Tuesday Lisa (1) flew from London to Madrid. She (2) .... up	fly, get
at six o'clock in the morning and (3) .... a cup of coffee. At 6.30	have
she (4) .... home and (5) .... to the airport. When she	leave, drive
(6) ...., she (7) .... the car and then (8) .... to the airport	arrive, park, go
café where she (9) .... breakfast. Then she (10) .... through	have, go
passport control and (11) .... for her flight. The plane (12)	wait, depart
on time and (13) .... in Madrid two hours later. Finally she	arrive
(14) .... a taxi from the airport to her hotel in the centre of Madrid.	take

11.4 Write sentences about the past (**yesterday / last week** etc.).

1 Jim always goes to work by car. Yesterday he went to work by car.
2 Rachel often loses her keys. She .... last week.
3 Kate meets her friends every evening. She .... yesterday evening.
4 I usually buy two newspapers every day. Yesterday I ....
5 We usually go to the cinema on Sundays. Last Sunday we ....
6 I eat an orange every day. Yesterday I ....
7 Tom always has a shower in the morning. This morning he ....
8 Our friends come to see us every Friday. They .... last Friday.

11.5 Write sentences about what <u>you</u> did yesterday.

1 I played volleyball yesterday.
2 ....
3 ....
4 ....
5 ....
6 ....

UNIT 12

I didn't ... Did you ... ? (past simple negative and questions)

A

We use **did** in past simple negatives and questions:

infinitive	*positive*		*negative*			*question*		
play	I	play**ed**	I		play		I	play?
start	we	start**ed**	we		start		we	start?
watch	you	watch**ed**	you	**did not**	watch		you	watch?
have	they	**had**	they	**(didn't)**	have	**did**	they	have?
see	he	**saw**	he		see		he	see?
do	she	**did**	she		do		she	do?
go	it	**went**	it		go		it	go?

B

do/does *(present)* → **did** *(past)*:

- I **don't** watch television very often.
- I **didn't** watch television **yesterday**.
- **Does** she often go away?
- **Did** she go away **last week**?

C

We use **did/didn't** + *infinitive* (**watch/play/go** *etc.*):

I watch**ed**	*but*	**I didn't** watch	(*not* 'I didn't watched')
they **went**		**did** they **go**?	(*not* 'did they went?')
he **had**		he **didn't have**	
you **did**		**did** you **do**?	

- I play**ed** tennis yesterday but I **didn't win**.
- '**Did** you **do** the shopping?' 'No, I **didn't have** time.'
- We **went** to the cinema but we **didn't enjoy** the film.

D

Study the word order in questions:

	did +	*subject* +	*infinitive*	
	Did	your sister	**phone**	you?
What	**did**	you	**do**	yesterday evening?
How	**did**	the accident	**happen**?	
Where	**did**	your parents	**go**	for their holiday?

E

short answers

Yes,	I/we/you/they he/she/it	**did.**

No,	I/we/you/they he/she/it	**didn't.**

- '**Did you** see Joe yesterday?' 'No, **I didn't**.'
- '**Did it** rain on Sunday?' 'Yes, **it did**.'
- '**Did Helen** come to the party?' 'No, **she didn't**.'
- '**Did your parents** have a good holiday?' 'Yes, **they did**.'

worked/got/went etc. (past simple) ⇒ UNIT 11

EXERCISES

12.1 Complete these sentences with the verb in the negative.

1 I saw Barbara but I *didn't see* Jane.
2 They worked on Monday but they .... on Tuesday.
3 We went to the post office but we .... to the bank.
4 She had a pen but she .... any paper.
5 Jack did French at school but he .... German.

12.2 Write questions with **Did ...?**

1 I watched TV last night. And you? *Did you watch TV last night?*
2 I enjoyed the party. And you? ....
3 I had a good holiday. And you? ....
4 I finished work early. And you? ....
5 I slept well last night. And you? ....

12.3 What did you do yesterday? Write positive or negative sentences.

1 (watch TV) *I watched TV. OR I didn't watch TV.*
2 (get up before 7 o'clock) I ....
3 (have a shower) ....
4 (buy a magazine) ....
5 (eat meat) ....
6 (go to bed before 10.30) ....

12.4 Write B's questions. Use:

arrive cost go go to bed late happen have a nice time ~~stay~~ win

1 A: We went to New York last month. B: Where *did you stay?* A: With some friends.	5 A: We came home by taxi. B: How much .... ? A: Ten pounds.
2 A: I was late this morning. B: What time .... ? A: Half past nine.	6 A: I'm tired this morning. B: .... ? A: No, but I didn't sleep very well.
3 A: I played tennis this afternoon. B: .... ? A: No, I lost.	7 A: We went to the beach yesterday. B: .... ? A: Yes, it was great.
4 A: I had a nice holiday. B: Good. Where .... ? A: To the mountains.	8 A: The window is broken. B: How .... ? A: I don't know.

12.5 Put the verb in the correct form – positive, negative or question.

1 We went to the cinema but the film wasn't very good. We *didn't enjoy* it. (enjoy)
2 Tim .... some new clothes yesterday – two shirts, a jacket and a pullover. (buy)
3 '.................................... yesterday?' 'No, it was a nice day.' (rain)
4 The party wasn't very good, so we .... long. (stay)
5 It was very warm in the room, so I .... a window. (open)
6 'Did you go to the bank this morning?' 'No, I .... time.' (have)
7 'I cut my hand this morning.' 'How .... that?' (do)

UNIT 13

I was doing (past continuous)

A

It is 6 o'clock now.
Sarah **is** at home.
She **is watching** television.

At 4 o'clock she **wasn't** at home.
She **was** at the sports club.

She **was playing** tennis.
She **wasn't watching** television.

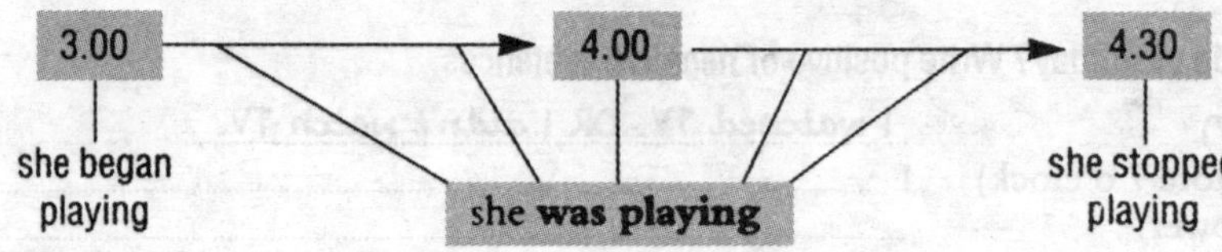

B

was/were + -ing is the *past continuous:*

positive

I he she it	**was**	doing watch**ing** play**ing** runn**ing** liv**ing**
we you they	**were**	*etc.*

negative

I he she it	**was not (wasn't)**	doing watch**ing** play**ing** runn**ing** liv**ing**
we you they	**were not (weren't)**	*etc.*

question

was	I he she it	doing? watch**ing**? play**ing**? runn**ing**? liv**ing**?
were	we you they	*etc.*

- What **were** you **doing** at 11.30 yesterday? **Were** you **working**?
- 'What did he say?' 'I don't know. I **wasn't listening**.'
- It **was raining**, so we didn't go out.
- In 1985 we **were living** in Canada.
- Today she's wearing a skirt, but yesterday she **was wearing** trousers.
- I woke up early yesterday. It was a beautiful morning. The sun **was shining** and the birds **were singing**.

Spelling (live → **living** / run → **running** / lie → **lying** *etc.*) ⇒ Appendix 5:

C

am/is/are + -ing *(present)* → **was/were + -ing** *(past):*

- **I'm** work**ing** (now). — **I was** work**ing** at 10.30 **last night**.
- **It isn't** rain**ing** (now). — **It wasn't** rain**ing** when we went out.
- What **are** you **doing** (now)? — What **were** you **doing** at three o'clock?

was/were ⇒ UNIT 10 **I was doing** and **I did** (past continuous and simple) ⇒ UNIT 14

EXERCISES

13.1 Look at the pictures. Where were these people at 3 o'clock yesterday afternoon? And what were they doing? Write two sentences for each picture.

1 *Ann was at home. She was watching TV.*
2 Carol and Jack .... They ....
3 Tom ....
4 ....
5 ....
6 And you? I ....

13.2 Sarah did a lot of things yesterday morning. Look at the pictures and complete the sentences.

1 At 9.45 *she was washing her car.*
2 At 11.45 she ....
3 At 9 o'clock ....
4 At 12.50 ....
5 At 8.15 ....
6 At 10.30 ....

13.3 Complete the questions. Use **was/were -ing**. Use **what/where/why** if necessary.

1 (you/live) *Where were you living* ... in 1990? — In London.
2 (you/do) .... at 2 o'clock? — I was asleep.
3 (it/rain) .... when you got up? — No, it was sunny.
4 (Ann/drive) .... so fast? — Because she was in a hurry.
5 (Tim/wear) .... a suit yesterday? — No, a T-shirt and jeans.

13.4 Look at the picture. You saw Joe in the street yesterday afternoon. What was he doing? Write positive or negative sentences.

1 (wear / a jacket) *He wasn't wearing a jacket.*
2 (carry / a bag) ....
3 (go / to the dentist) ....
4 (eat / an ice-cream) ....
5 (carry / an umbrella) ....
6 (go / home) ....
7 (wear / a hat) ....
8 (ride / a bicycle) ....

UNIT 14

I was doing (past continuous) and I did (past simple)

A

Jack was reading a book. The phone rang. He stopped reading. He answered the phone.

What **happened**? The phone **rang**. *(past simple)*

What **was** Jack **doing** when the phone rang?
He **was reading** a book. *(past continuous)*

What **did** he **do** when the phone rang?
He **stopped** reading and **answered** the phone. *(past simple)*

Jack began reading *before* the phone rang.
So: **When** the phone rang, he **was reading**.

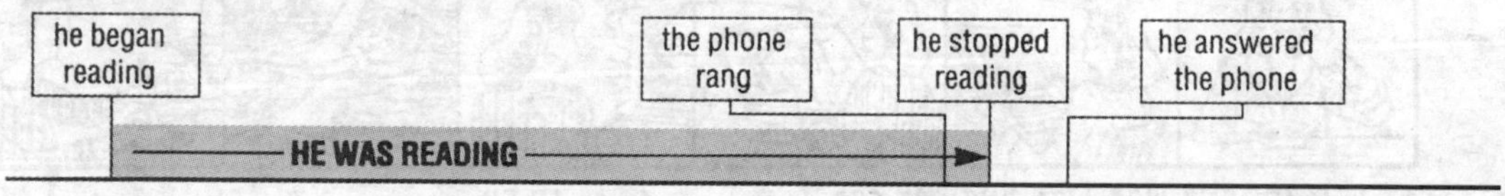

B

past simple

- A: What **did** you **do** yesterday morning?
  B: We **played** tennis. (from 10 to 11.30)

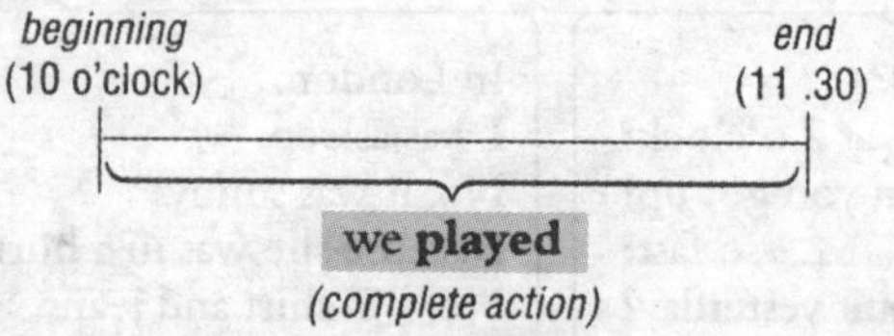

- Jack **read** a book yesterday. (= from beginning to end)
- **Did** you **watch** the film on television last night?
- It **didn't rain** while we were on holiday.

past continuous

- A: What **were** you **doing** at 10.30?
  B: We **were playing** tennis.

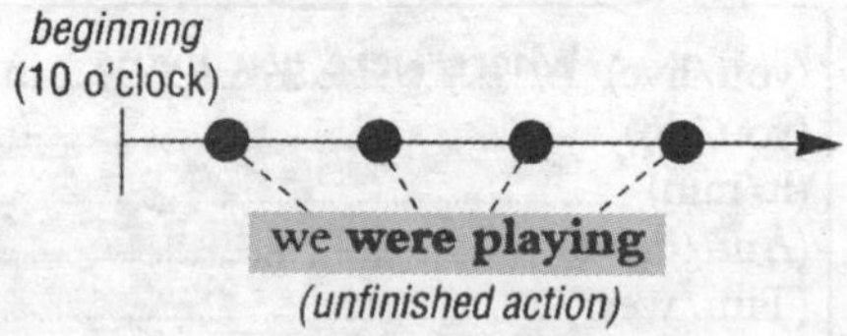

- Jack **was reading** a book when the phone rang.
- **Were** you **watching** television when I phoned you?
- It **wasn't raining** when I got up.

- I **started** work at 9 o'clock and **finished** at 4.30. At 2.30 I **was working**.
- It **was raining** when we **went** out. (= it started raining *before* we went out)
- I **saw** Lucy and Steve this morning They **were waiting** at the bus stop.
- Jenny **fell** asleep while she **was reading**.

I **did** (past simple) ⇒ UNITS 11-12 I **was doing** (past continuous) ⇒ UNIT 13 **while** ⇒ UNIT 98

EXERCISES

14.1 Look at the pictures and put the verbs in the correct form, past continuous or past simple.

1

Carol ....broke.... (break) her arm last week. It .... (happen) when she .... (paint) her room. She .... (fall) off the ladder.

2

The train .... (arrive) at the station and Paula .... (get) off. Two friends of hers, John and Jenny, ... (wait) to meet her.

3

Yesterday Sue .... (walk) along the road when she .... (meet) Jim. He .... (go) to the station to catch a train and he .... (carry) a bag. They .... (stop) to talk for a few minutes.

14.2 Put the verb into the past continuous or past simple.

1 A: What ....were you doing.... (you/do) when the phone ....rang.... (ring)?
B: I ....was watching.... (watch) television.

2 A: Was Jane busy when you went to see her?
B: Yes, she .... (study).

3 A: What time .... (the post / arrive) this morning?
B: It .... (come) while I .... (have) breakfast.

4 A: Was Margaret at work today?
B: No, she .... (not/go) to work. She was ill.

5 A: How fast .... (you/drive) when the police .... (stop) you?
B: I don't know exactly but I .... (not/drive) very fast.

6 A: .... (your team / win) the football match yesterday?
B: No, the weather was very bad, so we .... (not/play).

7 A: How .... (you/break) the window?
B: We .... (play) football. I .... (kick) the ball and it .... (hit) the window.

8 A: .... (you/see) Jenny last night?
B: Yes, she .... (wear) a very nice jacket.

9 A: What .... (you/do) at 2 o'clock this morning?
B: I was asleep.

10 A: I .... (lose) my key last night.
B: How .... (you/get) into your room?
A: I .... (climb) in through a window.

UNIT 15

I have done (present perfect 1)

A

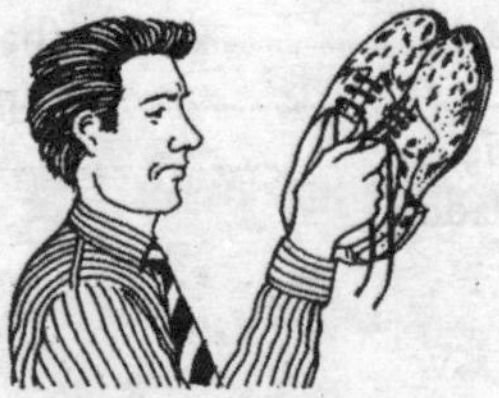

His shoes are dirty.

He is cleaning his shoes.

He **has cleaned** his shoes.
(= his shoes are clean *now*)

They are at home.

They are going out.

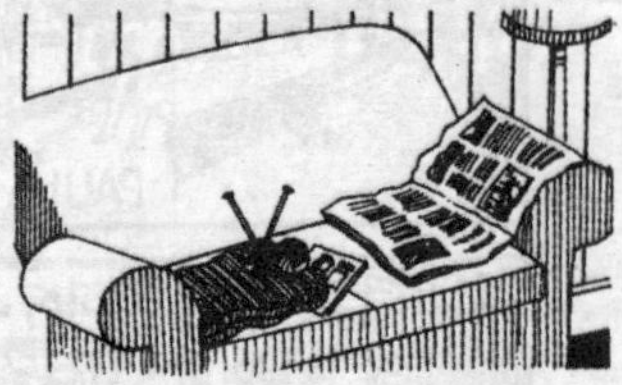

They **have gone** out.
(= they are not at home *now*)

B

has cleaned / **have gone** *etc.* is the *present perfect* (**have** + *past participle*):

<table>
<tr><td></td><td></td><td>past participle</td></tr>
<tr><td>I
we
you
they</td><td>have ('ve)
have not (haven't)</td><td rowspan="2">cleaned
finished
started
lost
done
been
gone</td></tr>
<tr><td>he
she
it</td><td>has ('s)
has not (hasn't)</td></tr>
</table>

<table>
<tr><td>have</td><td>I
we
you
they</td><td rowspan="2">cleaned?
finished?
started?
lost?
done?
been?
gone?</td><td rowspan="2">regular verbs (cleaned?, finished?, started?)
irregular verbs (lost?, done?, been?, gone?)</td></tr>
<tr><td>has</td><td>he
she
it</td></tr>
</table>

Regular verbs: The past participle is **-ed** (the same as the *past simple*):
clean → I have clean**ed**   finish → we have finish**ed**   start → she has start**ed**

Irregular verbs: The past participle is sometimes the same as the past simple and sometimes different (⇒ Appendix 2-3). For example:

the same:	buy → I **bought** / I have **bought**	have → he **had** / he has **had**
different:	break → I **broke** / I have **broken**	see → you **saw** / you have **seen**
	fall → it **fell** / it has **fallen**	go → they **went** / they have **gone**

C

We use the present perfect for *an action in the past* with a result *now*:

- **I've lost** my passport. (= I can't find my passport *now*)
- 'Where's Linda?' 'She**'s gone** to bed.' (= she is in bed *now*)
- We**'ve bought** a new car. (= we have a new car *now*)
- It's Rachel's birthday tomorrow and I **haven't bought** her a present.
- 'Bob is on holiday.' 'Oh, where **has** he **gone**?'
- Can I take this newspaper? **Have** you **finished** with it?

 present perfect ⇒ UNITS 16-19 present perfect and past simple ⇒ UNIT 20 irregular verbs ⇒ UNIT 24, APPENDIX 2-3

EXERCISES

15.1 Look at the pictures. What has happened? Choose from:

go to bed ~~**clean his shoes**~~ **stop raining** **close the door** **fall down** **have a bath**

before *now*

1  He has cleaned his shoes.

2  She ....

3 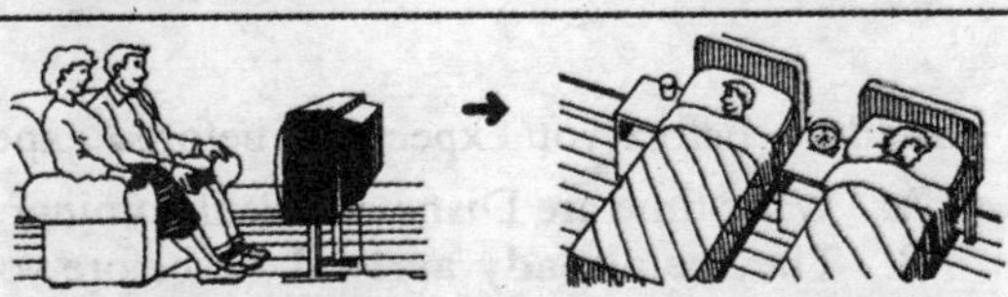 They ....

4  It ....

5 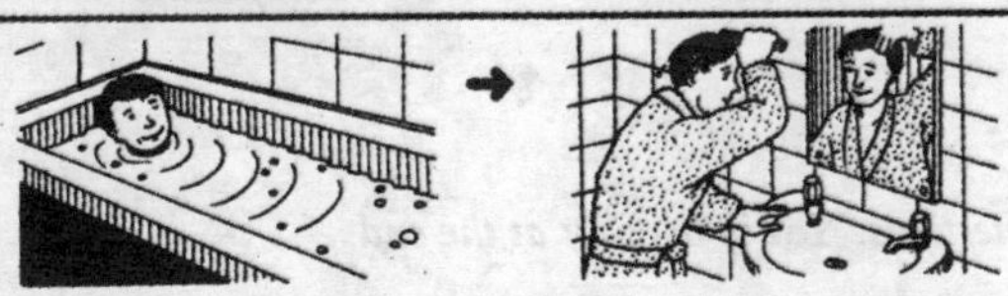 He ....

6 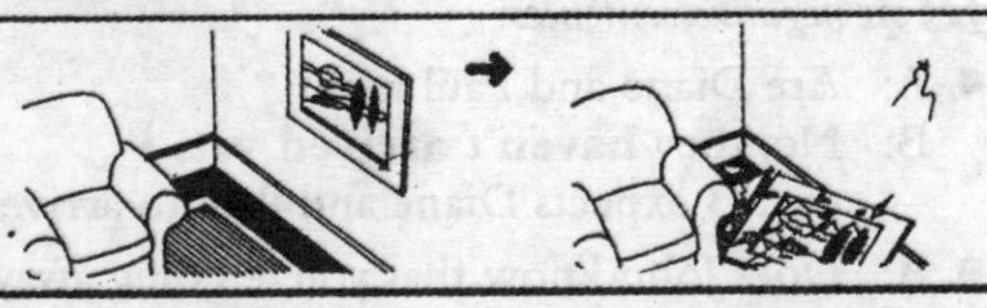 The ....

15.2 Complete the sentences with a verb from the list.

break **buy** **decide** ~~**finish**~~ **forget** **go** **go** **invite** **see** **not/see** **take** **tell**

1 'Can I have this newspaper?' 'Yes, I 've finished with it.'
2 I .... some new shoes. Do you want to see them?
3 'Where is Liz?' 'She .... out.'
4 I'm looking for Paula. .... you .... her?
5 Look! Somebody .... that window.
6 'Does Lisa know that you're going away?' 'Yes, I .... her.'
7 I can't find my umbrella. Somebody .... it.
8 I'm looking for Sarah. Where .... she .... ?
9 I know that woman but I .... her name.
10 Sue is having a party tonight. She .... a lot of people.
11 What are you going to do? .... you .... ?
12 Where are my glasses?' 'I don't know. I .... them.'

UNIT 16

I've just ... I've already ... I haven't ... yet (present perfect 2)

A I've just ...

They **have just arrived.**

just = a short time ago

- A: Are Jane and David here?
  B: Yes, they**'ve just arrived.**
- A: Are you hungry?
  B: No, **I've just had** dinner.
- A: Is Tom here?
  B: No, I'm afraid he**'s just gone.**
  (= he **has** just gone)

B I've already ...

already = before you expected / before I expected

- A: What time are Diane and Paul coming?
  B: They**'ve already arrived.** (= before you expected)
- It's only nine o'clock and Ann **has already gone** to bed. (= before I expected)
- A: John, this is Mary.
  B: Yes, I know. We**'ve already met.**

C I haven't ... yet / Have you ... yet?

yet = until now

You can use **yet** in *negative sentences* and *questions*. **Yet** is usually *at the end*.

The film **hasn't started yet.**

yet in *negative sentences*:

- A: Are Diane and Paul here?
  B: No, they **haven't arrived yet.**
  (but B expects Diane and Paul to arrive soon)
- A: Does John know that you're going away?
  B: No, I **haven't told** him **yet.**
  (but B is going to tell him soon)
- Margaret has bought a new dress but she **hasn't worn** it **yet.**

yet in *questions*:

- A: **Have** Diane and Paul **arrived yet?**
  B: No, not yet. We're still waiting for them.
- A: **Has** Linda **started** her new job **yet?**
  B: No, she starts next week.
- A: This is my new dress.
  B: Oh, it's nice. **Have** you **worn** it **yet?**

present perfect ⇒ UNITS 15, 17-20 word order ⇒ UNIT 93 **still, yet** and **already** ⇒ UNIT 94

EXERCISES

16.1 Write a sentence with **just** for each picture.

1 *They've just arrived.*
2 He ....
3 They ....
4 The race ....

16.2 Complete the sentences. Use **already** + present perfect.

1	What time is Paul arriving?	*He's already arrived.*
2	Do Sue and Bill want to see the film?	No, they .... it.
3	Don't forget to phone Tom.	I ....
4	When is Martin going away?	He ....
5	Do you want to read the newspaper?	I ....
6	When does Linda start her new job?	She ....

16.3 Write a sentence with **just** (**They've just ... / She's just ...** etc.) or a negative sentence with **yet** (**They haven't ... yet / She hasn't ... yet** etc.).

(she / go / out)
She hasn't gone out yet.

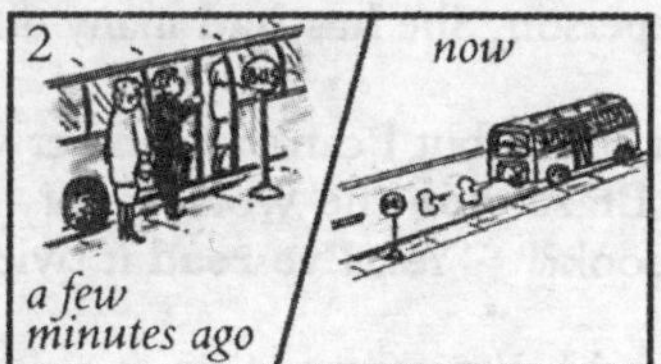

(the bus / go) The bus ....
....

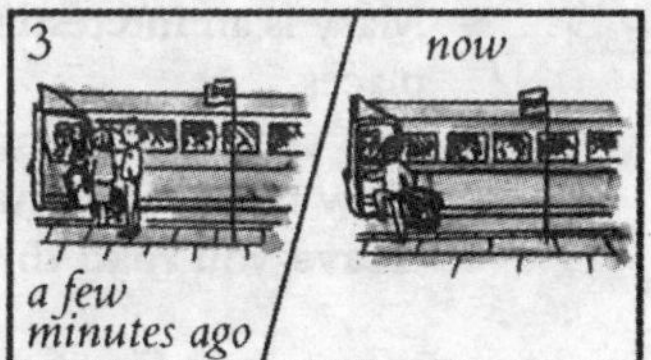

(the bus / go) ....
....

(he / open / it) ....
....

(they / finish / their dinner)
....

(it / stop / raining) ....
....

16.4 Write questions with **yet**.

1 Your friend has got a new job. Perhaps she has started it. You ask her:
Have you started your new job yet?

2 Your friend has some new neighbours. Perhaps he has met them. You ask him:
.... you ....

3 Your friend must write a letter. Perhaps she has written it now. You ask her:
....

4 Tom was trying to sell his car. Perhaps he has sold it now. You ask a friend about Tom:
....

UNIT 17

Have you ever ... ? (present perfect 3)

A

We use the *present perfect* (**have been / have had / have played** *etc.*) when we talk about a time from the past until now – for example, a person's life:

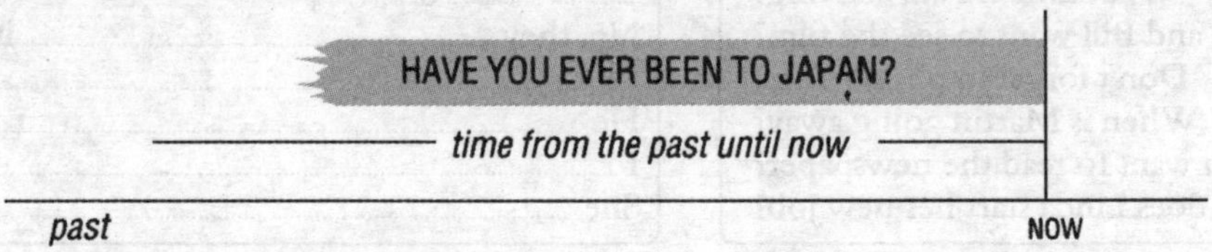

- **'Have** you **been** to France?' (*in your life*) 'No, I **haven't**.'
- **I've been** to Canada but I **haven't been** to the United States.
- Mary is an interesting person. She **has had** many different jobs and **has lived** in many places.
- **I've seen** that woman before but I can't remember where.
- How many times **has** Brazil **won** the World Cup?
- **'Have** you **read** this book?' 'Yes, **I've read** it twice.' (**twice** = two times)

B

present perfect + **ever** (in questions) and **never**:

- **'Has** Ann **ever been** to Australia?' 'Yes, once.' (**once** = one time)
- **'Have** you **ever played** golf?' 'Yes, I often play golf.'
- My mother **has never travelled** by air.
- I've **never ridden** a horse.
- 'Who is that man?' 'I don't know. **I've never seen** him before.'

C

gone and **been**

Bill **has gone** to Spain.
(= he is in Spain *now*)

two weeks later

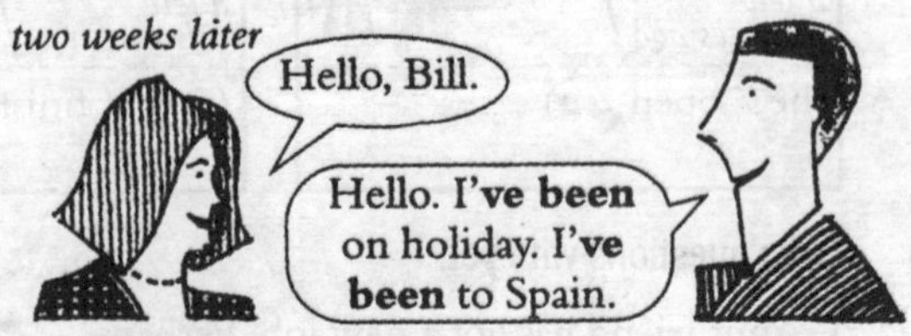

Bill **has been** to Spain.
(= he went to Spain but *now he is back*)

Compare:

- I can't find Susan. Where **has** she **gone**? (= Where is she now?)
- Oh, hello Susan! I was looking for you. Where **have** you **been**?

present perfect ⇒ UNITS 15-16, 18, 20   present perfect and past simple ⇒ UNIT 20

EXERCISES

17.1 You are asking Helen questions beginning **Have you ever ... ?** Write the questions.

	Question	Helen
1	(London?) Have you ever been to London?	No, never.
2	(play / golf?) Have you ever played golf?	Yes, many times.
3	(Australia?) Have	No, never.
4	(lose / your passport?)	Yes, once.
5	(fly / in a helicopter?)	No, never.
6	(eat / Chinese food?)	Yes, a few times.
7	(New York?)	Yes, twice.
8	(drive / a bus?)	No, never.
9	(break / your leg?)	Yes, once.

17.2 Write sentences about Helen. (Look at her answers in Exercise 17.1.)

1 (New York) Helen has been to New York twice.
2 (Australia) Helen ....
3 (Chinese food) ....
4 (drive / a bus) ....

Now write about yourself. How often have you done these things?

5 (New York) I ....
6 (play / tennis) ....
7 (fly / in a helicopter) ....
8 (be / late for work or school) ....

17.3 Mary is 65 years old. She has had an interesting life. What has she done?

~~have~~	be
do	write
travel	meet

all over the world	a lot of interesting things
~~many different jobs~~	a lot of interesting people
ten books	married three times

1 She has had many different jobs.
2 She ....
3 ....
4 ....
5 ....
6 ....

17.4 Put in **gone** or **been**.

1 Bill is on holiday at the moment. He's gone .... to Spain.
2 'Where's Jill?' 'She's not here. I think she's .... to the bank.'
3 Hello, Sue. Where have you .... ? Have you .... to the bank?
4 'Have you ever .... to Mexico?' 'No, never.'
5 My parents aren't at home this evening. They've .... out.
6 There's a new restaurant in town. Have you .... to it?
7 Ann knows Paris well. She's .... there many times.
8 Helen was here earlier but I think she's .... now.

UNIT 18

How long have you ... ? (present perfect 4)

A

Jill is on holiday in Ireland. She is there now.

She arrived in Ireland on Monday.
Today is Thursday.

How long **has she been** in Ireland?

She **has been** in Ireland { **since Monday.** / **for three days.**

Compare **is** and **has been**:

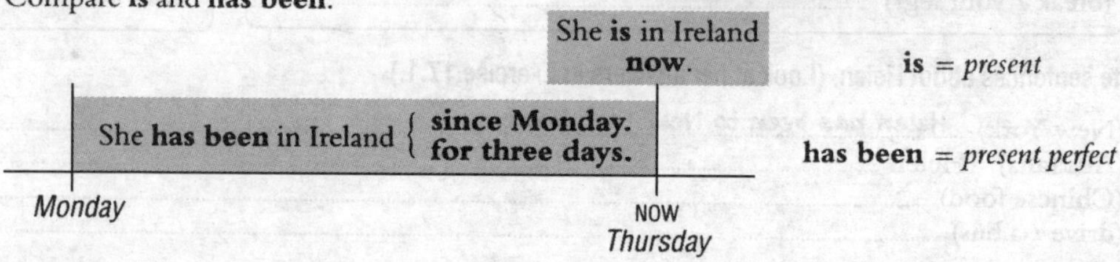

B

Compare:

present simple	*present perfect simple* (**have been/have lived/have known** *etc.*)
Mark and Liz **are** married.	They **have been** married **for** five years. (*not* 'They are married for five years.')
Are you married?	**How long have** you **been** married? (*not* 'How long are you married?')
Do you **know** Sarah?	**How long have** you **known** her? (*not* 'How long do you know her?')
I **know** Sarah.	**I've known** her **for** a long time. (*not* 'I know her for ...')
Linda **lives** in London.	**How long has** she **lived** in London? She **has lived** there **all her life**.
I **have** a car.	**How long have** you **had** your car? **I've had** it **since** April.

present continuous	*present perfect continuous* (**have been + ing**)
I'm learn**ing** German.	**How long have** you **been** learn**ing** German? (*not* 'How long are you learning German?') **I've been** learn**ing** German **for** two years.
David **is** watch**ing** TV.	**How long has** he **been** watch**ing** TV? He's **been** (= He **has been**) watch**ing** TV **since** 5 o'clock.
It's rain**ing**.	It's **been** (= It **has been**) rain**ing** **all day**.

for and **since** ⇒ UNITS 19, 97

EXERCISES

18.1 Complete these sentences.

1 Jill is in hospital. She has been in hospital since Monday.
2 I know Sarah. I have known her for a long time.
3 Linda and Frank are married. They .... married since 1989.
4 Brian is ill. He .... ill for the last few days.
5 We live in Scott Road. We .... there for ten years.
6 Catherine works in a bank. She .... in a bank for five years.
7 Alan has a headache. He .... a headache since he got up this morning.
8 I'm learning English. I .... English for six months.

18.2 Make questions with **How long ... ?**

1	Jill is on holiday.	How long has she been on holiday ?
2	Mike and Judy are in Brazil.	How long .... ?
3	I know Margaret.	How long .... you .... ?
4	Diana is learning Italian.	.... ?
5	My brother lives in Canada.	.... ?
6	I'm a teacher.	.... ?
7	It is raining.	.... ?

18.3

Look at the pictures and complete the sentences. Your sentence must end with one of these:

for ten minutes   **all day**   **all her life**   **~~for ten years~~**   **since he was 20**   **since Sunday**

1 They have been married for ten years.
2 She ....
3 They ....
4 The sun ....
5 She ....
6 He ....

18.4 Which is right?

1 Mark ~~is~~ / has been in Canada since April.   has been is right
2 Jane is a good friend of mine. I know / have known her very well.
3 Jane is a good friend of mine. I know / have known her for a long time.
4 'Sorry I'm late. How long are you / have you been waiting?'   'Not long. Only five minutes.'
5 Martin works / has worked in a hotel now. He likes his job very much.
6 Linda is reading the newspaper. She is / has been reading it for two hours.
7 'How long do you live / have you lived in this house?'   'About ten years.'
8 'Is that a new coat?'   'No, I have / I've had this coat for a long time.'
9 Tom is / has been in Spain at the moment. He is / has been there for the last three days.

UNIT 19

for since ago

A for and since

We use **for** and **since** to say *how long*:

- Jill is in Ireland. She **has been** there { **for three days.** / **since Monday.** }

We use **for** + *a period* of time (**three days / two years** *etc.*):

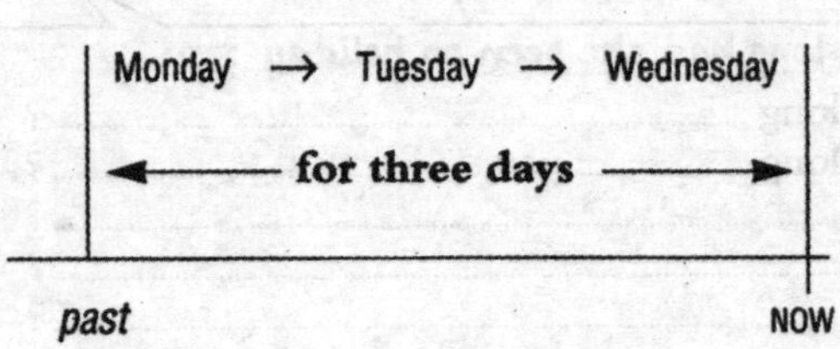

for	
three days	ten minutes
an hour	two hours
a week	four weeks
a month	six months
five years	a long time

- Richard has been in Canada **for six months.** (*not* 'since six months')
- We've been waiting **for two hours.** (*not* 'since two hours')
- I've lived in London **for a long time.**

We use **since** + *the start* of the period (**Monday / 9 o'clock** *etc.*):

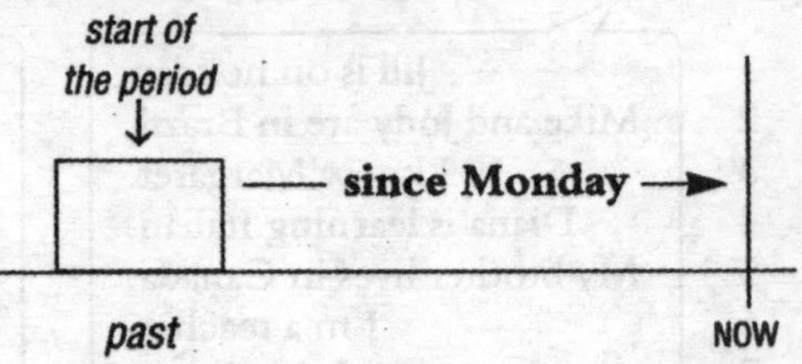

since	
Monday	Wednesday
9 o'clock	12.30
24 July	Christmas
January	I was ten years old
1985	we arrived

- Richard has been in Canada **since January.** (= from January to now)
- We've been waiting **since 9 o'clock.** (= from 9 o'clock to now)
- I've lived in London **since I was ten years old.**

B ago

ago = *before now:*

- Susan started her new job **three weeks ago.** (= three weeks before now)
- 'When did Tom go out?' **'Ten minutes ago.'** (= ten minutes before now)
- I had dinner **an hour ago.**
- Life was very different **a hundred years ago.**

We use **ago** with the *past* (**started/did/had/was** *etc.*).

Compare **ago** and **for**:

- **When did** Jill **arrive** in Ireland?
  She **arrived** in Ireland **three days ago.**
- **How long has** she **been** in Ireland?
  She **has been** in Ireland **for three days.**

present perfect + for/since ⇒ UNIT 18 from/until/since/for ⇒ UNIT 97 for and during ⇒ UNIT 98

EXERCISES

19.1 Write **for** or **since**.

1 Jill has been in Ireland *since* Monday.
2 Jill has been in Ireland *for* three days.
3 My aunt has lived in Australia .... 15 years.
4 Margaret is in her office. She has been there .... 7 o'clock.
5 India has been an independent country .... 1947.
6 The bus is late. We've been waiting .... 20 minutes.
7 Nobody lives in those houses. They have been empty .... many years.
8 Mike has been ill .... a long time. He has been in hospital .... October.

19.2 Answer these questions. Use **ago**.

1 When was your last meal? *Three hours ago.*
2 When was the last time you were ill? ....
3 When did you last go to the cinema? ....
4 When was the last time you were in a car? ....
5 When was the last time you went on holiday? ....

19.3 Complete the sentences. Use the words in brackets (...) + **for** or **ago**.

1 Jill arrived in Ireland *three days ago.* (three days)
2 Jill has been in Ireland *for three days.* (three days)
3 Linda and Frank have been married .... (20 years)
4 Linda and Frank got married .... (20 years)
5 Dan arrived .... (ten minutes)
6 We had lunch .... (an hour)
7 Silvia has been learning English .... (six months)
8 Have you known Lisa ....? (a long time)
9 I bought these shoes .... (a few days)

19.4 Complete the sentences with **for** or **since**.

1 Jill is in Ireland now. She arrived there three days ago. *She has been there for three days.*
2 Jack is here. He arrived here on Tuesday. He has ....
3 It's raining. It started an hour ago. It's been ....
4 I know Sue. I first met Sue two years ago. I've ....
5 I have a camera. I bought it in 1989. I've ....
6 They are married. They got married six months ago.
They've ....
7 Liz is studying medicine at university. She started three years ago.
She has ....
8 Dave plays the piano. He started when he was seven years old.
Dave has ....

19.5 Write sentences about yourself. Begin with the words in brackets (...).

1 (I've lived) ....
2 (I've been) ....
3 (I've been learning) ....
4 (I've known) ....
5 (I've had) ....

UNIT 20

I have done (present perfect) and **I did** (past simple)

A

With a *finished time* (**yesterday / last week** *etc.*), we use the past (**arrived/saw/was** *etc.*):

past simple + finished time

We **arrived**	yesterday. last week. at 3 o'clock. in 1991. six months ago.

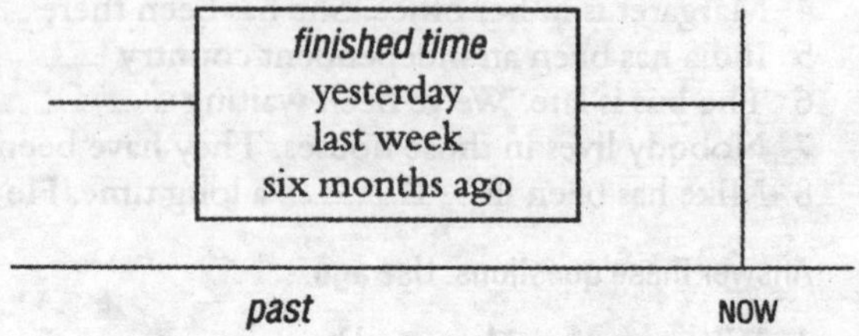

Do *not* use the present perfect (**have arrived / have done / have been** *etc.*) with a finished time:

- I **saw** Paula **yesterday**. (*not* 'I have seen')
- Where **were** you **on Sunday afternoon**? (*not* 'Where have you been')
- We **didn't have** a holiday **last year**. (*not* 'We haven't had')
- 'What **did** you **do last night**?' '**I stayed** at home.'
- William Shakespeare **lived from 1564 to 1616**. He **was** a writer. He **wrote** many plays and poems.

Use the past simple to ask **When … ?** or **What time … ?**:

- **When did** they **arrive**? (*not* 'When have they arrived?')

B

Compare:

present perfect

- I **have lost** my key. (= I can't find it *now*)
- Bill **has gone** home. (= he isn't here *now*)
- **Have** you **seen** Ann? (= where is she *now*?)

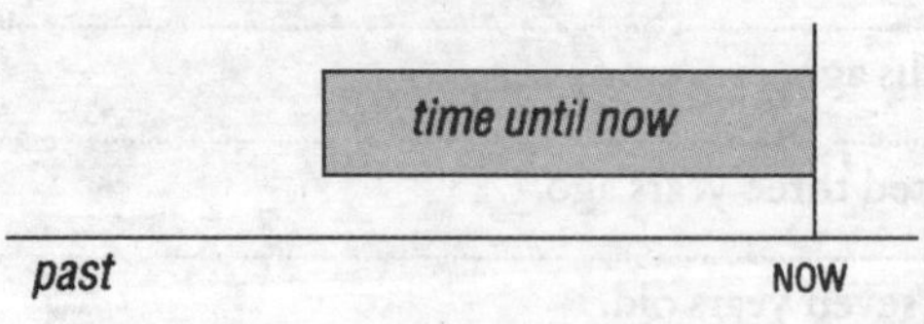

- **Have** you **ever been** to Spain? (= in your life, until *now*)
- My friend is a writer. He **has written** many books.
- The letter **hasn't arrived** yet.
- **We've lived** in Singapore for six years. (= we live there now)

past simple

- I **lost** my key **last week**.
- Bill **went** home **ten minutes ago**.
- **Did** you **see** Ann **on Saturday**?

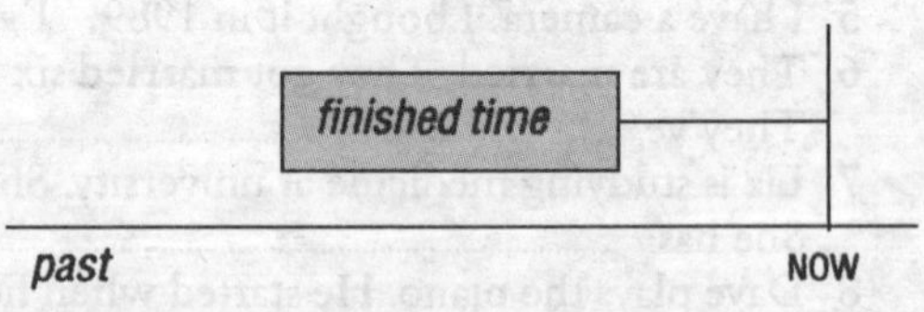

- **Did** you **go** to Spain **last year**?
- Shakespeare **wrote** many plays and poems.
- The letter **didn't arrive yesterday**.
- We **lived** in Glasgow **for six years** but now we live in Singapore.

past simple ⇒ UNITS 11-12 present perfect ⇒ UNITS 15-18

EXERCISES

20.1 Use the words in brackets (...) to answer the questions.

1	Have you seen Ann?	(5 minutes ago)	Yes, I saw her 5 minutes ago.
2	Have you started your new job?	(last week)	Yes, I .... last week.
3	Have your friends arrived?	(at 5 o'clock)	Yes, they ....
4	Has Sarah gone away?	(on Friday)	Yes, ...
5	Have you worn your new shoes?	(yesterday)	Yes, ...

20.2 Right or wrong? Correct the verbs that are wrong. (The verbs are underlined.)

1 I've lost my key. I can't find it. RIGHT
2 Have you seen Ann yesterday? WRONG: Did you see
3 I've finished my work at 2 o'clock. ....
4 I'm ready now. I've finished my work. ....
5 What time have you finished your work? ....
6 Sue isn't here. She's gone out. ....
7 Jim's grandmother has died in 1989. ....
8 Where have you been last night? ....

20.3 Put the verb in the present perfect or past simple.

1 My friend is a writer. He has written (write) many books.
2 We didn't have (not/have) a holiday last year.
3 I .... (play) tennis yesterday afternoon.
4 What time .... (you/go) to bed last night?
5 .... (you/ever/meet) a famous person?
6 The weather .... (not/be) very good yesterday.
7 My hair is wet. I .... (just/wash) it.
8 I .... (wash) my hair before breakfast this morning.
9 Kathy travels a lot. She .... (visit) many countries.
10 'Is Sonia here?' 'No, she .... (not/come) yet.'

20.4 Put the verb in the present perfect or past simple.

1 A: Have you ever been (you/ever/be) to Florida? B: Yes, we went (go) there on holiday two years ago. A: .... (you/have) a good time? B: Yes, it .... (be) great.	3 Rose works in a factory. She .... (work) there for six months. Before that she .... (be) a waitress in a restaurant. She .... (work) there for two years but she .... (not/enjoy) it very much.
2 A: Where's Alan? .... (you/see) him? B: Yes, he .... (go) out a few minutes ago. A: And Julia? B: I don't know. I .... (not/see) her.	4 A: Do you know Martin's sister? B: I .... (see) her a few times but I .... (never/speak) to her. .... (you/ever/speak) to her? A: Yes. I .... (meet) her at a party last week. She's very nice.

UNIT 21 is done   was done (passive 1)

A

The office **is cleaned** every day.

The office **was cleaned** yesterday.

Compare active and passive:

Somebody **cleans** the office every day. *(active)*

The office **is cleaned** every day. *(passive)*

Somebody **cleaned** the office yesterday. *(active)*

The office **was cleaned** yesterday. *(passive)*

B

The passive is:

				past participle	
present simple	**am/is/are**	(not)	+	**cleaned**	**done**
past simple	**was/were**			**invented**	**built**
				injured	**taken** *etc.*

The past participle of regular verbs is **-ed** (cleaned/damaged *etc.*).
For a list of *irregular* past participles **(done/built/taken** etc.), see Appendix 2–3.

- Butter **is made** from milk.
- Oranges **are imported** into Britain.
- How often **are** these rooms **cleaned**?
- I **am** never **invited** to parties.

- This house **was built** 100 years ago.
- These houses **were built** 100 years ago.
- When **was** the telephone **invented**?
- We **weren't invited** to the party last week.
- '**Was** anybody **injured** in the accident?' 'Yes, two people **were taken** to hospital.'

C

was/were born

- I **was born** in London in 1962. (*not* 'I am born')
- Where **were** you **born**?

D

Passive + **by** ...

- We were woken up **by a loud noise**. (= The noise woke us up.)
- The telephone was invented **by Alexander Bell** in 1876.
- My brother was bitten **by a dog** last week.

is being done / has been done ⇒ UNIT 22   irregular verbs ⇒ UNIT 24, APPENDIX 2-3   **by** ⇒ UNIT 104
active and passive ⇒ APPENDIX 1

EXERCISES

21.1 Write sentences from the words in brackets (...). Sentences 1-7 are present.

1 (the office / clean / every day) The office is cleaned every day.
2 (these rooms / clean / every day?) Are these rooms cleaned every day?
3 (glass / make / from sand) Glass ....
4 (stamps / sell / in a post office) ....
5 (this room / not / use / very often) ....
6 (we / allow / to park here?) ....
7 (how / this word / pronounce?) ....

Sentences 8-15 are past.

8 (the office / clean / yesterday) The office was cleaned yesterday.
9 (the house / paint / last month) The house ....
10 (three people / injure / in the accident) ....
11 (my bicycle / steal / a few days ago) ....
12 (when / this bridge / build?) ....
13 (you / invite / to the party last week?) ....
14 (how / these windows / break?) ....
15 (I / not / wake up / by the noise) ....

21.2 Correct these sentences.

1 This house built 100 years ago. This house was built ...
2 Football plays in most countries of the world. ....
3 Why did the letter send to the wrong address? ....
4 A garage is a place where cars repair. ....
5 Where are you born? ....
6 How many languages are speaking in Switzerland? ....
7 Somebody broke into our house but nothing stolen. ....
8 When was invented the bicycle? ....

21.3 Complete the sentences. Use the passive (present or past) of these verbs:

~~**clean**~~ **damage** **find** **give** **invite** **make** **make** **show** **steal** ~~**take**~~

1 The room is cleaned every day.
2 I saw an accident yesterday. Two people were taken to hospital.
3 Paper .... from wood.
4 There was a fire at the hotel last week. Two of the rooms ....
5 'Where did you get this picture?' 'It .... to me by a friend of mine.'
6 Many American programmes .... on British television.
7 'Did Jim and Sue go to the wedding?' 'No. They .... but they didn't go.'
8 'How old is this film?' 'It .... in 1965.'
9 My car .... last week but the next day it .... by the police.

21.4 Where were they born?

1 (Ian / Edinburgh) Ian was born in Edinburgh.
2 (Sally / Birmingham) Sally ....
3 (her parents / Ireland) Her ....
4 (you / ???) I ....
5 (your mother / ???) ....

UNIT 22 is being done has been done (passive 2)

A

is/are being ... *(present continuous passive)*

Somebody **is painting** the door. *(active)*

The door **is being painted.** *(passive)*

- My car is at the garage. It **is being repaired.** (= somebody is repairing it)
- Some new houses **are being built** opposite the park. (= somebody is building them)

Compare the *present continuous* and *present simple*:

- The office **is being cleaned** <u>at the moment</u>. *(continuous)*
  The office **is cleaned** <u>every day</u>. *(simple)*
- In Britain football matches **are** usually **played** on Saturday, but no matches **are being played** next Saturday.

For the present continuous and present simple, see Units 8 and 26.

B

has/have been ... *(present perfect passive)*

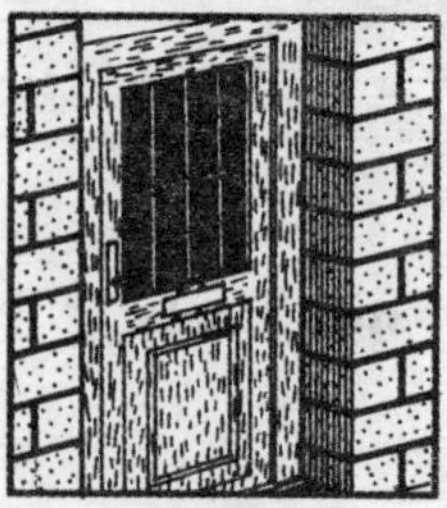

BEFORE

NOW

Somebody **has painted** the door. *(active)*

The door **has been painted.** *(passive)*

- My key **has been stolen**. (= somebody has stolen it)
- My keys **have been stolen**. (= somebody has stolen them)
- I'm not going to the party. I **haven't been invited.** (= nobody has invited me)
- **Has** this shirt **been washed**? (= Has somebody washed it?)

Compare the *present perfect* and *past simple:*

- The room is clean now. It **has been cleaned**. *(present perfect)*
  The room **was cleaned** <u>yesterday</u>. *(past simple)*
- I can't find my keys. I think they**'ve been stolen**. *(present perfect)*
  My keys **were stolen** <u>last week</u>. *(past simple)*

For the present perfect and past simple, see Unit 20.

EXERCISES

22.1 What's happening?

1 *The car is being repaired.* ....
2 A bridge ....
3 The windows ....
4 The grass ....

22.2 Look at the pictures. What is happening or what has happened? Use the present continuous (**is/are being ...**) or the present perfect (**has/have been ...**).

1 (the office / clean) *The office is being cleaned.*
2 (the shirts / iron) *The shirts have been ironed.*
3 (the window / break) The window ....
4 (the roof / repair) The roof ....
5 (the car / damage) ....
6 (the houses / knock / down) ....
7 (the trees / cut / down) ....
8 (they / invite / to a party) ....

22.3 Use the words in brackets (...) to complete the sentences. (Units 21 and 22)

1 I can't use my office at the moment. It *is being painted* (paint).
2 We didn't go to the party. We *weren't invited* (not/invite).
3 The washing machine was broken but it's OK now. It .... (repair)
4 The washing machine .... (repair) yesterday afternoon.
5 A factory is a place where things .... (make).
6 How old are these houses? When .... (they/build)?
7 A: .... (the computer / use) at the moment?
B: Yes, Jim is using it.
8 I've never seen these flowers before. What .... (they/call)?
9 Some trees .... (blow) down in the storm last night.
10 The bridge is closed at the moment. It .... (damage) last week and it .... (not/repair) yet.

UNIT 23

be/have/do in present and past tenses

A

be (= **am/is/are/was/were**) + **-ing** (**cleaning/working** *etc.*)

am/is/are + -ing
(present continuous)
⇒ Units 3-4 and 26

- Please be quiet. **I'm working.**
- It **isn't raining** at the moment.
- What **are** you **doing** this evening?

was/were + -ing
(past continuous)
⇒ Unit 13

- I **was working** when she arrived.
- It **wasn't raining**, so we went out.
- What **were** you **doing** at three o'clock?

B

be + *past participle* (**cleaned/made/eaten** *etc.*)

am/is/are + *past participle*
(passive present simple)
⇒ Unit 21

- The room **is cleaned** every day.
- **I'm** never **invited** to parties.
- Oranges **are imported** into Britain.

was/were + *past participle*
(passive past simple)
⇒ Unit 21

- The room **was cleaned** yesterday.
- These houses **were built** 100 years ago.
- How **was** the window **broken**?
- Where **were** you **born**?

C

have/has + *past participle* (**cleaned/lost/eaten/been** *etc.*)

have/has + *past participle*
(present perfect)
⇒ Units 15-18

- **I've cleaned** my room.
- Tom **has lost** his passport.
- Barbara **hasn't been** to Canada.
- Where **have** Paul and Linda **gone**?

D

do/does/did + *infinitive* (**clean/like/eat/go** *etc.*)

do/does + *infinitive*
(present simple negative and questions)
⇒ Units 6-7

- I like coffee but I **don't like** tea.
- Chris **doesn't go** out very often.
- What **do** you usually **do** at weekends?
- **Does** Barbara **live** alone?

did + *infinitive*
(past simple negative and questions)
⇒ Unit 12

- I **didn't watch** TV yesterday.
- It **didn't rain** last week.
- What time **did** Paul and Linda **go** out?

irregular verbs ⇒ UNIT 24, APPENDIX 2-3

EXERCISES

23.1 Put in **is/are/do/does.**

1 Do you work in the evenings?
2 Where are they going?
3 Why .... you looking at me?
4 .... Bill live near you?
5 .... you like cooking?
6 .... the sun shining?
7 What time .... the shops close?
8 .... Ann working today?
9 What .... this word mean?
10 .... you feeling all right?

23.2 Put in **am not / isn't / aren't / don't / doesn't**. All these sentences are negative.

1 Tom doesn't work in the evenings.
2 I'm very tired. I .... want to go out this evening.
3 I'm very tired. I .... going out this evening.
4 George .... working this week. He's on holiday.
5 My parents are usually at home. They .... go out very often.
6 Barbara has travelled a lot but she .... speak any foreign languages.
7 You can turn off the television. I .... watching it.
8 There's a party next week but we .... going.

23.3 Put in **was/were/did/have/has.**

1 Where were your shoes made?
2 .... you go out last night?
3 What .... you doing at 10.30?
4 Where .... your mother born?
5 .... Barbara gone home?
6 What time .... she go?
7 When .... these houses built?
8 .... Jim arrived yet?
9 Why .... you go home early?
10 How long .... they been married?

23.4 Put in **is/are/was/were/have/has.**

1 Joe has lost his passport.
2 This bridge .... built ten years ago.
3 .... you finished your work yet?
4 This town is always clean. The streets .... cleaned every day.
5 Where .... you born?
6 I .... just made some coffee. Would you like some?
7 Glass .... made from sand.
8 This is a very old photograph. It .... taken a long time ago.
9 Joe .... bought a new car.

23.5 Complete the sentences. Choose from the list and put the verb into the correct form.

damage eat enjoy ~~go~~ go away listen open pronounce ~~rain~~ understand use

1 I'm going to take an umbrella with me. It's raining .
2 Why are you so tired? Did you go to bed late last night?
3 Where are the chocolates? Have you .... them all?
4 How is your new job? Are you .... it?
5 My car was badly .... in the accident but I was OK.
6 Chris has got a car but she doesn't .... it very often.
7 Mary isn't at home. She has .... for a few days.
8 I don't .... the problem. Can you explain it again?
9 Martin is in his room. He's .... to music.
10 I don't know how to say this word. How is it .... ?
11 How do you .... this window? Can you show me?

UNIT
24
Regular and irregular verbs

A

Regular verbs

The past simple and past participle of *regular* verbs is **-ed**:

clean → clean**ed** live → liv**ed** paint → paint**ed** study → studi**ed**

Past simple (⇒ Unit 11)

- I **cleaned** my shoes yesterday.
- Charlie **studied** engineering at university.

Past participle

Present perfect = **have/has** + *past participle* (⇒ Units 15–18):

- I **have cleaned** my shoes.
- Jane **has lived** in London for ten years.

Passive = **be (is / are / were / has been** *etc.*) + *past participle* (⇒ Units 21–22):

- These rooms **are cleaned** every day.
- My car **has been repaired**.

B

Irregular verbs

The past simple and past participle of *irregular* verbs are *not* **-ed**:

	make	break	cut
past simple	**made**	**broke**	**cut**
past participle	**made**	**broken**	**cut**

Sometimes the past simple and past participle are *the same*. For example:

	make	find	buy	cut
past simple / *past participle*	**made**	**found**	**bought**	**cut**

- I **made** a cake yesterday. *(past simple)*
- I **have made** some coffee. *(past participle – present perfect)*
- Butter **is made** from milk. *(past participle – passive present)*

Sometimes the past simple and past participle are *different*. For example:

	break	know	begin	go
past simple	**broke**	**knew**	**began**	**went**
past participle	**broken**	**known**	**begun**	**gone**

- Somebody **broke** this window last night. *(past simple)*
- Somebody **has broken** this window. *(past participle – present perfect)*
- This window **was broken** last night. *(past participle – passive past)*

list of irregular verbs ⇒ APPENDIX 2-3 spelling (regular verbs) ⇒ APPENDIX 5

EXERCISES

24.1 Write the past simple / past participle of these verbs. (The past simple and past participle are the same for all the verbs in this exercise.)

1 make made	6 enjoy	11 hear ....
2 cut cut	7 buy	12 put ....
3 get	8 sit	13 catch ....
4 bring	9 leave	14 watch ....
5 pay	10 happen	15 understand ....

24.2 Write the past simple and past participle of these verbs.

1 break	broke	broken	6 run	....	....	11 take	....	....
2 begin	....	....	7 speak	....	....	12 go	....	....
3 eat	....	....	8 write	....	....	13 give	....	....
4 drink	....	....	9 come	....	....	14 throw	....	....
5 drive	....	....	10 know	....	....	15 forget	....	....

24.3 Put the verb in the right form.

1 I washed my hands because they were dirty. (wash)
2 Somebody has broken this window. (break)
3 I feel good. I .... very well last night. (sleep)
4 We .... a very good film yesterday. (see)
5 It .... a lot while we were on holiday. (rain)
6 I've .... my bag. (lose) Have you .... it? (see)
7 Rosa's bicycle was .... last week. (steal)
8 I .... to bed early because I was tired. (go)
9 Have you .... your work yet? (finish)
10 The shopping centre was .... about 20 years ago. (build)
11 Ann .... to drive when she was 18. (learn)
12 I've never .... a horse. (ride)
13 Julia is a good friend of mine. I've .... her for a long time. (know)
14 Yesterday I .... and .... my leg. (fall / hurt)

24.4 Complete these sentences. Choose from the list and put the verb into the correct form.

cost drive fly ~~make~~ meet sell speak swim tell think wake up win

1 I have made some coffee. Would you like some?
2 Have you .... John about your new job?
3 We played basketball on Sunday. We didn't play very well but we ....
4 I know Gary but I've never .... his wife.
5 We were .... by loud music in the middle of the night.
6 Stephanie jumped into the river and .... to the other side.
7 'Did you like the film?' 'Yes, I .... it was very good.'
8 Many different languages are .... in the Philippines.
9 Our holiday .... a lot of money because we stayed in an expensive hotel.
10 Have you ever .... a very fast car?
11 All the tickets for the concert were .... very quickly.
12 A bird .... in through the open window while we were having our dinner.

I used to ...

A

DAVE A FEW YEARS AGO

DAVE TODAY

Dave **used to work** in a factory. Now he **works** in a supermarket.

Dave **used to work** in a factory = he worked in a factory before but he doesn't work there now:

←---- he **used to** work ----→ | ←---------- he works ----------→

past | NOW

B

You can say **I used to work** ... / **she used to have** ... / **they used to be** ... *etc.*:

I/you/we/they he/she/it	**used to**	**be** **work** **have** **play** *etc.*

- When I was a child, I **used to like** chocolate.
- I **used to read** a lot of books but I don't read much these days.
- Liz has got short hair now but it **used to be** very long.
- They **used to live** in the same street as us, so we often **used to see** them. But we don't see them very often these days.
- Ann **used to have** a piano but she sold it a few years ago.

The negative is **I didn't use to** ... :
- When I was a child I **didn't use to like** tomatoes.

The question is **did you use to** ... ?:
- Where **did** you **use to live** before you came here?

C

We use **used to** ... only for the *past*. You cannot say 'I use to ...' *(present)*:
- I **used to play** tennis. These days I **play** golf. (*not* 'I use to play golf')
- We usually **get** up early. (*not* 'We use to get up early.')

EXERCISES

25.1 Look at the pictures. Complete the sentences with **used to ...** .

She used to have long hair.

He .... football.

.... a taxi driver.

.... in the country.

....

This building ....

25.2 Karen works very hard and has very little free time. A few years ago, things were different.

KAREN A FEW YEARS AGO

Do you do any sport?	Yes, I go swimming every day and I play volleyball.
Do you go out in the evenings?	Yes, most evenings.
Do you play a musical instrument?	Yes, the guitar.
Do you like reading?	Yes, I read a lot.
Do you travel much?	Yes, I go away two or three times a year.

KAREN NOW

Write sentences about Karen with **used to ...** .

1 She used to go swimming every day.
2 She ....
3 ....
4 ....
5 ....
6 ....

25.3 Complete these sentences. Use **used to** or the present simple (**I play / he lives** etc.).

1 I used to play tennis. I stopped playing a few years ago.
2 Do you do any sport?' 'Yes, I play basketball.
3 'Have you got a car?' 'No, I .... one but I sold it.'
4 George .... a waiter. Now he's the manager of a hotel.
5 'Do you go to work by car?' 'Sometimes but most days I .... by train.'
6 When I was a child, I never .... meat, but I eat it now.
7 Mary loves watching TV. She .... TV every evening.
8 We .... near the airport but we moved to the city centre a few years ago.
9 Normally I start work at 7 o'clock, so I .... up very early.
10 What games .... you .... when you were a child?

UNIT 26

What are you doing tomorrow?

A

They **are playing** tennis (**now**). He **is playing** tennis **tomorrow**.

We use **am/is/are + -ing** *(present continuous)* for something happening now:

- 'Where are Sue and Caroline?' 'They**'re playing** tennis in the park.'
- Please be quiet. **I'm working.**

We also use **am/is/are + -ing** for the *future* (tomorrow / next week *etc.*):

- Andrew **is playing** tennis tomorrow.
- **I'm** not **working** next week.

B

I am doing something tomorrow = I have *arranged* to do it, I have a plan to do it:

- Alice **is going** to the dentist on Friday.
  (= she has an appointment to see the dentist)
- We**'re having** a party next weekend.
- **Are** you **meeting** Bill this evening?
- What **are** you **doing** tomorrow evening?
- **I'm** not **going** out tonight. **I'm staying** at home.

You can also say 'I'm **going to** do something' (⇒ Unit 27).

C

Do *not* use the present simple (**I stay / do you go** etc.) for plans and arrangements:

- **I'm staying** at home this evening. (*not* 'I stay')
- **Are** you **going** out tonight? (*not* 'Do you go')
- Ann **isn't coming** to the party next week. (*not* 'Ann doesn't come')

But we use the present simple for timetables, programmes, trains, buses etc.:

- The train **arrives** at 7.30.
- What time **does** the film **finish**?

Compare:

present continuous – usually for people	*present simple* – timetables, programmes etc.
• **I'm going** to a concert tomorrow. • What time **are** you **leaving**?	• The concert **starts** at 7.30. • What time **does** your train **leave** ?

EXERCISES

26.1 Look at the pictures. What are these people doing next Friday?

1 Andrew is playing tennis on Friday.
2 Richard .... to the cinema.
3 Barbara ....
4 .... lunch with Ken.
5 ....

26.2 Write questions. All the sentences are future.

1 (you / go / out / tonight?) Are you going out tonight?
2 (you / work / next week?) ....
3 (what / you / do / tomorrow evening?) ....
4 (what time / your friends / arrive?) ....
5 (when / Liz / go / on holiday?) ....

26.3 Write sentences about yourself. What are you doing in the next few days?

1 I'm staying at home tonight.
2 I'm going to the theatre on Monday.
3 ....
4 ....
5 ....
6 ....

26.4 Put the verb in the present continuous (**he is leaving** etc.) or present simple (**the train leaves** etc.).

1 'Are you going (you/go) out this evening?' 'No, I'm too tired.'
2 We're going (we/go) to a concert this evening. It starts (it/start) at 7.30.
3 Do you know about Sally? .... (she/get) married next month!
4 A: My parents .... (go) on holiday next week.
B: Oh, that's nice. Where .... (they/go)?
5 Silvia is doing an English course at the moment. The course .... (finish) on Friday.
6 There's a football match tomorrow but .... (I/not/go).
7 .... (I/go) out with some friends tonight. Why don't you come too? .... (we/meet) at John's house at 8 o'clock.
8 A: How .... (you/get) home after the party tomorrow? By taxi?
B: No, I can go by bus. The last bus .... (leave) at midnight
9 A: Do you want to go to the cinema tonight?
B: Yes, what time .... (the film / begin)?
10 A: What .... (you/do) on Monday afternoon?
B: .... (I/work).

UNIT 27

I'm going to …

A

I'm going to (do something)

She **is going to watch** TV this evening.

We use **am/is/are going to…** for the *future:*

I	**am**	(not) **going to**	do …
he/she/it	**is**		drink …
we/you/they	**are**		watch …

am	I	**going to**	buy … ?
is	he/she/it		eat … ?
are	we/you/they		wear … ?

B

I am going to do something = I have decided to do it, my intention is to do it:

I decided to do it ——— **I'm going to do it** ———→

past — NOW — *future*

- **I'm going to buy** some books tomorrow.
- Sarah **is going to sell** her car.
- **I'm not going to have** breakfast this morning. I'm not hungry.
- What **are you going to wear** to the party tonight?
- 'Your hands are dirty.' 'Yes, I know. **I'm going to wash** them.'
- **Are** you **going to invite** John to your party?

We also use the present continuous (**I am doing**) for the future, usually for arrangements (⇒ Unit 26):

- **I am playing** tennis with Julia tomorrow.

C

Something **is going to happen**

Something **is going to happen** = it is clear *now* that it is sure to happen:

- Look at the sky! **It's going to rain.**
  (black clouds *now* → rain)
- Oh dear! It's 9 o'clock and I'm not ready.
  I'm going to be late.
  (9 o'clock *now* and not ready → late)

EXERCISES

27.1 What are these people saying?

27.2 Complete the sentences. Use **going to** + one of these verbs:

eat do give lie down stay walk ~~wash~~ watch ~~wear~~

1 My hands are dirty. *I'm going to wash* them.
2 What *are you going to wear* to the party tonight?
3 I don't want to go home by bus. I ....
4 John is going to London next week. He .... with some friends.
5 I'm hungry. I .... this sandwich.
6 It's Sharon's birthday next week. We .... her a present.
7 Sue says she's feeling very tired. She .... for an hour.
8 There's a good film on TV this evening. .... you .... it?
9 What .... Rachel .... when she leaves school?

27.3 Look at the pictures. What is going to happen?

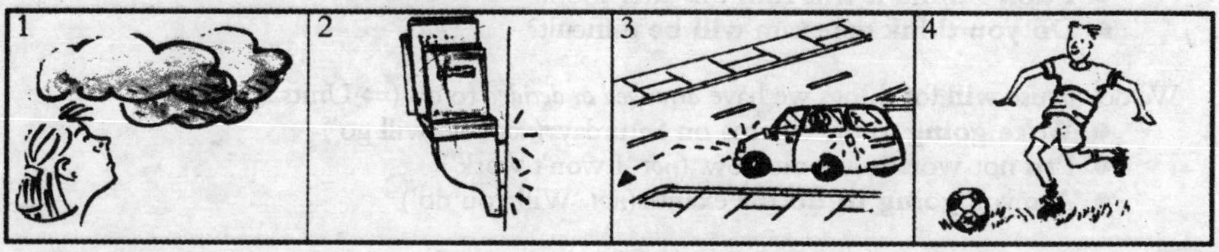

1 *It's going to rain.*
2 The shelf ....
3 The car ....
4 He ....

27.4 What are you going to do today or tomorrow? Write three sentences.

1 I'm ....
2 ....
3 ....

UNIT **28**

will/shall (1)

A

Sarah goes to work every day. She is always there from 8.30 until 4.30.

It is 11 o'clock now. Sarah **is** at work.

At 11 o'clock yesterday, she **was** at work.

At 11 o'clock tomorrow, she **will be** at work.

will + *infinitive* (**will be / will win / will come** *etc.*):

I/we/you/they he/she/it	**will ('ll)** **will not (won't)**	**be** **win** **eat** **come** *etc.*

will	I/we/you/they he/she/it	**be?** **win?** **eat?** **come?** *etc.*

'll = will: **I'll** (I will) / you**'ll** / she**'ll** *etc.*
won't = will not: I **won't** (= I will not) / you **won't** / she **won't** *etc.*

B

We use **will** for the *future* (**tomorrow / next week** *etc.*):

- Sue travels a lot. Today she is in Madrid. Tomorrow she**'ll be** in Rome. Next week she**'ll be** in Tokyo.
- You can phone me this evening. **I'll be** at home.
- Leave the old bread in the garden. The birds **will eat** it.
- **We'll** probably **go** out this evening.
- **Will** you **be** at home this evening?
- I **won't be** here tomorrow. (= I will not be here)
- Don't drink coffee before you go to bed. You **won't sleep**.

We often say **I think ... will ...** :

- **I think** Diana **will pass** the exam.
- **I don't think** it **will rain** this afternoon.
- **Do you think** the exam **will be** difficult?

C

We do *not* use **will** for things we have *arranged or decided* to do (⇒ Units 26-27):

- **We're going** to the cinema on Saturday. (*not* 'We will go')
- **I'm** not **working** tomorrow. (*not* 'I won't work')
- **Are** you **going to do** the exam? (*not* 'Will you do')

D

Shall

You can say **I shall** (= I will) and **we shall** (= we will):

- **I shall be** late tomorrow. *or* **I will (I'll) be** late tomorrow.
- I think **we shall win.** *or* I think **we will (we'll) win.**

But *do not* use **shall** with **you/they/he/she/it**:

- **Tom will** be late. (*not* 'Tom shall be')

EXERCISES

28.1 Helen is travelling in Europe. Complete the sentences with **she was**, **she's** or **she'll be**.

1 Yesterday she was in Paris.
2 Tomorrow .... in Amsterdam.
3 Last week .... in Barcelona.
4 Next week .... in London.
5 At the moment .... in Brussels.
6 Three days ago .... in Munich.
7 At the end of her trip .... very tired.

28.2 Where will you be? Write sentences about yourself. Use:

I'll be ... *or* **I'll probably be ...** *or* **I don't know where I'll be.**

1 (at 10 o'clock tomorrow)
I'll probably be on the beach. OR I'll be at work. OR I don't know where I'll be.
2 (one hour from now) ....
3 (at midnight tonight) ....
4 (at 3 o'clock tomorrow afternoon) ....
5 (two years from now) ....

28.3 Put in **will ('ll)** or **won't**.

1 Don't drink coffee before you go to bed. You won't sleep.
2 'Are you ready yet?' 'Not yet. I .... be ready in five minutes.'
3 I'm going away for a few days. I'm leaving tonight, so I .... be at home tomorrow.
4 It .... rain, so you don't need to take an umbrella.
5 A: I don't feel very well this evening.
B: Well, go to bed early and you .... feel better in the morning.
6 It's Bill's birthday next Monday. He .... be 25.
7 I'm sorry I was late this morning. It .... happen again.

28.4 Write sentences beginning **I think ...** or **I don't think ...**.

1 (Diana will pass the exam) I think Diana will pass the exam.
2 (Diana won't pass the exam) I don't think Diana will pass the exam.
3 (we'll win the game) I ....
4 (I won't be here tomorrow) ....
5 (Sue will like her present) ....
6 (they won't get married) ....
7 (you won't enjoy the film) ....

28.5 Which is right? (Study Unit 26 before you do this exercise.)

1 ~~We'll go~~ / We're going to the theatre tonight. We've got tickets. We're going is right
2 'What will you do / are you doing tomorrow evening?' 'Nothing. I'm free.'
3 They'll go / They're going away tomorrow morning. Their train is at 8.40.
4 I'm sure she'll lend / she's lending us some money. She's very rich.
5 'Why are you putting on your coat?' 'I'll go / I'm going out.'
6 Do you think Claire will phone / is phoning us tonight?
7 Steve can't meet us on Saturday. He'll work / He's working.
8 Will / Shall you be at home tomorrow evening?

UNIT 29

will/shall (2)

A

You can use **I'll** … (**I will**) when you *offer* or *decide* to do something:

- 'My bag is very heavy.' **'I'll carry** it for you.'
- **'I'll phone** you tomorrow, OK?' 'OK, goodbye.'

We often say **I think I'll** … / **I don't think I'll** … when we decide to do something:

- I'm tired. **I think I'll go** to bed early tonight.
- It's a nice day. **I think I'll sit** in the garden.
- It's raining. **I don't think I'll go** out.

Do *not* use the present simple (**I go** / **I phone** *etc.*) in sentences like these:

- **I'll phone** you tomorrow, OK? (*not* 'I phone you')
- I think **I'll go** to bed early. (*not* 'I go to bed')

B

Do *not* use **I'll** … for something you decided before (⇒ Units 26–27):

- **I'm working** tomorrow. (*not* 'I'll work')
- There's a good film on TV tonight. **I'm going to watch** it. (*not* 'I'll watch')
- What **are** you **doing** at the weekend? (*not* 'What will you do')

C

Shall I … ? **Shall we … ?**

Shall I/we … ? = Do you think this is a good thing to do? Do you think this is a good idea?

- It's very warm in this room. **Shall I open** the window?
- **'Shall I phone** you this evening?' 'Yes, please.'
- I'm going to a party tonight. What **shall I wear**?

- It's a nice day. **Shall we go** for a walk?
- Where **shall we go** for our holidays this year?
- 'Let's go out this evening.' 'OK, what time **shall we meet**?'

What are you doing tomorrow? ⇒ UNIT 26 **I'm going to …** ⇒ UNIT 27 **will/shall (1)** ⇒ UNIT 28
Let's ⇒ UNIT 52

EXERCISES

29.1 Complete the sentences. Use **I'll (I will)** + one of these verbs:

~~carry~~ do eat send show sit stay

1 My bag is very heavy. — *I'll carry* .... it for you.
2 Enjoy your holiday. — Thank you. .... you a postcard.
3 I don't want this banana. — Well, I'm hungry. .... it.
4 Do you want a chair? — No, it's OK. .... on the floor.
5 Did you phone Jenny? — Oh no, I forgot. .... it now.
6 Are you coming with me? — No, I don't think so. .... here.
7 How do you use this camera? — Give it to me and .... you.

29.2 Complete the sentences. Use **I think I'll ...** or **I don't think I'll ...** + one of these verbs:

buy ~~go~~ have play

1 It's cold today. *I don't think I'll go* out.
2 I'm hungry. I .... something to eat.
3 I feel tired. .... tennis.
4 This camera is too expensive. .... it.

29.3 Which is right?

1 ~~I phone~~ / I'll phone you tomorrow, OK? *I'll phone* is right
2 I haven't done the shopping yet. I do / I'll do it later.
3 I like sport. I watch / I'll watch a lot of sport on TV.
4 I need some exercise. I think I go / I'll go for a walk.
5 Jim is going to buy / will buy a new car. He told me last week.
6 'This letter is for Rose.' 'OK. I give / I'll give / I'm going to give it to her.'
7 A: Are you doing / Will you do anything this evening?
B: Yes, I'm going / I'll go out with some friends.

29.4 Write sentences with **Shall I ... ?** Choose words from Box A and Box B.

A		B	
turn on	make	some sandwiches	the television
turn off	~~open~~	~~the window~~	the light

1 It's very warm in this room. — *Shall I open the window?*
2 This programme isn't very good. — ....
3 I'm hungry. — ....
4 It's dark in this room. — ....

29.5 Write sentences with **Shall we ... ?** Choose words from Box A and Box B.

A		B	
what	where	buy	invite
~~what time~~	who	go	~~meet~~

1 Let's go out tonight. — OK, *what time shall we meet?*
2 Let's have a holiday. — OK, ...
3 Let's spend some money. — OK, ...
4 Let's have a party. — OK, ...

UNIT 30 might

A

He **might go** to New York.
(= it is possible that he will go to New York)

It **might rain**.
(= it is possible that it will rain)

might + *infinitive* (**might go / might be / might rain** *etc.*):

I/we/you/they he/she/it	**might** (not)	**be** **go** **play** **come** *etc.*

B

I might ... = it is possible that I will ... :

- I **might go** to the cinema this evening. (= it is possible that I will go)
- A: When is Barbara going to phone you?
  B: I don't know. She **might phone** this afternoon.
- Take an umbrella with you. It **might rain**.
- Buy a lottery ticket. You **might be** lucky. (= perhaps you will be lucky)
- 'Are you going out tonight?' **'I might.'** (= I might go out)

Study the difference:

- **I'm playing** tennis tomorrow. *(sure)*
  I **might play** tennis tomorrow. *(possible)*
- Barbara **is going to phone** later. *(sure)*
  Barbara **might phone** later. *(possible)*

C

The negative is **might not**:

- I **might not go** to work tomorrow. (= it is possible that I will not go)
- Sue **might not come** to the party. (= it is possible that she will not come)

D

may

You can use **may** in the same way. **I may** ... = **I might** ... :

- I **may go** to the cinema this evening. (= I might go)
- Sue **may not come** to the party. (= Sue might not come)

May I ... ? = Is it OK to ... / Can I ...?:

- **May I** ask a question? (= Can I ask?)
- **'May I** sit here?' 'Yes, of course.'

will ⇒ UNITS 28-29 can ⇒ UNIT 31

EXERCISES

30.1 Write sentences with **might**.

1 (it's possible that I'll go to the cinema) *I might go to the cinema.*
2 (it's possible that I'll see you tomorrow) I ....
3 (it's possible that Ann will forget to phone) ....
4 (it's possible that it will snow today) ....
5 (it's possible that I'll be late tonight) ....

Write sentences with **might not**.

6 (it's possible that Mary will not be here) ....
7 (it's possible that I won't have time to meet you) ....

30.2 Somebody is asking you about your plans. You have some ideas but you are not sure. Choose from the list and write sentences with **I might**.

fish **go away** **~~Italy~~** **Monday** **new car** **taxi**

1 Where are you going for your holidays? — I'm not sure. *I might go to Italy.*
2 What are you doing at the weekend? — I don't know. I ....
3 When will you see Ann again? — I'm not sure. ....
4 What are you going to have for dinner? — I don't know. ....
5 How are you going to get home tonight? — I'm not sure. ....
6 I hear you won some money. What are you going to do with it? — I haven't decided yet. ....

30.3 You ask Bill questions about his plans. Sometimes he is sure but usually he is not sure.

1 Are you playing tennis tomorrow? — Yes, in the afternoon.
2 Are you going out in the evening? — Possibly.
3 Are you going to get up early? — Perhaps.
4 Are you working tomorrow? — No, I'm not.
5 Will you be at home tomorrow morning? — Maybe.
6 Are you going to watch television? — I might.
7 Are you going out in the afternoon? — Yes, I am.
8 Are you going shopping? — Perhaps.

Now write about Bill. Use **might** where necessary.

1 *He's playing tennis tomorrow afternoon.*
2 *He might go out this evening.*
3 He ....
4 ....
5 ....
6 ....
7 ....
8 ....

30.4 Write three things that you might do tomorrow.

1 ....
2 ....
3 ....

UNIT 31

can and could

A

He **can play** the piano.

can + *infinitive* (**can do / can play / can come** *etc.*):

I/we/you/they he/she/it	**can** **cannot (can't)**	**do** **play** **see** **come** *etc.*

can	I/we/you/they he/she/it	**do?** **play?** **see?** **come?** *etc.*

B

I can do something = I *know how* to do it or *it is possible* for me to do it:

- I **can play** the piano. My brother **can play** the piano too.
- Sarah **can speak** Italian but she **can't speak** Spanish.
- '**Can** you **swim**?' 'Yes, but I'm not a very good swimmer.'
- '**Can** you **change** twenty pounds?' 'I'm sorry, I **can't**.'
- I'm having a party next week but Paul and Jenny **can't come.**

C

For the past (**yesterday / last week** etc.), we use **could/couldn't:**

- When I was young, I **could run** very fast.
- Before Anna came to Britain, she **couldn't understand** much English. Now she **can understand** everything.
- I was tired last night but I **couldn't sleep.**
- I had a party last week but Paul and Jenny **couldn't come.**

D

Can you ... ? Could you ... ? Can I ... ? Could I ... ?

We use **Can you ... ?** or **Could you ... ?** when we ask people to do things:

- **Can you** open the door, please? *or* **Could you** open the door, please?
- **Can you** wait a moment, please? *or* **Could you** wait ... ?

We use **Can I have ... ?** or **Could I have ... ?** to ask for something:

- *(in a shop)* **Can I have** these postcards, please? *or* **Could I have** ... ?

Can I ... ? or **Could I ... ?** = is it OK to do something?:

- Tom, **can I** borrow your umbrella? *or* Tom, **could I** borrow your umbrella?
- *(on the phone)* Hello, **can I** speak to Gerry, please? *or* ... **could I** speak ... ?

May I ... ? ⇒ UNIT 30

EXERCISES

31.1 Ask Steve if he can do these things:

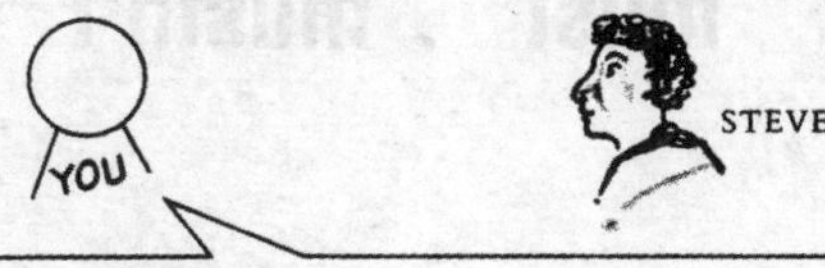

1 Can you swim?
2 ....
3 ....
4 ....
5 ....
6 ....

Can you do these things? Write sentences about yourself. Use **I can** or **I can't**.

7 I .... 9 .... 11 ....
8 .... 10 .... 12 ....

31.2 Complete these sentences. Use **can** or **can't** + one of these verbs:

~~come~~ find hear see speak

1 I'm sorry but we *can't come* to your party next Saturday.
2 I like this hotel room. You .... the mountains from the window.
3 You are speaking very quietly. I .... you.
4 Have you seen my bag? I .... it.
5 Catherine got the job because she .... five languages.

31.3 Complete these sentences. Use **can't** or **couldn't** + one of these verbs:

eat decide find go go ~~sleep~~

1 I was tired but I *couldn't sleep.*
2 I wasn't hungry yesterday. I .... my dinner.
3 Ann doesn't know what to do. She ....
4 I wanted to speak to Martin yesterday but I .... him.
5 Jim .... to the concert next Saturday. He has to work.
6 Paula .... to the meeting last week. She was ill.

31.4 What do you say in these situations? Use **can** or **could.** Use the words in brackets (...).

UNIT 32

must mustn't needn't

A

must + *infinitive* (**must do** / **must see** *etc.*):

I/we/you/they he/she/it	**must**	**do** **stop** **go** **write** *etc.*

B

Use **must** when you think it is necessary to do something:

- The windows are very dirty. I **must clean** them.
- It's a fantastic film. You **must see** it.
- We **must** go to the bank today. We haven't got any money.

For the past (**yesterday** / **last week** *etc.*), we use **had to** … (*not* **must**):

- We **had to go** to the bank yesterday. (*not* 'We must go … yesterday')
- I **had to walk** home last night. There were no buses. (*not* 'I must walk')

C

mustn't (= must not)

I **mustn't** (do something) = it is necessary *not* to do it, it is the wrong thing to do:

- I **must hurry**. I **mustn't be** late.
- I **mustn't forget** to phone Julia. (= I **must remember** to phone her)
- Be happy! You **mustn't be** sad. (= don't be sad)
- You **mustn't touch** the pictures. (= don't touch the pictures)

D

needn't (= need not)

I **needn't** (do something) = it is *not necessary* to do it, I don't need to do it:

- I **needn't clean** the windows. They aren't very dirty.
- You **needn't go** to the bank today. I can give you some money.

You can also say **don't need to …** (= needn't):

- I **don't need to clean** the windows.
- You **don't need to go** to the bank today.

Compare **needn't** and **mustn't**:

- You **needn't** go. You can stay here if you want.
- You **mustn't** go. You must stay here.

I have to … ⇒ UNIT 34

EXERCISES

UNIT **32**

32.1 Complete the sentences. Use **must** + one of these verbs:

be ~~**go**~~ **go** **learn** **meet** **wash** **win**

1 We *must go* to the bank today. We haven't got any money.
2 Marilyn is a very interesting person. You .... her.
3 My hands are dirty. I .... them.
4 You .... to drive. It will be very useful.
5 I .... to the post office. I need some stamps.
6 The game tomorrow is very important for us. We ....
7 You can't always have things immediately. You .... patient.

32.2 Put in **I must** or **I had to**.

1 *I had to* go to the bank yesterday to get some money.
2 It's late. .... go now.
3 I don't usually work on Saturdays but last Saturday .... work.
4 .... get up early tomorrow. I've got a lot to do.
5 I went to London by train last week. The train was full and .... stand all the way.
6 I was nearly late for my appointment this morning. .... run to get there on time.
7 I forgot to phone David yesterday. .... phone him later today.

32.3 Complete the sentences. Use **mustn't** or **needn't** + one of these verbs:

~~**clean**~~ **forget** **hurry** **lose** **wait** **write**

1 The windows aren't very dirty. You *needn't clean* them.
2 We have a lot of time. We ....
3 Keep these documents in a safe place. You .... them.
4 I'm not ready yet but you .... for me. You can go now and I'll come later.
5 We .... to turn off the lights before we leave.
6 I .... the letter now. I can do it tomorrow.

32.4 Find the sentences with the same meaning.

1 We can leave the meeting early.	A We must stay until the end.	1 *D*
2 We must leave the meeting early.	B We couldn't stay until the end.	2 ....
3 We mustn't leave the meeting early.	C We can't stay until the end.	3 ....
4 We needn't leave the meeting early.	D We needn't stay until the end.	4 ....
5 We had to leave the meeting early.	E We can stay until the end.	5 ....

32.5 Put in **must / had to / mustn't / needn't**.

1 You *needn't* go. You can stay here if you want.
2 It's a fantastic film. You *must* see it.
3 We've got enough food, so we .... go shopping.
4 We didn't have any food yesterday, so we .... go shopping.
5 I want to know what happened. You .... tell me.
6 You .... tell Sue what happened. I don't want her to know.
7 I .... hurry or I'll be late.
8 'Why were you so late?' 'I .... wait half an hour for a bus.'
9 We .... decide now. We can decide later.

UNIT

33 should

A

should + *infinitive* (**should do** / **should watch** *etc.*):

I/we/you/they he/she/it	**should** **shouldn't**	**do** **stop** **go** **watch** *etc.*

B

(You) **should** do something = it is a good thing to do, it is the right thing to do:

- Tom **should go** to bed earlier. He goes to bed very late and he's always tired.
- It's a good film. You **should go** and see it.
- When you play tennis, you **should** always **watch** the ball.

C

(You) **shouldn't** do something = it is *not* a good thing to do. **Shouldn't** = should not:

- Tom **shouldn't go** to bed so late.
- You watch TV all the time. You **shouldn't watch** TV so much.

D

We often use **think** with **should**:

I think … should … :

- **I think** Carol **should buy** some new clothes.
  (= I think it is a good idea.)
- It's late. **I think** I **should go** home now.
- A: Shall I buy this coat?
  B: Yes, I **think** you **should**.

I don't think … should … :

- **I don't think** you **should work** so hard.
  (= I don't think it is a good idea.)
- **I don't think** we **should go** yet. It's too early.

Do you think … should … ?:

- **Do you think I should buy** this hat?
- What time **do you think** we **should go** home?

E

Must is stronger than **should**:

- It's a **good** film. You **should** go and see it.
- It's a **fantastic** film. You **must** go and see it.

F

Another way to say **should** … is **ought to** … :

- It's a good film. You **ought to go** and see it. (= you should go)
- I think Carol **ought to buy** some new clothes. (= Carol should buy)

shall ⇒ UNITS 28-29 **must** ⇒ UNIT 32

EXERCISES

33.1 Complete the sentences. Use **you should** + one of these verbs:

clean **go** **take** **visit** ~~**watch**~~ **wear**

1 When you play tennis, you should watch the ball.
2 It's late and you're very tired. .... to bed.
3 .... your teeth twice a day.
4 If you have time, ... the Science Museum. It's very interesting.
5 When you're driving, ... a seat belt.
6 It's too far to walk from here to the station. .... a taxi.

33.2 Write about the people in the pictures. Use **He/She shouldn't ... so ...** .

1 She shouldn't watch TV so much.
2 He ....
3 .... hard.
4 ....

33.3 You ask a friend for advice. Write questions with **Do you think I should ... ?**

1 You are in a shop. You are trying on a jacket. (buy?)
You ask your friend: Do you think I should buy this jacket?
2 You can't drive. (learn?)
You ask your friend: Do you think ....
3 You don't like your job. (get another job?)
You ask your friend: ....
4 You are going to have a party. (invite Gary?)
You ask your friend: ....

33.4 Write sentences with **I think ... should ...** or **I don't think ... should ...**

1 It's late. (go home now) I think we should go home now.
2 That coat is too big for you. (buy it) I don't think you should buy it.
3 You don't need your car. (sell it) ....
4 Diane needs a rest. (have a holiday) ....
5 Sally and Colin are too young. (get married) ....
6 You're not well this morning. (go to work) ....
7 James isn't well today. (go to the doctor) ....
8 The hotel is too expensive for us. (stay there) ....

33.5 What do you think? Write sentences with **should**.

1 I think everybody should learn another language.
2 I think everybody ....
3 I think ....
4 I don't think ....
5 I think I should ....

UNIT 34

I have to ...

A

I have to do something = it is necessary for me to do it, I am obliged to do it

I/we/you/they	**have**	**to do** **to work**
he/she/it	**has**	**to go** **to wear** *etc.*

- I'll be late for work tomorrow. I **have to go** to the dentist.
- Jill starts work at 7 o'clock, so she **has to get** up at 6.
- You **have to pass** a test before you can get a driving licence.

B

The past (**yesterday** / **last week** *etc.*) is **had to** ... :

- I was late for work yesterday. I **had to go** to the dentist.
- We **had to walk** home last night. There were no buses.

C

In questions and negatives we use **do/does** (present) and **did** (past):

present

do	I/we/you/they	**have to** ... ?
does	he/she/it	

I/we/you/they	**don't**	**have to** ...
he/she/it	**doesn't**	

past

did	I/we/you/they he/she/it	**have to** ... ?

I/we/you/they he/she/it	**didn't have to** ...

- What time **do you have to go** to the dentist tomorrow?
- **Does** Jill **have to work** on Sundays?
- Why **did** they **have to leave** the party early?

I **don't have to** (do something) = it is *not* necessary to do it:

- I'm not working tomorrow, so I **don't have to get** up early.
- Ian **doesn't have to work** very hard. He's got an easy job.
- We **didn't have to wait** very long for the bus.

D

must and **have to**

Use **must** or **have to** when you say what *you* think is necessary, when you give *your* opinion:

- It's a fantastic film. You **must** see it. *or* You **have** to see it.

When you are *not* giving your personal opinion, use **have to** (*not* **must**):

- Jill won't be at work this afternoon. She **has to** go to the doctor. (this is not my personal opinion – it is a fact)
- In many countries, men **have to** do military service. (this is not my opinion – it is the law in those countries)

must / mustn't / needn't ⇒ UNIT 32

EXERCISES

34.1 Complete the sentences. Use **have to** or **has to** + one of these verbs:

do **read** **speak** **travel** ~~**wear**~~

1 My eyes are not very good. I have to wear glasses.
2 At the end of the course all the students .... a test.
3 Mary is studying literature. She .... a lot of books.
4 Albert doesn't understand much English. You .... very slowly to him.
5 Kate is not often at home. She .... a lot in her job.

34.2 Complete the sentences. Use **have to** or **had to** + one of these verbs:

answer **buy** **change** **go** ~~**walk**~~

1 We had to walk home last night. There were no buses.
2 It's late. I .... now. I'll see you tomorrow.
3 I went to the supermarket after work yesterday. I .... some food.
4 This train doesn't go all the way to London. You .... at Bristol.
5 We did an exam yesterday. We .... six questions out of ten.

34.3 Complete the questions. Some are present and some are past.

1	I have to get up early tomorrow.	What time do you have to get up?
2	George had to wait a long time.	How long ....?
3	Liz has to go somewhere.	Where ....?
4	We had to pay a lot of money.	How much ....?
5	I have to do some work.	What exactly ....?

34.4 Write sentences with **don't/doesn't/didn't have to ...** .

1 Why are you going out? You don't have to go out.
2 Why is Ann waiting? She ....
3 Why did you get up early? You ....
4 Why is Paul working so hard? He ....
5 Why do you want to leave now? We ....

34.5 Which is correct? Sometimes **must** and **have to** are both correct.

1 It's a great film. You must see / have to see it. both are correct
2 In many countries, men ~~must do~~ / have to do military service. have to do is correct
3 You can't park your car here for nothing. You must pay / have to pay.
4 I didn't have any money with me last night, so I must borrow / had to borrow some.
5 I eat too much chocolate. I really must stop / have to stop.
6 'Why is Paula going now?' 'She must meet / has to meet somebody.'
7 What's wrong? You must tell / have to tell me. I want to help you.

34.6 Write some things that you (or your friends or family) have to do or had to do.

1 (every day) I have to travel ten miles every day.
2 (every day) ....
3 (tomorrow) ....
4 (yesterday) ....

Would you like ... ?   I'd like ...

A

Would you like ... ? = Do you want ... ?

We use **Would you like ... ?** to *offer* things:

- A: **Would you like** some coffee?
  B: No, thank you.
- A: **Would you like** a chocolate?
  B: Yes, please.
- A: What **would you like,** tea or coffee?
  B: Tea, please.

We use **Would you like to ... ?** to *invite* somebody:

- **Would you like to go** for a walk?
- A: **Would you like to have** dinner with us on Sunday?
  B: Yes, **I'd love to.** (= I would love to have dinner with you)
- What **would you like to do** this evening?

B

I'd like ... is a polite way to say 'I want'. **I'd** like = **I would** like:

- I'm thirsty. **I'd like** a drink.
- *(in a tourist office)* **I'd like** some information about hotels, please.
- **I'd like to see** the film on television this evening.

C

Would you like ... ? and **Do you like ... ?**

Would you like ... ? / I'd like ...	**Do you like ... ? / I like ...**

Would you like some tea? = Do you want some tea?	**Do you like** tea? = Do you think tea is nice?
• A: **Would you like** to go to the cinema tonight? (= Do you want to go *tonight*?) B: Yes, I'd love to.	• A: **Do you like** going to the cinema? *(in general)* B: Yes, I go to the cinema a lot.
• **I'd like** an orange, please. (= Can I have an orange?)	• **I like** oranges. *(in general)*
• What **would you like** to do next weekend?	• What **do you like** to do at weekends?

like to do and **like -ing** ⇒ UNIT 51   **I would** do something **if** ... ⇒ UNIT 112

EXERCISES

35.1 What are the people in the pictures saying? Use **Would you like ... ?**

35.2 What do you say to Sue in these situations? Use **Would you like to ... ?**

1 You want to go to the cinema tonight. Perhaps Sue will go with you. (go)
You say: *Would you like to go to the cinema tonight?*

2 You want to play tennis tomorrow. Perhaps Sue will play too. (play)
You say: ....

3 You've got some holiday photographs. Sue hasn't seen them yet. (see)
You say: ....

4 You have an extra ticket for a concert next week. Perhaps Sue will go. (go)
You say: ....

5 It's raining and Sue is going out. She hasn't got an umbrella but you have one. (borrow)
You say: ....

35.3 Which is right?

1 '~~Do you like~~ / Would you like a chocolate?' 'Yes, please.' *Would you like is right*
2 'Do you like / Would you like bananas?' 'Yes, I love them.'
3 'Do you like / Would you like an ice-cream?' 'No, thank you.'
4 'What do you like / would you like to drink?' 'A glass of water, please.'
5 'Do you like / Would you like to go out for a walk?' 'Not now. Perhaps later.'
6 I like / I'd like tomatoes but I don't eat them very often.
7 What time do you like / would you like to have dinner this evening?
8 'Do you like / Would you like something to eat?' 'No, thanks. I'm not hungry.'
9 'Do you like / Would you like your new job?' 'Yes, I'm enjoying it.'
10 I'm tired. I like / I'd like to go to sleep now.

UNIT 36

there is there are

A

There's a man on the roof.

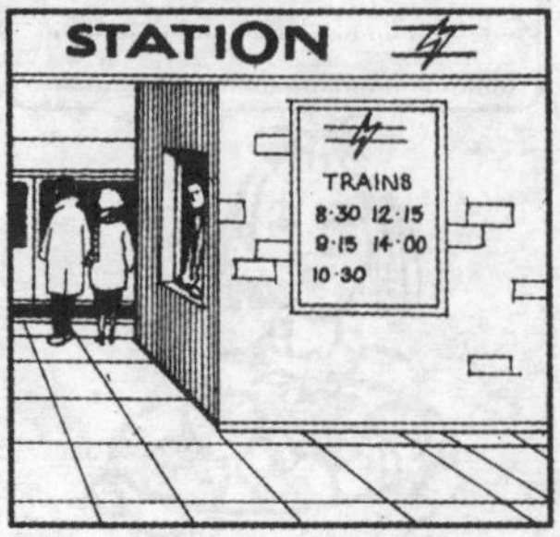

There's a train at 10.30.

There are seven days in a week.

singular

there is ...	**(there's)**
is there ... ?	
there is not ...	**(there isn't** *or* **there's not)**

- **There's** a big tree in the garden.
- **There's** a good film on TV tonight.
- A: Have you got any money?
  B: Yes, **there's** some in my bag.
- A: Excuse me, **is there** a hotel near here?
  B: Yes, **there is**. / No, **there isn't**.
- We can't go skiing. **There isn't** any snow.

plural

there are ...	
are there ... ?	
there are not ...	**(there aren't)**

- **There are** some big trees in the garden.
- **There are** a lot of accidents on this road.
- A: **Are there** any letters for me today?
  B: Yes, **there are**. / No, **there aren't**.
- This restaurant is very quiet. **There aren't** many people here.
- How many players **are there** in a football team?
- **There are** 11 players in a football team.

B

there is and it is

there is

There's a book on the table.
(*not* 'It's a book on the table.')

it is

I like this book. **It's** interesting.
(**it** = this book)

Compare:

- 'What's **that noise**?' '**It's** a train.' (**it** = that noise)
  There's a train at 10.30. **It**'s a fast train. (**it** = the 10.30 train)
- **There's** a lot of salt in this soup.
  I don't like **this soup. It**'s too salty. (**it** = this soup)

there was / were / has been etc. ⇒ UNIT 37   **it and there** ⇒ UNIT 38   **some and any** ⇒ UNIT 75

EXERCISES

36.1 Kenham is a small town. Look at the information in the box and write sentences about Kenham with **There is/are** or **There isn't/aren't**.

1	a castle?	No
2	any restaurants?	Yes (a lot)
3	a hospital?	Yes
4	a swimming pool?	No
5	any cinemas?	Yes (two)
6	a university?	No
7	any big hotels?	No

1 There isn't a castle.
2 There are a lot of restaurants.
3 ......
4 ......
5 ......
6 ......
7 ......

36.2 Write sentences about your town (or a town that you know). Use **There is/are/isn't/aren't**.

1 There are a few restaurants.
2 There's a big park.
3 ......
4 ......
5 ......
6 ......

36.3 Put in **there is / there isn't / is there / there are / there aren't / are there**.

1 Kenham isn't an old town. There aren't any old buildings.
2 Look! ...... a photograph of your brother in the newspaper!
3 'Excuse me, ... a bank near here?' 'Yes, at the end of the street.'
4 ...... five people in my family: my parents, my two sisters and me.
5 'How many students ...... in the class?' 'Twenty.'
6 'Can we take a photograph?' 'No, ... a film in the camera.'
7 '...... a bus from the city centre to the airport?' 'Yes. Every 20 minutes.'
8 '...... any problems?' 'No, everything is OK.'
9 ...... nowhere to sit down. ...... any chairs.

36.4 Write sentences with **There are ...** . Choose from the boxes.

~~seven~~	twenty-six
nine	thirty
fifteen	fifty

letters	~~days~~
players	days
planets	states

September	the solar system
the USA	~~a week~~
a rugby team	the English alphabet

1 There are seven days in a week.
2 ......
3 ......
4 ......
5 ......
6 ......

36.5 Put in **there's / is there / it's / is it**.

1 'There's a train at 10.30.' 'Is it a fast train?'
2 I'm not going to buy this shirt. ...... very expensive.
3 'What's wrong?' '...... something in my eye.'
4 ...... a red car outside the house. ...... yours?
5 '...... anything on television tonight?' 'Yes, ... a film at 8.15.'
6 'What's that building?' '...... a school.'
7 '...... a restaurant in this hotel?' 'No, I'm afraid not.'

UNIT 37

there was/were there has/have been there will be

A there was / there were *(past)*

There is a train every hour.

The time now is 11.15.
There was a train at 11 o'clock.

Compare:

there is/are *(present)*	**there was/were** *(past)*
• **There is** a good film on TV tonight. • We are staying at a very big hotel. **There are** 250 rooms. • **Are there** any letters for me this morning? • I'm hungry but **there isn't** anything to eat.	• **There was** a good film on TV last night. • We stayed at a very big hotel. **There were** 250 rooms. • **Were there** any letters for me yesterday? • When I got home, I was hungry but **there wasn't** anything to eat.

B there has been / there have been *(present perfect)*

- Look! **There's been** an accident.
  (**there's been** = there **has** been)
- This road is very dangerous. **There have been** many accidents.

Compare **there was** *(past)*:

- **There was** an accident **last night**.
  (*not* 'There has been an accident last night.')

For *past simple* and *present perfect* see Unit 20.

C there will be

- Do you think **there will be** a lot of people at the party on Saturday?
- The manager of the company is leaving, so **there will be** a new manager soon.
- I'm going away tomorrow. I'll do my packing today because **there won't be** time tomorrow.
  (**there won't be** = there **will not** be)

was/were ⇒ UNIT 10 **has/have been** ⇒ UNITS 15-18 **will** ⇒ UNIT 28 **there is/are** ⇒ UNIT 36
there and **it** ⇒ UNITS 36, 38 **some** and **any** ⇒ UNIT 75

EXERCISES

37.1 Look at the two pictures. Now the room is empty but what was in the room last week? Write sentences with **There was ...** or **There were ...** + the words in the list.

an armchair	**a carpet**	**some flowers**	**a sofa**
some books	~~**a clock**~~	**three pictures**	**a small table**

1 There was a clock on the wall near the window.
2 .... on the floor.
3 .... on the wall near the door.
4 .... in the middle of the room.
5 .... on the table.
6 .... on the shelves.
7 .... in the corner near the door.
8 .... opposite the door.

37.2 Put in **there was / there wasn't / was there / there were / there weren't / were there.**

1 I was hungry but there wasn't anything to eat.
2 Were there any letters for me yesterday?
3 .... a football match on TV last night. Did you see it?
4 'We stayed at a very nice hotel.' 'Did you? .... a swimming pool?'
5 'Did you buy any eggs?' 'No, ... any in the shop.'
6 The wallet was empty. .... any money in it.
7 '.......................... many people at the meeting?' 'No, very few.'
8 We didn't visit the museum. .... enough time.
9 I'm sorry I'm late. .... a lot of traffic.
10 Twenty years ago .... many tourists here. Now there are a lot.

37.3 Put in **there + is / are / was / were / has been / have been / will be.**

1 There was a good film on TV yesterday evening.
2 .... 24 hours in a day.
3 .... a party at the club last Friday but I didn't go.
4 'Where can I buy a newspaper?' '.......................... a shop at the end of the street.'
5 'Why are those policemen outside the bank?' '.......................... a robbery.'
6 When we arrived at the cinema, ... a long queue to see the film.
7 When you arrive tomorrow, ... somebody at the station to meet you.
8 Ten years ago .... 500 children at the school. Now .... more than a thousand.
9 Last week I went back to the town where I was born. It's very different now. .... a lot of changes.
10 I think everything will be OK. I don't think .... any problems.

UNIT **38**

It ...

A

We use **it** for *time/day/distance/weather:*

time

- What time is **it**?
- **It**'s half past ten.
- **It**'s late.
- **It**'s time to go home.

day

- What day is **it**?
- **It**'s Thursday.
- **It**'s 16 March.
- **It** was my birthday yesterday.

distance

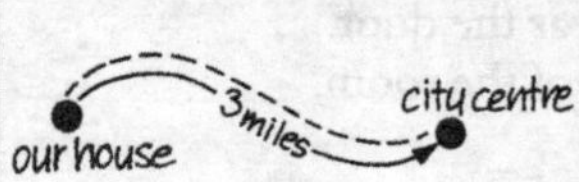

- **It**'s three miles from our house to the city centre.
- How far is **it** from London to Bristol?
- **It**'s a long way from here to the station.
- We can walk home. **It** isn't far.

We use **far** in *questions* (**is it far**?) and negatives (**it isn't far**).
We use **a long way** in *positive sentences* (**it's a long way**).

weather

- **It**'s raining. **It** isn't raining. Is **it** snowing?
- **It** rains a lot here. **It** didn't rain yesterday.
  Does **it** snow very often?
- **It**'s warm/hot/cold/fine/cloudy/windy/sunny/foggy/dark *etc.*
- **It**'s a nice day today.

Compare **it** and **there**:

- **It rains** a lot in winter.
  There is a lot of rain in winter.
- **It** was very **windy**.
  There was **a strong wind** yesterday.

B

It's nice to ... *etc.*

It's	**easy / difficult / impossible / dangerous / safe** **expensive / interesting / nice / wonderful / terrible** *etc.*	**to ...**

- **It** 's nice **to see you again**. (**it** = to see you again)
- **It**'s impossible **to understand her**. (**it** = to understand her)
- **It** wasn't easy **to find your house**. (**it** = to find your house)

C

Don't forget **it**:

- **It**'s raining again. (*not* 'Is raining again')
- Is **it** true that you are going away? (*not* 'Is true that ...')

there is → UNIT 36

EXERCISES

38.1 Write about the weather in the pictures. Use **It's ...** .

1 *It's raining.* ....
2 ....
3 ....
4 ....
5 ....
6 ....

38.2 Put in **it is (it's)** or **is it**.

1 What time *is it* ?
2 We must go now. .... very late.
3 .... true that Bill can fly a helicopter?
4 'What day .... today? Tuesday?' 'No, ... Wednesday.'
5 .... ten kilometres from the airport to the city centre.
6 .... possible to phone you at your office?
7 'Do you want to walk to the restaurant?' 'I don't know. How far .... ?'
8 .... Linda's birthday today. She's 27.
9 I don't believe it! .... impossible.

38.3 Write questions with **How far ... ?**

1 (here / the station) *How far is it from here to the station?*
2 (the hotel / the beach) How ....
3 (New York / Washington) ....
4 (your house / the airport) ....

38.4 Put in **it** or **there**.

1 *It* rains a lot in winter.
2 *There* was a strong wind yesterday.
3 .... was a nice day yesterday.
4 We can't go skiing. .... isn't any snow.
5 ....'s hot in this room. Open a window.
6 I was afraid because .... was very dark.
7 .... was a storm last night. Did you hear it?
8 ....'s a long way from here to the nearest shop.

38.5 Complete the sentences. Choose from the boxes.

it's	easy	dangerous	to	work in this office	~~get up early~~
	~~difficult~~	nice		visit different places	go out alone
	impossible	interesting		see you again	make friends

1 If you go to bed late, *it's difficult to get up early* in the morning.
2 Hello, Jill. .... How are you?
3 .... There is too much noise.
4 Everybody is very nice at work. ....
5 I like travelling. ....
6 A lot of cities are not safe. .... at night.

UNIT 39

I am   I don't etc.

A

She isn't tired but **he is.**
(**he is** = he is tired)

He likes tea but **she doesn't.**
(**she doesn't** = she doesn't like tea)

In these examples, it is not necessary to repeat words ('he is *tired*', 'she doesn't *like tea*').

You can use these verbs in the same way:

am/is/are
was/were
have/has
do/does/did
can
will
might
must

- I haven't got a car but my sister **has.** (= my sister has got a car)
- A: Please help me.
  B: I'm sorry. I **can't**. (= I can't help you)
- A: Are you tired?
  B: **I was**, but **I'm not** now. (= I was tired but I'm not tired now)
- A: Do you think Ann will phone this evening?
  B: She **might**. (= she might phone)
- A: Are you going now?
  B: Yes, I'm afraid I **must.** (= I must go)

You *cannot* use **'m/'s/'ve** *etc.* (short forms) in this way. You must use **am/is/have** *etc.*:
- She isn't tired but he **is.** (*not* ... but he's)

But you *can* use **isn't / haven't / won't** *etc.* (negative short forms):
- My sister has got a car but I **haven't**.
- 'Are you and Jim working tomorrow?' 'I am but Jim **isn't**.'

B

You can use **I am / I'm not** *etc.* after **Yes** and **No**:
- 'Are you tired?' 'Yes, I **am**. / No, **I'm not**.'
- 'Will Alan be here tomorrow?' 'Yes, he **will**. / No, he **won't**.'
- 'Is there a bus to the airport?' 'Yes, there **is**. / No, there **isn't**.'

C

We use **do/does** for the *present simple*: (⇒ Units 6–7)
- I don't like hot weather but Sue **does**. (= Sue likes hot weather)
- Sue works hard but I **don't**. (= I don't work hard)
- 'Do you enjoy your work?' 'Yes, I **do**.'

We use **did** for the *past simple*: (⇒ Unit 12)
- A: Did you and John enjoy the film?
  B: I **did** but John **didn't**. (= I enjoyed it but John didn't enjoy it)
- 'I enjoyed the film.' 'I **did** too.' (= I enjoyed it too)
- 'Did it rain yesterday?' 'No, it **didn't**.'

have you? / don't you? etc. ⇒ UNIT 40   **so am I / neither do I** etc ⇒ UNIT 41

EXERCISES

39.1 Complete these sentences. Use only one verb (**is/have/can** etc.) each time.

1 Kate wasn't hungry but we were.
2 I'm not married but my brother ....
3 Bill can't help you but I ....
4 I haven't seen the film but Tom ....
5 Diane won't be here but Chris ....
6 You weren't late but I ....

39.2 Complete these sentences with a negative verb (**isn't/haven't/can't** etc.).

1 My sister can play the piano but I can't.
2 Ann is working today but I ....
3 I was working but my friends ....
4 Richard has got a car but I ....
5 I'm ready to go but Tom ....
6 I've got a key but Sally ....

39.3 Complete these sentences with **do/does/did** or **don't/doesn't/didn't**.

1 I don't like hot weather but Sue does.
2 Sue likes hot weather but I don't.
3 My mother wears glasses but my father ....
4 You don't know Paul very well but I ....
5 I didn't enjoy the party but my friends ....
6 I don't watch TV much but Peter ....
7 Kate lives in London but her parents ....
8 You had a shower this morning but I ....

39.4 Complete the sentences. Write about yourself and other people. (See the example.)

1 I didn't go out last night but my friends did.
2 I like .... but ....
3 I don't .... but ....
4 I'm ....
5 I haven't ....

39.5 Put in a verb, positive or negative.

1 'Are you tired?' 'I was earlier but I'm not now.'
2 John is happy today but he .... yesterday.
3 The post office isn't open yet but the shops ....
4 I haven't got a video camera but I know somebody who ....
5 I would like to help you but I'm afraid I ....
6 I don't usually go to work by car but I .... yesterday.
7 A: Have you ever been to the United States?
B: No, but Sandra .... She went there on holiday last year.
8 'Do you and Ann watch TV a lot?' 'I .... but Ann doesn't.'
9 I've been invited to the party but Kate ....
10 'Do you think Diane will pass her exams?' 'Yes, I'm sure she ....'
11 'Are you going out this evening?' 'I .... I don't know for sure.'

39.6 Answer these questions about yourself. Use **Yes, I have. / No, I'm not.** etc.

1 Are you British? No, I'm not.
2 Have you got a car? ....
3 Do you feel well? ....
4 Is it snowing? ....
5 Are you hungry? ....
6 Do you like classical music? ....
7 Will you be in Paris tomorrow? ....
8 Have you ever been in hospital? ....
9 Did you buy anything yesterday? ....
10 Were you asleep at 3 a.m.? ....

Have you? Are you? Don't you? etc.

A

You can say **have you? / is it? / can't he?** etc. to show that you are interested or surprised:

- '**You're** late.' 'Oh, **am I?** I'm sorry.'
- '**I was** ill last week.' '**Were you?** I didn't know that.'
- '**It's** raining again.' '**Is it?** It was sunny ten minutes ago.'
- '**There's** a letter for you.' '**Is there?** Where is it?'

- '**Bill can't** drive.' '**Can't he?** I didn't know that.'
- '**I'm not** hungry.' '**Aren't you?** I am.'
- '**Sue isn't** at work today.' '**Isn't she?** Is she ill?'

Use **do/does** for the *present simple* and **did** for the *past simple:*

- '**I speak** four languages.' '**Do you?** Which ones?'
- '**Tom doesn't** eat meat.' '**Doesn't he?** Does he eat fish?'
- '**Linda got** married last week.' '**Did she?** Really?'

B

Question tags

You can use **have you? / is it? / can't she?** *etc.* at the end of a sentence.
These 'mini-questions' are *question tags.*

a *positive* sentence → a *negative* question tag
a *negative* sentence → a *positive* question tag

positive → *negative*

It's a beautiful day,	**isn't it?**	Yes, it's lovely.
Sally lives in London,	**doesn't she?**	Yes, that's right.
You closed the window,	**didn't you?**	Yes, I think so.
Those shoes are nice,	**aren't they?**	Yes, very nice.
Tom will be here soon,	**won't he?**	Yes, probably.

negative → *positive*

That isn't your car,	**is it?**	No, my car is white.
You haven't met my mother,	**have you?**	No, I haven't.
Sally doesn't smoke,	**does she?**	No, she doesn't.
You won't be late,	**will you?**	No, I'm never late.

I am / I don't etc. ⇒ UNIT 39

EXERCISES

40.1 Answer with **Do you? / Doesn't she? / Did they?** etc.

1	I speak four languages.	Do you ?	Which ones?
2	I work in a bank.	.... ?	I work in a bank too.
3	I didn't go to work yesterday.	.... ?	Were you ill?
4	Jill doesn't like me.	.... ?	Why not?
5	You look tired.	.... ?	I feel fine.
6	Julia phoned me last night.	.... ?	What did she say?

40.2 Answer with **Have you? / Haven't you? / Did she? / Didn't she?** etc.

1	I've bought a new car.	Have you ?	What make is it?
2	Tim doesn't eat meat.	Doesn't he ?	Does he eat fish?
3	I've lost my key.	.... ?	When did you last have it?
4	Sue can't drive.	.... ?	She should learn.
5	I was born in Italy.	.... ?	I didn't know that.
6	I didn't sleep well last night.	.... ?	Was the bed uncomfortable?
7	There's a film on TV tonight.	.... ?	Are you going to watch it?
8	I'm not happy.	.... ?	Why not?
9	I met Paula last week.	.... ?	How is she?
10	Margaret works in a factory.	.... ?	What kind of factory?
11	I won't be here next week.	.... ?	Where will you be?
12	The clock isn't working.	.... ?	It was working yesterday.

40.3 Complete these sentences with a question tag (**isn't it? / haven't you?** etc.).

1	It's a beautiful day, isn't it ?	Yes, it's lovely.
2	These flowers are nice, ... ?	Yes, what are they?
3	Judy was at the party, ... ?	Yes, but I didn't speak to her.
4	You've been to Paris, ... ?	Yes, many times.
5	You speak German, ... ?	Yes, but not very well.
6	Martin looks tired, ... ?	Yes, he works very hard.
7	You'll help me, ... ?	Yes, of course I will.

40.4 Complete these sentences with a question tag, positive (**is it? / do you?** etc.) or negative (**isn't it? / don't you?** etc.).

1	You haven't got a car, have you ?	No, I can't drive.
2	You aren't tired, ... ?	No, I feel fine.
3	Carol is a very nice person, ... ?	Yes, everybody likes her.
4	You can play the piano, ... ?	Yes, but I'm not very good.
5	You don't know Mike's sister, ... ?	No, I've never met her.
6	Sally went to university, ... ?	Yes, she studied economics.
7	The film wasn't very good, ... ?	No, it was terrible.
8	Ann lives near you, ... ?	That's right. In the same street.
9	You won't tell anybody what I said, ... ?	No, of course not.

UNIT 41

too/either so am I / neither do I etc.

A **too** and **either**

We use **too** and **either** at the end of a sentence.

We use **too** after a *positive* verb:	We use **either** after a *negative* verb:
● A: I'm happy. B: **I'm** happy **too**. ● A: I enjoyed the film. B: **I enjoyed** it **too**. ● Mary is a doctor. Her husband **is** a doctor **too**.	● A: I'm not happy. B: I'm **not** happy **either**. (*not* 'I'm not … too') ● A: I can't cook. B: I **can't either**. (*not* 'I can't too') ● Bill doesn't watch TV. He does**n't** read newspapers **either**.

B **so am I / neither do I** etc.

so **neither**	**am/is/are …** **was/were …** **do/does …** **did …** **have/has …** **can …** **will …** **would …**

so am I = I am too **so have I** = I have too (*etc.*):	**neither am I** = I'm not either **neither can I** = I can't either (*etc.*):
● A: **I'm** working. B: **So am I.** (= I'm working too) ● A: **I was** late for work today. B: **So was John**. (= John was late too) ● A: **I work** in a bank. B: **So do I.** ● A: **We went** to the cinema last night. B: Did you? **So did we.** ● A: **I'd** like to go to Australia. B: **So would I.**	● A: **I haven't** got a key. B: **Neither have I**. (= I haven't either) ● A: **Ann can't** cook. B: **Neither can Tom.** (= Tom can't either) ● A: **I won't** (= will not) be here tomorrow. B: **Neither will I.** ● A: **I never go** to the cinema. B: **Neither do I.** You can also use **Nor** … (= Neither …): ● A: I'm not married. B: **Nor am I.** *or* **Neither am I.**

Note that we say: So **am I** (*not* 'So I am'), Neither **have I** (*not* 'Neither I have').

I am / I don't etc. ⇒ UNIT 39

EXERCISES

41.1 Put in **too** or **either**.

1	I'm happy.	I'm happy too .
2	I'm not hungry.	I'm not hungry ....
3	I'm going out.	I'm going out ....
4	It rained on Saturday.	It rained on Sunday ....
5	Jenny can't drive a car.	She can't ride a bicycle ....
6	I don't like shopping.	I don't like shopping ....
7	Jane's mother is a teacher.	Her father is a teacher ....

41.2 Answer with **So ... I** (**So am I / So do I / So can I** etc.).

1	I went to bed late last night.	So did I.
2	I'm thirsty.	....
3	I've just had dinner.	....
4	I need a holiday.	....
5	I'll be late tomorrow.	....
6	I was very tired this morning.	....

Answer with **Neither**.

7	I can't go to the party.	....
8	I didn't phone Alex last night.	....
9	I haven't got any money.	....
10	I'm not going out tomorrow.	....
11	I don't know what to do.	....

41.3 You are talking to Maria. Write true sentences about yourself. Where possible, use **So ... I** or **Neither ... I**.
Look at these examples carefully:

MARIA

I'm tired. — you can answer: So am I. or I'm not.

I don't work hard. — you can answer: Neither do I. or I do.

1	I'm learning English.	....
2	I can ride a bicycle.	....
3	I'm not American.	....
4	I like cooking.	....
5	I don't like cold weather.	....
6	I slept well last night.	....
7	I've never been to Scotland.	....
8	I don't write letters very often.	....
9	I'm going out tomorrow evening.	....
10	I haven't got a headache.	....
11	I didn't watch TV last night.	....
12	I often go to the cinema.	....

UNIT 42

isn't haven't don't etc. (negatives)

A

We use **not** (**n't**) in negative sentences:

positive	→ *negative*	
am	**am not** (**'m not**)	**I'm not** tired.
is	**is not** (**isn't** *or* **'s not**)	It **isn't** (*or* It**'s not**) raining.
are	**are not** (**aren't** *or* **'re not**)	They **aren't** (*or* They**'re not**) here.
was	**was not** (**wasn't**)	Julian **wasn't** hungry.
were	**were not** (**weren't**)	The shops **weren't** open.
have	**have not** (**haven't**)	I **haven't** finished my work.
has	**has not** (**hasn't**)	Sue **hasn't** got a car.
will	**will not** (**won't**)	We **won't** be here tomorrow.
can	**cannot** (**can't**)	George **can't** drive.
could	**could not** (**couldn't**)	I **couldn't** sleep last night.
must	**must not** (**mustn't**)	I **mustn't** forget to phone Ann.
should	**should not** (**shouldn't**)	You **shouldn't** work so hard.
would	**would not** (**wouldn't**)	I **wouldn't** like to be an actor.

B

don't/doesn't/didn't

Present simple negative: I/we/you/they **do not** (**don't**) / he/she/it **does not** (**doesn't**) } **work/live/go** *etc.*

Past simple negative: I/they/he/she *(etc.)* **did not** (**didn't**) **work/live/go** *etc.*

positive	→ *negative*
I **want** to go out.	→ I **don't want** to go out.
They **work** hard.	→ They **don't work** hard.
Liz **plays** the guitar.	→ Liz **doesn't play** the guitar.
My father **likes** his job.	→ My father **doesn't like** his job.
I **got** up early this morning.	→ I **didn't get** up early this morning.
They **worked** hard yesterday.	→ They **didn't work** hard yesterday.
We **played** tennis.	→ We **didn't play** tennis.
Diane **had** a bath.	→ Diane **didn't have** a bath.

Don't ...

Look!	→ **Don't look!**
Wait for me.	→ **Don't wait** for me.

Sometimes **do** is the main verb (**don't do** / **doesn't do** / **didn't do**):

Do something!	→ **Don't do** anything!
Sue **does** a lot at weekends.	→ Sue **doesn't do** much at weekends.
I **did** what you said.	→ I **didn't do** what you said.

present simple negative ⇒ UNIT 6   past simple negative ⇒ UNIT 12   **Why isn't/don't ... ?** ⇒ UNIT 43

EXERCISES

42.1 Make these sentences negative.

1 He's gone away. *He hasn't gone away.*
2 They're married. ....
3 I've had dinner. ....
4 It's cold today. ....
5 We'll be late. ....
6 You should go. ....

42.2 Make these sentences negative. Use **don't/doesn't/didn't**.

1 She saw me. *She didn't see me.*
2 I like cheese. ....
3 They understood. ....
4 He lives here. ....
5 Go away! ....
6 I did the shopping. ....

42.3 Make these sentences negative.

1 She can swim. *She can't swim.*
2 They've arrived. ....
3 I went to the bank. ....
4 He speaks German. ....
5 We were angry. ....
6 He'll be pleased. ....
7 Phone me tonight. ....
8 It rained yesterday. ....
9 I could hear them. ....
10 I believe you. ....

42.4 Complete these sentences with a negative verb (**isn't/haven't/don't** etc.).

1 They aren't rich. They *haven't* got much money.
2 'Would you like something to eat?' 'No, thank you. I .... hungry.'
3 I .... find my glasses. Have you seen them?
4 George .... write letters very often. He prefers to use the phone.
5 We can walk to the station from here. It .... very far.
6 'Where's Jill?' 'I .... know. I .... seen her today.'
7 Be careful! .... fall!
8 We went to the cinema last night. I .... like the film very much.
9 I've been to Spain many times but I .... been to Portugal.
10 Julia .... be here tomorrow. She's going away.
11 'Who broke that window?' 'Not me. I .... do it.'
12 We didn't see what happened. We .... looking at the time.

42.5 You ask Gary some questions. His answers are always 'Yes' or 'No'. Write sentences about Gary, positive or negative.

YOU	GARY		
Are you married?	No.	1	*He isn't married.*
Do you live in London?	Yes.	2	*He lives in London.*
Were you born in London?	No.	3	....
Do you like London?	No.	4	....
Would you like to live in the country?	Yes.	5	....
Can you drive?	Yes.	6	....
Have you got a car?	No.	7	....
Do you read newspapers?	No.	8	....
Are you interested in politics?	No.	9	....
Do you watch TV most evenings?	Yes.	10	....
Did you watch TV last night?	No.	11	....
Did you go out last night?	Yes.	12	....

UNIT 43

is it … ? have you … ? do they … ? etc. (questions 1)

A

positive: **you are** **You are** eating.

question: **are you** **Are you** eating? What **are you** eating?

In questions, the first verb (**is/are/have** *etc.*) is before the subject:

positive subject + verb		*question* verb + subject
I **am** late.	→	**Am I** late?
That seat **is** free.	→	**Is that seat** free?
She **was** angry.	→	Why **was she** angry?
David **has** gone.	→	Where **has David** gone?
You **have** got a car.	→	**Have you** got a car?
They **will** be here soon.	→	When **will they** be here?
Paula **can** swim.	→	**Can Paula** swim?

Be careful with word order: the subject is after the first verb:

- Where **has David** gone? (*not* 'Where has gone David?')
- **Are those people** waiting for something? (*not* 'Are waiting … ?')
- When **was the telephone** invented? (*not* 'When was invented … ?')

B

do … ? / does … ? / did … ?

Present simple questions: **do** I/we/you/they / **does** he/she/it } **work/live/go** *etc.*

Past simple questions: **did** you/she/they *(etc.)* **work/live/go** *etc.*

positive		*question*
They **work** hard.	→	**Do** they **work** hard?
You **watch** television.	→	How often **do** you **watch** television?
Chris **works** hard.	→	**Does** Chris **work** hard?
She **gets up** early.	→	What time **does** she **get** up?
They **worked** hard.	→	**Did** they **work** hard?
You **had** dinner.	→	What **did** you **have** for dinner?
She **got** up early.	→	What time **did** she **get** up?

Sometimes **do** is the main verb (**do** you **do** / **did** he **do** *etc.*):

- What **do** you usually **do** at weekends?
- 'What **does** your brother **do**?' 'He works in a bank.'
- 'I broke my finger last week.' 'How **did** you **do** that?' (*not* 'How did you that?')

C

Why isn't … ? / Why don't … ? *etc.* (**Why** + *negative*):

- Where's John? **Why isn't he** here? (*not* 'Why he isn't here?')
- **Why can't Paula** come to the meeting tomorrow? (*not* 'Why Paula can't … ?')
- **Why didn't you** phone me last night?

present simple questions ⇒ UNIT 7 past simple questions ⇒ UNIT 12 questions 2-3 ⇒ UNITS 44-45
what/which/how … ? ⇒ UNITS 46-47

EXERCISES

43.1 Write questions.

1	I can swim.	(and you?)	Can you swim?
2	I work hard.	(and Jim?)	Does Jim work hard?
3	I was late this morning.	(and you?)	....
4	I've got a key.	(and Ann?)	....
5	I'll be here tomorrow.	(and you?)	....
6	I'm going out this evening.	(and Paul?)	....
7	I like my job.	(and you?)	....
8	I live near here.	(and Linda?)	....
9	I enjoyed my holiday.	(and you?)	....
10	I had a shower this morning.	(and you?)	....

43.2 You are talking to a friend about driving. Write the full questions.

1	(have / a car?) Have you got a car?	Yes, I have.
2	(use / a lot?) .... it	Yes, nearly every day.
3	(use / yesterday?)	Yes, to go to work.
4	(enjoy driving?)	Not very much.
5	(a good driver?)	I think I am.
6	(ever / have / an accident?)	No, never.

43.3 Put the words in the right order. All the sentences are questions.

1. (has / gone / where / David?) Where has David gone?
2. (working / Rachel / is / today?) Is Rachel working today?
3. (the children / what / are / doing?) What ....
4. (made / is / how / cheese?) ....
5. (to the party / coming / is / your sister?) ....
6. (you / the truth / tell / don't / why?) ....
7. (your guests / have / yet / arrived?) ....
8. (leave / what time / your train / does?) ....
9. (your car / in the accident / was / damaged?) ....
10. (to work / Ann / why / go / didn't?) ....

43.4 Complete the questions.

1	I want to go out.	Where do you want to go?
2	Ann and Paul aren't going to the party.	Why aren't they going?
3	I'm reading.	What ....
4	Sue went to bed early.	What time ....
5	My parents are going on holiday.	When ....
6	I met Tom a few days ago.	Where ....
7	Tina has gone away.	Where ....
8	I can't come to the party.	Why ....
9	I need some money.	How much ....
10	Angela doesn't like me.	Why ....
11	It rains sometimes.	How often ....
12	I did the shopping.	When ....

UNIT 44

Who saw you? Who did you see? (questions 2)

A

Sylvia saw Paul.

Who saw Paul?
Sylvia. (Sylvia saw him.)

Who did Sylvia **see**?
Paul. (She saw Paul.)

Sylvia saw Paul

subject	*object*
Somebody saw Paul.	Sylvia saw **somebody**.
Who saw Paul?	**Who** did Sylvia see?
Sylvia. (Sylvia saw him.)	Paul. (She saw Paul.)
'**who**' is the *subject* '**Paul**' is the *object*	'**who**' is the *object* '**Sylvia**' is the *subject*

B

In these questions, **who/what** is the *subject:*

- **Who lives** in this house? (= *somebody* lives in it – who?)
  (*not* 'Who does live?')
- **What happened**? (= *something* happened – what?)
  (*not* 'What did happen?)
- **What's happening**? (What's = What **is**)
- **Who's got** my key? (Who's = Who **has**)

In these questions, **who/what** is the *object:*

- Who did **you** meet yesterday? (= **you** met *somebody* – who?)
- What did **Paul** say? (= **Paul** said *something* – what?)
- Who are **you** phoning?
- What was **Sylvia** wearing?

Compare:

- George likes oranges. → **Who likes** oranges? – George.
  What does George like? – Oranges.
- Jill won some money. → **Who won** some money? – Jill.
  What did Jill win? – A hundred pounds.

C

Use **who** for people (somebody). Use **what** for things, ideas *etc.* (something):

- **Who** is your favourite **singer**?
- **What** is your favourite **song**?

questions ⇒ UNITS 43, 45 what/which/how ⇒ UNIT 46

EXERCISES

44.1 Make questions with **who** or **what**. In these questions, **who/what** is the subject.

1	Somebody broke the window.	*Who broke the window?*
2	Something fell off the shelf.	What ....
3	Somebody wants to see you.	.... me?
4	Somebody took my umbrella.	....
5	Something made me ill.	....
6	Somebody is coming.	....

44.2 Make questions with **who** or **what** (subject or object).

1	I bought something.	*What did you buy?*
2	Somebody lives in this house.	*Who lives in this house?*
3	I phoned somebody.	....
4	Something happened last night.	....
5	Somebody knows the answer.	....
6	Somebody did the washing-up.	....
7	Jill did something.	....
8	Something woke me up.	....
9	Somebody saw the accident.	....
10	I saw somebody.	....
11	Somebody has got my pen.	....
12	This word means something.	....

44.3 You want the missing information (**XXXXX**). Write questions with **who** or **what**.

1	I lost **XXXXX** yesterday but fortunately **XXXXX** found it and gave it back to me.	*What did you lose?* *Who found it?*
2	**XXXXX** phoned me last night. She wanted **XXXXX**.	....
3	I needed some advice, so I asked **XXXXX**. He said **XXXXX**.	....
4	I hear that **XXXXX** got married last week. **XXXXX** told me.	....
5	I met **XXXXX** on my way home this evening. She told me **XXXXX**.	....
6	Steve and I played tennis yesterday. **XXXXX** won. After the game we **XXXXX**.	....
7	It was my birthday last week and I had some presents. **XXXXX** gave me a book and Catherine gave me **XXXXX**.	....

UNIT 45

Who is she talking to? What is it like? (questions 3)

A

Julia is talking to somebody.

Who is she talking **to**?

In questions beginning **Who ... ? / What ... ? / Where ... ? / Which ... ?**, prepositions (**to/from/with** *etc.*) usually go at the end:

- '**Where** are you **from**?' 'I'm from Thailand.'
- 'John was afraid.' '**What** was he afraid **of**?'
- '**Who** do these books belong **to**?' 'They're mine.'
- Tom's father is in hospital.' '**Which hospital** is he **in**?'
- 'Kate is going on holiday.' '**Who with**?' / '**Who** is she going **with**?'
- 'I want to talk to you.' '**What about**?' / '**What** do you want to talk to me **about**?'

B

What is it like? / What are they like? *etc.*

What's (= What is) **it like?** = tell me something about it – is it good or bad, big or small, old or new? *etc.*

When we say '**What is it like?**', **like** is a *preposition*. It is *not* the verb **like** ('**Do** you **like** your new house?' *etc.*).

- A: There's a new restaurant in our street.
  B: **What's** it **like**? Is it good?
  A: I don't know. I haven't eaten there yet.
- A: **What's** your new teacher **like**?
  B: She's very good. We learn a lot.
- A: I met Linda's parents yesterday.
  B: Did you? **What** are they **like**?
  A: They're very friendly.
- A: Did you have a nice holiday? **What** was the weather **like**?
  B: It was lovely. The sun shone every day.

questions ⇒ UNITS 43-44 what/which/how ⇒ UNIT 46 prepositions ⇒ UNITS 99-106

EXERCISES

45.1 You want the missing information (**XXXXX**). Write questions with **who** or **what**.

1 The letter is from **XXXXX**.	*Who is the letter from?*
2 I'm looking for a **XXXXX**.	What .... you ....
3 I went to the cinema with **XXXXX**.	....
4 The film was about **XXXXX**.	....
5 I gave the money to **XXXXX**.	....
6 The book was written by **XXXXX**.	....

45.2 Complete the questions for the pictures. Use one of these verbs + a preposition:

listen **look** **talk** ~~**talk**~~ **wait** **write**

1 *Who is she talking to?*
2 What ....
3 Who ....
4 What ....
5 What ....
6 Which bus ....

45.3 Write questions beginning **Which ... ?**

1 Tom's father is in hospital.	*Which hospital is he in?*
2 We stayed at a hotel.	.... you ....
3 Jack plays for a football team.	....
4 I went to school in this town.	....

45.4 You want some information about another country. You ask somebody who has been there. Ask questions with **What is/are ... like?**

1 (the roads) *What are the roads like?*
2 (the food) ....
3 (the people) ....
4 (the weather) ....

45.5 Ask questions with **What was/were ... like?**

1 Your friend has just come back from holiday. Ask about the weather.
What was the weather like?
2 Your friend has just come back from the cinema. Ask about the film.
....
3 Your friend has just finished an English course. Ask about the lessons.
....
4 Your friend has just come back from holiday. Ask about the hotel.
....

UNIT **46**

What ... ? Which ... ? How ... ?

A

What + *noun* (**What colour ... ? / What kind ... ?** *etc.*)

- **What colour** is your car?
- **What colour** are your eyes?
- **What size** is this shirt?
- **What make** is your TV set?
- **What time** is it?
- **What day** is it today?
- **What kind** of job do you want? (*or* **What type** of job ... ? / **What sort** of job ... ?)

What *without a noun:*

- **What**'s your favourite colour?
- **What** do you want to do this evening?

B

Which + *noun* (things or people):

- **Which train** did you catch – the 9.50 or the 10.30?
- **Which doctor** did you see – Doctor Ellis, Doctor Gray or Doctor Hill?

We use **which** *without a noun* for things, not people:

- **Which** is bigger – Canada or Australia?

We use **who** for people *(without a noun)*:

- **Who** is taller – Bill or Gerry? (*not* 'Which is taller?')

C

What or **which?**

We use **which** when we are thinking about a small number of possibilities (perhaps 2, 3 or 4):

- We can go this way or that way.
  Which way shall we go?
- There are four umbrellas here.
  Which is yours?

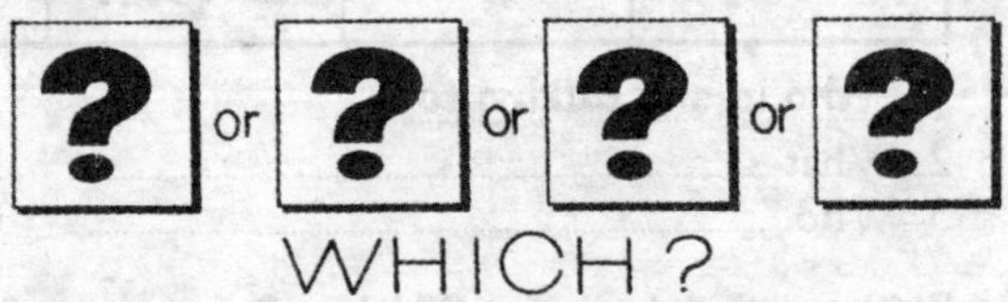

What is more general:

- **What** is the capital of Argentina?
- **What sort** of music do you like?

Compare:

- **What colour** are his eyes? (*not* 'Which colour?')
  Which colour do you prefer, **pink or yellow**?
- **What** is the longest river in the world?
  Which is the longest river – **the Mississippi, the Amazon or the Nile**?

D

How ... ?

- '**How** was the party last night?' 'It was great.'
- '**How** do you usually go to work?' 'By bus.'

You can use **how** + *adjective/adverb* (**how tall / how old / how often** *etc.*):

'**How**
- **tall** are you?' 'I'm 1 metre 70.'
- **big** is the house?' 'Not very big.'
- **old** is your mother?' 'She's 45.'
- **far** is it from here to the airport?' 'Five kilometres.'
- **often** do you use your car?' 'Every day.'
- **long** have they been married?' 'Ten years.'
- **much** was the meal?' 'Twenty pounds.'

questions ⇒ UNITS 43-45 **How long does it take ... ?** ⇒ UNIT 47 **which one(s)** ⇒ UNIT 74

EXERCISES

46.1 Write questions with **what**.

1	I've got a new TV set.	(make?)	*What make is it?*
2	I want a job.	(kind?)	*What kind of job do you want?*
3	I've got a new sweater.	(colour?)	What ....
4	I got up early this morning.	(time?)	.... get up?
5	I like music.	(type?)	....
6	I want to buy a car.	(kind?)	....

46.2 Complete the questions. Use **Which ... ?**

46.3 Put in **what/which/who**.

1 *What* is that man's name?
2 *Which* way shall we go? Left or right?
3 You can have tea or coffee. .... do you prefer?
4 '.............. day is it today?' 'Friday.'
5 This is a nice house. .... room is yours?
6 .... is your favourite sport?
7 .... is more expensive, meat or fish?
8 .... is older, Ann or George?
9 .... kind of camera have you got?
10 A: Mary has got three cameras.
B: .... camera does she use most?
11 .... nationality are you?

46.4 Complete the questions with **How** + adjective or adverb (**high/long** etc.).

1	*How high* is Mount Everest?	Nearly 9000 metres.
2	.... is it to the station?	It's about two kilometres from here.
3	.... is Helen?	She's 26.
4	.... do the buses run?	Every ten minutes.
5	.... is the water in the pool?	Two metres.
6	.... have you lived here?	Nearly three years.

46.5 Write questions with **How ... ?**

1 Are you 1 metre 70? 1.75? 1.80? *How tall are you?*
2 Is this box one kilogram? Two? Three? ....
3 Are you 20 years old? 22? 25? ....
4 Did you spend £10? £15? £20? ....
5 Do you watch TV every day? Once a week? Never?
....
6 Is it 1000 miles from Paris to Moscow? 1500? 2000?
....

UNIT 47

How long does it take … ?

A

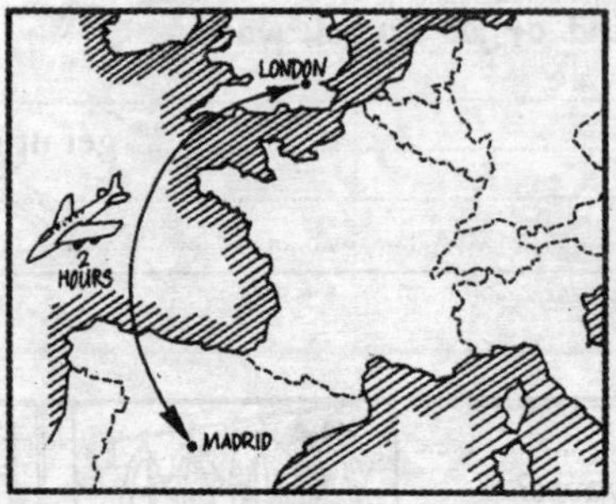

How long **does it take**		by plane by train by car		?
It takes	two hours ten minutes a long time		from … to …	

How long **does it take** by plane from London to Madrid?

It takes two hours.

- How long **does it take** by train from London to Manchester?
- **It takes** two hours by train from London to Manchester.
- How long **does it take** by car from your house to the station?
- **It takes** ten minutes by car from my house to the station.

B

How long	**does** **did** **will**	**it take**	(you) (Ann) (them)	**to … ?**

It	**takes** **took** **will take**	(me) (Ann) (them)	a week a long time three hours	**to …**

I started reading the book on Monday.
I finished it on Wednesday evening.

It **took me** three days **to read** it.

- How long **does it take to fly** from London to Madrid?
- **It takes** a long time **to learn** a language.
- **It doesn't take** long **to cook** an omelette.
- **It takes me** 20 minutes **to get** to work.

- 'I came by train.' 'Did you? How long **did it take** (to get here)?'
- **It took Tom** an hour **to do** his shopping.
- **Did it take you** a long time **to find** a job?

- How long **will it take me** to learn to drive?
- **It will take us** an hour **to cook** the dinner.

EXERCISES

47.1 Look at the pictures and write questions with **How long ... ?**

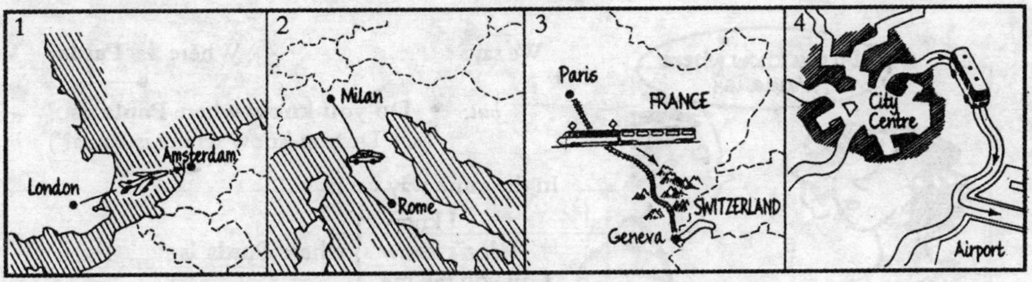

1 How long does it take by plane from London to Amsterdam?
2 ....
3 ....
4 ....

47.2 How long does it take to do these things? Write full sentences.

1 fly from your city/country to London
It takes two hours to fly from Madrid to London.
2 fly from your city/country to New York
....
3 study to be a doctor in your country
....
4 walk from your home to the nearest shop
....
5 get from your home to the nearest airport
....

47.3 Write questions with **How long did it take ... ?**

1 (She found a place to live.) How long did it take her to find a place to live?
2 (I walked to the station.) .... you ....
3 (He cleaned the windows.) ....
4 (I learnt to ski.) ....
5 (They repaired the car.) ....

47.4 Read the situations and write sentences with **It took ...** .

1 I read a book last week. I started reading it on Monday. I finished it three days later.
It took me three days to read the book.
2 We walked home last night. We left at 10 o'clock and we arrived home at 10.20.
....
3 I learnt to drive last year. I had my first driving lesson in January. I passed my driving test six months later. ....
4 Mark drove to London yesterday. He left home at 8 o'clock and got to London at 10.
....
5 Linda began looking for a job a long time ago. She got a job last week.
....
6 *(write a true sentence about yourself)*
....

UNIT 48

Do you know where ... ?
I don't know what ... etc.

A

We say: Where **is** **Paula**?

but: **Do you know** where **Paula** **is** ?
(*not* 'Do you know where is Paula?')

In the same way we say:

I know
I don't know } where **Paula is**
Can you tell me

Compare:

Who **are those people**?	*but*	**Do you know** / **Can you tell me**	who **those people are**	?
How old **is Linda**?			how old **Linda is**	
What time **is it**?			what time **it is**	
Where **can I** go?			where **I can** go	
How much **is this camera**?		**I know** / **I don't know** / **I don't remember**	how much **this camera is**	
When **are you** going away?			when **you're** going away	
Where **have they** gone?			where **they have** gone	
What **was Ann** wearing?			what **Ann was** wearing	

B

Questions with **do/does/did** (*present simple* and *past simple*):

Where **does he live** ?

Do you know where **he lives** ? (*not* 'Do you know where does he live?')

Compare:

How **do aeroplanes** fly?	*but*	**Do you know**	how **aeroplanes fly**	?
What **does Jane** want?		**I don't know**	what **Jane wants**	
Why **did she** go home?		**I don't remember**	why **she went** home	
Where **did I** put the key?		**I know**	where **I put** the key	

C

Questions beginning **Is ... ? / Do ... ? / Can ... ?** *etc.* (*yes/no questions*):

Compare:

Question					
Is Jack at home?	*but*	**Do you know**	**if** *or* **whether**	**Jack is** at home	?
Have they got a car?				**they've** got a car	
Can Brian swim?		**I don't know**		**Brian can** swim	
Do they live near here?				**they live** near here	
Did anybody see you?				**anybody saw** you	

You can use **if** *or* **whether** in these sentences:

- Do you know **if** they've got a car? *or* Do you know **whether** they've got a car?

EXERCISES

48.1 Answer these questions with **I don't know where/when/why ... etc.**

1 Have your friends gone home? (where) *I don't know where they've gone.*
2 Is Kate in her office? (where) I don't know ......
3 Is the castle very old? (how old) ......
4 Will Paul be here soon? (when) ......
5 Was he angry because I was late? (why) ......
6 Has Sally lived here a long time? (how long) ......

48.2 Complete the sentences.

1 (How do aeroplanes fly?) Do you know *how aeroplanes fly?*
2 (Where does Susan work?) I don't know ......
3 (What did Peter say?) Do you remember ......?
4 (Why did he go home early?) I don't know ......
5 (What time does the film begin?) Do you know ......?
6 (How did the accident happen?) I don't remember ......

48.3 Which is right?

1 Do you know what time ~~is it~~ / it is? Do you know what time it is? is right
2 Why are you / you are going away?
3 I don't know where are they / they are going.
4 Can you tell me where is the museum / the museum is?
5 Where do you want / you want to go for your holidays?
6 Do you know what do elephants eat / elephants eat?

48.4 Write questions with **Do you know if ... ?**

1 (Have they got a car?) *Do you know if they've got a car?*
2 (Are they married?) Do you know ......
3 (Does Sue know Bill?) ......
4 (Will George be here tomorrow?) ......
5 (Did he pass his exam?) ......

48.5 Write questions beginning **Do you know ... ?**

1 (What does Ann want?) *Do you know what Ann wants?*
2 (Where is Paula?) Do ......
3 (Is she working today?) ......
4 (What time does she start work?) ......
5 (Are the shops open tomorrow?) ......
6 (Where do Sarah and Tim live?) ......
7 (Did they go to Ann's party?) ......

48.6 Use your own ideas to complete these sentences.

1 Do you know why *the bus was late* ?
2 Do you know what time ......?
3 Excuse me, can you tell me where ......?
4 I don't know what ......
5 Do you know if ......?

UNIT 49

She said that ... He told me that ...

A

Last week you went to a party. A lot of your friends were there. Here are some things they said to you:

Today you meet Paul. You tell him about the party. *You* tell *Paul* what *your friends* said:

DIANE  I'm enjoying my new job. / My **father isn't** very well.	**am** / **is** → **was**	Diane said that **she was** enjoying her new job. She said that **her father wasn't** very well.
SARAH, TIM  **We're** going to buy a house.	**are** → **were**	Sarah and Tim said that **they were** going to buy a house.
PETER  **I have** to go early. / **My sister has** gone to Australia.	**have** / **has** → **had**	Peter said that **he had** to go early. He said that **his sister had** gone to Australia.
ANN  I **can't** find a job.	**can** → **could**	Ann said that **she couldn't** find a job.
STEVE  **I'll** phone you.	**will** → **would**	Steve said that **he would** phone me.
ANGELA  **I don't** like my job. / **My son doesn't** like school.	**do** / **does** → **did**	Angela said that **she didn't** like her job. She said that **her son didn't** like school.
MIKE  **You look** tired. / YOU  **I feel** fine.	**look** → **looked**; **feel** → **felt**; *etc.* *(present)* → *etc.* *(past)*	Mike said that **I looked** tired. I said that **I felt** fine.

B

say and **tell**

say (→ said)
- He **said** that he was tired. (*not* 'He said me')
- What did she **say to** you? (*not* 'say you')

Do *not* say: 'he said me', 'I said Ann' *etc.*

tell (→ told)
- He **told me** that he was tired. (*not* 'He told that ...')
- What did she **tell you**? (*not* 'tell to you')

Do *not* say: 'he told to me', 'I told to Ann' *etc.*

C

You can say:
- He said **that** he was tired. *or* He said he was tired. (*without* 'that')
- Ann told me **that** she didn't like her job. *or* Ann told me she didn't like her job.

 I told him to ⇒ UNIT 52

EXERCISES

49.1 Read what these people say and write sentences with **He/She /They said (that)** … .

1 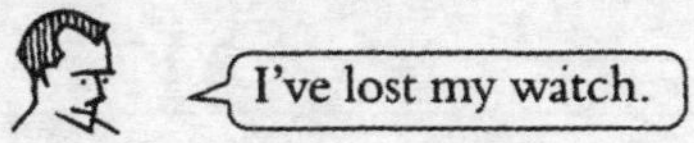

He said he had lost his watch.

2 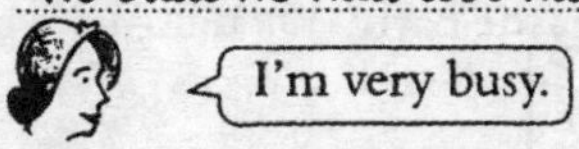

....

3 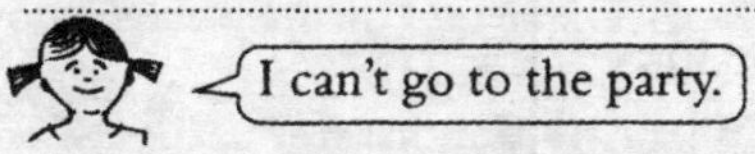

....

4 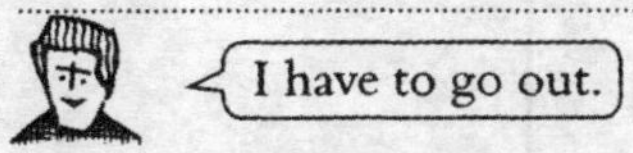

....

5 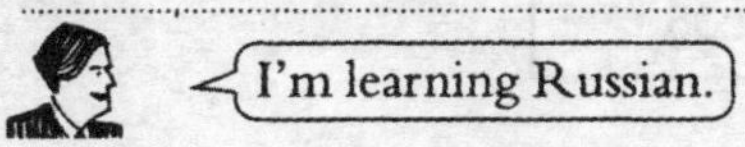

....

6 

....

7 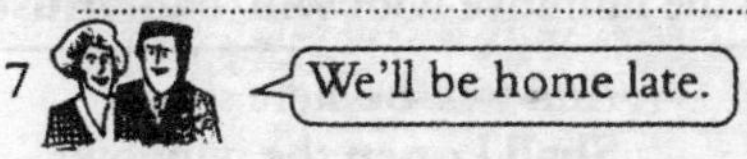

....

8 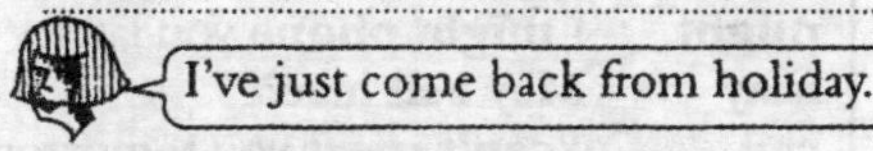

....

9 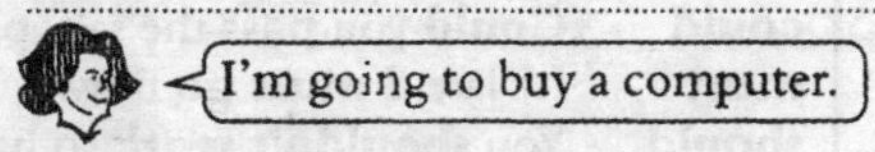

....

10 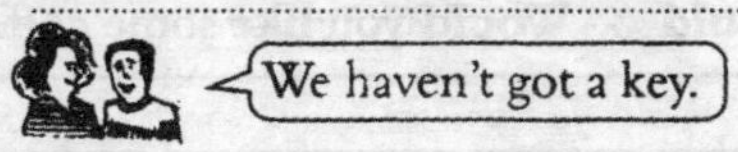

....

49.2 Use the pictures to complete the sentences.

1 I met Diane last week. She said she was enjoying her new job.
2 Betty didn't want anything to eat. She said ....
3 I wanted to borrow Mike's ladder but he said ....
4 Sally was invited to the party but she said ....
5 Sharon told me she didn't want the picture. She said ....
6 Martin has just gone away on holiday. He said ....
7 I was looking for Robert. Linda said ....
8 'Why did Steve stay at home?' 'He said ....'
9 'Has Mary gone out?' 'I think so. She said ....'

49.3 Put in **say/said** or **tell/told**.

1 He said he was tired.
2 What did she tell you?
3 Ann .... she didn't like Peter.
4 Jack .... me that you were ill.
5 Please don't .... Jim what happened.
6 Did Lucy .... she would be late?
7 The woman .... she was a reporter.
8 The woman .... us she was a reporter.
9 They asked me a lot of questions but I didn't .... them an thing.
10 They asked me a lot of questions but I didn't .... anything.

UNIT 50

work/working go/going do/doing

A work/go/be *etc. (infinitive)*

We use the infinitive with **will/can/must** *etc.*:

will	Ann **will be** here soon.	⇒ Units 28–29
shall	**Shall** I **open** the window?	
might	I **might phone** you later.	⇒ Unit 30
may	**May** I **sit** here?	
can	I **can't meet** you tomorrow.	⇒ Unit 31
could	**Could** you **pass** the salt, please?	
must	It's late. I **must go** now.	⇒ Unit 32
should	You **shouldn't work** so hard.	⇒ Unit 33
would	**Would** you **like** some coffee?	⇒ Unit 35

do/does *(present simple)*	**Do** you **work**? They **don't work** very hard. Tina **doesn't know** many people. How much **does** it **cost**?	⇒ Units 6–7
did *(past simple)*	What time **did** the train **leave**? We **didn't sleep** well.	⇒ Unit 12

B to work / to go / to be *etc.* (to + *infinitive*)

(I'm) **going to...**	**I'm going to play** tennis tomorrow. What **are** you **going to do**?	⇒ Unit 27
(I) **have to...**	**I have to go** now. Everybody **has to eat.**	⇒ Unit 34
(I) **want to...**	Do you **want to go** out? They don't **want to come** with us.	⇒ Unit 51
(I) **would like to...**	**I'd like to talk** to you. **Would** you **like to go** out?	⇒ Unit 35
(I) **used to...**	Dave **used to work** in a factory.	⇒ Unit 25

C working/going/playing *etc.*

am/is/are + -ing *(present continuous)*	Please be quiet. **I'm working.** Tom **isn't working** today. What time **are** you **going** out?	⇒ Units 3–4, 8, 26
was/were + -ing *(past continuous)*	It **was raining**, so we didn't go out. What **were** you **doing** when the phone rang?	⇒ Units 13–14

verbs + to ... and -ing (I want to do / I enjoy doing) ⇒ UNIT 51   go + -ing ⇒ UNIT 54

EXERCISES

50.1 Complete the sentences. Write: **... phone Paul** or **... to phone Paul**.

1 I'll phone Paul .
2 I'm going to phone Paul .
3 Can you .... Paul?
4 Shall I .... ?
5 I'd like ....
6 Do you have .... ?
7 You should ....
8 I want ....
9 I might ....
10 You must ....

50.2 Complete the sentences with a verb from the box. Sometimes you need the infinitive (**work/go** etc.) and sometimes you need **-ing** (**working/going** etc.).

do/doing	get/getting	~~sleep/sleeping~~	watch/watching
eat/eating	go/going	stay/staying	wear/wearing
fly/flying	listen/listening	wait/waiting	~~work/working~~

1 Please be quiet. I'm working .
2 I feel tired today. I didn't sleep very well last night.
3 What time do you usually .... up in the morning?
4 'Where are you ....?' 'To the bank.'
5 Did you .... television last night?
6 Look at that plane! It's .... very low.
7 You can turn off the radio. I'm not .... to it.
8 They didn't .... anything because they weren't hungry.
9 My friends were .... for me when I arrived.
10 'Does Sharon always .... glasses?' 'No, only for reading.'
11 'What are you .... this evening?' 'I'm .... at home.'

50.3 Put the verb in the correct form. Choose:
the infinitive (**work/go** etc.) or **to ... (to work / to go** etc.) or **-ing (working/going** etc.)

1 Shall I open the window? (open)
2 It's late. I have to go now. (go)
3 Ann isn't working this week. She's on holiday. (work)
4 I'm tired. I don't want .... out. (go)
5 It might ...., so take an umbrella with you. (rain)
6 What time do you have .... tomorrow morning? (leave)
7 I'm afraid I can't .... you. (help)
8 My brother is a student. He's .... physics. (study)
9 Would you like .... on a trip round the world? (go)
10 When you saw Janet, what was she ....? (wear)
11 When you go to London, where are you going ....? (stay)
12 I'm hungry. I must .... something to eat. (have)
13 'Where's George?' 'He's .... a bath.' (have)
14 I used .... a car but I sold it last year. (have)
15 He spoke very quietly. I couldn't .... him. (hear)
16 You don't look well. I don't think you should .... to work today. (go)
17 I don't know what he said. I wasn't .... to him. (listen)
18 I'm sorry I'm late. I had .... a phone call. (make)
19 I want .... what happened. (know) You must .... me. (tell)
20 May I .... your phone? (use)

UNIT **51**

to … (I want to do) and -ing (I enjoy doing)

A

verbs + **to …** (I want to do)

want	**plan**	**decide**	**try**	
hope	**expect**	**offer**	**forget**	**+ to … (to do / to work / to be** *etc.***)**
need	**promise**	**refuse**	**learn**	

- What do you **want to do** this evening?
- It's not very late. We **don't need to go** home yet.
- Tina has **decided to sell** her car.
- You **forgot to switch** off the light when you went out.
- My brother is **learning to drive**.
- I **tried to read** my book but I was too tired.

B

verbs + **-ing** (I enjoy doing)

enjoy	**stop**	**suggest**	**+ -ing (doing / working / being** *etc.***)**
mind	**finish**		

- I **enjoy** dancing. (*not* 'enjoy to dance')
- I don't **mind** getting up early.
- Has it **stopped** raining?
- Sonia **suggested** going to the cinema.

C

verbs + **-ing** *or* **to…**

like	**love**	**start**	**continue**	**+ -ing (doing** *etc.***)** *or* **to … (to do** *etc.***)**
prefer	**hate**	**begin**		

- Do you **like** getting up early? *or* Do you **like to get** up early?
- I **prefer** travelling by car. *or* I **prefer to travel** by car.
- Ann **loves** dancing. *or* Ann **loves to dance**.
- I **hate** being late. *or* I **hate to be** late.
- It **started** raining. *or* It **started to rain**.

D

would like to … *(etc.)*

would like	**would love**	**+ to … (to do / to work / to be** *etc.***)**
would prefer	**would hate**	

- Julia **would like to meet** you. (*not* 'would like meeting')
- **I'd love to go** to Australia. (**I'd** = **I would**)
- '**Would you like to sit down?**' 'No, **I'd prefer to stand**, thank you.'
- **I wouldn't like to be** a teacher.

would like ⇒ UNIT 35 **I want you to …** ⇒ UNIT 52 **go + -ing** ⇒ UNIT 54
preposition + -ing ⇒ UNIT 105

EXERCISES

51.1 Put the verb in the right form, **to ...** or **-ing**.

1 I enjoy dancing (dance).
2 What do you want to do (do) tonight.
3 Goodbye! I hope .... (see) you again soon.
4 I learnt .... (swim) when I was five years old.
5 Have you finished .... (clean) the kitchen?
6 I'm tired. I want .... (go) to bed.
7 Do you enjoy .... (visit) other countries?
8 The weather was nice, so I suggested .... (go) for a walk by the river.
9 Where's Bill? He promised .... (be) here on time.
10 I'm not in a hurry. I don't mind .... (wait).
11 What have you decided .... (do)?
12 George was very angry and refused .... (speak) to me.
13 Where's Ann? I need .... (ask) her something.
14 I was very upset and started .... (cry).
15 I'm trying .... (work). Please stop .... (talk).

51.2 Complete the sentences using **to ...** or **-ing**. Use one of these verbs:

go help ~~live~~ lose rain read see send ~~take~~ wait walk watch

1 I like London but I wouldn't like to live there.
2 I like taking (OR to take) photographs when I'm on holiday.
3 Linda has a lot of books. She enjoys ....
4 I'm surprised that you're here. I didn't expect .... you.
5 Don't forget .... us a postcard when you're on holiday.
6 'Shall we get a taxi to the cinema?' 'If you like, but it isn't far. I don't mind ....'
7 This ring is very beautiful. I'd hate .... it.
8 Julia had a lot to do, so I offered .... her.
9 What shall we do this afternoon? Would you like .... to the beach?
10 When I'm tired in the evenings, I like .... television.
11 'Shall we go now?' 'No, I'd prefer .... a few minutes.'
12 I'm not going out until it stops ....

51.3 Complete the answers to the questions.

1	Do you usually get up early?	Yes, I like getting (OR to get) up early .
2	Do you ever go to museums?	Yes, I love ....
3	Do you often write letters?	No, I don't like ....
4	Have you ever been to New York?	No, but I'd love .... one day.
5	Do you often travel by train?	Yes, I enjoy ....
6	Shall we eat at home or go to a restaurant?	I don't mind .... a restaurant but I'd prefer .... home.

51.4 Complete these sentences. Write about yourself. Use **to ...** or **-ing**.

1 I enjoy ....
2 I don't like ....
3 If it's a nice day tomorrow, I'd like ....
4 When I'm on holiday, I like ....
5 I don't mind .... but ....
6 I wouldn't like ....

UNIT 52

I want you to ... I told you to ...

A

I want you to ...

The woman **wants to go.**

The man **doesn't want** the woman **to go.** He **wants** her **to stay.**

We say:

I want { **you** / **somebody** / **Ann** } **to do something**

- **I want you to be** happy. (*not* 'I want that you are happy')
- They didn't **want anybody to know** their secret.
- Do you **want me to lend** you some money?

We use **would like** in the same way:

- **Would** you **like me to lend** you some money?

B

We also use this structure (*verb* + somebody + **to** ...) with:

ask
tell
advise
expect
persuade
teach

	verb	+ somebody	+ **to** ...	
Sue	**asked**	a friend	**to lend**	her some money.
I	**told**	you	**to be**	careful.
What do you	**advise**	me	**to do?**	
I didn't	**expect**	them	**to be**	here.
We	**persuaded**	George	**to come**	with us.
I	**taught**	my brother	**to swim.**	

C

I told you to ... / I told you not to ...

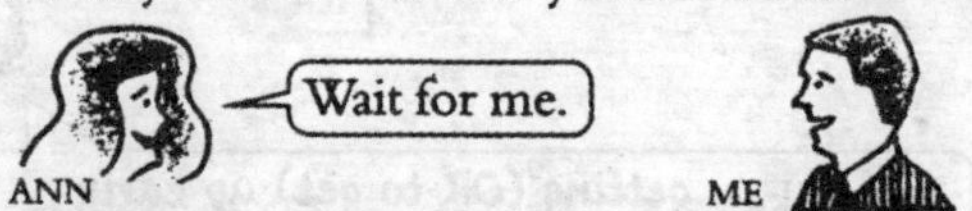

→ Ann **told** me **to wait** for her.

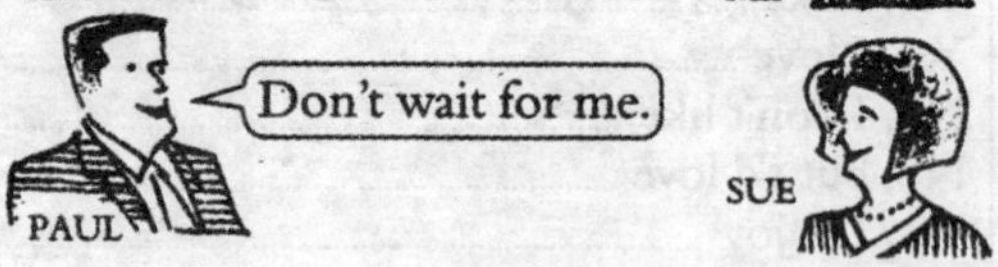

→ Paul **told** Sue **not to wait** for him.

D

make and **let**

After **make** and **let**, we do *not* use **to**:

- He's very funny. He **makes** me **laugh.** (*not* 'makes me to laugh')
- At school our teacher **made** us **work** very hard.
- Sue **let** me **use** her computer because mine wasn't working (*not* 'let me to use')

You can say **Let's** ... (= **Let us**) when you want people to do things with you:

- Come on! **Let's dance.**
- 'Shall we go out tonight?' 'No, I'm tired. **Let's stay** at home.'

He told me that ... ⇒ UNIT 49

EXERCISES

52.1 Write sentences beginning **I want you ... / I don't want you ... / Do you want me ... ?**

1 (you must come with me) *I want you to come with me.*
2 (listen carefully) I want ....
3 (please don't be angry) I don't ....
4 (shall I wait for you?) Do you ....
5 (don't phone me tonight) ....
6 (you must meet Sarah) ....

52.2 Look at the pictures and complete the sentences.

1 Dan persuaded *me to go to the cinema.*
2 I wanted to get to the station. A woman told ....
3 Brian wasn't well. I advised ....
4 Linda had a lot of luggage. She asked ....
5 I was busy. I told ....
6 I wanted to make a phone call. Paul let ....
7 Sue is going to phone later. I told ....
8 Ann's mother taught ....

52.3 Complete these sentences with the verbs in the list. Sometimes **to** is necessary (**to go / to wait** etc.); sometimes **to** is not necessary (**go/wait** etc.).

arrive borrow get go go make repeat tell think wait

1 Please stay here. I don't want you *to go*.
2 I didn't hear what she said, so I asked her .... it.
3 'Shall we begin?' 'No, let's .... a few minutes.'
4 Are they already here? I expected them .... much later.
5 Kevin's parents didn't want him .... married.
6 I want to stay here. You can't make me .... with you.
7 'Is that your bicycle?' 'No, it's John's. He let me .... it.'
8 Mary can't come to the party. She told me .... you.
9 Would you like a drink? Would you like me .... some coffee?
10 'Ann doesn't like me.' 'What makes you .... that?'

UNIT 53

I went to the shop to ...

A

Paula wanted a newspaper, so she went to the shop.

Why did she go to the shop?
To buy a newspaper.

She went to the shop **to buy** a newspaper.

to ... (**to buy** / **to see** *etc.*) tells us *why* a person does something:

- 'Why are you going out?' '**To get** some bread.'
- Ann went to the station **to meet** her friend.
- Sue turned on the television **to watch** the news.
- I'd like to go to Spain **to learn** Spanish.

money/time to (do something):

- We need some **money to buy** food.
- I haven't got **time to watch** television.

B

to ... and **for** ...

to + *verb* (**to buy** / **to see** *etc.*)	**for** + *noun* (**for a newspaper** / **for food** *etc.*)
• I went to the shop **to buy** a newspaper. (*not* 'for buy')	• I went to the shop **for a newspaper.**
• They're going to Scotland **to see** their friends.	• They're going to Scotland **for a holiday.**
• We need some money **to buy** food.	• We need some money **for food.**

C

wait for ...

- Please **wait for me.**
- Are you **waiting for the bus**?

wait to (do something):

- Hurry up! I'm **waiting to go.**
- Are you **waiting to see** the doctor?

wait for (somebody/something) **to** ... :

- I can't go out yet. I'm **waiting for John to phone.**
- Are you **waiting for the doctor to come**?

go to ... and go for ... ⇒ UNIT 54 **something to eat / nothing to do etc.** ⇒ UNIT 78
enough to/for ... ⇒ UNIT 90 **too ... to/for ...** ⇒ UNIT 91

EXERCISES

53.1 Write sentences beginning **I went to ...** . Choose from the boxes.

~~the station~~	the post office	buy some food	get some stamps
the café	the supermarket	~~catch a train~~	meet a friend

1 *I went to the station to catch a train.*
2 I went ....
3 ....
4 ....

53.2 Finish the sentences. Choose from the box.

to open this door	to wake him up	to see who it was
~~to watch the news~~	to read the newspaper	to get some fresh air

1 I turned on the television *to watch the news.*
2 Alice sat down in an armchair ....
3 Do I need a key ....?
4 I went for a walk by the river ....
5 I knocked on the door of David's room ....
6 The doorbell rang, so I looked out of the window ....

53.3 Use your own ideas to finish these sentences. Use **to ...** .

1 I went to the shop *to buy a newspaper.*
2 I'm very busy. I haven't got time ....
3 I phoned Ann ....
4 I'm going out ....
5 I borrowed some money ....

53.4 Put in **to** or **for**.

1 Paula went to the shop *to* buy some bread.
2 We went to a restaurant .... have dinner.
3 Robert wants to go to university .... study economics.
4 I'm going to London .... an interview next week.
5 I'm going to London .... visit some friends of mine.
6 Have you got time .... a cup of coffee?
7 I got up late this morning. I didn't have time .... wash.
8 Everybody needs money .... live.
9 The office is very small. There's space only .... a desk and chair.
10 A: Excuse me, are you waiting .... use the phone?
B: No, I'm waiting .... somebody.

53.5 Finish these sentences. Choose from:

~~John / phone~~   **it / to arrive**   **you / tell me**   **the film / begin**

1 I can't go out yet. I'm waiting *for John to phone.*
2 I sat down in the cinema and waited ....
3 We called an ambulance and waited ....
4 'Do you know what to do?' 'No, I'm waiting ....'

UNIT **54**

go to ... go on ... go for ... go -ing

A

go to ... (**go to work** / **go to London** / **go to a concert** *etc.*)

- What time do you usually **go to work**?
- I'm **going to France** next week.
- Tom didn't want to **go to the concert**.
- 'Where's Ann?' 'She's **gone to bed**.'
- **I went to the dentist** last week.

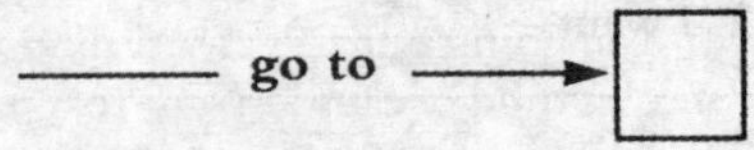

go to sleep = start to sleep:

- I was very tired and **went to sleep** quickly.

go home (*without* **to**)

- I'm **going home** now. (*not* 'going to home')

B

go on ...

go on	holiday a trip a tour an excursion a cruise strike

- We're **going on holiday** next week.
- Children often **go on school trips**.
- When we were in Scotland, we **went on a lot of excursions** to different places.
- The workers have **gone on strike**. (= they are refusing to work)

C

go for ...

go (somewhere) **for**	a walk a run a swim a drink a meal a holiday

- 'Where's Ann?' 'She's **gone for a walk**.'
- Do you **go for a run** every day?
- The sea looks nice. Let's **go for a swim**.
- We **went for a drink** after work yesterday.
- Shall we **go** out **for a meal**? I know a good restaurant.
- They've **gone** to Scotland **for a holiday**.
  (We say **'on holiday'** *but* **'for a** holiday'.)

D

go + -ing

We use **go + -ing** for many sports (**swimming** / **skiing** *etc.*) and also **shopping**:

I **go** he is **going** we **went** they have **gone** she wants to **go**	shopp**ing** swimm**ing** fish**ing** sail**ing** ski**ing** jogg**ing** *etc.*

- Are you **going shopping** this afternoon?
- It's a nice day. Let's **go swimming**. (*or* Let's **go for a** swim.)
- Rachel has a small boat and she often **goes sailing**.
- **I went jogging** before breakfast this morning.

EXERCISES

54.1 Put in **to/on/for** where necessary.

1 I'm going ...to... France next week.
2 Rachel often goes ...... sailing.
3 Sue went ...... Mexico last year.
4 Would you like to go ...... the cinema this evening?
5 Jack goes ...... jogging every morning.
6 I'm going out ...... a walk. Do you want to come?
7 I'm tired because I went to a party last night and went ...... bed very late.
8 Martin is going ...... holiday ...... Italy next week.
9 The weather was warm and the river was clean, so we went ...... a swim.
10 There will be no buses next week because the bus drivers are going ...... strike.
11 I need some stamps, so I'm going ...... the post office.
12 It's late. I must go ...... home now.
13 Would you like to go ...... a tour of the city?
14 Shall we go out ...... a meal this evening?
15 My parents are going ...... a cruise this summer.

54.2 Use the pictures to complete the sentences. Use **go/goes/going/went + -ing**.

RACHEL DIANE GEORGE LINDA PETER SHEILA

1 Rachel has a boat. She often ...goes sailing... .
2 Last Saturday Diane went ....
3 George ...... every day.
4 Linda is going on holiday next month. She is ....
5 Peter is going out later. He has to ....
6 Sheila ...... after work yesterday evening.

54.3 Use the words in the box to finish these sentences. Use **to/on/for** if necessary.

home	shopping	holiday	~~a swim~~	sleep
a walk	Portugal	riding	the bank	skiing

1 The sea looks nice. Let's go ...for a swim... .
2 'Is Ann at home?' 'No, she's gone ...... to get some money.'
3 I'm going ...... now. I have to buy some presents.
4 I was very tired last night. I sat down in an armchair and went ....
5 I wasn't enjoying the party, so I went ...... early.
6 We live near the mountains. In winter we go ...... every weekend.
7 Richard has got a horse. He often goes ....
8 The weather is nice. Shall we go ...... in the park?
9 A: Are you going ...... soon?
B: Yes, next month. We're going ....

UNIT
55 get

A

get a letter / **get a job** *etc.* (**get** + *noun*) = receive/buy/fetch/find:

you **don't have** something → you **get** it → you **have** it

- 'Did you **get** my letter?' 'Yes, I **got** it yesterday.' (= *receive*)
- I like your pullover. Where did you **get** it? (= *buy*)
- (*on the phone*) 'Hello, can I speak to Ann, please?' 'One moment. I'll **get** her.' (= *fetch*)
- It's difficult to **get** a job at the moment. (= *find*)

also **get a bus** / **a train** / **a taxi** (= take a bus/train etc.):

- 'Did you come here on foot?' 'No, I **got** the bus.'

B

get hungry / **get cold** / **get tired** *etc.* (**get** + *adjective*) = become:

you're **not hungry** → you **get hungry** → you **are hungry**

- If you don't eat, you **get hungry**.
- Drink your coffee. It**'s getting cold**.
- I'm sorry your mother is ill. I hope she **gets better** soon.
- We **got** very **wet** because we didn't have an umbrella.

also **get married**
get dressed (= put your clothes on)
get lost (= lose your way)

- Linda and Frank are **getting married** soon.
- I got up and **got dressed** quickly.
- We went for a walk and **got lost**.

C

get to a place = arrive:

- I usually **get to work** before 8.30. (= *arrive at work*)
- We left London at 10 o'clock and **got to Manchester** at 12.45.
- How did you **get here**? By bus?

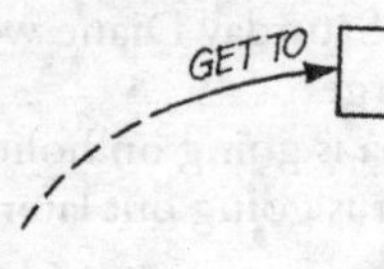

get home (*without* **to**):

- What time did you **get home** last night?

D

get in/out/on/off

get in (a car) | **get out** (**of** a car) | **get on** | **get off** (a bus / a train / a plane)

- Kate **got in the car** and drove away. (*You can also say:* Kate got **into** the car ...)
- A car stopped and a man **got out**. (*but* A man got out **of the car**.)
- We **got on the bus** outside the hotel and **got off** in Church Street.

get to ⇒ UNIT 101 **in/out/on/off** ⇒ UNITS 103, 107 **get up** ⇒ UNIT 107 **get on** ⇒ APPENDIX 6

EXERCISES

55.1 Complete these sentences. Use **get(s)** and choose from the box.

a taxi	~~my letter~~	some milk	a doctor
your jacket	a good salary	a ticket	the job

1 I wrote to you last week. Did you *get my letter* ?
2 Where did you .... ? It's very nice.
3 Quick! This man is ill. We must ....
4 I don't want to walk home. Let's ....
5 I had an interview with the manager but I didn't ....
6 When you go out, can you .... ?
7 'Are you going to the concert?' 'Yes, if I can ....'
8 Margaret has got a well-paid job. She ....

55.2 Complete these sentences. Use **getting** + one of these words:

dark **late** ~~**cold**~~ **ready** **married**

1 Drink your coffee. It's *getting cold.*
2 Turn on the light. It's ....
3 'I'm .... next week.' 'Oh, really? Congratulations!'
4 'Where's Sally?' 'She's .... to go out.'
5 It's .... It's time to go home.

55.3 Complete the sentences. Use **get/got** + one of these words:

angry **better** ~~**hungry**~~ **lost** **married** **nervous** **old** **wet**

1 If you don't eat, you *get hungry.*
2 Don't go out in the rain. You'll ....
3 My brother .... last year. His wife's name is Julia.
4 Why did you .... with me? I didn't do anything wrong.
5 We tried to find the hotel but we ....
6 Everybody wants to stay young but we all ....
7 The beginning of the film wasn't very good but it ....
8 Most people .... before examinations.

55.4 Write sentences with **I left ... and got to ...** .

1 home / 7.30 → work / 8.15 *I left home at 7.30 and got to work at 8.15.*
2 London / 10.15 → Bristol / 11.45
I left London at 10.15 and ....
3 the party / 11.15 → home / midnight
....
4 **Write a true sentence about yourself.**
I left ....

55.5 Put in **got in / got out of / got on / got off**.

1 Kate *got in* the car and drove away.
2 I .... the bus and walked to my house from the bus stop.
3 Ann .... the car, shut the door and went into a shop.
4 I made a stupid mistake. I .... the wrong train.

UNIT **56**

do and **make**

A

Do is a general word for actions:

- What are you **doing** this evening? (*not* 'What are you making?')
- 'Shall I open the window?' 'No, it's OK. I'll **do** it.'
- Julia's job is very boring. She **does** the same thing every day.
- I **did** a lot of things yesterday.

What do you do? = What's your job?:

- 'What do you **do**?' 'I work in a bank.'

B

Make = produce/create. For example:

She's **making** coffee. He has **made** a cake. They **make** umbrellas. It was **made** in France.

Compare **do** and **make**:

- **I did** a lot of things yesterday. I **cleaned** my room, I **wrote** some letters and I **made** a cake.
- A: What do you **do** in your free time? Sport? Reading? Hobbies?
  B: I **make clothes**. I **make** dresses and jackets. I also **make** toys for children.

C

Expressions with **do**

do	an exam (examination) / a test
	a course
	homework
	(somebody) a favour
	exercises
	housework

- I'm **doing my driving test** next week.
- John has just **done a training course**.
- Have the children **done their homework**?
- Ann, could you **do me a favour**?
- I go for a run and **do exercises** every morning.
- I hate **doing housework**, especially cleaning.

also **do the shopping / the washing / the washing-up / the ironing / the cooking** *etc.*:

- **I did the washing** but I didn't **do the shopping**.

D

Expressions with **make**

make	a mistake
	an appointment
	a phone call
	a list
	a noise
	a bed

- I'm sorry, **I made a mistake**.
- I must **make an appointment** to see the doctor.
- Excuse me, I have to **make a phone call**.
- Have you **made a shopping list**?
- It's late. We mustn't **make a noise**.
- Sometimes I forget to **make my bed** in the morning.

We say **make a film** *but* **take a photograph**:

- When was **this film made**? *but* When was **this photograph taken**?

do/does/did (negatives and questions) ⇒ UNITS 42-43 **make** somebody do something ⇒ UNIT 52

EXERCISES

56.1 Put in **make/making/made** or **do/doing/did/done**.

1 'Shall I open the window?' 'No, it's OK. I'll ...do... it.'
2 What did you .... at the weekend? Did you go away?
3 Do you know how to .... bread?
4 Paper is .... from wood.
5 Richard didn't help me. He sat in an armchair and .... nothing.
6 'What do you ....?' 'I'm a doctor.'
7 I asked you to clean the bathroom. Have you .... it?
8 'What do they .... in that factory?' 'Shoes.'
9 I'm .... some coffee. Would you like some?
10 Why are you angry with me? I didn't .... anything wrong.
11 'What are you .... tomorrow afternoon?' 'I'm working.'

56.2 What are these people doing?

1 He's making a cake.
2 They ....
3 He ....
4 ....
5 ....
6 ....
7 ....
8 ....
9 ....
10 ....
11 ....
12 ....

56.3 Put in **make** or **do** in the correct form.

1 I hate ...doing... housework, especially cleaning.
2 Why do you always .... the same mistake?
3 'Can you .... me a favour?' 'It depends what it is.'
4 'Have you .... your homework?' 'Not yet.'
5 I need to see the dentist but I haven't .... an appointment.
6 I'm .... a course in photography at the moment. It's very good.
7 The last time I .... an exam was ten years ago.
8 When you've finished Exercise 1, you can .... Exercise 2.
9 There's something wrong with the car. The engine is .... a strange noise.
10 It was a bad mistake. It was the worst mistake I've ever ....
11 Let's .... a list of all the things we have to .... today.

UNIT **57**

have

A have and have got (⇒ Unit 9)

I've got (something) or **I have** (something) = it is mine:

- **I've got** a new car. *or* I **have** a new car.
- Sue **has got** long hair. *or* Sue **has** long hair.
- **Have** they **got** any children? *or* **Do** they **have** any children?
- Tim **hasn't got** a job. *or* Tim **doesn't have** a job.
- How much time **have** you **got**? *or* How much time **do** you **have**?

also

I've got / **I have**	a headache / (a) toothache / a stomach ache / a pain (in my leg *etc.*)
	a cold / a cough / a sore throat / a temperature / flu *etc.*

- **I've got** a headache. *or* I **have** a headache.
- **Have** you **got** a cold? *or* **Do** you **have** a cold?

The past is: **I had** (*without* 'got') / **I didn't have** / **Did you have**? *etc.*:

- When I first met Sue, she **had** short hair.
- He **didn't have** any money because he **didn't have** a job.
- How much time **did** you **have**?

B have breakfast / have a shower *etc.*

In these expressions **have** = eat/drink/take etc. You *cannot* use 'have got'.

have	breakfast / lunch / dinner
	a meal / a sandwich / a pizza *etc.*
	a cup of coffee / a glass of milk *etc.*
	something to eat/drink

- 'Where's Ann?' 'She's **having** lunch.'
- I **don't** usually **have** breakfast.
- I **had** three cups of coffee this morning.
- '**Have** a biscuit!' 'Oh, thank you.'

We also use **have** (*not* 'have got') in these expressions:

have	a bath / a shower
	a rest / a holiday / a party
	a nice time / a good journey *etc.*
	a walk / a swim / a game (of tennis *etc.*)
	a dream / an accident
	a baby
	a look (at …)

- I **had** a shower this morning.
- We**'re having** a party next week. You must come.
- Enjoy your holiday. **Have** a nice time!
- **Did** you **have** a good time in London?
- Sandra has just **had** a baby.
- Can I **have** a look at your newspaper?

C

Compare **I've got** and **I have**:

- **I've got** / **I have** a new shower. It's very good.
  (You can use **I've got** *or* **I have** *in this sentence.)*
- I **have** a shower every morning. (*not* '**I've got**')
- A: Where's Paul?
  B: He**'s having** a shower. (= he's washing now)

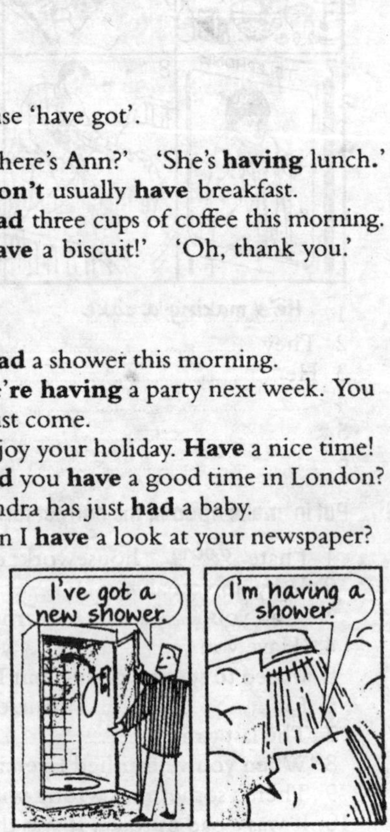

EXERCISES

57.1 Put in the correct form of **have** or **have got**.

1 I didn't have time to do the shopping yesterday. (I / not / have)
2 'Has Lisa got (OR Does Lisa have) a car?' 'No, she can't drive.' (Lisa / have?)
3 He can't open the door. .... a key. (he / not / have)
4 .... a cold last week. He's better now. (George / have)
5 What's wrong? .... a headache? (you / have?)
6 We wanted to go by taxi but we .... enough money. (we / not / have)
7 Liz is very busy. .... much free time. (she / not / have)
8 .... any problems when you were on holiday? (you / have?)

57.2 What are these people doing? Choose from the list:

a rest **a cup of tea** **a bath** **~~breakfast~~** **dinner** **a nice time**

1 They're having breakfast.
2 She ....
3 He ....
4 They ....
5 ....
6 ....

57.3 What do you say in these situations?

1 Ann is going on holiday. What do you say to her before she goes?
Have a nice holiday!
2 You meet Claire at the airport. She has just got off her plane. Ask her about the flight.
Did you have a good flight?
3 Tom is going on a long journey. What do you say to him before he leaves?
....
4 It's Monday morning. You are at work. Ask Paula about her weekend.
....
5 Paul has just come home after playing tennis with a friend. Ask him about the game.
....
6 Rachel is going out for a meal tonight. What do you say to her before she goes?
....

57.4 Complete the sentences. Use **have/had** and choose from the list.

an accident **a glass of water** **a look** **a walk** **~~a party~~** **something to eat**

1 We had a party a few weeks ago. We invited fifty people.
2 'Shall we ....?' 'No, I'm not hungry.'
3 I was thirsty, so I ....
4 I like to get up early and .... before breakfast.
5 Tina is a very good driver. She has never ....
6 There's something wrong with the engine of my car. Can you .... at it?

UNIT
58

I/me he/him they/them etc.

A *People*

subject	**I**	**we**	**you**	**he**	**she**	**they**
object	**me**	**us**	**you**	**him**	**her**	**them**

subject			*object*
I	**I** know Ann.	Ann knows **me.**	**me**
we	**We** know Ann.	Ann knows **us.**	**us**
you	**You** know Ann.	Ann knows **you.**	**you**
he	**He** knows Ann.	Ann knows **him.**	**him**
she	**She** knows Ann.	Ann knows **her.**	**her**
they	**They** know Ann.	Ann knows **them.**	**them**

B *Things*

subject	**it**	**they**
object	**it**	**them**

- I don't want **this book.** You can have **it**.
- I don't want **these books**. You can have **them.**
- Diane never drinks **milk**. She doesn't like **it**.
- I never go to **parties.** I don't like **them.**

C

We use **me/her/them** *etc. (object)* after a preposition (**for/to/with** *etc.*):

- This letter isn't **for me**. It's **for you**.
- Who is that woman? Why are you looking **at her**?
- We're going to the cinema. Do you want to come **with us?**
- Sue and Kevin are going to the cinema. Do you want to go **with them?**
- 'Where's the newspaper?' 'You're sitting **on it**.'

give it/them to ... :

- I want that book. Please give **it to me**.
- Robert wants these books. Can you give **them to him**, please?

my/his/their etc. ⇒ UNIT 59 **Give me that book / Give it to me** ⇒ UNIT 95

EXERCISES

58.1 Finish the sentences with **him/her/them**.

1 I don't know those girls. Do you know *them* ?
2 I don't know that man. Do you know .... ?
3 I don't know those people. Do you know .... ?
4 I don't know David's wife. Do you know .... ?
5 I don't know Mr Stevens. Do you know .... ?
6 I don't know Sarah's parents. Do you know .... ?
7 I don't know the woman with the black coat. Do you know .... ?

58.2 Complete the sentences. Use **I/me/you/she/her** etc.

1 **I** want to see **her** but *she* doesn't want to see *me* .
2 **They** want to see **me** but .... don't want to see ....
3 **She** wants to see **him** but .... doesn't want to see ....
4 **We** want to see **them** but .... don't want to see ....
5 **He** wants to see **us** but .... don't want to see ....
6 **They** want to see **her** but .... doesn't want to see ....
7 **I** want to see **them** but .... don't want to see ....
8 **You** want to see **her** but .... doesn't want to see ....

58.3 Write sentences beginning **I like ... , I don't like ...** or **Do you like ... ?**

1 I don't eat tomatoes. *I don't like them.*
2 George is a very nice man. I like ....
3 This jacket isn't very nice. I don't ....
4 This is my new car. Do .... ?
5 Mrs Clark is not very friendly. I ....
6 These are my new shoes. .... ?

58.4 Complete the sentences. Use **I/me/he/him** etc.

1 Who is that woman? Why are you looking at *her* ?
2 'Do you know that man?' 'Yes, I work with ....'
3 Where are the tickets? I can't find ....
4 I can't find my keys. Where are .... ?
5 We're going out. You can come with ....
6 Margaret likes music. .... plays the piano.
7 I don't like dogs. I'm afraid of ....
8 I'm talking to you. Please listen to ....
9 Where is Ann? I want to talk to ....
10 My brother has a new job. .... doesn't like .... very much.

58.5 Complete the sentences.

1 I want that book. Can you *give it to me* ?
2 He wants the key. Can you give .... ?
3 She wants the keys. Can you .... ?
4 I want that letter. Can you .... ?
5 They want the money. Can you .... ?
6 We want the photographs. Can you .... ?

my/his/their etc.

A

I → **my**	I	like	**my**	job.
we → **our**	We	like	**our**	jobs.
you → **your**	You	like	**your**	job.
he → **his**	He	likes	**his**	job.
she → **her**	She	likes	**her**	job.
they → **their**	They	like	**their**	jobs.
it → **its**	Oxford (= it) is famous for **its** university.			

We use **my/your/his** *etc. + a noun:*

my hands　　**his** mother　　**her** new car
our house　　**your** best friend　　**their** room

B

his/her/their

DIANE

her car
(= Diane's car)

her husband
(= Diane's husband)

her children
(= Diane's children)

ANDY

his bicycle

his sister

his parents

MR AND MRS THOMSON

their son

their daughter

their children

C

its and it's

its　　Oxford is famous for **its** university.
it's (= it **is**)　　I like Oxford. **It's** a nice city. (= It **is** a nice city.)

mine/yours etc. ⇒ UNIT 60　　**I/me/my/mine** ⇒ UNIT 61

EXERCISES

59.1 Finish these sentences.

1 I'm going to wash my hands.
2 She's going to wash ....
3 We're going to wash ....
4 He's going to wash ....
5 They're going to wash ....
6 Are you going to wash .... ?

59.2 Finish these sentences.

1 He lives with his parents.
2 They live with .... parents.
3 We .... parents.
4 Julia lives ....
5 I .... parents.
6 John ....
7 Do you live .... ?
8 Most children ....

59.3 Look at the family tree and complete the sentences with **his/her/their**.

1 I saw Liz with her husband, Philip.
2 I saw Ann and Ted with .... children.
3 I saw Ted with .... wife, Ann.
4 I saw George with .... brother, Bill.
5 I saw Ann with .... brother, Bill.
6 I saw Liz and Philip with .... son, Bill.
7 I saw Ann with .... parents.
8 I saw Diana and Robert with .... parents.

59.4 Put in **my/our/your/his/her/their/its**.

1 Do you like your job?
2 I know Mr Watson but I don't know .... wife.
3 Mr and Mrs Baker live in London. .... son lives in Australia.
4 We're going to have a party. We're going to invite all .... friends.
5 Ann is going out with .... friends this evening.
6 I like tennis. It's .... favourite sport.
7 'Is that .... car?' 'No, I haven't got a car.'
8 I want to phone Ann. Do you know .... phone number?
9 Do you think most people are happy in .... jobs?
10 I'm going to wash .... hair before I go out.
11 This is a beautiful tree. .... leaves are a beautiful colour.
12 John has a brother and a sister. .... brother is 25 and .... sister is 21.

59.5 Complete the sentences. Use **my/his/their** etc. with one of these words:

coat **homework** **house** **husband** ~~**job**~~ **key** **name**

1 Jim doesn't enjoy his job. It's not very interesting.
2 I can't open the door. I haven't got ....
3 Sally is married. .... works in a bank.
4 It's very cold today. Put on .... when you go out.
5 'What are the children doing?' 'They're doing ....'
6 'Do you know that man?' 'Yes, but I don't know ....'
7 We live in Barton Street. .... is at the end on the left.

UNIT 60 Whose is this? It's mine/yours/hers etc.

A

I	→	**my**	→	**mine**
we	→	**our**	→	**ours**
you	→	**your**	→	**yours**
he	→	**his**	→	**his**
she	→	**her**	→	**hers**
they	→	**their**	→	**theirs**

It's **my** money.	It's **mine.**
It's **our** money.	It's **ours.**
It's **your** money.	It's **yours.**
It's **his** money.	It's **his.**
It's **her** money.	It's **hers.**
It's **their** money.	It's **theirs.**

B

We use **my/your** *etc. + a noun* (**my hands / your book** *etc.*):

- **My hands** are cold.
- Is this **your book**?
- Ann gave me **her umbrella**.
- It's **their problem**, not **our problem**.

We use **mine/yours** *etc. without a noun:*

- Is this book **mine** or **yours**? (= my book or your book)
- I didn't have an umbrella, so Ann gave me **hers**. (= her umbrella)
- It's their problem, not **ours**. (= not our problem)
- We went in our car and they went in **theirs**. (= their car)

You can use **his** *with or without a noun:*

- 'Is this **his camera** or **hers**?' 'It's **his**.'

C

a friend **of mine** / a friend **of his** / some friends **of yours** *etc.*

- I went out to meet a friend **of mine**. (*not* 'a friend of me')
- Tom was with a friend **of his**. (*not* 'a friend of him')
- Are those people friends **of yours**? (*not* 'friends of you')

D

Whose ... ?

- **Whose book** is this? (= Is it your book? his book? my book? *etc.*)

You can use **whose** *with or without a noun:*

- **Whose money** is this? / **Whose** is this? } It's mine.
- **Whose shoes** are these? / **Whose** are these? } They're John's.

my/his/their etc. ⇒ UNIT 59 **I/me/my/mine** ⇒ UNIT 61 **Ann's camera / my brother's car** ⇒ UNIT 63

EXERCISES

60.1 Finish the sentences with **mine/yours** etc.

1 It's your money. It's ...yours...
2 It's my bag. It's ....
3 It's our car. It's ....
4 They're her shoes. They're ....
5 It's their house. It's ....
6 They're your books. They're ....
7 They're my glasses. They're ....
8 It's his coat. It's ....

60.2 Choose the right word.

1 It's their/~~theirs~~ problem, not ~~our~~/ours. — their and ours are right
2 This is a nice camera. Is it your/yours?
3 That's not my/mine umbrella. My/Mine is black.
4 Whose books are these? Your/Yours or my/mine?
5 Catherine is going out with her/hers friends this evening.
6 My/Mine room is bigger than her/hers.
7 They've got two children but I don't know their/theirs names.
8 Can we use your washing machine? Our/Ours is broken.

60.3 Finish these sentences. Use **friend(s) of mine/yours** etc.

1 I went to the cinema with a ...friend of mine...
2 They went on holiday with some ...friends of theirs...
3 She's going out with a friend ....
4 We had dinner with some ....
5 I played tennis with a ....
6 Tom is going to meet a ....
7 Do you know those people? Are they ....?

60.4 Look at the pictures. What are the people saying?

UNIT 61

I/me/my/mine

	I *etc.* (⇒ Unit 58)	**me** *etc.* (⇒ Unit 58)	**my** *etc.* (⇒ Unit 59)	**mine** *etc.* (⇒ Unit 60)
	**I** know Tom.	Tom knows **me**.	It's **my** car.	It's **mine**.
	**We** know Tom.	Tom knows **us**.	It's **our** car.	It's **ours**.
	**You** know Tom.	Tom knows **you**.	It's **your** car.	It's **yours**.
	**He** knows Tom.	Tom knows **him**.	It's **his** car.	It's **his**.
	**She** knows Tom.	Tom knows **her**.	It's **her** car.	It's **hers**.
	**They** know Tom.	Tom knows **them**.	It's **their** car.	It's **theirs**.

- 'Do **you** know that man?' 'Yes, **I** know **him** but **I** can't remember **his name**.'
- **She** was very pleased because **we** invited **her** to stay with **us** at **our house**.
- A: Where are the children? Have **you** seen **them**?
  B: Yes, **they** are playing with **their friends** in the park.
- That's **my pen**. Can you give it to **me**, please?
- 'Is this **your umbrella**?' 'No, it's **yours**.'
- **He** didn't have an umbrella, so **she** gave **him hers**. (= she gave her umbrella to him)
- **I'm** meeting a friend of **mine** this evening. (*not* 'a friend of me')

myself/yourself etc. ⇒ UNIT 62 **Give me that book / Give it to me** ⇒ UNIT 95

EXERCISES

61.1 Answer the questions in the same way.

1

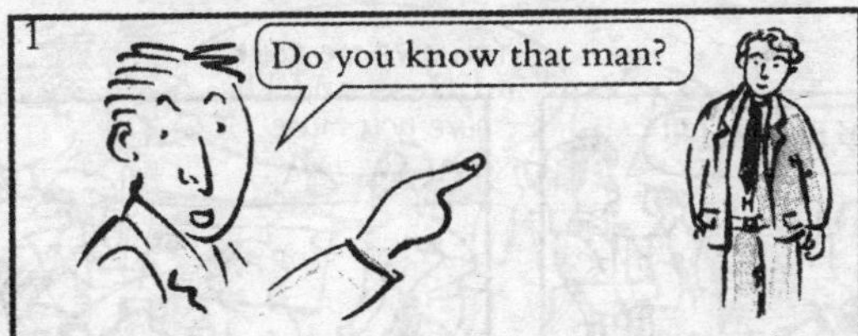

Yes, I know him but I can't remember his name.

2

Yes, I know .... but I can't remember ....

3

Yes, I .... but I .... names.

4

Yes, I .... but ....

61.2 Finish these sentences in the same way.

1 We invited her to stay with us at our house.
2 He invited us to stay with .... house.
3 They invited me to stay with .... house.
4 I invited them ....
5 She invited us ....
6 Did you invite him .... ?

61.3 Complete the sentences in the same way.

1 I gave him my address and he gave me his.
2 I gave her .... address and she gave me ....
3 He gave me .... address and I gave ....
4 We gave them .... address and they gave ....
5 She gave him .... address and ....
6 You gave us .... address and ....
7 They gave you .... address and ....

61.4 Put in **him/her/yours** etc.

1 Where's Ann? Have you seen her ?
2 Where are my keys? Where did I put .... ?
3 This letter is for Bill. Can you give it to .... ?
4 We wrote to John but he didn't answer .... letter.
5 'I can't find my pen. Can I use .... ?' 'Yes, of course.'
6 We're going to the cinema. Why don't you come with .... ?
7 Did your sister pass .... exams?
8 Some people talk about .... jobs all the time.
9 Last night I went out for a meal with a friend of ....

UNIT 62

myself/yourself/themselves etc.

A

He's looking at **himself**.

Help **yourself**!

They're enjoying **themselves**.

I	→	**me**	→	**myself**
he	→	**him**	→	**himself**
she	→	**her**	→	**herself**
you	→	**you**	→	**yourself** / **yourselves**
we	→	**us**	→	**ourselves**
they	→	**them**	→	**themselves**

- **I** looked at **myself** in the mirror.
- **He** cut **himself** with a knife.
- **She** fell off her bike but she didn't hurt **herself**.
- Please help **yourself**. *(one person)*
- Please help **yourselves**. *(two or more people)*
- We had a good holiday. **We** enjoyed **ourselves**.
- They had a nice time. **They** enjoyed **themselves**.

B

Compare:

me/him/them *etc.*

She is looking at **him**
different people

- You never talk to **me**.
- I didn't pay for **them**.
- Did I hurt **you**?

myself/himself/themselves *etc.*

He is looking at **himself**
the same person

- Sometimes I talk to **myself**.
- They paid for **themselves**.
- Be careful. Don't hurt **yourself**.

C

by myself / by yourself *etc.* = alone:

- I went on holiday **by myself**. (= I went alone)
- 'Was she with friends?' 'No, she was **by herself**.'

D

each other

- Jill and Ann are good friends. They know **each other** well. (= Jill knows Ann / Ann knows Jill)
- Paul and I live near **each other**. (= he lives near me / I live near him)

Compare **each other** and **-selves**:

- Steve and Sue looked at **each other**. (= he looked at her / she looked at him)

- Steve and Sue looked at **themselves**. (= he looked at himself / she looked at herself)

EXERCISES

62.1 Finish the sentences with **myself/yourself** etc.

1 He looked at himself in the mirror.
2 I'm not angry with you. I'm angry with ....
3 Margaret had a nice time in London. She enjoyed ....
4 My friends had a nice time in London. They enjoyed ....
5 I picked up a very hot plate and burnt ....
6 He never thinks about other people. He only thinks about ....
7 I want to know more about you. Tell me about .... *(one person)*
8 Goodbye! Have a nice holiday and look after .... ! *(two people)*

62.2 Write sentences with **by myself / by yourself** etc.

1 I went on holiday alone.	I went on holiday by myself.
2 When I saw him, he was alone.	When I saw him, he ....
3 Don't go out alone.	Don't ....
4 I went to the cinema alone.	I ....
5 My sister lives alone.	My sister ....
6 Many people live alone.	Many people ....

62.3 Write sentences with **each other**.

1 They like each other.
2 They can't ....
3 They ....

4 ....
5 ....
6 ....

62.4 Complete the sentences. Use: **each other** or **ourselves/yourselves/themselves** or **us/you/them.**

1 Paul and I live near each other .
2 Who are those people? Do you know them ?
3 You can help Tom and Tom can help you. So you and Tom can help ....
4 There's food in the kitchen. If you and Chris are hungry, you can help ....
5 We didn't go to Ann's party. She didn't invite ....
6 When we go on holiday, we always enjoy ....
7 Mary and Jane were at school together but they never see .... now.
8 Diane and I are very good friends. We've known .... for a long time.
9 'Did you see David and Diane at the party?' 'Yes, but I didn't speak to ....'
10 Many people talk to .... when they're alone.

UNIT 63

-'s (**Ann's** camera / **my brother's** car etc.)

A

Ann's camera
(**her** camera)

my **brother's** car
(**his** car)

the **manager's** office
(**his** *or* **her** office)

We normally use **-'s** for *people*:

- I stayed at **my sister's** house. (*not* 'the house of my sister')
- Have you met **Mr Kelly's** wife? (*not* 'the wife of Mr Kelly')
- Are you going to **James's** party?
- Paul is **a man's** name. Paula is **a woman's** name.

You can use **-'s** without a noun after it:

- Mary's hair is longer than **Ann's**. (= Ann's hair)
- 'Whose umbrella is this?' 'It's **my mother's**.' (= my mother's umbrella)
- 'Where were you last night?' 'I was at **Paul's**.' (= Paul's house)

B

friend's *and* friends'

my friend**'s** house = *one friend*
(= **his** house *or* **her** house)

We write **-'s** after
friend/student/mother etc. *(singular)*:

my mother**'s** car *(one mother)*
my father**'s** car *(one father)*

my friends**'** house = *two or more friends*
(= **their** house)

We write **-'** after
friend**s**/student**s**/parent**s** etc. *(plural)*:

my parents**'** car *(two parents)*

C

We use **of** ... for *things, places* etc.:

- Look at the roof **of that building**. (*not* 'that building's roof')
- We didn't see the beginning **of the film**. (*not* 'the film's beginning')
- What's the name **of this village**?
- Do you know the cause **of the problem**?
- You can sit in the back **of the car**.
- Madrid is the capital **of Spain**.

mine/yours etc. ⇒ UNIT 60 **whose** ... ? ⇒ UNIT 60 **-'s (he's / Mary's** etc.) ⇒ APPENDIX 4.5

EXERCISES

63.1 Look at the family tree. Write sentences about the people in the family.

Mary and Brian are married.
They have a son, James, and a daughter, Julia.
Julia is married to Paul.
Julia and Paul have a son, Daniel.

1 (Brian/husband) Brian is Mary's husband.
2 (Julia/mother) Julia is Daniel's mother.
3 (Mary/wife) Mary is .... wife.
4 (James/brother) James ....
5 (James/uncle) .... uncle.
6 (Julia/wife) Julia ....
7 (Mary/grandmother) ....
8 (Julia/sister) ....
9 (Paul/husband) ....
10 (Paul/father) ....
11 (Daniel/nephew) ....

63.2 Look at the pictures and answer the questions. Use one word only.

1  Whose is this? Alice's
2  Whose is this? ....
3  And this? ....
4  And these? ....
5  And this? ....
6  And these? ....

63.3 Are these sentences OK? Correct the sentences where necessary.

1 I stayed at the house of my sister. — my sister's house
2 What is the name of this village? — OK
3 Do you like the colour of this coat? ....
4 Do you know the phone number of Bill? ....
5 The job of my brother is very interesting. ....
6 Write your name at the top of the page. ....
7 For me the morning is the best part of the day. ....
8 The favourite colour of Paula is blue. ....
9 When is the birthday of your mother? ....
10 The house of my parents isn't very big. ....
11 The walls of this house are very thin. ....
12 The car stopped at the end of the street. ....
13 Are you going to the party of Silvia next week? ....
14 The manager of the hotel is on holiday at the moment. ....

UNIT 64

a/an ...

A

He's got **a** camera.

She's waiting for **a** taxi.

It's **a** beautiful day.

a ... = one thing or person:

- Alice works in **a bank**. (*not* 'in bank')
- Can I ask **a question**? (*not* 'ask question')
- I haven't got **a car**.
- There's **a woman** at the bus stop.

B

an (*not* 'a') before **a/e/i/o/u**:

- Do you want **an** apple or **a** banana?
- I'm going to buy **a** hat and **an** umbrella.
- There was **an** interesting programme on TV last night.

also **an hour** (**h** is not pronounced: an (h)our)
but **a university** (pronounced *yuniversity*)
a European country (pronounced *yuropean*)

another (= **an** + **other**) is *one* word:

- Can I have **another** cup of tea?

C

We use **a/an** ... when we say what a thing or a person is. For example:

- The sun is **a star**.
- Football is **a game**.
- Dallas is **a city in Texas**.
- A mouse is **an animal**. It's **a small animal**.
- Joe is **a very nice person**.

We use **a/an** ... for *jobs* etc.:

- A: What's your job?
  B: I'm **a dentist**. (*not* 'I'm dentist.')
- 'What does Mark do?' 'He's **an engineer**.'
- Would you like to be **a teacher**?
- Beethoven was **a composer**.
- Picasso was **a famous painter**.
- Are you **a student**?

a car / some money (countable/uncountable) ⇒ UNITS 66-67 **a and the** ⇒ UNIT 68

EXERCISES

64.1 Write a or an.

1 ...an... old book
2 .... window
3 .... horse
4 .... airport
5 .... new airport
6 .... organisation
7 .... university
8 .... hour
9 .... economic problem

64.2 What are these things? Choose from the list.

~~bird~~	fruit	mountain	river	musical instrument
flower	game	planet	tool	vegetable

1 A duck is ...a bird... .
2 A carrot is ....
3 Tennis is ....
4 A hammer is ....
5 Everest is ....
6 Jupiter is ....
7 A pear is ....
8 The Amazon is ....
9 A rose is ....
10 A trumpet is ....

64.3 What are their jobs? Choose from the list and finish the sentences.

~~dentist~~ electrician nurse photographer private detective shop assistant taxi driver

1 ...She's a dentist....
2 He's ....
3 She ....
4 ....
5 ....
6 ....
7 ....
8 And you? I'm ....

64.4 Make sentences. Choose from Box A and Box B. Use **a/an** where necessary.

A

~~I want to ask you~~	Barbara works in
Tom never wears	Ann wants to learn
I can't ride	Jim lives in
My brother is	This evening I'm going to

B

old house	artist
party	~~question~~
bookshop	foreign language
hat	bicycle

1 ...I want to ask you a question....
2 ....
3 ....
4 ....
5 ....
6 ....
7 ....
8 ....

UNIT 65 flower(s) bus(es) (singular and plural)

A

The plural of a noun is usually -**s**:

singular (= one) → *plural* (= two or more)
a flower → **some** flower**s**
a week → **two** week**s**
a nice place → **many** nice place**s**
this shop → **these** shop**s**

a flower

some flower**s**

Spelling (⇒ Appendix 5):

-**s** / -**sh** / -**ch** / -**x**	→	-**es**	bu**s** → bus**es**	di**sh** → dish**es**	
			chur**ch** → church**es**	bo**x** → box**es**	
		also	potato → potato**es**	tomato → tomato**es**	
-**y**	→	-**ies**	bab**y** → bab**ies**	dictionar**y** → dictionar**ies**	
			part**y** → part**ies**		
but -**ay** / -**ey** / -**oy**	→	-**ys**	d**ay** → d**ays**	monk**ey** → monk**eys**	b**oy** → b**oys**
-**f** / -**fe**	→	-**ves**	shel**f** → shel**ves**	kni**fe** → kni**ves**	wi**fe** → wi**ves**

B

These things are plural in English:

scissors **glasses** **trousers** **jeans** **shorts** **tights** **pyjamas**

- Do you wear **glasses**?
- Where **are** the **scissors**? I need **them**.

You can also say **a pair of scissors** / **a pair of trousers** / **a pair of pyjamas** *etc.*:

- I need **a** new **pair of jeans**. *or* I need **some** new **jeans**. (*not* 'a new jeans')

C

Some plurals do *not* end in -**s**:

this **man** → these **men**	one **foot** → two **feet**	that **sheep** → those **sheep**
a **woman** → some **women**	a **tooth** → all my **teeth**	a **fish** → a lot of **fish**
a **child** → many **children**	a **mouse** → some **mice**	

also: a **person** → **two people** / **some people** / **a lot of people** *etc.*

- **She**'s a nice **person**.

but

- **They** are nice **people**. (*not* 'nice persons')

D

People is plural (= they), so we say **people are** / **people have** *etc.*:

- **A lot of people speak** English. (*not* 'speaks')
- I like **the people** here. **They are** very friendly.

Police is plural:

- '**The police are** here.' 'Why? What **do they** want?'

EXERCISES

65.1 Write the plural.

1 flower flowers	5 umbrella	9 family ......
2 boat	6 address	10 foot ......
3 woman	7 knife	11 holiday ......
4 city	8 sandwich	12 potato ......

65.2 Look at the pictures and complete the sentences.

1 There are a lot of sheep in the field.
2 George is cleaning his ....
3 There are three ...... at the bus stop.
4 Jill has got two ....
5 There are a lot of ...... in the river.
6 The ...... are falling from the tree.

65.3 Some of these sentences are right but most are wrong. Correct the sentences that are wrong.

1 I'm going to buy some flowers. OK
2 I need a new jeans. I need a new pair of jeans. OR I need some new jeans.
3 It's a lovely park with a lot of beautiful tree. ......
4 There was a woman in the car with two mens. ......
5 Sheep eat grass. ......
6 David is married and has three childs. ......
7 Most of my friend are student. ......
8 He put on his pyjama and went to bed. ......
9 We went fishing but we didn't catch many fish. ......
10 Do you know many persons in this town? ......
11 I like your trouser. Where did you get it? ......
12 The town centre is usually full of tourist. ......
13 I don't like mice. I'm afraid of them. ......
14 This scissor isn't very sharp. ......

65.4 Which is right? Complete the sentences.

1 It's a nice place. Many people go there for a holiday. (**go** *or* **goes**?)
2 Some people ...... always late. (**is** *or* **are**?)
3 The president is not popular. The people ...... like him. (**don't** *or* **doesn't**?)
4 A lot of people ...... television every day. (**watch** *or* **watches**?)
5 Three people ...... injured in the accident. (**was** *or* **were**?)
6 How many people ...... in that house? (**live** *or* **lives**?)
7 ...... the police carry guns in your country? (**Do** *or* **Does**?)
8 The police ...... looking for the stolen car. (**is** *or* **are**?)
9 I need my glasses but I can't find .... (**it** *or* **them**?)
10 I'm going to buy ...... new jeans today. (**a** *or* **some**?)

UNIT 66

a car / some money (countable/uncountable 1)

A noun can be *countable* or *uncountable.*

A

Countable nouns

For example: (a) **car** (a) **man** (a) **key** (a) **house** (a) **flower** (an) **idea** (an) **accident**

You can use **one/two/three** (*etc.*) + *countable nouns* (you can *count* them):

one car

two cars

three **men**

four **houses**

Countable nouns can be *singular* (= one) or *plural* (= two or more):

singular:	**a car**	**my car**	**the car** *etc.*		
plural:	**cars**	**two cars**	**the cars**	**some cars**	**many cars** *etc.*

- I've got **a car.**
- There aren't **many cars** in the car park.
- New **cars** are very expensive.

You *cannot* use the singular (**car/house/key** *etc.*) alone. You need **a/an** (⇒ Unit 64):

- We can't get in without **a key.** (*not* 'without key')

B

Uncountable nouns

For example: **water** **air** **rice** **salt** **plastic** **money** **music** **tennis**

water

salt

money

music

You *cannot* say **one/two/three** (*etc.*) + these things: ~~one water~~ ~~two musics~~

Uncountable nouns have only *one* form:
money the **money** my **money** some **money** much **money** *etc.*

- I've got **some money.**
- There isn't **much money** in the box.
- **Money** isn't everything.

You *cannot* use **a/an** + *uncountable nouns:* ~~a~~ **money** ~~a~~ **music**

But you can say **a piece of ... / a glass of ...** *etc.* + *uncountable noun:*

a glass of water	**a can of** oil	**a bar of** chocolate
a piece of cheese	**a bottle of** milk	**a piece of** music
a bowl of rice	**a cup of** coffee	**a game of** tennis

a/an ⇒ UNIT 64 countable/uncountable 2 ⇒ UNIT 67

EXERCISES

66.1 What are these things? Some are countable and some are uncountable. Write **a/an** if necessary.
The names of these things are:

bucket	**envelope**	**milk**	~~**salt**~~	~~**spoon**~~	**toothpaste**
egg	**jug**	**money**	**sand**	**toothbrush**	**wallet**

66.2 Some of these sentences are right, but some of them need **a/an**. Put in **a/an** where necessary.

1 I haven't got watch. a watch
2 Do you like cheese? OK
3 Ann never wears hat. ....
4 Are you looking for job? ....
5 Mary doesn't eat meat. ....
6 Mary eats apple every day. ....
7 I'm going to party tonight. ....
8 Music is wonderful thing. ....
9 Jamaica is island. ....
10 I don't need key. ....
11 Everybody needs food. ....
12 I've got good idea. ....
13 Can you drive car? ....
14 Do you want cup of coffee? ....
15 I don't like coffee without milk. ....
16 Don't go out without umbrella. ....

66.3 What are the things in the pictures? Write **a ... of ...** for each picture. Use the words in the boxes.

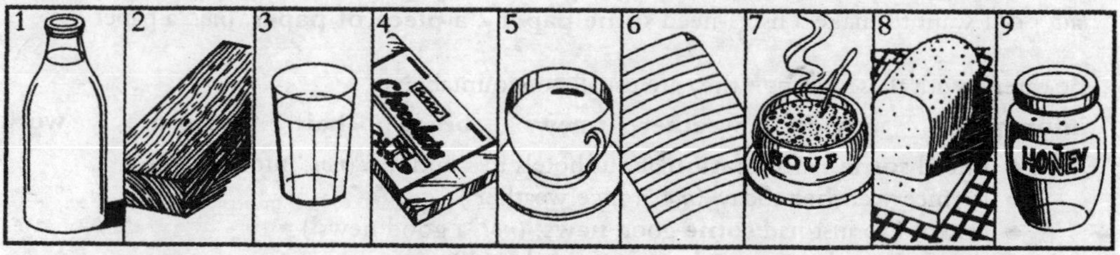

bar	cup	loaf
~~bottle~~	glass	piece
bowl	jar	piece

bread	~~milk~~	tea
chocolate	paper	water
honey	soup	wood

1 a bottle of milk
2 ....
3 ....
4 ....
5 ....
6 ....
7 ....
8 ....
9 ....

UNIT 67

a car / some money (countable/uncountable 2)

A

a/an and **some**

a/an + *singular countable noun* (**car/apple/shoe** *etc.*):
- I need **a** new **car**.
- Would you like **an apple**?

an apple

some + *plural countable nouns* (car**s**/apple**s**/shoe**s** *etc.*):
- I need **some** new **shoes**.
- Would you like **some apples**?

some apples

some + *uncountable nouns* (**water/money/music** *etc.*):
- I need **some money**.
- Would you like **some cheese**?
- (*or* Would you like **a piece of** cheese?)

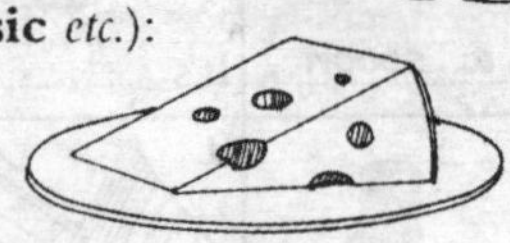

some cheese *or* **a piece of** cheese

Compare **a** and **some**:
- Linda bought **a hat, some shoes** and **some perfume**.
- I read **a newspaper**, wrote **some letters** and listened to **some music**.

B

Many nouns are *sometimes* countable and *sometimes* uncountable. For example:

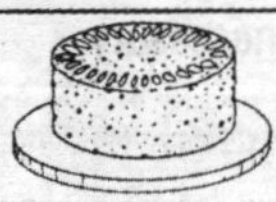

a cake

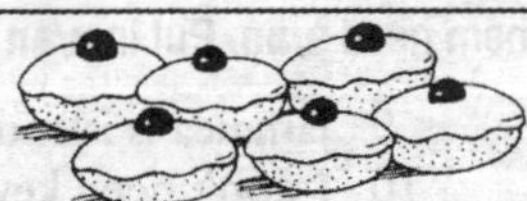

some cakes

some cake *or* **a piece of cake**

a chicken

some chickens

some chicken *or* **a piece of chicken**

Compare **a paper** (= a newspaper) and **some paper**:
- I want something to read. I'm going to buy **a paper**.

but
- I want to make a list. I need **some paper / a piece of paper**. (*not* 'a paper')

C

Be careful with these nouns – they are usually uncountable:

information **advice** **weather** **news** **bread** **hair** **furniture** **work**

- I need **some information** about hotels in London. (*not* 'informations')
- It's nice **weather** today. (*not* 'a nice weather')
- Listen! I've just had **some** good **news**. (*not* 'a good news')
- I'm going to buy **some bread**. (*not* 'a bread')
- Sue has got very long **hair**. (*not* 'hairs')
- They've got **some** very nice **furniture** in their house. (*not* 'furnitures')
- 'Do you like your job?' 'Yes, but it's hard **work**.' (*not* 'a hard work')

We say **a job** (*but not* 'a work'):
- I've got **a** new **job**. (*not* 'a new work')

 countable/uncountable 1 ⇒ UNIT 66 **some** and **any** ⇒ UNIT 75

EXERCISES

67.1 What did you buy? Use the pictures to make sentences (**I bought ...**).

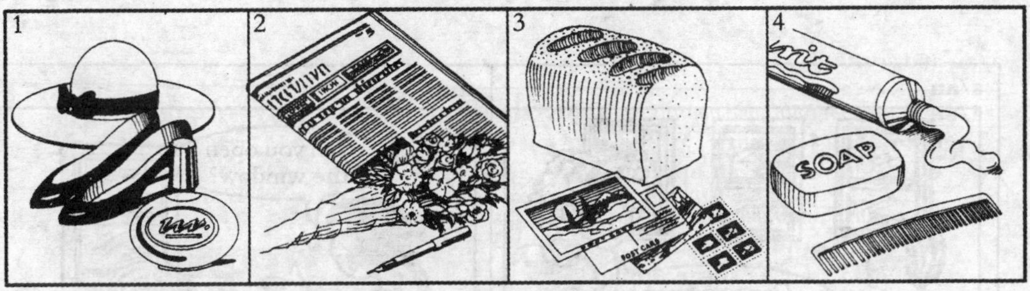

1 I bought some perfume, a hat and some shoes.
2 I bought ....
3 ....
4 ....

67.2 Write sentences with **Would you like a ... ?** or **Would you like some ... ?**

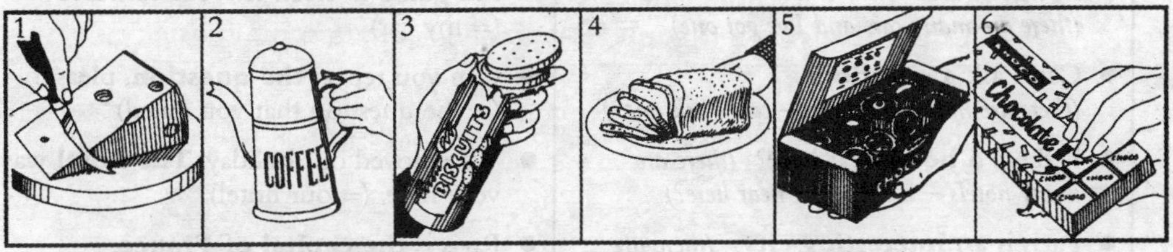

1 Would you like some cheese?
2 Would you like ....?
3 Would ....?
4 ....?
5 ....?
6 ....?

67.3 Put in **a/an** or **some**.

1 I read a book and listened to some music.
2 I need .... money. I want to buy .... food.
3 We met .... interesting people at the party.
4 I'm going to open .... window to get .... fresh air.
5 She didn't eat much for lunch – only .... apple and .... bread.
6 We live in .... big house. There's .... nice garden with .... beautiful trees.
7 I'm going to make a table. First I need .... wood.
8 Listen to me carefully. I'm going to give you .... advice.
9 I want to write a letter. I need .... paper and .... pen.

67.4 Which is right?

1 I'm going to buy some new ~~shoe~~/shoes. shoes is right
2 Martin has got brown eye/eyes.
3 Paula has got short black hair/hairs.
4 The tourist guide gave us some information/informations about the town.
5 We're going to buy some new chair/chairs.
6 We're going to buy some new furniture/furnitures.
7 It's difficult to get a work/job at the moment.
8 We had lovely weather / a lovely weather when we were on holiday.

UNIT 68

a/an and the

A

a/an	the
 There are *three* windows here. **a window** = window 1 or 2 or 3	 There is only *one* window here – **the** window.
• I've got **a car**. *(there are many cars and I've got one)*	• I'm going to clean **the car** tomorrow. (= my car)
• Can I ask **a question**? *(there are many questions – can I ask one?)*	• Can you repeat **the question**, please? (= the question that you asked)
• Is there **a hotel** near here? *(there are many hotels – is there one near here?)*	• We enjoyed our holiday. **The hotel** was very nice. (= our hotel)
• Paris is **an interesting city**. *(there are many interesting cities and Paris is one)*	• Paris is **the capital of France**. *(there is only one capital of France)*
• Lisa is **a student**. *(there are many students and Lisa is one)*	• Lisa is **the youngest student** in her class. *(there is only one youngest student in her class)*

Compare **a** and **the**:

- I bought **a jacket** and **a shirt**. **The jacket** was cheap but **the shirt** was expensive.
  (= **the** jacket and **the shirt that I bought**)

B

We say **the** … when it is clear which thing or person we mean. For example:

the door / the ceiling / the floor / the carpet / the light *etc. (of a room)*
the roof / the garden / the kitchen / the bathroom *etc. (of a house)*
the centre / the station / the airport / the town hall *etc. (of a town)*

- 'Where's Tom?' 'In **the kitchen**.'
  (= the kitchen in this house or flat)
- Turn off **the light** and close **the door**.
  (= the light and the door of the room)
- Do you live far from **the centre**?
  (= the centre of your town)
- I'd like to speak to **the manager**, please.
  (= the manager of this shop *etc.*)

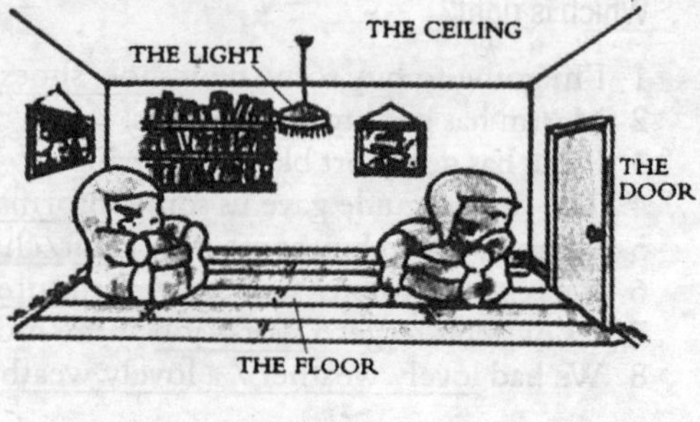

a/an ⇒ UNIT 64 the ⇒ UNITS 69-72

EXERCISES

68.1 Put in a/an or the.

1 We enjoyed our holiday. ..The.. hotel was very nice.
2 'Can I ask ..a.. question?' 'Of course. What do you want to ask?'
3 You look very tired. You need .... holiday.
4 'Where's Tom?' 'He's in .... bathroom.'
5 Jane is .... interesting person. You must meet her.
6 A: Excuse me, can you tell me how to get to .... city centre?
B: Yes, go straight on and then take .... next turning left.
7 A: Shall we go out for .... meal this evening?
B: Yes, that's .... good idea.
8 It's .... nice morning. Let's go for .... walk.
9 Amanda is .... student. When she finishes her studies, she wants to be .... journalist. She lives with two friends in .... flat near .... college where she is studying. .... flat is small but she likes it.
10 Peter and Mary have got two children, ... boy and .... girl. .... boy is seven years old and .... girl is three. Peter works in .... factory. Mary hasn't got .... job at the moment.

68.2 Complete the sentences. Use a or the + one of these words:

airport cup ~~door~~ floor picture radio

68.3 Put in a/an or the where necessary.

1 Don't forget to (turn off light) when you go out. ..turn off the light..
2 Enjoy your holiday and don't forget to send me postcard. ....
3 What is name of this village? ....
4 Canada is very big country. ....
5 What is largest city in Canada? ....
6 I like this room but I don't like colour of carpet. ....
7 'Are you OK?' 'No, I've got headache.' ....
8 We live in old house near station. ....
9 What is name of director of film we saw last night? ....

UNIT 69

the ...

A

We use **the** when it is clear which thing or person we mean:

- What is **the name** of this street? (this street has only one name)
- Who is **the best player** in your team?
- Can you tell me **the time**, please? (= the time *now*)
- My office is on **the first floor**. (= the first floor of the building)

Don't forget **the**:

- Do you live near **the city centre**? (*not* 'near city centre')
- Excuse me, where is **the nearest bank**? (*not* 'where is nearest ...')

B

the same ...

- We live in **the same street**. (*not* 'in same street')
- 'Are these two books different?' 'No, they're **the same**.' (*not* 'they're same')

C

We say:

the sun / the moon / the world / the sky / the sea / the country:

- **The sky** is blue and **the sun** is shining.
- Do you live in a town or in **the country**?

the police / the fire brigade / the army (of a city, country etc.):

- My brother is a soldier. He's in **the army**.

the top / the end / the middle / the left etc.:

- Write your name at **the top of** the page.
- My house is at **the end of** this street.
- The table is in **the middle of** the room.
- Do you drive on **the right** or on **the left** in your country?

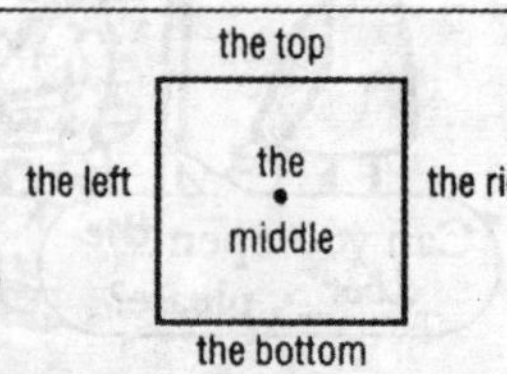

(play) **the piano / the guitar / the trumpet** etc. (musical instruments):

- Paula is learning to play **the piano**.

the radio:

- I listen to **the radio** a lot.

D

We do *not* use **the** with:

television:

- I watch **television** a lot.
- What's on **television** tonight?

but • Can you turn off **the television**? (= the TV set)

breakfast / lunch / dinner:

- What did you have for **breakfast**? (*not* 'the breakfast')
- **Dinner** is ready!

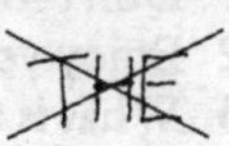

next / last + week/month/year/summer/Monday etc.:

- I'm not working **next week**. (*not* 'the next week')
- Did you have a holiday **last summer**? (*not* 'the last summer')

a/an and the ⇒ UNIT 68   the ⇒ UNITS 70-72   the oldest / the most expensive etc. ⇒ UNIT 89

EXERCISES

69.1 Put in **the** where necessary. Write OK if the sentence is already correct.

1 What is (name) of this street? *the name*
2 What's on television tonight? *OK*
3 Our apartment is on second floor. ....
4 Would you like to go to moon? ....
5 Which is best hotel in this town? ....
6 What time is lunch? ....
7 How far is it to city centre? ....
8 We're going away at end of May. ....
9 What are you doing next weekend? ....
10 I didn't like her first time I met her. ....
11 I'm going out after dinner. ....
12 What's biggest city in world? ....
13 My sister got married last month. ....
14 My dictionary is on top shelf on right. ....
15 We live in country about five miles from nearest village. ....

69.2 Complete the sentences. Use: **the same** + **age colour problem ~~street~~ time.**

1 I live in North Street and you live in North Street. We live in *the same street.*
2 I arrived at 8.30 and you arrived at 8.30. We arrived at ....
3 Jim is 25 and Sue is 25. Jim and Sue are ....
4 My shirt is dark blue and so is my jacket. My shirt and jacket are ....
5 I've got no money and you've got no money. We've got ....

69.3 Look at the pictures and complete the sentences. Use **the** if necessary.

1 *The sun* is shining.
2 She's playing ....
3 They're having ....
4 He's listening to ....
5 They're watching ....
6 They're swimming in ....

69.4 Complete these sentences. Choose from the list. Use **the** if necessary.

capital ~~dinner~~ police lunch middle name sky television

1 We had *dinner* at a restaurant last night.
2 We stayed at a very nice hotel but I don't remember ....
3 .... is very clear tonight. You can see all the stars.
4 Did you see the film on .... last night?
5 Somebody was trying to break into the shop so I called ....
6 Tokyo is .... of Japan.
7 'What did you have for ....?' 'A salad.'
8 I woke up in .... of the night.

UNIT 70 go to work go home go to the cinema

A

She's **at work**.

They're going **to school**.

He's **in bed**.

We say:

(go) **to work**, (be) **at work**, start **work**, finish **work**:
- Goodbye! I'm **going to work** now. (*not* 'to the work')
- I **finish work** at 5 o'clock every day.

(go) **to school**, (be) **at school**, start **school**, leave **school** *etc.*:
- What did you learn **at school** today? (*not* 'at the school')
- Some children don't like **school**.

(go) **to university/college**, (be) **at university/college**:
- Helen wants to **go to university** when she **leaves school**.
- What did you study **at college**?

(go) **to hospital**, (be) **in hospital**:
- Jack was in an accident. He had to go **to hospital**.

(go) **to prison**, (be) **in prison**:
- Why is he **in prison**? What did he do?

(go) **to church**, (be) **in/at church**:
- David usually **goes to church** on Sundays.

(go) **to bed**, (be) **in bed**:
- I'm tired. I'm **going to bed**. (*not* 'to the bed')
- 'Where's Jill?' 'She's **in bed**.'

(go) **home**, (be) **at home** *etc.*:
- I'm tired. I'm **going home**. (*not* 'to home')
- Are you going out tonight or are you **staying at home**?

~~THE~~

B

We say:

(go to) **the cinema / the theatre / the bank / the post office**:
- I never go to **the theatre** but I often go to **the cinema**.
- 'Are you going to **the bank**?' 'No, **the post office**.'

(go to) **the doctor, the dentist**:
- You're not well. Why don't you go to **the doctor**?
- I'm going to **the dentist** tomorrow.

also **the station / the airport / the city centre** (⇒ Unit 68)

THE

the ⇒ UNITS 68-69, 71-72 **in/at** ⇒ UNITS 99-100 **to/in/at** ⇒ UNIT 101 (at) **home** ⇒ UNIT 101

EXERCISES

70.1 Where are these people? Complete the sentences. Sometimes you need **the**.

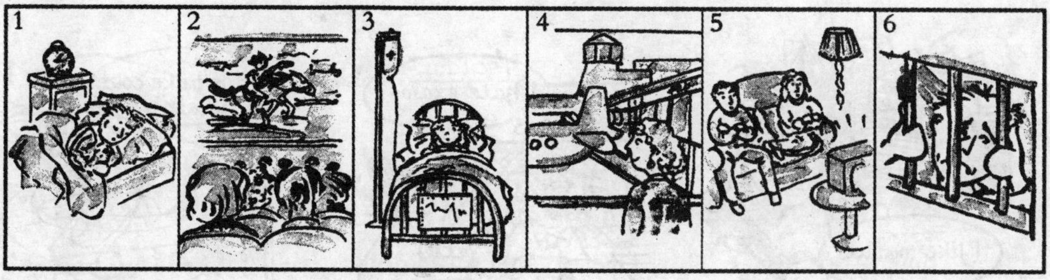

1 He's in bed.

2 They're at ....

3 She's in ....

4 She's at ....

5 They're at ....

6 He's in ....

70.2 Complete the sentences. Choose from the list. Use **the** if necessary.

~~bank~~ bed ~~church~~ home post office school station

1 I need some money. I must go to the bank.
2 David usually goes to church on Sundays.
3 In Britain, children go to .... from the age of five.
4 There were a lot of people at .... waiting for the train.
5 I phoned you last night but you weren't at ....
6 I'm going to .... now. Goodnight!
7 I'm going to .... to get some stamps.

70.3 Complete the sentences. Sometimes you need **the**.

1 If you want to catch a plane, you go to the airport.
2 If you want to see a film, you go to ....
3 If you are tired and you want to sleep, you ....
4 If you rob a bank and the police catch you, you ....
5 If you have a problem with your teeth, you ....
6 If you want to study after you leave school, you ....
7 If you are injured in an accident, you ....

70.4 Put in **the** where necessary. Write *OK* if the sentence is complete.

1 We went to cinema last night. to the cinema
2 I finish work at 5 o'clock every day. OK
3 Mary wasn't feeling well yesterday, so she went to doctor. ....
4 I wasn't feeling well this morning, so I stayed in bed. ....
5 Why is Angela always late for work? ....
6 'Where are the children?' 'They're at school.' ....
7 We've got no money in bank. ....
8 When I was younger, I went to church every Sunday. ....
9 What time do you usually get home from work? ....
10 Do you live far from city centre? ....
11 'Where shall we meet?' 'At station.' ....
12 Jim is ill. He's in hospital. ....
13 Margaret takes her children to school every day. ....
14 Would you like to go to university? ....
15 Would you like to go to theatre this evening? ....

UNIT
71

I like **music** I hate **exams**

A

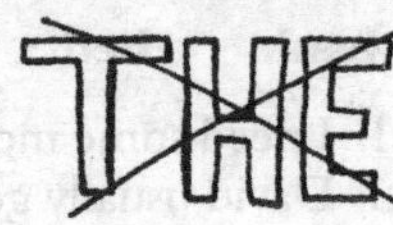

Do not use **the** for *general ideas:*

- I like **music**, especially **classical music**.
  (*not* 'the music … the classical music')
- We don't eat **meat** very often. (*not* 'the meat')
- **Life** is not possible without **water**. (*not* 'The life … the water')
- I hate **exams**. (*not* 'the exams')
- Do you know a shop that sells **foreign newspapers**?
- I'm not very good at writing **letters**.

Do not use **the** for games and sports:

- My favourite sports are **tennis** and **skiing**. (*not* 'the tennis … the skiing')

Do not use **the** for languages or academic subjects (**history/geography/physics/biology** *etc.*):

- Do you think **English** is difficult? (*not* 'the English')
- Tom's brother is studying **physics** and **chemistry**.

B

flowers or **the flowers**?

Compare:

• **Flowers** are beautiful. (= flowers *in general*)	• This is a lovely garden. **The flowers** are beautiful. (= the flowers *in this garden*)
• I don't like **cold weather**. (= cold weather *in general*)	• **The weather** isn't very good today. (= the weather *today*)
• We don't eat **fish** very often. (= fish *in general*)	• We had a very nice meal last night. **The fish** was very good. (= the fish *we ate last night*)
• Are you interested in **history**? (= history *in general*)	• Are you interested in **the history** of your country?

the ⇒ UNITS 68-70, 72

EXERCISES

71.1 What do you think about these things?

dogs	big cities	motor racing	TV quiz shows	exams	parties
museums	tea	basketball	computer games	loud music	hard work

Choose seven of these things and write sentences beginning:

I like ... **I don't like ...** **I love ...** **I hate ...** **I don't mind ...** (= it's OK)

1 *I hate exams.*
2 ....
3 ....
4 ....
5 ....
6 ....
7 ....
8 ....

71.2 Are you interested in these things? Write sentences with:

I'm (very) interested in ...	I know a lot about ...	I don't know much about ...
I'm not interested in ...	I know a little about ...	I don't know anything about ...

1 (history) *I'm very interested in history.*
2 (politics) I ....
3 (sport) ....
4 (art) ....
5 (astronomy) ....
6 (economics) ....

71.3 Which is right?

1 My favourite sport is tennis / ~~the tennis~~. tennis is right
2 I like this hotel. ~~Rooms~~ / The rooms are very nice. The rooms is right
3 Everybody needs friends / the friends.
4 Jane doesn't go to parties / the parties very often.
5 I went shopping this morning. Shops / The shops were very busy.
6 'Where's milk / the milk?' 'It's in the fridge.'
7 I don't like milk / the milk. I never drink it.
8 'Do you do any sports?' 'Yes, I play football / the football.'
9 These days a lot of people use computers / the computers.
10 We went for a swim in the river. Water / The water was very cold.
11 I don't like swimming in cold water / the cold water.
12 Excuse me, can you pass salt / the salt, please?
13 I like this town. I like people / the people here.
14 Vegetables / The vegetables are good for you.
15 'Where are children / the children?' 'They're in the garden.'
16 I can't sing this song. I don't know words / the words.
17 I enjoy taking photographs / the photographs. It's my hobby.
18 I must show you photographs / the photographs that I took when I was on holiday.
19 English / The English is used a lot in international business / the international business.
20 Money / The money doesn't always bring happiness / the happiness.

UNIT 72

the ... (names of places)

A

Places (continents, countries, states, islands, towns etc.)

In general we do *not* use **the** + names of places:

~~THE~~
- **France** is a very large country. (*not* 'the France')
- **Cairo** is the capital of **Egypt**.
- **Corsica** is an island in the Mediterranean.
- **Peru** is in **South America**.

But we use **the** in names with 'republic'/'states'/'kingdom':

THE **the Republic** of Ireland (*or* **the** Irish **Republic**)
the United **States** of America (**the** USA) **the** United **Kingdom** (**the** UK)

B

the -s (plural names)

We use **the** + *plural* names of countries/islands/mountains:

THE **the** Netherlands **the** Canary Islands **the** Philippines **the** Andes

C

Seas, rivers etc.

We use **the** + names of oceans/seas/rivers/canals:

THE
the Atlantic (Ocean) **the** Mediterranean (Sea) **the** Amazon
the (River) Nile **the** Suez Canal **the** Black Sea

D

Places in towns (streets, buildings etc.)

In general we do *not* use **the** + names of streets, squares etc.:

~~THE~~
- Kevin lives in **Newton Street**.
- Where is **Highfield Road**, please?
- **Times Square** is in New York.

We do *not* use **the** + name of place (or person) + airport/station/university/castle etc.:

~~THE~~
Kennedy Airport **Victoria Station** **Cambridge University**
Westminster Abbey **Edinburgh Castle** **London Zoo**

But usually we use **the** + names of hotels, restaurants, pubs, cinemas, theatres, museums:

THE
the Hilton (Hotel) **the** Star of India (restaurant)
the Science Museum **the** Odeon (cinema)
the National Theatre **the** Tate Gallery (art gallery)

E

the ... of ...

We use **the** + names with ... **of** ...:

THE
the Republic **of** Ireland **the** Bank **of** England
the Great Wall **of** China **the** Tower **of** London

We say: **the north / the south / the east / the west / the middle** (of ...):

- I've been to **the north of Italy** but not to **the south**.

the ⇒ UNITS 68-71

EXERCISES

72.1 These are geography questions. Choose your answer from the box. Sometimes you need **The**.

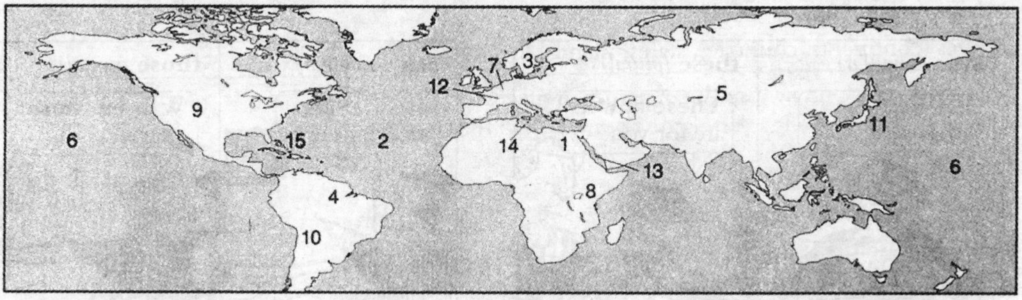

1 Cairo .... is the capital of Egypt.
2 The Atlantic .... is between Africa and America.
3 .... is a country in northern Europe.
4 .... is a river in South America.
5 .... is the largest continent in the world.
6 .... is the largest ocean.
7 .... is a river in Europe.
8 .... is a country in East Africa.
9 .... is between Canada and Mexico.
10 .... are mountains in South America.
11 .... is the capital of Japan.
12 .... are mountains in central Europe.
13 .... is between Saudi Arabia and Africa.
14 .... is an island in the Mediterranean.
15 .... are a group of islands near Florida.

Alps
Amazon
Andes
Asia
~~Atlantic~~
Bahamas
~~Cairo~~
Kenya
Malta
Pacific
Red Sea
Rhine
Sweden
Tokyo
United States

72.2 Put in **the** where necessary. If the sentence is already correct, write *OK*.

1 Kevin lives in Newton Street. OK
2 We went to see a play at National Theatre. at the National Theatre
3 Have you ever been to China? ....
4 Have you ever been to Philippines? ....
5 Have you ever been to south of France? ....
6 Can you tell me where Regal Cinema is? ....
7 Can you tell me where Merrion Street is? ....
8 Can you tell me where Museum of Modern Art is? ....
9 Europe is bigger than Australia. ....
10 Belgium is smaller than Netherlands. ....
11 Which river is longer – Mississippi or Nile? ....
12 Did you go to National Gallery when you were in London? ....
13 'Where did you stay?' 'At Park Hotel in Hudson Road.' ....
14 How far is it from Trafalgar Square to Victoria Station (*in London*)? ....
15 Rocky Mountains are in North America. ....
16 Texas is famous for oil and cowboys. ....
17 Panama Canal joins Atlantic Ocean and Pacific Ocean. ....
18 I hope to go to United States next year. ....
19 Mary comes from a small town in west of Ireland. ....
20 Alan studied physics at Manchester University. ....

UNIT 73

this/that/these/those

A

this — **this** picture (= this picture *here*)

these — **these** flowers (= these flowers *here*)

that — **that** picture (= that picture *there*)

those — **those** people (= those people *there*)

B

We use **this/that/these/those** *with a noun* (**this picture / that girl** *etc.*) or *without a noun*:

with a noun:
- **This hotel** is expensive but it's very nice.
- Who's **that girl**?' 'I don't know.'
- Do you like **these shoes**? I bought them last week.
- **Those apples** look nice. Can I have one?

without a noun:
- **This** is a nice hotel but it's very expensive.
- 'Excuse me, is **this** your bag?' 'Oh yes, thank you.'
- Who's **that**? (= Who is that person?)
- Which shoes do you like most? **These** or **those**?

C

that = something that *has happened:*
- 'I'm sorry I forgot to phone you.' '**That**'s all right.'
- **That** was a really nice meal. Thank you very much.

that = what somebody *has just said:*
- 'You're a teacher, aren't you?' 'Yes, **that**'s right.'
- 'Martin has got a new job.' 'Has he? I didn't know **that**.'
- 'I'm going on holiday next week.' 'Oh, **that**'s nice.'

D

We use **this is** ... and **is that** ... ? on the telephone:
- Hello, **this** is David. (**this** = the speaker)
- Is **that** Sarah? (**that** = the other person)

We use **this is** ... to *introduce* people:
- A: Brian, **this is** Chris.
  B: Hello, Chris – pleased to meet you.
  C: Hello.

this one / that one ⇒ UNIT 74

EXERCISES

73.1 Complete the sentences. Use **this/that/these/those** + these words:

birds **house** **plates** **postcards** **seat** ~~**shoes**~~

73.2 Write questions: **Is this/that your ... ?** or **Are these/those your ... ?**

73.3 Complete the sentences with **this is** or **that's** or **that**.

1 A: I'm sorry I'm late.
B: That's all right.

2 A: I can't come to the party tomorrow.
B: Oh, ... a pity. Why not?

3 *(on the telephone)*
Sue: Hello, Ann. .... Sue.
Ann: Oh, hello, Sue. How are you?

4 A: You're lazy.
B: .... not true!

5 A: Jill plays the piano very well.
B: Really? I didn't know ....

6 *Mark meets Paul's sister (Ann):*
Paul: Mark, ... my sister, Ann.
Mark: Hello, Ann.

7 A: I'm sorry I was angry yesterday.
B: .... OK. Forget it!

8 A: You're a friend of John's, aren't you?
B: Yes, ... right.

UNIT 74

one/ones

A

one (= a ...)

Would you like **one** ?
= Would you like **a chocolate** ?

one = a/an ... (a chocolate / an apple *etc.*)

- I need **a pen**. Have you got **one**? (**one = a pen**)
- A: Is there **a bank** near here?
  B: Yes, there's **one** at the end of this street. (**one = a bank**)

B

one and ones

one *(singular)*

Which **one**? = Which **hat**?

one = hat/car/girl *etc.*

this one / that one
- Which **car** is yours? **This one** or **that** one? (= this car or that **car**)

the one ...
- A: Which **hotel** did you stay at?
  B: **The one** opposite the station.

the ... one
- I don't like the black **coat** but I like **the brown one**.
- Don't buy that **camera**. Buy **the other one**.

a/an ... one
- This **cup** is dirty. Can I have **a clean one**?
- That biscuit was nice. I'm going to have **another one.**

ones *(plural)*

Which **ones**? = Which **flowers**?

ones = flowers/cars/girls *etc.*

these/those (usually *without* 'ones'):
- Which flowers do you want? **These** or **those**? (*not usually* 'these ones/those ones')

the ones ...
- A: Which **keys** are yours?
  B: **The ones** on the table.

the ... ones
- I don't like the red **shoes** but I like **the green ones**.
- Don't buy those **apples**. Buy **the other ones**.

some ... ones
- These **cups** are dirty. Can we have **some clean ones?**
- My **shoes** are very old. I'm going to buy **some new ones.**

which ... ? ⇒ UNIT 46 another ⇒ UNIT 64 this/that etc. ⇒ UNIT 73

EXERCISES

74.1 A asks B some questions. Use the information in the box to write B's answers. Use **one** (not '**a/an** ...') in the answers.

B doesn't need a car	B has just had a cup of coffee
there's a chemist in Mill Road	B is going to buy a bicycle
~~B hasn't got a pen~~	B hasn't got an umbrella

1 A: Can you lend me a pen? B: I'm sorry, *I haven't got one.*
2 A: Would you like to have a car? B: No, I don't ....
3 A: Have you got a bicycle? B: No, but ....
4 A: Can you lend me an umbrella? B: I'm sorry but ....
5 A: Would you like a cup of coffee? B: No, thank you. ....
6 A: Is there a chemist near here? B: Yes, ...

74.2 Complete the sentences. Use **a/an ... one**. Use the words in the list.

better **big** ~~**clean**~~ **different** **new** **old**

1 This cup is dirty. Can I have *a clean one* ?
2 I'm going to sell my car and buy ....
3 That's not a very good photograph but this is ....
4 I want today's newspaper. This is ....
5 This box is too small. I need ....
6 Why do we always go to the same restaurant? Let's go to ....

74.3 Use the information in the box to complete these conversations. Use **one/ones**.

the coat is black	I took the photographs on the beach last week
the girl is tall with long hair	the shoes are green
~~the hotel is opposite the station~~	the pictures are on the wall
the house has got a red door	the books are on the top shelf
the flowers are yellow	the man has got a moustache and glasses

1 A: We stayed at a hotel.
B: *Which one* ?
A: *The one opposite the station.*

2 A: Those shoes are nice.
B: .... ?
A: ....

3 A: That's a nice house.
B: .... ?
A: .... with ....

4 A: I like that coat.
B: .... ?
A ....

5 A: I like those pictures.
B: .... ?
A: ....

6 A: Are those your books?
B: .... ?
A: ....

7 A: Do you know that girl?
B: .... ?
A: ....

8 A: Those flowers are beautiful.
B: .... ?
A: ....

9 A: Who's that man?
B: .... ?
A: ....

10 A: Have you seen my photographs?
B: .... ?
A: ....

UNIT 75

some and **any**

A

some

Use **some** in *positive* sentences:
- I'm going to buy **some** clothes.
- There's **some** ice in the fridge.
- We did **some** exercises.

any

Use **any** in *negative* sentences:
- I'm **not** going to buy **any** clothes.
- There is**n't any** orange juice in the fridge.
- We did**n't** do **any** exercises.

B

any and **some** in questions

In most questions (but not all) we use **any**:
- Is there **any** ice in the fridge?
- Has he got **any** friends?
- Why didn't you buy **any** food?

We normally use **some** (*not* **any**) when we *offer* things (**Would you like ... ?**):
- A: Would you like **some** coffee?
  B: Yes, please.

or when we *ask for* things (**Can I have ... ?** *etc.*):
- A: Can I have **some** soup, please?
  B: Yes. Help yourself.
- A: Can you lend me **some** money?
  B: Sure. How much do you need?

C

some and **any** *without a noun*
- I didn't take any photographs but Ann took **some**. (= some photographs)
- You can have some coffee but I don't want **any**. (= any coffee)
- I've just made some coffee. Would you like **some**? (= some coffee)
- 'Where's your luggage?' 'I haven't got **any**.' (= any luggage)
- 'Are there any biscuits?' 'Yes, there are **some** in the kitchen.' (= some biscuits)

D

something / somebody (*or* **someone**)
- She said **something**.
- I saw **somebody** (*or* **someone**).
- Would you like **something** to eat?
- Quick! **Somebody**'s coming.

anything / anybody (*or* **anyone**)
- She did**n't** say **anything**.
- I did**n't** see **anybody** (*or* **anyone**).
- Are you doing **anything** this evening?
- Where's Ann? Has **anybody** seen her?

a and some ⇒ UNIT 67 **somebody/anything** etc. ⇒ UNIT 78

EXERCISES

75.1 Put in **some** or **any**.

1 I bought some cheese but I didn't buy any bread.
2 I'm going to the post office. I need .... stamps.
3 There aren't .... shops in this part of town.
4 George and Alice haven't got .... children.
5 Have you got .... brothers or sisters?
6 There are .... beautiful flowers in the garden.
7 Do you know .... good hotels in London?
8 'Would you like .... tea?' 'Yes, please.'
9 When we were on holiday, we visited .... very interesting places.
10 Don't buy .... rice. We don't need ....
11 I went out to buy .... milk but they didn't have .... in the shop.
12 I'm thirsty. Can I have .... water, please?

75.2 Complete the sentences. Use **some** or **any** + one of these words:

air	**cheese**	**help**	**letters**	**photographs**
batteries	**friends**	**languages**	**milk**	~~**shampoo**~~

1 I want to wash my hair. Is there any shampoo ?
2 This evening I'm going to write ....
3 I haven't got my camera, so I can't take ....
4 Do you speak .... foreign .... ?
5 Yesterday evening I went to a restaurant with .... of mine.
6 Can I have .... in my coffee, please?
7 The radio isn't working. There aren't .... in it.
8 It's hot in this office. I'm going out for .... fresh ....
9 'Would you like ....?' 'No, thank you. I've had enough to eat.'
10 I can do this job alone. I don't need ....

75.3 Complete the sentences. Use **some** or **any**.

1 Ann didn't take any photographs but I took some . (I/take)
2 'Where's your luggage?' 'I haven't got any .' (I/not/have)
3 'Do you need any money?' 'No, thank you. ....' (I/have)
4 'Can you lend me some money?' 'I'm sorry but ....' (I/not/have)
5 The tomatoes in the shop didn't look very good, so .... (I/not/buy)
6 There were some nice oranges in the shop, so .... (I/buy)

75.4 Put in **something/somebody/anything/anybody**.

1 She said something to me but I didn't understand it.
2 'What's wrong?' 'There's .... in my eye.'
3 Do you know .... about politics?
4 I went to the shop but I didn't buy ....
5 .... has broken the window. I don't know who.
6 There isn't .... in the bag. It's empty.
7 I'm looking for my keys. Has .... seen them?
8 Would you like .... to drink?
9 I didn't eat .... because I wasn't hungry.
10 This is a secret. Please don't tell ....

UNIT 76

not + any   no   none

A

The car park is empty.

There are**n't any** cars } in the car park.
There are **no** cars

How many cars are there in the car park?
None.

not (n't) + any

- There are**n't any** cars in the car park.
- Sally and Steve have**n't** got **any** children.
- You can have some coffee but I do**n't** want **any**.

no + *noun* (**no cars / no garden** *etc.*)
no ... = **not + any** *or* **not + a**:

- There are **no cars** in the car park. (= there are**n't any** cars)
- We've got **no coffee**. (= we have**n't** got **any** coffee)
- It's a nice house but there's **no garden**. (= there is**n't a** garden)

We use **no** ... especially after **have (got)** and **there is/are**.

negative verb + **any** = *positive verb* + **no**:

- They **haven't** got **any** children. *or* They**'ve** got **no** children.
  (*not* 'They haven't got no children')
- There **isn't any** sugar in your coffee. *or* There**'s no** sugar in your coffee.

B

no and **none**

Use **no** + *noun* (**no money / no children** *etc.*):

- We've got **no money**.
- Everything was OK. There were **no problems.**

Use **none** alone (*without* a noun):

- 'How much money have you got?' **'None.'** (= no money)
- 'Were there any problems?' 'No, **none**.' (= no problems)

C

none and **no-one**

none = 0 (zero)
None is an answer for **How much?/ How many?** *(things or people)*:

- **'How much** money have you got?' **'None.'** (= no money)
- **'How many** people did you meet?' **'None.'** (= no people)

no-one = nobody (⇒ Unit 77)
No-one is an answer for **Who?**:

- **'Who** did you meet?' **'No-one.'** (*or* **Nobody**.)

negatives ⇒ UNIT 42   some and any ⇒ UNIT 75   anybody/nobody/nothing etc. ⇒ UNITS 77-78

EXERCISES

76.1 Write these sentences again with **no**.

1 We haven't got any money. *We've got no money.*
2 There aren't any shops near here. There are ....
3 Carol hasn't got any free time. ....
4 There isn't a light in this room. ....

Write these sentences again with **any**.

5 We've got no money. *We haven't got any money.*
6 There's no tea in the pot. ....
7 There are no buses today. ....
8 Tom has got no brothers or sisters. ....

76.2 Put in **no** or **any**.

1 There's *no* sugar in your coffee.
2 My brother is married but he hasn't got .... children.
3 Sue doesn't speak .... foreign languages.
4 I'm afraid there's .... coffee. Would you like some tea?
5 'Look at those birds!' 'Birds? Where? I can't see .... birds.'
6 'Do you know where Jane is?' 'No, I've got .... idea.'

Put in **no**, **any** or **none**.

7 There aren't .... pictures on the wall.
8 The weather was cold but there was .... wind.
9 I wanted to buy some oranges but they didn't have .... in the shop.
10 Everything was correct. There were .... mistakes.
11 'How much luggage have you got?' '..........'
12 'How much luggage have you got?' 'I haven't got ....'

76.3 Complete the sentences. Use **any** or **no** + one of these words:

answer **difference** **film** **friends** **furniture** **heating** **money** **photographs** ~~**problems**~~ **questions**

1 Everything was OK. There were *no problems* .
2 They want to go on holiday but they've got ....
3 I'm not going to answer ....
4 He's always alone. He's got ....
5 There is .... between these two machines. They're exactly the same.
6 There wasn't .... in the room. It was completely empty.
7 I tried to phone you yesterday but there was ....
8 The house is cold because there isn't ....
9 I can't take .... There's .... in the camera.

76.4 Write short answers (one or two words) to these questions. Use **none** where necessary.

1 How many letters did you write yesterday? *Two. OR A lot. OR None.*
2 How many sisters have you got? ....
3 How much coffee did you drink yesterday? ....
4 How many photographs have you taken today? ....
5 How many legs has a snake got? ....

UNIT 77

not + anybody/anyone/anything nobody/no-one/nothing

A

not + anybody/anyone
nobody/no-one
(for people)

- There **isn't** { **anybody** / **anyone** } in the room.
- There **is** { **nobody** / **no-one** } in the room.
- A: **Who** is in the room?
  B: **Nobody**. / **No-one**.

any**body** = any**one**   no**body** = no-**one**
(-**body** and -**one** are the same)

not + anything
nothing
(for things)

- There **isn't anything** in the bag.
- There **is nothing** in the bag.
- A: **What**'s in the bag?
  B: **Nothing**.

B

not + anybody/anyone
- I do**n't** know **anybody** (*or* **anyone**) here.

nobody = not + anybody
no-one = not + anyone
- I'm lonely. I've got **nobody** to talk to.
  (= I have**n't** got **anybody**.)
- The house is empty. There is **no-one** in it.
  (= There is**n't anyone** in it.)

not + anything
- I **can't** remember **anything**.

nothing = not + anything
- She said **nothing**.
  (= She did**n't** say **anything**.)
- There's **nothing** to eat.
  (= There is**n't anything** to eat.)

C

You can use **nobody/no-one/nothing** at the beginning of a sentence or alone (to answer a question):

- The house is empty. **Nobody** lives there.
  (*not* 'Anybody lives there')
- 'Who did you speak to?' **'No-one.'**
- **Nothing** happened.
  (*not* 'Anything happened')
- 'What did you say?' **'Nothing.'**

D

Remember: *negative verb* + **anybody/anyone/anything**
positive verb + **nobody/no-one/nothing**

- He does**n't** know **anything**. (*not* 'He doesn't know nothing')
- Do**n't** tell **anybody**. (*not* 'Don't tell nobody')
- There **is nothing** to do in this town. (*not* 'There isn't nothing')

some and any ⇒ UNIT 75   **any and no** ⇒ UNIT 76   **somebody/anything/nowhere etc.** ⇒ UNIT 78

EXERCISES

77.1 Write these sentences again with **nobody/no-one** or **nothing**.

1 There isn't anything in the bag. *There's nothing in the bag.*
2 There isn't anybody in the office. There's ....
3 I haven't got anything to do. I ....
4 There isn't anything on TV. ....
5 There wasn't anyone at home. ....
6 We didn't find anything. ....

77.2 Write these sentences again with **anybody/anyone** or **anything**.

1 There's nothing in the bag. *There isn't anything in the bag.*
2 There was nobody on the bus. There wasn't ....
3 I've got nothing to read. ....
4 I've got no-one to help me. ....
5 She heard nothing. ....
6 We've got nothing for dinner. ....

77.3 Answer these questions with **nobody/no-one** or **nothing**.

1a What did you say? *Nothing.*
2a Who saw you? *Nobody.*
3a What do you want? ....
4a Who did you meet? ....
5a Who knows the answer? ....
6a What did you buy? ....
7a What happened? ....
8a Who was late? ....

Now answer the same questions with full sentences.
Use **nobody/no-one/nothing** or **anybody/anyone/anything**.

1b *I didn't say anything.*
2b *Nobody saw me.*
3b I don't ....
4b I ....
5b .... the answer.
6b ....
7b ....
8b ....

77.4 Complete the sentences. Use **nobody/no-one/nothing/anybody/anyone/anything**.

1 That house is empty. *Nobody* lives there.
2 Jack has a bad memory. He can't remember *anything* .
3 Be quiet! Don't say ....
4 I didn't know about the meeting. .... told me.
5 'What did you have to eat?' '.......... . I wasn't hungry.'
6 I didn't eat .... I wasn't hungry.
7 Jenny was sitting alone. She wasn't with ....
8 I'm afraid I can't help you. There's .... I can do.
9 I don't know .... about car engines.
10 The museum is free. It doesn't cost .... to go in.
11 I heard a knock on the door but when I opened it there was .... there.
12 She spoke very fast. I didn't understand ....
13 'What are you doing this evening?' '.......... . Why?'
14 Helen has gone away. .... knows where she is. She didn't tell .... where she was going.

somebody/anything/nowhere etc.

A

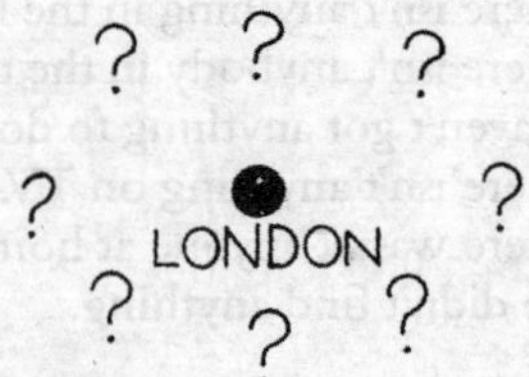

Somebody (or **someone**) has broken the window.

somebody/someone = *a person but we don't know who*

She has got **something** in her mouth.

something = *a thing but we don't know what*

Tom lives **somewhere** near London.

somewhere = *in/to a place but we don't know where*

B

people (**-body** *or* **-one**)

somebody *or* **someone**
anybody *or* **anyone**
nobody *or* **no-one**

- There is **somebody** (*or* **someone**) in the garden.
- Is there **anybody** (*or* **anyone**) in the garden?
- There is**n't anybody** (*or* **anyone**) in the garden.
- There is **nobody** (*or* **no-one**) in the garden.

-body and **-one** are the same: **somebody = someone, nobody = no-one** *etc.*

things (**-thing**)

something
anything
nothing

- She said **something** but I didn't understand her.
- Are you doing **anything** at the weekend?
- I was angry but I did**n't** say **anything**.
- 'What did you say?' **'Nothing.'**

places (**-where**)

somewhere
anywhere
nowhere

- They live **somewhere** in the south of England.
- Did you go **anywhere** interesting for your holidays?
- I'm staying here. I'm **not** going **anywhere**.
- I don't like this town. There is **nowhere** to go.

C

something/anybody *etc.* + *adjective* (**big/cheap/interesting** *etc.*)

- Did you meet **anybody interesting** at the party?
- We always go to the same place. Let's go **somewhere different**.
- 'What's that letter?' 'It's **nothing important**.'

D

something/anybody *etc.* **+ to ...**

- I'm hungry. I want **something to eat**. (= something that I can eat)
- He hasn't got **anybody to talk** to. (= anybody that he can talk to)
- There is **nowhere to go** in this town. (= nowhere where people can go)

some and any ⇒ UNIT 75 **any and no** ⇒ UNIT 76 **anybody/nothing** etc. ⇒ UNIT 77
everything/-body/-where ⇒ UNIT 79

EXERCISES

78.1 Put in **somebody** (or **someone**) / **something** / **somewhere**.

1	She said *something.*	What did she say?
2	I've lost	What have you lost?
3	They went	Where did they go?
4	I'm going to phone	Who are you going to phone?

78.2 Put in **nobody** (or **no-one**) / **nothing** / **nowhere**.

1a	What did you say?	*Nothing.*
2a	Where are you going?	....
3a	What do you want?	....
4a	Who are you looking for?	....

Now answer the same questions with full sentences. Use **not + anybody/anything/anywhere**.

1b *I didn't say anything.* 3b ....
2b I'm not .... 4b ....

78.3 Put in **somebody/anything/nowhere** etc.

1 It's dark. I can't see *anything* .
2 Tom lives *somewhere* near London.
3 Do you know .... about computers?
4 'Listen!' 'What? I can't hear ....'
5 'What are you doing here?' 'I'm waiting for ....'
6 Please listen carefully. There's .... I want to tell you.
7 'Did .... see the accident?' 'No, ...'
8 We weren't hungry, so we didn't eat ....
9 'What's going to happen?' 'I don't know. .... knows.'
10 'Do you know .... in London?' 'Yes, a few people.'
11 'What's in that cupboard?' .... It's empty.'
12 I'm looking for my glasses. I can't find them ....
13 I don't like cold weather. I want to live .... warm.
14 Is there .... interesting on television tonight?
15 Have you ever met .... famous?

78.4 Complete the sentences. Choose from Box A and Box B.

A

something	anything	nothing
somewhere	anywhere	nowhere

You can use these words more than once.

B

do	drink	eat	go
play	read	sit	stay

1 We don't go out very much because there's *nowhere to go* .
2 There isn't any food in the house. We haven't got ....
3 I'm bored. I've got ....
4 'Why are you standing?' 'Because there isn't ....'
5 'Would you like .... ?' 'Yes, please – a glass of orange juice.'
6 All the hotels were full. There was ....
7 I want .... I'm going to buy a magazine.
8 Children need ....

UNIT 79

every and all

A

every

Every house in the street is the same.

every house in the street = **all the houses** in the street

We use **every** + *singular noun* (**every house / every country** *etc.*):

- Alice has been to **every country** in Europe.
- **Every summer** we have a holiday by the sea.
- She looks different **every time** I see her.

Use a *singular verb* after **every** ... :

- **Every house** in the street **is** the same. (*not* 'are the same')
- **Every country has** a national flag. (*not* 'have')

Compare **every** and **all**:

• **Every student** in the class passed the exam.	• **All** the students in the class passed the exam.
• **Every country has** a national flag.	• **All countries have** a national flag.

B

every day and **all day**

every day = on all days:

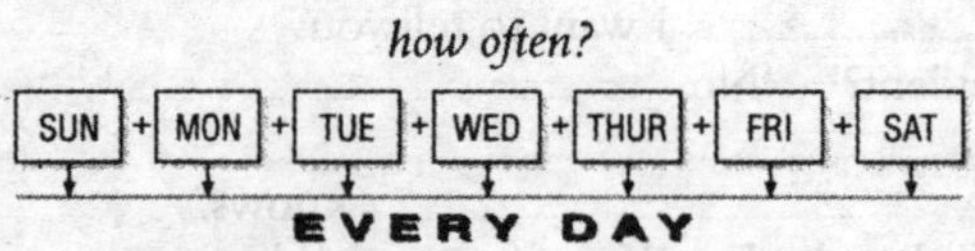

- A: How often do you read a newspaper?
  B: **Every day.**
- Bill watches TV for about two hours **every evening.** (= on all evenings)

also **every morning/night/summer** *etc.*

all day = the complete day:

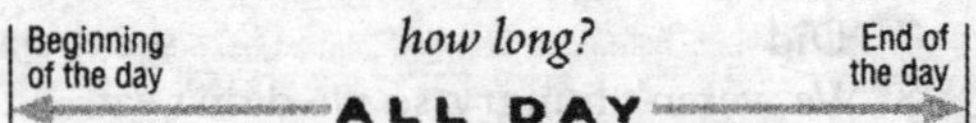

- The weather was bad yesterday. It rained **all day.**
- I was tired after work yesterday, so I watched TV **all evening.** (= the complete evening)

also **all morning/night/summer** *etc.*

C

everybody (*or* **everyone**) / **everything** / **everywhere**

everybody or **everyone** *(people)*
everything *(things)*
everywhere *(places)*

- **Everybody** (*or* **Everyone**) needs friends. (= all people need friends)
- Have you got **everything** you need? (= all the things you need)
- I've lost my watch. I've looked **everywhere** for it. (= I've looked in all places)

Use a *singular verb* after **everybody/everyone/everything**:

- **Everybody has** problems. (*not* 'Everybody have')

all ⇒ UNIT 80

EXERCISES

79.1 Complete the sentences. Use **every** + one of these words:

day **room** ~~**student**~~ **time** **word**

1 Every student in the class passed the exam.
2 My job is very boring. .... is the same.
3 Kate is a very good tennis player. When we play, she wins ....
4 .... in the hotel has a private bathroom.
5 'Did you understand what she said?' 'Most of it but not ....'

79.2 Complete the sentences with **every day** or **all day**.

1 Yesterday it rained all day.
2 I buy a newspaper .... but sometimes I don't read it.
3 I'm not going out tomorrow. I'll be at home ....
4 I usually drink about four cups of coffee ....
5 Paula was ill yesterday, so she stayed in bed ....
6 Last year we went to the seaside for a week and it rained ....
7 I'm tired now because I've been working hard ....

79.3 Put in **every** or **all**.

1 Bill watches TV for about two hours every evening.
2 Barbara gets up at 6.30 .... morning.
3 The weather was nice yesterday, so we sat in the garden .... afternoon.
4 I'm going away on Monday. I'll be away .... week.
5 'How often do you go skiing?' '.......... year. Usually in March.'
6 A: Were you at home at 10 o'clock yesterday?
B: Yes, I was at home .... morning. I went out after lunch.
7 My sister likes cars. She buys a new one .... year.
8 I saw Jack at the party. He wasn't very friendly. He didn't speak to me .... evening.
9 We go away on holiday for two or three weeks .... summer.

79.4 Put in **everybody/everything/everywhere**.

1 Everybody needs friends.
2 Chris knows .... about computers.
3 I like the people here. .... is very friendly.
4 This is a nice hotel. It's comfortable and .... is very clean.
5 Kevin never uses his car. He goes .... by motor-bike.
6 Let's have dinner. .... is hungry.
7 Sue's house is full of books. There are books ....
8 You are right. .... you say is true.

79.5 Put in a verb (one word).

1 Everybody has problems.
2 Are you ready yet? Everybody .... waiting for you.
3 The house is empty. Everyone .... gone out.
4 George is very popular. Everybody .... him.
5 This town is completely different. Everything .... changed.
6 I arrived home very late. I came in quietly because everyone .... asleep.
7 Everybody .... mistakes!

all most some any no/none

A

Compare:

children/money/books *etc.* (in general):	**the** children / **the** money / **these** books *etc.*:
• **Children** like playing. (= children in general) • **Money** isn't everything. (= money in general) • I enjoy reading **books**. • Everybody needs **friends**.	• Where are **the children**? (= our children) • I want to buy a car but I haven't got **the money**. (= the money for a car) • Have you read **these books**? • I often go out with **my friends**.

B

most/most of ... , some/some of ... *etc.*

most/some *etc.* **+ noun:**

all **most** **some** **any** **no**	~~**of**~~	**cities** **children** **books** **money**

most of/some of *etc.* **+ the/this/my** ... *etc.*

all	**(of)**	**the** ... **this/that** ... **these/those** ... **my/your** ... *etc.*
most **some** **any** **none**	**of**	

all **most** **some** **any** **no / none / not + any**

- **Most children** like playing. (= children in general)
- I don't want **any money**.
- **Some books** are better than others.
- He's got **no friends**.
- **All cities** have the same problems. (= cities in general)

Do not use **of** in these sentences:

- **Most people** drive too fast. (*not* 'Most of people')
- **Some birds** can't fly. (*not* 'Some of birds')

- **Most of the children at this school** are under 11 years old.
- I don't want **any of this money**.
- **Some of these books** are very old.
- **None of my friends** live near me.

We say **all the** ... / **all my** ... *etc.* (usually without **of**):

- **All the students in our class** passed the exam.
- Silvia has lived in London **all her life**.

C

all of it / most of them / none of us *etc.*

all **most** **some** **any** **none**	**of**	**it** **them** **us** **you**

- You can have **some of this cake** but not **all of it**.
- A: Do you know those people?
B: **Most of them,** but not **all of them**.
- **Some of us** are going out tonight. Why don't you come with us?
- I've got a lot of books but I haven't read **any of them**.
- 'How many of these books have you read?' **'None of them.'**

the ... **(children / the children** etc.) ⇒ UNIT 71 **some** and **any** ⇒ UNIT 75 **no/none/any** ⇒ UNIT 76
all and **every** ⇒ UNIT 79

EXERCISES

80.1 Complete the sentences. Use the word in brackets (**some/most** etc.). Sometimes you need **of** (**some of / most of** etc.).

1 Most....... children like playing. (most)
2 Some of...... this money is yours. (some)
3 .... people never stop talking. (some)
4 .... the shops in the city centre close at 6.30. (most)
5 You can change your money in .... banks. (most)
6 I don't like .... the pictures in the living room. (any)
7 He's lost .... his money. (all)
8 .... my friends are married. (none)
9 Do you know .... the people in this photograph? (any)
10 .... birds can fly. (most)
11 I enjoyed .... the film but I didn't like the ending. (most)
12 .... sports are very dangerous. (some)
13 We can't find anywhere to stay. .... the hotels are full. (all)
14 You must have .... this cheese. It's delicious. (some)
15 The weather was bad when we were on holiday. It rained .... the time. (most)

80.2 Look at the pictures and answer the questions. Use **all/most/some/none + of them / of it.**

1 How many of the people are women? Most of them.
2 How many of the boxes are on the table? ....
3 How many of the men are wearing hats? ....
4 How many of the windows are open? ....
5 How many of the people are standing? ....
6 How much of the money is Ben's? ....

80.3 Right or wrong? Correct the sentences that are wrong? Write *OK* if the sentence is correct.

1 Most of children like playing. Most children
2 All the students failed the exam. OK
3 Some of people work too hard. ....
4 Some of questions in the exam were very easy. ....
5 I haven't seen any of those people before. ....
6 All of insects have six legs. ....
7 Have you read all these books? ....
8 Most of students in our class are very nice. ....
9 Most of my friends are going to the party. ....
10 I'm very tired this morning – I was awake most of night. ....

UNIT 81

both   either   neither

A

We use **both/either/neither** to talk about *two* things or people:

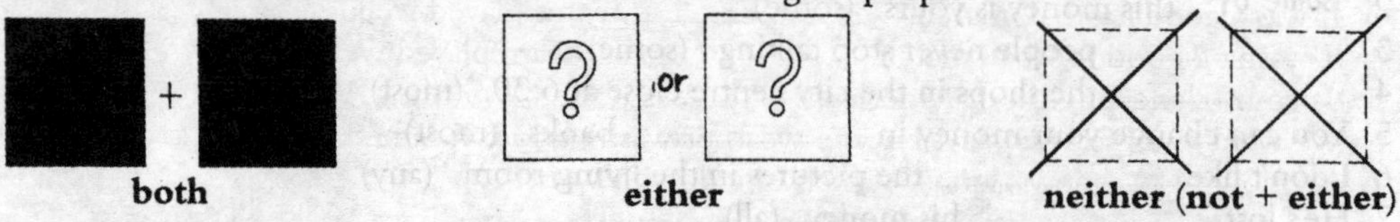

- Rosemary has two children. **Both** are married. (**Both** = the two children)
- Would you like tea or coffee? You can have **either**. (= tea *or* coffee)
- A: Do you want to go to the cinema or the theatre?
  B: **Neither**. I want to stay at home. (**Neither** = *not* the cinema *or* the theatre)

Compare **either** and **neither**:

- 'Would you like **tea or coffee**?' {
  '**Either**. I don't mind.' (= tea *or* coffee)
  'I do**n't** want **either**.' (*not* 'I don't want neither')
  '**Neither**.' (= *not* tea *or* coffee)

B

both/either/neither + *noun*

both	+	*plural:*	**both**	**windows/books/children** *etc.*
either **neither**	+	*singular:*	**either** **neither** }	**window/book/child** *etc.*

- Last year I went to Paris and Rome. I liked **both cities** very much.
- First I worked in an office, and later in a shop. **Neither job** was very interesting.
- There are two ways from here to the station. You can go **either way**.

C

both of ... / **either of** ... / **neither of** ...

both **either** **neither**	**of**	**the** ... **these / those** ... **my / your / Ann's** ... *etc.*

- **Neither of my parents** is English.
- I have**n't** read **either of these books**.

You can say **both** (of) **the** ... / **both** (of) **those** ... / **both** (of) **my** ... *etc.* (*with or without* **of**):

- I like **both of those pictures**. *or* I like **both those pictures**.
- **Both of Ann's sisters** are married. *or* **Both Ann's sisters** are married.

D

both of them / **neither of us** *etc.* + *noun*

both **either** **neither**	**of**	**them** **us** **you**

- Ann has got two sisters. **Both of them are** married.
- Tom and I didn't eat anything. **Neither of us was** hungry.
- Who are those two people? I do**n't** know **either of them**.

I can't either / neither can I ⇒ UNIT 41

EXERCISES

81.1 Put in **both/either/neither**. Use **of** where necessary.

1 Last year I went to Paris and Rome. I liked ...both... cities very much.
2 There were two pictures on the wall. I didn't like ...either of... them.
3 It was a good football match. .... teams played well.
4 It wasn't a good football match. .... team played well.
5 'Is your friend English or American?' '.................... . She's Australian.'
6 We went away for two days but the weather wasn't good. It rained on .... days.
7 A: I bought two newspapers. Which one do you want?
B: .... It doesn't matter which one.
8 I invited Diana and Mike to the party but .... them came.
9 'Do you go to work by car or by bus?' '.................... . I always walk.'
10 'Which jacket do you prefer, this one or that one?' 'I don't like .... them.'
11 'Do you work or are you a student?' '.................... . I've got a job and I study too.'
12 Paula and I didn't know the time because .... us had a watch.
13 Ann has got two sisters and a brother. .... sisters are married.
14 Ann has got two sisters and a brother. I've met her brother but I haven't met .... her sisters.

81.2 Complete the sentences for the pictures. Use **Both ...** and **Neither ...** .

1 ...Both cups are... empty.
2 .... are open.
3 .... wearing a hat.
4 .... cameras.
5 .... to the airport.
6 .... right.

81.3 A man and a woman answered some questions. Their answers were the same. Write sentences with **Both/Neither of them ...** .

1 Are you married?	No	No	1	Neither of them is married.
2 How old are you?	21	21	2	Both of them are 21.
3 Are you a student?	Yes	Yes	3	.... students.
4 Have you got a car?	No	No	4	.... a car.
5 Where do you live?	London	London	5	....
6 Do you like cooking?	Yes	Yes	6	....
7 Can you play the piano?	No	No	7	....
8 Do you read newspapers?	Yes	Yes	8	....
9 Are you interested in sport?	No	No	9	....

UNIT 82 a lot much many

A

a lot of money

not much money

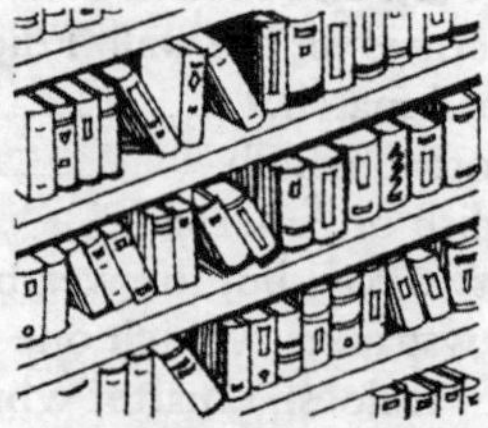
a lot of books

not many books

We use **much** + *uncountable noun:*
much food / much money *etc.*:
- Did you buy **much food**?
- We haven't got **much luggage.**
- How **much money** do you want?
- A: Have you got any **money**?
  B: I've got some but **not much.**

We use many + *plural noun:*
many books / many people *etc.*:
- Did you buy **many books**?
- We don't know **many people.**
- How **many photographs** did you take?
- A: Did you take any **photographs**?
  B: I took some but **not many.**

We use **a lot of** + *all types of noun:*
- We bought **a lot of food.**
- Paula hasn't got **a lot of** free **time.**
- We bought **a lot of books.**
- Did they ask you **a lot of questions**?

Note that we say:
- There **is** a lot of **food/money/water** … (*singular verb*)
- There **are** a lot of **trees/shops/people** … (*plural verb*)
- A lot of **people speak** English. (*not* 'speaks')

B

We use **much** in questions and negative sentences, but *not usually* in positive sentences:
- Do you drink **much coffee / a lot of coffee**?
- I don't drink **much coffee / a lot of coffee.**

but
- I drink **a lot of coffee**. (*not* 'I drink much coffee.')
- 'Do you drink **much** coffee?' 'Yes, **a lot**.' (*not* 'much')

We use **many** and **a lot of** in all types of sentences:
- Have you got **many friends / a lot of friends**?
- We haven't got **many friends / a lot of friends.**
- We've got **many friends / a lot of friends.**

C

much and **a lot** *without* a noun
- Diane spoke to me but she didn't say **much.**
- 'Do you watch TV **much**?' 'No, **not much.**' (= not often)
- We like films, so we go to the cinema **a lot.** (*not* 'much' – See section B)
- I don't like him very **much.**

countable/uncountable ⇒ UNITS 66-67

EXERCISES

82.1 Put in **much** or **many**.

1 Did you buy *much* food?
2 There aren't .... hotels in this town.
3 We haven't got .... petrol.
4 Were there .... people on the train?
5 Did .... students fail the examination?
6 Paula hasn't got .... money.
7 I wasn't very hungry. I didn't eat ....
8 I haven't seen George for .... years.

Put in **How much** or **How many**.

9 .... people are coming to the party?
10 .... milk do you want in your coffee?
11 .... bread did you buy?
12 .... players are there in a football team?

82.2 Complete the sentences. Use **much** or **many** with one of these words:

~~books~~ countries luggage people time times

1 I don't read very much. I haven't got *many books* .
2 Quick! We must hurry. We haven't got ....
3 Do you travel a lot? Have you been to .... ?
4 Tina hasn't lived here very long, so she doesn't know ....
5 'Have you got .... ?' 'No, only this bag.'
6 I know Paris very well. I've been there ....

82.3 Complete the sentences with **a lot of** + one of these:

accidents ~~books~~ fun interesting things traffic

1 I like reading. I have *a lot of books.*
2 We enjoyed our visit to the museum. We saw ....
3 This road is very dangerous. There are ....
4 We enjoyed our holiday. We had ....
5 It took me a long time to drive here. There was ....

82.4 In some of these sentences **much** is not natural. Change the sentences or write *OK*.

1 Do you drink much coffee? *OK*
2 I drink much tea. *a lot of tea*
3 It was a cold winter. We had much snow. ....
4 There wasn't much snow last winter. ....
5 It costs much money to travel around the world. ....
6 We had a cheap holiday. It didn't cost much. ....
7 Do you know much about computers? ....
8 'Have you got any luggage?' 'Yes, much.' ....

82.5 Write sentences about these people. Use **much** and **a lot**.

1 Jim loves films. (go to the cinema) *He goes to the cinema a lot.*
2 Linda thinks TV is boring. (watch TV) *She doesn't watch TV much.*
3 Tina is a good tennis player. (play tennis) She ....
4 Martin doesn't like driving. (use his car) He ....
5 Paul spends most of the time at home. (go out) ....
6 Sue has been all over the world. (travel) ....

UNIT 83 (a) little (a) few

A

a little water

(a) **little** + *uncountable noun:*

(a) **little water**
(a) **little money**
(a) **little time**
(a) **little soup**

a few books

(a) **few** + *plural noun:*

(a) **few** books
(a) **few** questions
(a) **few people**
(a) **few** days

B

a little = some but not much:

- She didn't eat anything but she drank **a little water**.
- I speak **a little Spanish**. (= some Spanish but not much)
- A: Can you speak Spanish?
  B: **A little**.

a few = some but not many:

- Last night I wrote **a few letters**.
- We're going away for **a few days**.
- I speak **a few words** of Spanish.
- A: Are there any shops in the village?
  B: Yes, **a few**.

C

~~**a**~~ **little** (*without* **a**) = nearly no ... *or* nearly nothing:

- There was **little food** in the fridge. It was nearly empty.

You can say **very little**:

- Dan is very thin because he eats **very little**. (= nearly nothing)

~~**a**~~ **few** (*without* **a**) = nearly no ... :

- There were **few people** in the park. It was nearly empty.

You can say **very few**:

- Your English is very correct. You make **very few mistakes**.

D

little and **a little**:

a little is a *positive* idea:

- They have **a little** money, so they're not poor. (= they have some money)

~~**a**~~ **little** is a *negative* idea:

- They have **little** money. They are very poor. (= nearly no money)

few and **a few**:

a few is a *positive* idea:

- I've got **a few** friends, so I'm not lonely. (= I've got some friends)

~~**a**~~ **few** is a *negative* idea:

- I'm sad and I'm lonely. I've got **few** friends. (= nearly no friends)

countable/uncountable ⇒ UNITS 66-67

EXERCISES

83.1 Answer the questions with **a little** or **a few**.

1 'Have you got any money?' 'Yes, a little.'
2 'Have you got any envelopes?' 'Yes, ...'
3 'Do you want sugar in your coffee?' 'Yes, ..., please.'
4 'Did you take any photographs when you were on holiday?' 'Yes, ...'
5 'Does your friend speak English?' 'Yes, ...'
6 'Are there any factories in this town?' 'Yes, ...'

83.2 Put in **a little** or **a few** + one of these words:

air **chairs** **days** **friends** **~~letters~~** **milk** **Russian** **times**

1 Last night I wrote a few letters to my family and friends.
2 Can I have .... in my coffee, please?
3 'When did Julia go away?' '.. ago.'
4 'Do you speak any foreign languages?' 'I can speak ....'
5 'Are you going out alone?' 'No, I'm going with ....'
6 'Have you ever been to Rome?' 'Yes, ...'
7 There wasn't much furniture in the room – just a table and ....
8 I'm going out for a walk. I need .... fresh ....

83.3 Complete the sentences. Use **very little** or **very few** + one of these words:

coffee **hotels** **~~mistakes~~** **people** **rain** **time** **work**

1 Your English is very good. You make very few mistakes.
2 I drink .... I don't like it.
3 The weather here is very dry in summer. There is ....
4 It's difficult to find a place to stay in this town. There are ....
5 We must hurry. We've got ....
6 The town is very quiet at night. .... go out.
7 Some people in the office are very lazy. They do ....

83.4 Put in **little / a little / few / a few**.

1 There was little food in the fridge. It was nearly empty.
2 'When did Sarah go out?' '................................ minutes ago.'
3 I can't decide now. I need .... time to think about it.
4 There was .... traffic, so we arrived earlier than we expected.
5 The bus service isn't very good at night – there are .... buses after 9 o'clock.
6 'Would you like some soup?' 'Yes, ... please.'
7 I'd like to practise my English more but I have .... opportunity.

83.5 Right or wrong? Correct the sentences where necessary. Write *OK* if the sentence is correct.

1 We're going away (for few days) next week. for a few days
2 Everybody needs little luck. ....
3 I can't talk to you now – I've got few things to do. ....
4 I eat very little meat – I don't like it very much. ....
5 Excuse me, can I ask you few questions? ....
6 There were little people on the bus – it was nearly empty. ....

UNIT 84

old/nice/interesting etc. (adjectives)

A *adjective + noun* (**nice day / blue eyes** *etc.*)

adjective +	*noun*
It's a **nice**	**day** today.
Laura has got **brown**	**eyes.**
There's a very **old**	**bridge** in this village.
Do you like **Italian**	**food**?
I don't speak any **foreign**	**languages.**
There are some **beautiful yellow**	**flowers** in the garden.

The adjective is *before* the noun:

- They live in a **modern house.** (*not* 'a house modern')
- Have you met any **famous people**? (*not* 'people famous')

The ending of an adjective is always the same:

a **different place**   **different** places (*not* 'differents')

B **be** (**am/is/was** *etc.*) + *adjective*

- The weather **is nice** today.
- These flowers **are** very **beautiful**.
- **Are** you **cold**? Shall I close the window?
- **I'm hungry.** Can I have something to eat?
- The film **wasn't** very **good**. It **was boring**.
- Please **be quiet**. I'm reading.

C **look/feel/smell/taste/sound** + *adjective*

- 'You **look tired**.' 'Yes, I **feel tired**.'
- George told me about his new job. It **sounds** very **interesting**.
- Don't cook that meat. It doesn't **smell good**.

Compare:

He	**is** **feels** **looks**	**tired.**

They	**are** **look** **sound**	**American.**

It	**is** **smells** **tastes**	**good.**

get + adjective (**get hungry/tired** etc.) ⇒ UNIT 55   **something/anybody** + adjective ⇒ UNIT 78

EXERCISES

84.1 Put the words in the right order.

1 (new / live in / house / they / a) They live in a new house.
2 (like / jacket / I / that / green) I ....
3 (music / like / do / classical / you?) Do .... ?
4 (had / wonderful / a / I / holiday) ....
5 (went to / restaurant / a / Chinese / we) ....

84.2 The words in the box are adjectives (**black/foreign** etc.) or nouns (**air/job** etc.). Use an adjective and a noun to complete each sentence.

air	clouds	~~foreign~~	holiday	job	~~languages~~	sharp
black	dangerous	fresh	hot	knife	long	water

1 Do you speak any foreign languages ?
2 Look at those .... It's going to rain.
3 Sue works very hard and she's very tired. She needs a ....
4 I want to have a bath but there's no ....
5 Can you open the window? We need some ....
6 I need a .... to cut these onions.
7 Fire-fighting is a ....

84.3 Write sentences for the pictures. Choose from Box A and Box B.

A

feel(s)	look(s)	~~sound(s)~~
look(s)	smell(s)	taste(s)

\+ **B**

~~happy~~	ill	nice
horrible	new	surprised

1 You sound happy.

2 It ....

3 I ....

4 You ....

5 They ....

6 It ....

84.4 A and B don't agree. Complete B's sentences. Use the word in brackets (...).

	A	B	
1	You look tired.	Do I? I don't feel tired.	(feel)
2	This is a new coat.	Is it? It	(look)
3	I'm American.	Are you? You	(sound)
4	You look cold.	Do I? I	(feel)
5	These bags are heavy.	Are they? They	(look)
6	That soup looks good.	Does it? It	(taste)

UNIT 85 quickly/badly/suddenly etc. (adverbs)

A

He ate his dinner very **quickly**.

Suddenly the shelf fell down.

Quickly and **suddenly** are adverbs.

adjective + **-ly** → *adverb:*

adjective	quick	bad	sudden	careful	heavy	
adverb	quick**ly**	bad**ly**	sudden**ly**	careful**ly**	heav**ily**	*etc.*

Spelling (⇒ Appendix 5): eas**y** → eas**ily** heav**y** → heav**ily**

B

Adverbs tell you *how* something happens or *how* somebody does something:

- The train **stopped suddenly**.
- I **opened** the door **slowly**.
- Please **listen carefully**.
- I **understand** you **perfectly**.

It's **raining heavily**.

Compare:

adjective (⇒ Unit 84)	*adverb*
● Sue **is** very **quiet**.	● Sue **speaks** very **quietly**. (*not* 'speaks very quiet')
● **Be careful!**	● **Listen carefully**! (*not* 'listen careful')
● It was **a bad game**.	● Our team **played badly**. (*not* 'played bad')
● I **feel nervous**. (= I am nervous)	● I **waited nervously**.

C

hard fast late early These words are adjectives *and* adverbs:

● Sue's job **is** very **hard**.	● Sue **works** very **hard.** (*not* 'hardly')
● Ben is **a fast runner**.	● Ben can **run fast**.
● The bus **was late/early.**	● I **went** to bed **late/early**.

D

good *(adjective)* → **well** *(adverb)*

● Your English **is** very **good**.	● You **speak** English very **well**. (*not* 'very good')
● It was **a good game**.	● Our team **played well**.

But **well** is also an *adjective* (= not ill, in good health):

- 'How are you?' **'I'm** very **well**, thank you. And you?'

adjectives ⇒ UNIT 84

EXERCISES

85.1 Look at the pictures and complete the sentences with one of these adverbs:

angrily **badly** **dangerously** **fast** ~~**heavily**~~ **quietly**

1 It's raining heavily.
2 He sings very ....
3 They came in ....
4 She shouted at me ....
5 She can run very ....
6 He was driving ....

85.2 Choose a verb (Box A) + an adverb (Box B) to complete the sentences.

A

come	know	sleep	win
explain	~~listen~~	think	work

\+ **B**

~~carefully~~	clearly	hard	well
carefully	easily	quickly	well

1 I'm going to tell you something very important, so please listen carefully.
2 Ann! I need your help. .... !
3 They .... At the end of the day they're always tired.
4 I'm tired this morning. I didn't .... last night.
5 You're a much better tennis player than me. When we play, you always ....
6 .... before you answer the question.
7 I've met Alice a few times but I don't .... her very ....
8 Our teacher isn't very good. Sometimes he doesn't .... things very ....

85.3 Which is right?

1 Don't eat so ~~quick~~/quickly. It's not good for you. quickly is right
2 Why are you angry/angrily? I haven't done anything.
3 Can you speak slow/slowly, please?
4 Come on, Dave! Why are you always so slow/slowly?
5 Bill is a very careful/carefully driver.
6 Jane is studying hard/hardly for her examinations.
7 'Where's Diane?' 'She was here but she left sudden/suddenly.'
8 Please be quiet/quietly. I'm studying.
9 Some companies pay their workers very bad/badly.
10 Those oranges look nice/nicely. Can I have one?

85.4 Put in **good** or **well**.

1 Your English is very good. You speak English very well.
2 Jackie did very .... in her exams.
3 The party was very .... I enjoyed it very much.
4 Martin has a difficult job but he does it ....
5 How are your parents? Are they .... ?
6 Did you have a .... holiday? Was the weather .... ?

UNIT 86

old/older expensive/more expensive

A

old **older** heavy **heavier** expensive **more expensive**

Older / heavier / more expensive are *comparative* forms.
The comparative is **-er** (**older**) or **more ...** (**more expensive**).

B

-er (old**er**/heavi**er** *etc.*)

> Short words (1 syllable) → **-er**:
>
> **old** → older **slow** → slower **cheap** → cheaper
>
> **nice** → nicer **late** → later **big** → bigger
>
> *Spelling* (⇒ Appendix 5): big → bi**gg**er hot → ho**tt**er thin → thi**nn**er
>
> Words ending in **-y** → **-ier**:
>
> easy → eas**ier** heavy → heav**ier** early → earl**ier**

- Rome is **old** but Athens is **older**. (*not* 'more old')
- Is it **cheaper** to go by car or by train? (*not* 'more cheap')
- Helen wants a **bigger** car.
- This coat is OK but I think the other one is **nicer**.
- Don't write a letter. It's **easier** to phone. (*not* 'more easy')

far → further:

- 'How far is it to the station? A mile?' 'No, it's **further**. About two miles.'

C

more ...

> Long words (2/3/4 syllables) → **more ...** :
>
> careful → **more** careful polite → **more** polite
>
> expensive → **more** expensive interesting → **more** interesting

- You must be **more careful**.
- I don't like my job. I want to do something **more interesting**.
- Is it **more expensive** to go by car or by train?

D

good/well → better bad → worse

- The weather wasn't very **good** yesterday but it's **better** today.
- 'Do you feel **better** today?' 'No, I feel **worse**.'
- Which is **worse** – a headache or a toothache?

older than ... / more expensive than ... ⇒ UNIT 87 **the oldest / the most expensive** ⇒ UNIT 89

UNIT
86

EXERCISES

86.1 Look at the pictures and write the comparative (**older / more interesting** etc.).

1

heavy heavier

2

big ....

3

slow ....

4

expensive ....

5

high ....

6
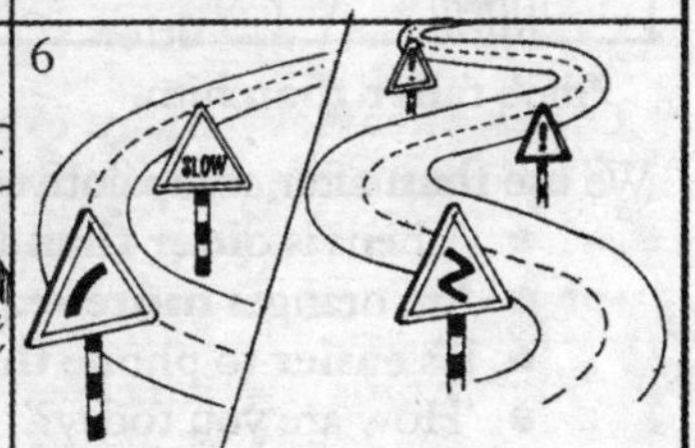

dangerous ....

86.2 Write the comparative.

1 old older
2 strong ....
3 happy ....
4 modern ....
5 important ....
6 good ....
7 large ....
8 serious ....
9 pretty ....
10 crowded ....

86.3 Write the opposite.

1 younger older
2 colder ....
3 cheaper ....
4 better ....
5 nearer ....
6 easier ....

86.4 Complete the sentences. Use a comparative.

1 Helen's car isn't very big. She wants a bigger one.
2 My job isn't very interesting. I want to do something more interesting.
3 You're not very tall. Your brother is ....
4 David doesn't work very hard. I work ....
5 My chair isn't very comfortable. Yours is ....
6 Your plan isn't very good. My plan is ....
7 These flowers aren't very nice. The blue ones are ....
8 My bag isn't very heavy. Your bag is ....
9 I'm not very interested in art. I'm .... in history.
10 It isn't very warm today. It was .... yesterday.
11 These tomatoes don't taste very good. The other ones tasted ....
12 Britain isn't very big. France is ....
13 London isn't very beautiful. Paris is ....
14 This knife isn't very sharp. Have you got a .... one?
15 People today aren't very polite. In the past they were ....

older than ... more expensive than ...

A

She's **taller than** him.

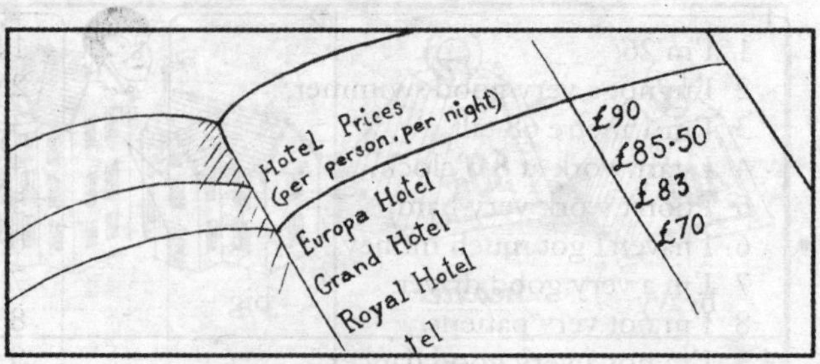

The Europa Hotel is **more expensive than** the Grand.

We use **than** after comparatives (**older than** ... / **more expensive than** ... *etc.*):

- Athens is **older than** Rome.
- Are oranges **more expensive than** bananas?
- It's **easier** to phone **than** to write a letter.
- 'How are you today?' 'Not bad. **Better than** yesterday.'
- The restaurant is **more crowded than** usual.

B

We say: than **me** / than **him** / than **her** / than **us** / than **them**. You can say:

- I can run faster **than him.** *or* I can run faster **than he can.**
- You are a better singer **than me.** *or* You are a better singer **than I am.**
- I got up earlier **than her.** *or* I got up earlier **than she did.**

C

more/less than ...

- A: How much did your shoes cost? £30?
  B: No, **more than** that. (= **more than** £30)
- The film was very short – **less than** an hour.
- They've got **more money than** they need.
- You go out **more than** me.

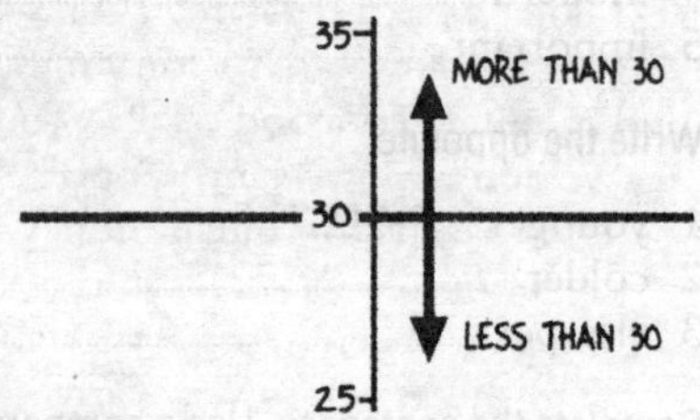

D

a bit older / much older etc.

Box A is **a bit bigger** than Box B.

Box C is **much bigger** than Box D.

a bit **much**	bigger older better more difficult more expensive	than ...

- Canada is **much bigger** than France.
- Jill is **a bit older** than Gary – she's 25 and he's 24½.
- The hotel was **much more expensive** than I expected.
- You go out **much more** than me.

old → older, expensive → more expensive ⇒ UNIT 86 **not as (old) as ⇒ UNIT 88**

EXERCISES

87.1 Write sentences about Liz and Ben. Use **than**.

LIZ

1 I'm 26.
2 I'm not a very good swimmer.
3 I'm 1 metre 68 tall.
4 I start work at 8 o'clock.
5 I don't work very hard.
6 I haven't got much money.
7 I'm a very good driver.
8 I'm not very patient.
9 I'm not a very good dancer.
10 I'm very intelligent.
11 I speak French very well.
12 I don't go to the cinema very much.

BEN

1 I'm 24.
2 I'm a very good swimmer.
3 I'm 1 metre 63 tall.
4 I start work at 8.30.
5 I work very hard.
6 I've got a lot of money.
7 I'm not a very good driver.
8 I'm very patient.
9 I'm a good dancer.
10 I'm not very intelligent.
11 I don't speak French very well.
12 I go to the cinema a lot.

1 *Liz is older than Ben.*
2 *Ben is a better swimmer than Liz.*
3 Liz is ....
4 Liz starts .... Ben.
5 Ben ....
6 Ben has got ....
7 Liz is a ....
8 Ben ....
9 Ben ....
10 Liz ....
11 Liz ....
12 Ben ....

87.2 Complete the sentences. Use **than**.

1 He isn't very tall. You *'re taller than him. (OR ... than he is.)*
2 She isn't very old. You're ....
3 I don't work very hard. You work ....
4 He doesn't watch TV very much. You ....
5 I'm not a very good cook. You ....
6 We don't know many people. You ....
7 They haven't got much money. You ....
8 I can't run very fast. You can ....
9 She hasn't been here very long. You ....
10 They didn't get up very early. You ....
11 He wasn't very surprised. You ....

87.3 Complete the sentences with **a bit** or **much** + a comparative (**older/better** etc.).

1 Jill is 25. Gary is 24½.
Jill is a bit older than Gary.
2 Jack's mother is 54. His father is 69.
Jack's mother ....
3 My camera cost £100. Yours cost £96.
My camera ....
4 Yesterday I felt terrible. Today I feel OK.
I feel ....
5 Today the temperature is 12 degrees. Yesterday it was ten degrees.
It's ....
6 Ann is an excellent tennis player. I'm not very good.
Ann ....

UNIT 88 not as ... as

A

not as ... as

She's old but she's **not as old as** he is.

Box A is**n't as big as** Box B.

- Rome **is not as old as** Athens. (= Athens is **older**)
- The Grand Hotel is**n't as expensive as** the Europa. (= the Europa is **more expensive**)
- I do**n't** play tennis **as often as** you. (= you play **more often**)
- The weather is better than it was yesterday. It is**n't as cold**. (= as cold **as it was yesterday**)

B

not as much as ... / not as many as ...

- I haven't got **as much money as** you. (= you've got **more money**)
- I don't know **as many people as** you. (= you know **more people**)
- I don't go out **as much as** you. (= you go out **more**)

C

Compare **not as ... as** and **than**:

- Rome is **not as old as** Athens.
  Athens is **older than** Rome. (*not* 'older as Rome')
- Tennis is**n't as popular as** football.
  Football is **more popular than** tennis.
- I **don't** go out **as much as you.**
  You go out **more than** me.

D

We say: as **me** / as **him** / as **her** *etc.* You can say:

- She's not as old **as him**. *or* She's not as old **as he is.**
- You don't work as hard **as me.** *or* You don't work as hard **as I do.**

E

We say **the same as** ... :

- The weather today is **the same as** yesterday.
- My hair is **the same colour as** yours.
- I arrived at **the same time as** Tim.

much/many ⇒ UNIT 82 **older than ... / more expensive than ...** ⇒ UNIT 87

EXERCISES

88.1 Look at the pictures and write sentences about A, B and C.

1 A is *bigger than C but not as big as B.*
2 A is .... B but not .... C.
3 C is .... A but ....
4 A is .... but ....
5 B has got ....
6 C works ....

88.2 Write sentences with **as ... as ...** .

1 Athens is older than Rome. Rome *isn't as old as Athens.*
2 My room is bigger than yours. Your room isn't ....
3 You got up earlier than me. I didn't ....
4 We played better than them. They ....
5 I've been here longer than you. You ....
6 She's more nervous than him. He ....

88.3 Put in **as** or **than**.

1 Athens is older *than* Rome.
2 I don't watch TV as much .... you.
3 You eat more .... me.
4 I feel better .... I felt yesterday.
5 Jim isn't as clever .... he thinks.
6 Belgium is smaller .... Switzerland.
7 Brazil isn't as big .... Canada.
8 I can't wait longer .... an hour.

88.4 Use the information to complete the sentences about Julia, Andrew and Caroline. Use **the same age / the same street** etc.

1 (age) *Andrew is the same age as Caroline.*
2 (street) Julia lives ....
3 (time) Julia got up ....
4 (colour) Andrew's ....

UNIT 89

the oldest   the most expensive

A

HOTEL PRICES IN KINTON
(per person . per night)

Europa Hotel	£95	Grosvenor	£60
Grand Hotel	£85·50	Bennetts	£58
Royal	£85	Carlton	£55
Astoria	£70	Star	£50
Palace	£65	Station	£45

Box A is **bigger than** Box B.

Box A is **bigger than** all the other boxes.

Box A is **the biggest** box.

The Europa Hotel is **more expensive than** the Grand.

The Europa Hotel is **more expensive than** all the other hotels in the town.

The Europa Hotel is **the most expensive** hotel in the town.

Bigg**er** / old**er** / **more** expensive *etc.* are *comparative* forms (⇒ Unit 86).
Bigg**est** / old**est** / **most** expensive *etc.* are *superlative* forms.

B

The superlative form is **-est** (**oldest**) *or* **most** ... (**most expensive**):

Short words (**old/cheap/nice** *etc.*) → **the -est**:

old → **the** old**est**   **cheap** → **the** cheap**est**   **nice** → **the** nic**est**
but **good** → **the best**   **bad** → **the worst**
Spelling (⇒ Appendix 5): big → the bigg**est**   hot → the hott**est**

Words ending in **-y** (**easy/heavy** *etc.*) → **the -iest**:

easy → **the** eas**iest**   heavy → **the** heav**iest**   pretty → **the** prett**iest**

Long words (**careful/expensive/interesting** *etc.*) → **the most** ...:

careful → **the most** careful   **interesting** → **the most** interesting

C

We say: **the** oldest ... / **the** most expensive ... *etc.* (with **the**):

- The church is very old. It's **the oldest** building in the town.
  (= it is old**er than** all the other buildings)
- What is **the longest** river in the world?
- Money is important but it isn't **the most important** thing in life.
- Excuse me, where is **the nearest** bank?

D

You can use **the oldest** / **the best** / **the most expensive** *etc. without* a noun:

- Ken is a good player but he isn't **the best** in the team.
  (**the best** = the best player)

E

superlative + **I've ever** ... / **you've ever** ... *etc.*

- The film was very bad. I think it's **the worst** film **I've ever seen.**
- What is **the most unusual** thing **you've ever done**?

present perfect + **ever** ⇒ UNIT 17   older / more expensive ⇒ UNITS 86-87

EXERCISES

89.1 Write sentences with comparatives (**older** etc.) and superlatives (**the oldest** etc.).

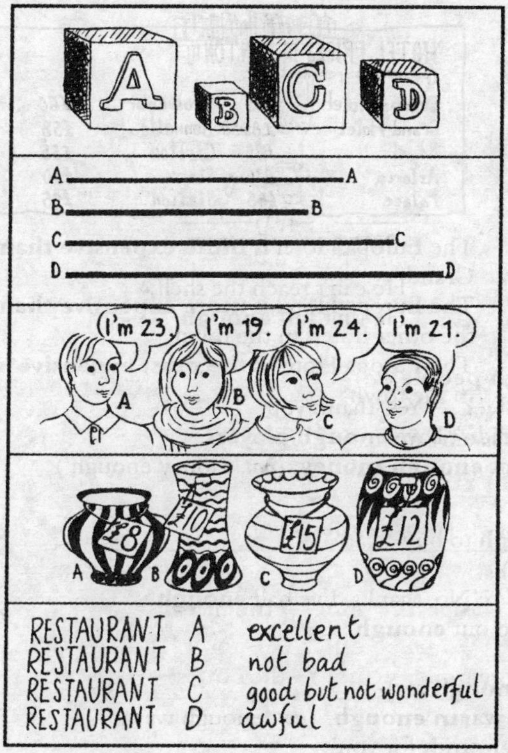

1 **(big/small)**
(A/D) A is bigger than D.
(A) A is the biggest.
(B) B is the smallest.

2 **(long/short)**
(C/A) C is .... A.
(D) D is ....
(B) B ....

3 **(young/old)**
(D/C) D ....
(B) ....
(C) ....

4 **(expensive/cheap)**
(D/A) ....
(C) ....
(A) ....

5 **(good/bad)**
(A/C) ....
(A) ....
(D) ....

89.2 Complete the sentences. Use a superlative (**the oldest** etc.).

1 This building is very old. It's the oldest building in the town.
2 It was a very happy day. It was .... of my life.
3 It's a very good film. It's .... I've ever seen.
4 She's a very popular singer. She's .... in the country.
5 It was a very bad mistake. It was .... I've ever made.
6 It's a very pretty village. It's .... I've ever seen.
7 It was a very cold day. It was .... of the year.
8 He's a very boring person. He's .... I've ever met.

89.3 Write sentences with a superlative (**the longest** etc.).

~~Sydney~~	Brazil	large	country	planet	the USA	the solar system
Everest	Jupiter	long	~~city~~	state	Africa	South America
Alaska	the Nile	high	river	mountain	the world	~~Australia~~

1 Sydney is the largest city in Australia.
2 Everest ....
3 ....
4 ....
5 ....
6 ....

UNIT **90**

enough

A

She can't buy a sandwich.
She hasn't got **enough money**.

He can't reach the shelf.
He isn't **tall enough**.

B

enough + *noun* (**enough money** / **enough people** *etc.*)

- 'Is there **enough sugar** in your coffee?' 'Yes, thank you.'
- We wanted to play football but we didn't have **enough players**.
- Why don't you buy a car? You've got **enough money**. (*not* 'money enough')

enough *without a noun:*

- I've got some money but not **enough** to buy a car.
  (= I need more money to buy a car)
- 'Would you like some more to eat?' 'No, thanks. I've had **enough**.'
- You're always at home. You don't go out **enough**.

C

adjective + **enough** (**good enough** / **tall enough** *etc.*)

- 'Shall we sit outside?' 'No, it isn't **warm enough**.' (*not* 'enough warm')
- Can you hear the radio? Is it **loud enough** for you?
- Don't buy that coat. It's nice but it isn't **long enough**. (= it's too short)

Remember:

enough + *noun*	*but*	*adjective* + **enough**
enough money		tall **enough**
enough time		good **enough**
enough people		old **enough**

D

We say:

enough for (somebody/something)	• This pullover isn't **big enough for me**. • I haven't got **enough money for a car**.
enough to (**do** something)	• I haven't got **enough money to buy** a car. (*not* 'for buy a car') • Is your English **good enough to have** a conversation? (*not* 'for have')
enough for (somebody/something) **to** (**do** something)	• There aren't **enough chairs for everybody to sit** down.

to ... and **for** ... ⇒ UNIT 53   **too** ⇒ UNIT 91

EXERCISES

90.1 Look at the pictures and complete the sentences. Use **enough** + one of these words:

chairs ~~**money**~~ **paint** **wind**

1 She hasn't got enough money.
2 There aren't ……………
3 She hasn't got ……………
4 There isn't ……………

90.2 Look at the pictures and complete the sentences. Use one of these adjectives + **enough**:

big **long** **strong** ~~**tall**~~

1 He isn't tall enough.
2 The car ……………
3 His legs aren't ……………
4 He ……………

90.3 Complete the sentences. Use **enough** with one of these words:

big **eat** **fruit** ~~**loud**~~ **old** **practise** ~~**sugar**~~ **time** **tired**

1 'Is there enough sugar in your coffee?' 'Yes, thank you.'
2 Can you hear the radio? Is it loud enough for you?
3 He can leave school if he wants – he's ……………
4 Did you have …………… to answer all the questions in the exam?
5 This house isn't …………… for a large family.
6 Tina is very thin. She doesn't …………… .
7 You don't eat …………… . You should eat more – it's good for you.
8 It's late but I don't want to go to bed now. I'm not …………… .
9 Lisa isn't a very good tennis player because she doesn't …………… .

90.4 Complete the sentences. Use **enough** with the words in brackets (…).

1 We haven't got enough money to buy a car. (money / buy)
2 This knife isn't …………… tomatoes. (sharp / cut)
3 The water wasn't …………… a bath. (warm / have)
4 Have we got …………… sandwiches? (bread / make)
5 We played well but not …………… the game. (well / win)
6 I don't have …………… newspapers. (time / read)

UNIT
91 too

A

His shoes are **too big** for him.

There is **too much** sugar in it.

B

too + *adjective / adverb* (**too big / too hard** *etc.*)

- Can you turn the radio down?
  It's **too loud**. (= louder than I want)
- I can't work. I'm **too tired**.
- I think you work **too hard**.

C

too much / too many = more than you want, more than is good:

- I don't like the weather here. There is **too much rain**. (= more rain than is good)
- Let's go to another restaurant. There are **too many people** here.
- Emily studies all the time. I think she studies **too much**.
- Traffic is a problem in this town. There are **too many cars**.

D

Compare **too** and **not enough**:

• The hat is **too big** for him. • The radio is **too loud**. Can you turn it down, please? • There's **too much sugar** in my coffee. (= more sugar than I want) • I don't feel very well. I ate **too much**.	• The hat is**n't big enough** for him. (= it's **too small**) • The radio is**n't loud enough**. Can you turn it up, please? • There's **not enough sugar** in my coffee. (= I need more sugar) • You're very thin. You do**n't** eat **enough**.

too big

not big enough

E

We say:

too ... **for** (somebody/something)	• These shoes are **too big for me**. • It's a small house – **too small for a large family**.
too ... **to** (**do** something)	• I'm **too tired to go** out. (*not* 'for go out') • It's **too cold to sit** outside.
too ... **for** (somebody/something) **to** (**do** something)	• She speaks **too fast for me to understand**.

to and **for** ⇒ UNIT 53 **much/many** ⇒ UNIT 82 **enough** ⇒ UNIT 90

EXERCISES

91.1 Look at the pictures and complete the sentences. Use **too** + one of these words:

big crowded fast heavy ~~loud~~ low

1 The radio is *too loud.*
2 The box is ....
3 The net is ....
4 She's driving ....
5 The ball is ....
6 The restaurant is ....

91.2 Put in **too / too much / too many / enough**.

1 You're always at home. You don't go out *enough*.
2 I don't like the weather here. There's *too much* rain.
3 I can't wait for them. I haven't got .... time.
4 There was nowhere to sit on the beach. There were .... people.
5 You're always tired. I think you work .... hard.
6 'Did you have .... to eat?' 'Yes, thank you.'
7 You drink .... coffee. It's not good for you.
8 You don't eat .... vegetables. You should eat more.
9 I don't like the weather here. It's .... cold.
10 Our team didn't play well. We made .... mistakes.
11 'Would you like some milk in your tea?' 'Yes, but not ....'

91.3 Complete the sentences. Use **too** or **enough** with the words in brackets.

1 I couldn't work. I *was too tired.* (tired)
2 Can you turn the radio up, please? It *isn't loud enough.* (loud)
3 I don't want to walk home. It's .... (far)
4 Don't buy anything in that shop. It .... (expensive)
5 You can't put all your things in this bag. It .... (big)
6 I couldn't do the exercise. It .... (difficult)
7 Your work needs to be better. It .... (good)
8 I can't talk to you now. I .... (busy)
9 I thought the film was boring. It .... (long)

91.4 Complete the sentences. Use **too** (+ adjective) + **to** (do something).

1 (I'm not going out / cold) *It's too cold to go out.*
2 (I'm not going to bed / early) It's ....
3 (they're not getting married / young) They're ....
4 (nobody goes out at night / dangerous) It's ....
5 (don't phone Ann now / late) It's ....
6 (I didn't say anything / surprised) I was ....

UNIT 92

He **speaks English** very well. (word order 1)

A

verb + object

Sue **reads** **a newspaper** every day.
subject *verb* *object*

The *verb* (**reads**) and the *object* (**a newspaper**) are usually together. We say:

- Sue **reads a newspaper** every day.

(*not* 'Sue reads every day a newspaper.')

	verb	*+ object*
He	**speaks**	**English** very well. (*not* 'He speaks very well English.')
	I like	**Italian food** very much. (*not* 'I like very much …')
Did you	**watch**	**television** all evening? (*not* 'Did you watch all evening …?')
We	**invited**	**a lot of people** to the party. (*not* 'We invited to the party … ')
Paul often	**wears**	**a black hat**. (*not* 'Paul wears often … ')
	I opened	**the door** quietly.
Why do you always	**make**	**the same mistake**?
I'm going to	**borrow**	**some money** from the bank.

B

place and time

We went **to a party** **last night.**
place *time*

Place (**to a party**) is usually before *time* (**last night**). We say:

- We went **to a party last night**. (*not* 'We went last night to a party.')

	place (*where?*)	*time* (*when? how long? how often?*)
Liz walks	**to work**	**every day**. (*not* '… every day to work')
Will you be	**at home**	**this evening?** (*not* '… this evening at home?')
I usually go	**to bed**	**early.** (*not* '… early to bed')
We arrived	**at the airport**	**at 7 o'clock.**
They've lived	**in the same house**	**for 20 years.**
Jim's father has been	**in hospital**	**since June**.

word order in questions ⇒ UNITS 43-45 **always/usually/often** etc. ⇒ UNIT 93

EXERCISES

92.1 Right or wrong? Correct the sentences that are wrong.

1 Did you watch all evening television? — Did you watch television all evening?
2 Sue reads a newspaper every day. — OK
3 I like very much this picture. — ....
4 Tom started last week his new job. — ....
5 I want to speak English fluently. — ....
6 Jane bought for her friend a present. — ....
7 I drink every day three cups of coffee. — ....
8 Don't eat your dinner too quickly! — ....
9 I borrowed from my brother fifty pounds. — ....

92.2 Put the words in order.

1 (the door / opened / I / quietly) — I opened the door quietly.
2 (two letters / I / this morning / wrote) — I ....
3 (passed / Paul / easily / the exam) — ....
4 (Ann / very well / French / doesn't speak) — ....
5 (a lot of work / did / I / yesterday) — ....
6 (London / do you know / well?) — ....
7 (we / enjoyed / very much / the party) — ....
8 (the problem / carefully / I / explained) — ....
9 (we / at the airport / some friends / met) — ....
10 (did you buy / in England / that jacket?) — ....
11 (every day / do / the same thing / we) — ....
12 (football / don't like / very much / I) — ....

92.3 Put the words in order.

1 (to work / every day / walks / Liz) — Liz walks to work every day.
2 (at the hotel / I / early / arrived) — I ....
3 (goes / every year / to Italy / Julia) — Julia ....
4 (we / since 1988 / here / have lived) — We ....
5 (in London / Sue / in 1960 / was born) — Sue ....
6 (didn't go / yesterday / Paul / to work) — Paul ....
7 (to the bank / yesterday afternoon / went / Ann)
Ann ....
8 (I / in bed / this morning / my breakfast / had)
I ....
9 (in October / Barbara / to university / is going)
Barbara ....
10 (I / a beautiful bird / this morning / in the garden / saw)
I ....
11 (many times / have been / my parents / to the United States)
My ....
12 (my umbrella / I / last night / left / in the restaurant)
I ....
13 (to the cinema / tomorrow evening / are you going?)
Are ....
14 (the children / I / took / this morning / to school)
I ....

UNIT 93

always/usually/often etc. (word order 2)

A

always	**often**	**ever**	**rarely**	**also**	**already**	**all**
usually	**sometimes**	**never**	**seldom**	**just**	**still**	**both**

These words (**always/never** *etc.*) are often with the verb in the middle of a sentence:

- My brother **never speaks** to me.
- She**'s always** late.
- Do you **often go** to restaurants?
- I **sometimes eat** too much. (*or* **Sometimes** I eat too much.)
- I don't want to go to the cinema. **I've already** seen the film.
- I've got three sisters. They**'re all** married.

B

always/never *etc.* go *before* the verb:

		verb
always		**go**
often	+	**play**
never		**feel**
etc.		*etc.*

- I **always go** to work by car. (*not* 'I go always')
- Ann **often plays** tennis. (*not* 'Ann plays often tennis')
- You **sometimes look** unhappy.
- They **usually have** dinner at 7 o'clock.
- We **rarely** (*or* **seldom) watch** television.
- Richard is a good footballer. He **also plays** tennis and volleyball. (*not* 'He plays also tennis')
- I've got three sisters. They **all live** in London.

but **always/never** *etc.* go *after* **am/is/are/was/were**:

am		
is		**always**
are	+	**often**
was		**never**
were		*etc.*

- I **am never** ill. (*not* 'I never am ill')
- They **are usually** at home in the evenings.
- It **is often** very cold here in winter.
- When I was a child, I **was always** late for school.
- 'Where's Linda?' 'She**'s still** in bed.'
- I've got two brothers. They**'re both** doctors.

C

always/never *etc.* go *between* two verbs (**have** ... **been** / **can** ... **find** *etc.*):

verb 1		*verb 2*
will / **can** / **do** / *etc.*	**always** / **often** / **never** / *etc.*	**go** / **find** / **remember** / *etc.*
have / **has**		**gone** / **been** / *etc.*

- I **will always remember** you.
- It **doesn't often rain** here.
- **Do** you **usually go** to work by car?
- I **can never find** my keys.
- **Have** you **ever been** to Rome?
- A: Where's Linda?
  B: She**'s just gone** out. (she's = she has)
- A: Where are your friends?
  B: They**'ve all gone** to the cinema.

always/never + present simple ⇒ UNIT 5 **just/already** + present perfect ⇒ UNIT 16 **all** ⇒ UNITS 79-80
both ⇒ UNIT 81 **still** ⇒ UNIT 94

EXERCISES

93.1 Look at Paul's answers to the questions and write sentences with **often/never** etc.

1	Do you ever play tennis?	Yes, often.	*Paul often plays tennis.*
2	Do you get up early?	Yes, always.	He ....
3	Are you ever late for work?	No, never.	He ....
4	Do you ever get angry?	Sometimes.	....
5	Do you ever go swimming?	Yes, often.	....
6	Are you at home in the evenings?	Yes, usually.	....

93.2 Write these sentences with the words in brackets (...).

1 My brother speaks to me. (never) *My brother never speaks to me.*
2 Susan is polite. (always) Susan ....
3 I finish work at 5 o'clock. (usually) I ....
4 Jill has started a new job. (just) Jill ....
5 I go to bed before midnight. (rarely) ....
6 The bus isn't late. (usually) ....
7 I don't eat fish. (often) ....
8 I will forget what you said. (never) ....
9 Have you lost your passport? (ever) ....
10 Do you work in the same place? (still) ....
11 They stay in the same hotel. (always) ....
12 Diane doesn't work on Saturdays. (usually) ....
13 Is Tina here? (already) ....
14 What do you have for breakfast? (usually) ....
15 I can remember his name. (never) ....

93.3 Write sentences with **also**. Use the words in brackets (...).

1 Do you play football? (tennis) *Yes, and I also play tennis.*
2 Do you speak Italian? (French) Yes, and I ....
3 Are you tired? (hungry) Yes, and ....
4 Have you been to England? (Ireland) Yes, ...
5 Did you buy any clothes? (some books) ....

93.4 Write sentences with **both** and **all**.

I live in London.
I play football.
I'm a student.
I've got a car.

I live in London.
I play football.
I'm a student.
I've got a car.

1 *They both live in London.*
They .... football.
.... students.
.... cars.

I'm married. I was born in England.
I live in New York.

2 They .... married.
They .... England.
....

UNIT 94

still yet already

A still

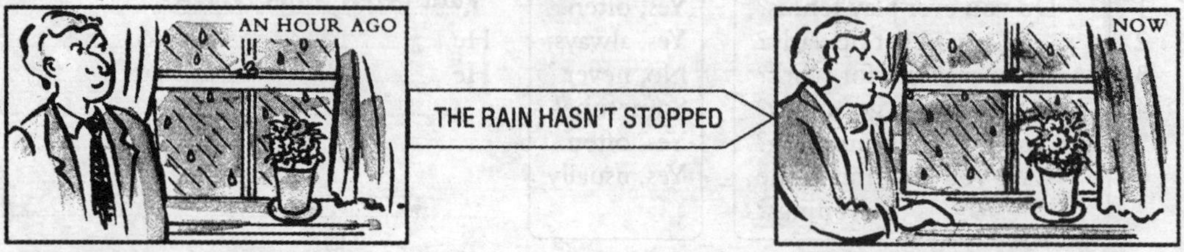

An hour ago it was raining. It is **still** raining now.

still = something is the same as before:

- I had a lot to eat but I'm **still** hungry. (= I was hungry before and I'm hungry now)
- 'Did you sell your car?' 'No, I've **still** got it.'
- 'Do you **still** live in Barcelona?' 'No, I live in Madrid now.'

B yet

Twenty minutes ago they were waiting for Bill.

They are **still** waiting for Bill.
Bill **hasn't come yet**.

yet = until now:
We use **yet** in *negative* sentences (He **hasn't** come yet.) and in *questions* (**Has he** come yet?).
Yet is usually at the end of a sentence:

- A: Where's Diane?
  B: She is**n't** here **yet**. (= she will be here but until now she hasn't come)
- A: What are you doing this evening?
  B: I do**n't** know **yet**. (= I will know later but I don't know at the moment)
- A: Are you ready to go **yet**?
  B: **Not yet**. Wait a moment. (= I will be ready but I'm not ready at the moment)
- A: Have you finished with the newspaper **yet**?
  B: No, I'm still reading it.

Compare **yet** and **still**:

- She hasn't gone **yet**. = She's **still** here. (*not* 'She is yet here')
- I haven't finished eating **yet**. = I'm **still** eating.

C

already = earlier than expected:

- 'What time is John arriving?' 'He's **already** here.' (= earlier than we expected)
- 'I'm going to tell you what happened.' 'That's not necessary. I **already** know.'
- Ann doesn't want to go to the cinema. She has **already** seen the film.

already/yet + present perfect ⇒ UNIT 16 word order (**still/already**) ⇒ UNIT 93

EXERCISES

94.1 You meet Lisa. The last time you saw her was two years ago. You ask her some questions with **still**.

LISA – TWO YEARS AGO

1 *Do you still play the piano?*
2 Do you ....
3 Are ....
4 ....
5 ....
6 ....

94.2 Write three sentences for each situation. Look at the example carefully.

before → *now*

1
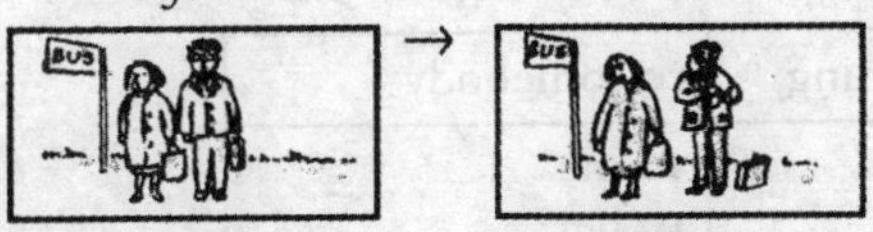

(before) *They were waiting for the bus.*
(still) *They are still waiting.*
(yet) *The bus hasn't come yet.*

2

(before) He was ....
(still) He ....
(yet) .... yet.

3
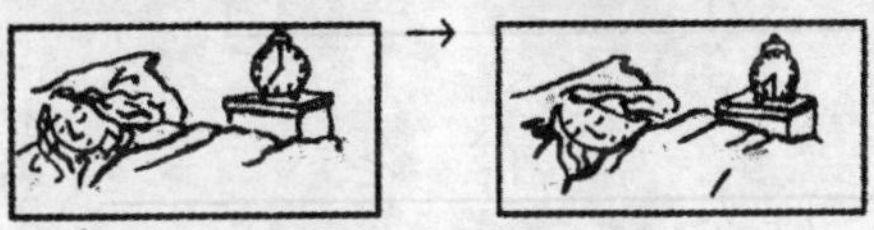

(before) She ....
(still) ....
(yet) ....

4
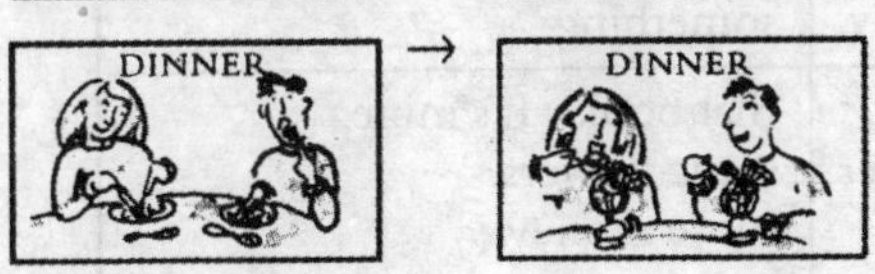

(before) They ....
(still) ....
(yet) ....

94.3 Write questions with **yet**.

1 You and Sue are going out together. You are waiting for her to get ready. Perhaps she is ready now. *You ask her:* *Are you ready yet?*
2 You are waiting for Ann to arrive. She wasn't here ten minutes ago. Perhaps she is here now. *You ask somebody:* .... Ann ....
3 Mary did an exam and is waiting for the results. Perhaps she has her results now. *You ask her:* .... you ....
4 A few days ago you spoke to Tom. He wasn't sure where to go on holiday. Perhaps he has decided now. *You ask him:* ....

94.4 Complete the sentences. Use **already**.

1 What time is John arriving?	*He's already* here.
2 Does Ann want to see the film?	No, she *has already seen* it.
3 I must see Julia before she goes.	It's too late. She ....
4 Do you need a pen?	No thanks. I .... one.
5 Shall I pay the bill?	No, it's OK. I ....
6 Shall I tell Paul about the meeting?	No, he .... I told him.

UNIT 95

Give me that book! Give it to me!

A

give	lend	pass	send	show

After these verbs (**give/lend** *etc.*), there are two possible structures:

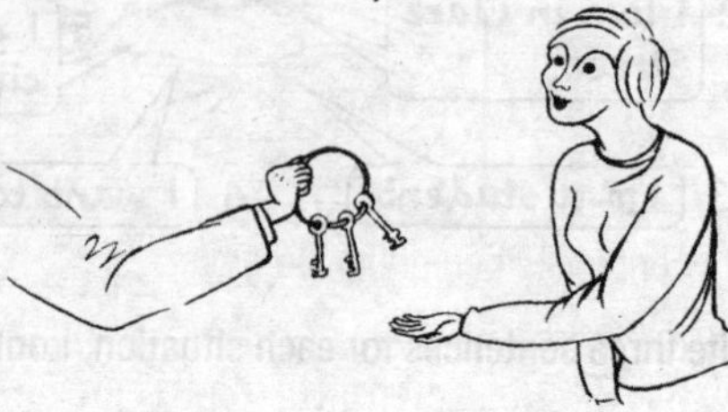

(**give**) **something to somebody**:

- I gave **the keys to Liz**.

(**give**) **somebody something**:

- I gave **Liz the keys**.

B

(**give**) **something to somebody**

	something	**to** somebody
That's my book. **Give**	it	**to** me.
These are Sue's keys. Can you **give**	them	**to** her?
Can you **give**	these flowers	**to** your mother?
I **lent**	my car	**to** a friend of mine.
Did you **send**	a postcard	**to** Kate?
We've seen these photos. You **showed**	them	**to** us.

C

(**give**) **somebody something**

	somebody	something
Give	me	that book. It's mine.
Tom **gave**	his mother	some flowers.
I **lent**	John	some money.
How much money did you **lend**	him?	
I **sent**	you	a postcard. Did you receive it?
Linda **showed**	us	her holiday photos.
Can you **pass**	me	the salt, please?

You can also say '**buy/get** somebody something':

- I **bought** my mother some flowers. (= I bought some flowers **for** my mother.)
- Can you **get** me a newspaper when you go out? (= get a newspaper **for** me)

D

Compare:

- I **gave** the keys **to Liz**.
  I **gave Liz** the keys. (*but not* 'I gave to Liz the keys.')
- That's my book. Can you **give** it **to me**?
  Can you **give me** that book? (*but not* 'give to me that book')

We prefer the first structure (**give** something **to** somebody) when the *thing* is **it or them**:

- I gave **it to her**. (*not* 'I gave her it')
- Here are the keys. Give **them to your father**. (*not* 'Give your father them')

it/him/them etc. ⇒ UNIT 58

EXERCISES

95.1 Mark had some things that he didn't want. He gave them to different people.

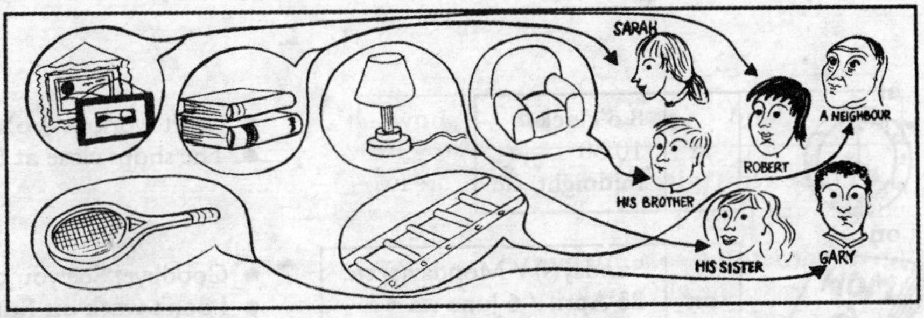

Write sentences beginning **He gave ...** .

1 What did Mark do with the armchair? *He gave it to his brother.*
2 What did he do with the tennis racket? He gave ....
3 What happened to the books? He ....
4 What about the lamp? ....
5 What did he do with the pictures? ....
6 And the ladder? ....

95.2 You wanted to give presents to your friends. You decided to give them the things in the pictures. Write a sentence for each person.

1 *I gave Paul a book.*
2 I gave ....
3 I ....
4 ....
5 ....
6 ....

95.3 Write questions beginning **Can you give me ... ? / Can you pass me ... ?** etc.

1 (you want the salt) (pass) *Can you pass me the salt?*
2 (you need an umbrella) (lend) Can you ....
3 (you want my address) (give) Can .... your ....
4 (you need ten pounds) (lend) ....
5 (you want some information) (send) ....
6 (you want to see the letter) (show) ....
7 (you want some stamps) (get) ....

95.4 Which is right?

1 ~~I gave to Liz the keys.~~ / I gave Liz the keys. *I gave Liz the keys is right*
2 I'll lend to you some money if you want. / I'll lend you some money if you want.
3 Did you send the letter me? / Did you send the letter to me?
4 I want to buy for you a present. / I want to buy you a present.
5 Can you pass to me the sugar, please?/ Can you pass me the sugar, please?
6 This is Ann's bag. Can you give it to her? / Can you give her it?
7 I showed to the policeman my identity card. / I showed the policeman my identity card.

UNIT 96

at 8 o'clock on Monday in April

A

at

at	8 o'clock 10.30 midnight *etc.*

- I start work **at 8 o'clock.**
- The shops close **at 5.30.**

on

on	Sunday(s) / Monday(s) *etc.* 25 April / 6 June *etc.* New Year's Day *etc.*

- Goodbye! See you **on Friday.**
- I don't work **on Sundays.**
- The concert is **on 22 November.**

in

in	April/June *etc.* 1985/1750 *etc.* summer/spring *etc.*

- I'm going on holiday **in October.**
- Emma left school **in 1993.**
- The garden is lovely **in spring.**

B

We say:

at the weekend **at night** **at Christmas / at Easter** **at the end of ...** **at the moment**

- Are you going away **at the weekend?**
- I can't sleep **at night.**
- Where will you be **at Christmas**? (*but* **on** Christmas **Day**)
- I'm going on holiday **at the end of** October.
- Are you busy **at the moment?**

C

in the morning / in the afternoon / in the evening

- I always feel good **in the morning.**
- Do you often go out **in the evening?**

but

on Monday morning / on Tuesday afternoon / on Friday evening / on Saturday night *etc.*:

- I'm meeting Jill **on Monday morning.**
- Are you doing anything **on Saturday evening?**

D

We do *not* use **at/on/in** before:

this ... (**this morning / this week** *etc.*) **last** ... (**last August / last week** *etc.*) **next** ... (**next Monday / next week** *etc.*) **every** ... (**every day / every week** *etc.*)

- Are you going out **this evening?**
- The garden was lovely **last summer.**
- I'm going on holiday **next Monday.** (*not* 'on next Monday')

E

in five minutes / in a few days / in six weeks / in two years *etc.*

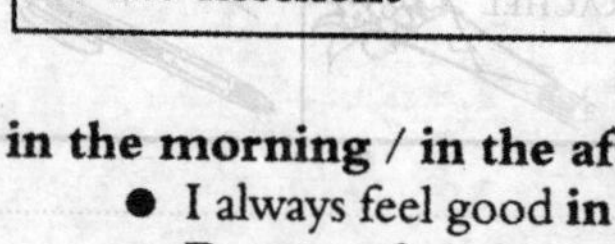

now **in five minutes**

- Hurry! The train leaves **in five minutes.** (= it leaves five minutes from now)
- Goodbye! I'll see you **in a few days.** (= a few days from now)

in/at/on (places) ⇒ **UNITS 99-100**

EXERCISES

96.1 Write **at/on/in**.

1 ..on.... 6 June
2 ..in.... the evening
3 .... half past two
4 .... Wednesday
5 1987
6 .... September
7 .... 24 September
8 .... Thursday
9 .... 11.45
10 .... Christmas Day
11 .... Christmas
12 .... the morning
13 .... Friday morning
14 .... Saturday night
15 .... night
16 .... the end of the day
17 .... the weekend
18 .... winter

96.2 Write **at/on/in**.

1 Goodbye! See you ..on.... Friday.
2 Where were you .... 28 February?
3 I got up .... 8 o'clock this morning.
4 I like getting up early .... the morning.
5 My sister got married .... May.
6 Diane and I first met .... 1979.
7 Did you go out .... Tuesday?
8 Did you go out .... Tuesday evening?
9 Do you often go out .... the evening?
10 Let's meet .... 7.30 tomorrow evening.
11 I often go away .... the weekend.
12 I'm starting my new job .... 3 July.
13 We often go to the beach .... summer.
14 George isn't here .... the moment.
15 Julia's birthday is .... January.
16 Do you work .... Saturdays?
17 The company started .... 1969.
18 I like to look at the stars .... night.
19 I'll send you the money .... the end of the month.

96.3 Look at Lisa's diary for next week and complete the sentences.

1 Lisa is going to the cinema **on Wednesday evening.**
2 She has to phone Chris ....
3 She isn't doing anything special ....
4 She's got a driving lesson ....
5 She's going to a party ....
6 She's meeting Sam ....

96.4 Write sentences with **in ...** .

1 It's 17.25 now. The train leaves at 17.30. **The train leaves in five minutes.**
2 It's Monday today. I'll phone you on Thursday. I'll .... days.
3 Today is 14 June. My exam is on 28 June. My ....
4 It's 3 o'clock now. Tom will be here at 3.30. Tom ....

96.5 Write **at/on/in** if necessary. Sometimes there is no preposition.

1 I'm leaving ..on.... Friday.
2 I'm leaving ..—.... next Friday. *(no preposition)*
3 I always feel tired .... the evening.
4 Will you be at home .... this evening?
5 We went to France .... last summer.
6 Laura was born .... 1975.
7 What are you doing .... the weekend?
8 I phone Robert .... every Sunday.
9 Shall we play tennis .... next Sunday?
10 I can't go to the party .... Sunday.
11 I'm going out. I'll be back .... an hour.
12 I don't often go out .... night.

UNIT 97

from ... to   until   since   for

A from ... to ...

- We lived in Canada **from** 1982 **to** 1990.
- I work **from** Monday **to** Friday.

You can also say **from** ... **until** ... :

- We lived in Canada **from** 1982 **until** 1990.

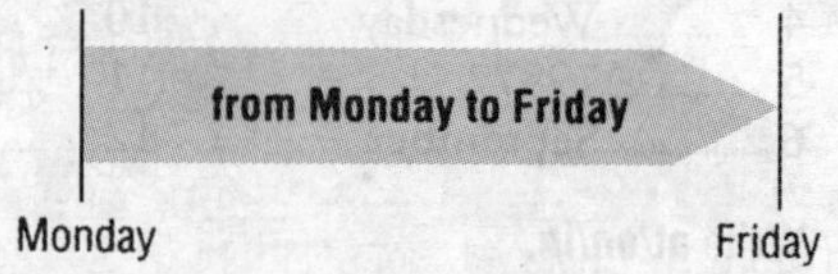

B until + *the end of a period*

until Friday   **until December**   **until 3 o'clock**   **until I come back**

- They're going away tomorrow. They'll be away **until Friday**.
- I went to bed early but I wasn't tired. I read a book **until 3 o'clock**.
- Wait here **until I come back**.

You can also say **till** (= **until**):

- Wait here **till** I come back.

Compare:

- '**How long** will you be away?' '**Until** Monday.'
- '**When** are you coming back?' '**On** Monday.'

C since + *a time in the past (to now)*

since Monday   **since 1968**   **since 2.30**   **since I arrived**

We use **since** after the *present perfect* (**have been / have done** *etc.*):

- John is in hospital. He has been in hospital **since Monday**. (= from Monday to now)
- Mr and Mrs Kelly have been married **since 1968**. (from 1968 to now)
- It has been raining **since I arrived**.

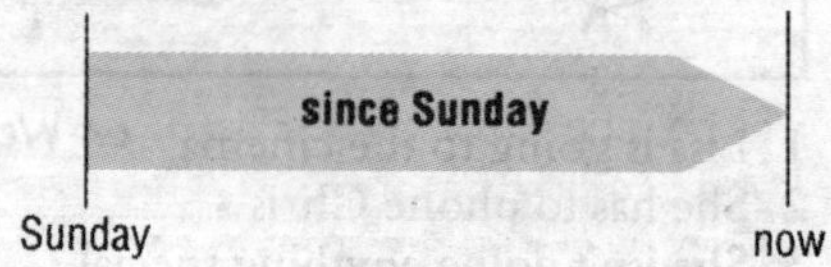

Compare:

- We lived in Canada **from** 1982 **to** 1990.
  We lived in Canada **until** 1990.
- Now we live in France. We came to France **in** 1990.
  We have lived in France **since** 1990. (= from 1990 until now)

We use **for** (*not* **since**) + *a period of time* (**three days / ten years** *etc.*):

- John has been in hospital **for three days**. (*not* 'since three days')

D for + *a period of time*

for three days   **for ten years**   **for ten minutes**   **for a long time**

- George stayed with us **for three days**.
- I'm going away **for a few weeks**.
- I'm going away **for the weekend**.
- They've been married **for ten years**.

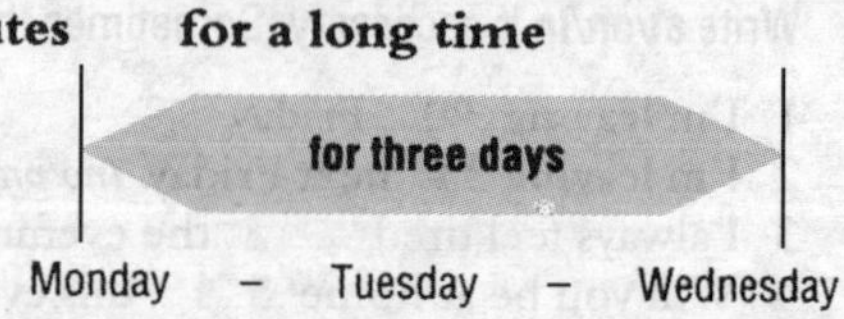

EXERCISES

97.1 Read the information about these people and complete the sentences. Use **from ... to / until / since**.

1 (Alex / Canada / 1982 – 1990) Alex lived in Canada from 1982 to 1990.
2 (Alex / Canada / → 1990) Alex lived in Canada .... 1990.
3 (Alex / England / 1990 →) Alex has lived in England ....
4 (Alice / France / → 1991) Alice lived in ....
5 (Alice / Switzerland / 1991 →) Alice has lived in ....
6 (Carol / a hotel / 1990 – 1993) Carol worked .... 1990 ....
7 (Carol / a restaurant / 1993 →) Carol has worked ....
8 (Gerry / a teacher / 1983 – 1989) Gerry was a ....
9 (Gerry / a salesman / 1989 →) Gerry has been ....

Now write sentences with **for**.

10 (Alex / Canada) Alex lived in Canada for eight years.
11 (Alex / England) Alex has lived in England ....
12 (Alice / Switzerland) Alice has ....
13 (Carol / a hotel) Carol worked ....
14 (Carol / restaurant) Carol ....
15 (Gerry / a teacher) Gerry ....
16 (Gerry / a salesman) Gerry ....

97.2 Put in **until/since/for**.

1 Mr and Mrs Kelly have been married since 1968.
2 I was tired this morning. I stayed in bed .... 10 o'clock.
3 We waited for Sue .... half an hour but she didn't come.
4 'Have you just arrived?' 'No, I've been here .... half past seven.'
5 'How long did you stay at the party last night?' '.......... midnight.'
6 David and I are good friends. We have known each other .... ten years.
7 I'm tired. I'm going to lie down .... a few minutes.
8 Don't open the door of the train .... the train stops.
9 This is my house. I've lived here .... I was seven years old.
10 Jack has gone away. He'll be away .... Wednesday.
11 Next week I'm going to Paris .... three days.
12 I usually finish work at 5.30, but sometimes I work .... six.
13 'How long have you known Ann?' '.......... we were at school together.'
14 Where have you been? I've been waiting for you .... twenty minutes.

UNIT **98**

before after during while

A

before **during** **after**

before the film

during the film

after the film

- Everybody is nervous **before exams**.
- I went to sleep **during the film**.
- We were tired **after our visit** to the museum.

B

before **while** **after**

before we played

while we were playing

after we played

- Don't forget to close the window **before you go** out.
- I often go to sleep **while I'm watching** television.
- They went home **after they did** the shopping.

C

during, **while** and **for**

We use **during** + *noun* (during **the film**). We use **while** + *verb* (while **I'm watching**):

- We didn't speak **during the meal**.

but
- We didn't speak **while we were eating**. (*not* 'during we were eating')

Use **for** (*not* 'during') + *a period of time* (**three days / two hours / a year** *etc.*):

- We played tennis **for two hours**. (*not* 'during two hours')
- I lived in London **for a year**. (*not* 'during a year')

D

You can use **before/after + -ing** (**before going / after eating** *etc.*):

- I always have breakfast **before going** to work. (= before I go to work)
- **After doing** the shopping, they went home. (= after they did)

Do *not* say 'before to go', 'after to do' etc.:

- **Before eating** the apple, I washed it carefully. (*not* 'before to eat')
- I started work **after reading** the newspaper. (*not* 'after to read')

past continuous (I was -ing) ⇒ UNITS 13-14 for ⇒ UNIT 97 prepositions + -ing ⇒ UNIT 105
before/after/while/when ⇒ UNIT 110

EXERCISES

98.1 Complete the sentences. Choose from the boxes.

before	during	+	the concert	~~the exam~~	they went to Australia
after	while		the course	lunch	you are waiting
			the end	the night	

1 Everybody was nervous before the exam.
2 I usually work four hours in the morning, and another two hours ....
3 The film was very boring. We left ....
4 Ann went to evening classes to learn German. She learnt a lot ....
5 My aunt and uncle lived in London ....
6 A: Somebody broke a window .... Did you hear anything?
B: No. I was asleep all the time.
7 Would you like to sit down .... ?
8 'Are you going home ....?' 'No, we're going to a restaurant.'

98.2 Put in **during/while/for**.

1 We didn't speak while we were eating.
2 We didn't speak during the meal.
3 George phoned .... you were out.
4 I stayed in Rome .... five days.
5 Sally wrote a lot of letters .... she was on holiday.
6 The students looked very bored .... the lesson.
7 I fell out of bed .... I was asleep.
8 Yesterday evening I watched TV .... three hours.
9 I don't usually watch TV .... the day.
10 Do you ever watch TV .... you are having dinner?

98.3 Complete the sentences. Use **-ing** (**doing** etc.).

1 After doing the shopping, they went home.
2 I felt sick after .... too much chocolate.
3 I'm going to ask you a question. Think carefully before .... it.
4 I felt awful when I got up this morning. I felt better after .... a shower.
5 After .... my work, I left the office and went home.
6 Before .... to a foreign country, it's a good idea to learn a few words of the language.

98.4 Write sentences with **before + -ing** and **after + -ing**.

1 They did the shopping. Then they went home.
After doing the shopping, they went home.
2 John left school. Then he worked in a bookshop for two years.
John worked ....
3 I read a few pages of my book. Then I went to sleep.
Before ....
4 We walked for three hours. We were very tired.
After ....
5 Let's have a cup of coffee. Then we'll go out.
Let's ....

UNIT 99

in at on (places 1)

A in

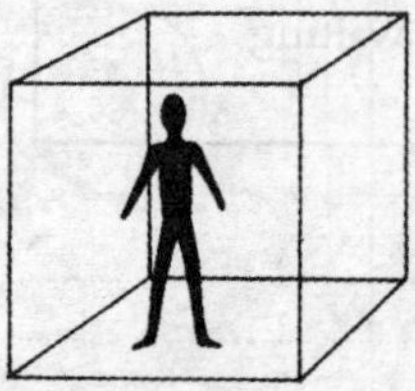

in a room
in a shop
in a car
in the water

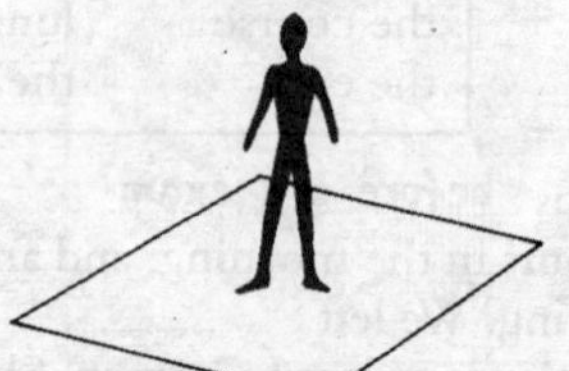

in a garden
in a town
in the city centre
in France

- 'Where's David?' **'In the kitchen. / In the garden. / In London.'**
- What's **in that box / in that bag / in that cupboard?**
- Angela works **in a shop / in a bank / in a factory**.
- I had a swim **in the river / in the sea**.
- Milan is **in the north of Italy**.
- I live **in a town** but I want to live **in the country**.

B at

at the bus stop

at the door

at the traffic lights

at her desk

- There's somebody **at the bus stop / at the door**.
- The car is waiting **at the traffic lights**.
- Julia is working **at her desk**.

at the top / at the bottom / at the end (of ...):

- Write your name **at the top of the page**.
- My house is **at the end of the street**.

at the top (of the page)

at the bottom (of the page)

C on

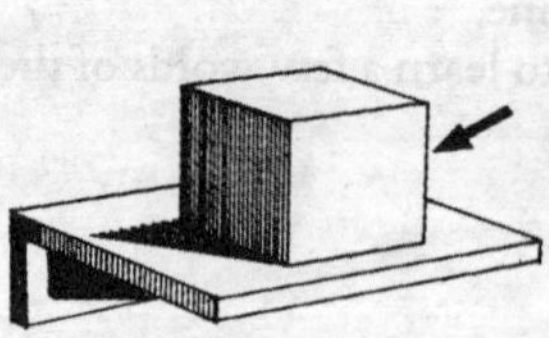

on a shelf
on a plate
on a balcony
on the floor *etc.*

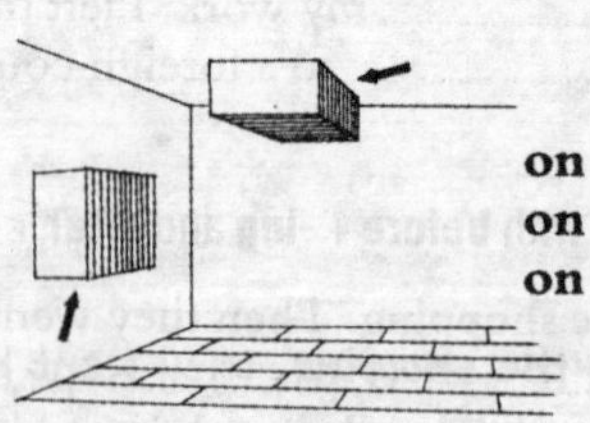

on a wall
on a door
on the ceiling *etc.*

- There are some books **on the shelf** and some pictures **on the wall**.
- There are a lot of apples **on those trees**.
- Don't sit **on the grass**. It's wet.
- There is a stamp **on the envelope**.

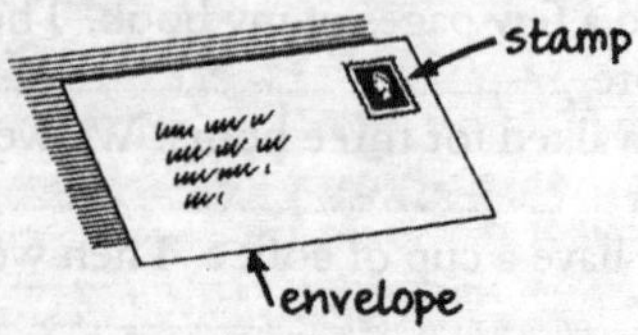

also **on a horse / on a bicycle / on a motor-bike**:

- Who is that man **on the motor-bike**?

in/at/on (places 2) ⇒ UNIT 100 **the top / the bottom** etc. ⇒ UNIT 69 **at/on/in** (time) ⇒ UNIT 96

EXERCISES

99.1 Look at the pictures and answer the questions. Use **in/at/on** + the words in brackets (...).

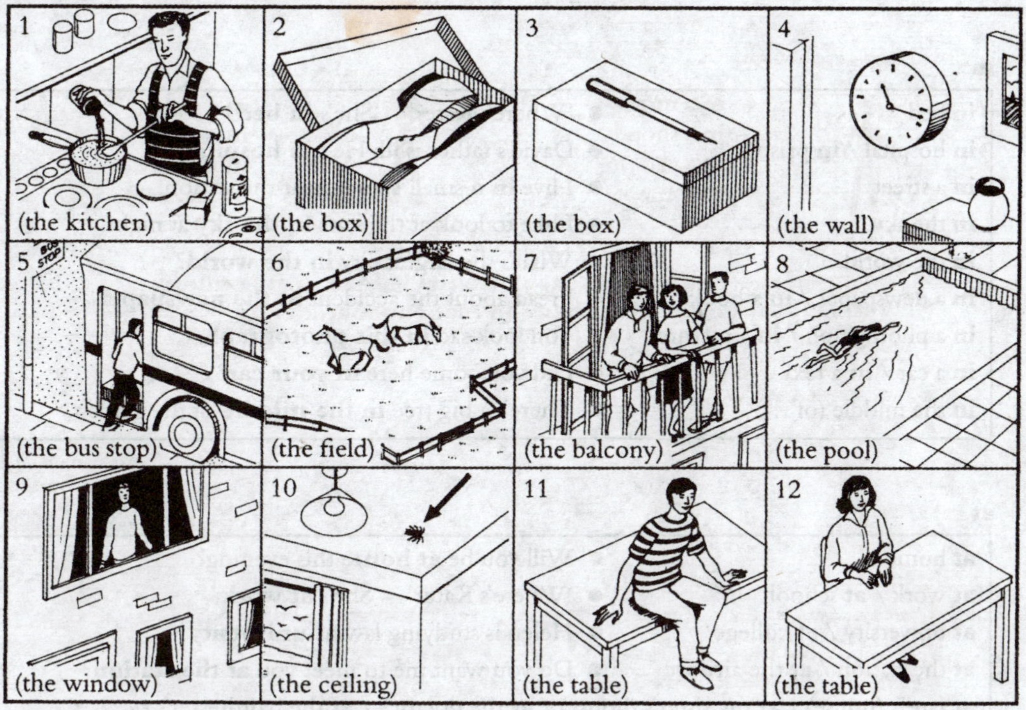

1 Where is he? In the kitchen.
2 Where are the shoes? ....
3 Where is the pen? ....
4 Where is the clock? ....
5 Where is the bus? ....
6 Where are the horses? ....
7 Where are they standing? ....
8 Where is she swimming? ....
9 Where is he standing? ....
10 Where is the spider? ....
11 Where is he sitting? ....
12 Where is she sitting? ....

99.2 Put in **in/at/on**.

1 Don't sit on the grass. It's wet.
2 What have you got .... your bag?
3 Look! There's a man .... the roof. What's he doing?
4 There are a lot of fish .... this river.
5 Our house is number 45 – the number is .... the door.
6 'Is the cinema near here?' 'Yes, turn left .... the traffic lights.'
7 I usually do my shopping .... the city centre.
8 My sister lives .... Brussels.
9 There's a small park .... the top of the hill.
10 I think I heard the doorbell. There's somebody .... the door.
11 Munich is a large city .... the south of Germany.
12 There are a few shops .... the end of the street.
13 It's difficult to carry a lot of things .... a bicycle.
14 I looked at the list of names. My name was .... the bottom of the list.
15 There is a mirror .... the wall .... the living room.

UNIT **100**

in at on (places 2)

A in

in bed	• 'Where's Kate?' 'She's **in bed**.'
in hospital / **in** prison	• David's father is ill. He's **in hospital.**
in a street	• I live **in a** small **street** near the station.
in the sky	• I like to look at the stars **in the sky** at night.
in the world	• What's the largest city **in the world**?
in a newspaper / **in** a book	• I read about the accident **in the newspaper**.
in a photograph / **in** a picture	• You look sad **in this photograph**.
in a car / **in** a taxi	• Did you come here **in your car**?
in the middle (of ...)	• There's a big tree **in the middle** of the garden.

B at

at home	• Will you be **at home** this evening?
at work / **at** school	• 'Where's Kate?' 'She's **at work**.'
at university / **at** college	• Helen is studying law **at university**.
at the station / **at** the airport	• Do you want me to meet you **at the station**?

at Jane's (house) / **at** my sister's (house) / **at** the doctor's / **at** the hairdresser's *etc.*

• 'Where were you yesterday?' '**At my sister's**.'

• I saw Tom **at the doctor's**.

at a concert / **at** a party / **at** a football match *etc.*

• There weren't many people **at the party**.

Often it is possible to use **in** or **at** for buildings (hotels, restaurants *etc.*):

• We stayed **at** a nice hotel. *or* We stayed **in** a nice hotel.

C on

on a bus

on the first floor

on the way from A to B

on a bus / **on** a train / **on** a plane / **on** a ship

• Did you come here **on the bus**?

on the ground floor / **on** the first floor *etc.*

• The office is **on the first floor**. (*not* 'in the first floor')

on the way (to ...) / **on the way** home

• I met Ann **on the way** to work / **on the way** home.

 in/at/on (places 1) ⇒ UNIT 99   to/in/at ⇒ UNIT 101   on the left/right ⇒ UNIT 102

EXERCISES

100.1 Look at the pictures and answer the questions. Use **in/at/on** + the words in brackets (...).

1 (hospital) 2 (the airport) 3 (bed) 4 (a ship) 5 (the sky) 6 (a party) 7 (the doctor's) 8 (the second floor) 9 (work) 10 (a plane) 11 (a taxi) 12 (a wedding)

1 Where is she? In hospital.
2 Where are they? ....
3 Where is he? ....
4 Where are they? ....
5 Where are the stars? ....
6 Where are they? ....
7 Where is Brian? ....
8 Where is the restaurant? ....
9 Where is she? ....
10 Where are they? ....
11 Where are they? ....
12 Where are they? ....

100.2 Put in **in/at/on**.

1 Helen is studying law at university.
2 There was a big table .... the middle of the room.
3 What is the longest river .... the world?
4 Were there many people .... the concert last night?
5 Will you be .... home tomorrow afternoon?
6 Who is that man .... this photograph? Do you know him?
7 Where are your children? Are they .... school?
8 George is coming by train. I'm going to meet him .... the station.
9 Charlie is .... hospital. He's going to have an operation tomorrow.
10 How many pages are there .... this book?
11 'Are you hungry after your journey?' 'No, I had a meal .... the train.'
12 I'm sorry I'm late. My car broke down .... the way here.
13 'Is Tom here?' 'No, he's .... his brother's.'
14 Don't believe everything you see .... the newspaper!
15 I walked to work but I came home .... the bus.

UNIT **101**

to in at (places 3)

A

to

go/come/return/walk *(etc.)* **to** …

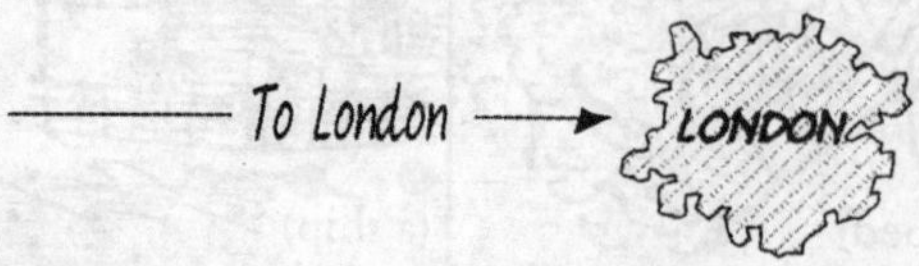

- We're **going to London** next week.
- I want to **go to Italy**.
- We **walked** from my house **to the city centre**.
- What time do you **go to bed**?

- The bus is **going to the airport**.
- Sally didn't **go to work** yesterday.
- I **went to a party** last night.
- You must **come to our house**.

in/at (⇒ Units 99–100)

be/stay/do something *(etc.)* **in** …

- Piccadilly Circus **is in London**.
- My brother **lives in Italy**.
- The main shops **are in the city centre**.
- I like **reading in bed**.

be/stay/do something *(etc.)* **at** …

- The bus **is at the airport**.
- Ann **wasn't at work** yesterday.
- **I met her at a party**.
- Ann **stayed at her brother's house**.

B

home

go/come/walk *(etc.)* **home** (*without* 'to'): • I'm tired. I'm **going home**. (*not* 'to home') • Did you **walk home**?	**be/stay/do something** *(etc.)* **at home**: • I'm **staying at home** this evening. • 'Where's Ann?' **'At home.'**

C

arrive and **get**

arrive in *a country or town* (**arrive in Italy / arrive in Paris** *etc.*):
- They **arrived in England** last week. (*not* 'arrived to England')

arrive at *other places* (**arrive at the station / arrive at work** *etc.*):
- What time did you **arrive at the hotel**? (*not* **'arrive to the hotel'**)

get to (a place):
- What time did you **get to the hotel**?
- What time did you **get to Paris**?

get home / arrive home (*no preposition*):
- I was tired when I **got home**. *or* I was tired when I **arrived home**.

been to ⇒ UNIT 17 **get (to …)** ⇒ UNIT 55 **in/at** ⇒ UNITS 99-100

EXERCISES

101.1 Write **to** or **in**.

1 I like reading *in* bed.
2 We're going .... Italy next month.
3 Sue is on holiday .... Italy at the moment.
4 I must go .... the bank today.
5 I was tired, so I stayed .... bed late.
6 What time do you usually go .... bed?
7 Does this bus go .... the centre?
8 Would you like to live .... another country?

101.2 Write **to** or **at** if necessary. Sometimes there is no preposition.

1 Paula didn't go *to* work yesterday.
2 I'm tired. I'm going .... home. *(no preposition)*
3 Ann is not very well. She has gone .... the doctor.
4 Would you like to come .... a party on Saturday?
5 'Is Liz .... home?' 'No, she's gone .... work.'
6 There were 20,000 people .... the football match.
7 Why did you go .... home early last night?
8 A boy jumped into the river and swam .... the other side.
9 There were a lot of people waiting .... the bus stop.
10 We had a good meal .... a restaurant and then we went back .... the hotel.

101.3 Write **to**, **at** or **in** if necessary. Sometimes there is no preposition.

1 I'm not going out this afternoon. I'm staying *at* home.
2 We're going .... a concert tomorrow evening.
3 I went .... New York last year.
4 How long did you stay .... New York?
5 Next year we hope to go .... Canada to visit some friends.
6 Shall we go .... the cinema this evening?
7 Is there a restaurant .... the station?
8 After the accident three people were taken .... hospital.
9 How often do you go .... the dentist?
10 'Is Diane here?' 'No, she's .... Ann's.'
11 My house is .... the end of the street on the left.
12 I went .... Mary's house but she wasn't .... home.
13 There were no taxis, so we had to walk .... home.
14 'What did you study .... university?' 'I didn't go .... university.'

101.4 Write **to**, **at** or **in** if necessary. Sometimes there is no preposition.

1 What time do you usually get .... work?
2 What time do you usually get .... home?
3 What time did you arrive .... the party?
4 When did you arrive .... London?
5 What time does the train get .... Paris?
6 We arrived .... home very late.

101.5 Complete these sentences about yourself. Use **to/in/at**.

1 At three o'clock this morning I was *in bed.*
2 Yesterday I went ....
3 At 11 o'clock yesterday morning I was ....
4 One day I'd like to go ....
5 I don't like going ....
6 At 9 o'clock yesterday evening I was ....

UNIT 102

under behind opposite etc. (prepositions)

A

next to (or **beside**) / **between** / **in front of** / **behind**

A is **next to** B. *or* A is **beside** B.
B is **between** A and C.
D is **in front of** B.
E is **behind** B.

also
A is **on the left**.
C is **on the right**.
B is **in the middle** (of the group).

B

opposite / **in front of**

A is sitting **in front of** B.
A is sitting **opposite** C.
C is sitting **opposite** A.

C

by (= next to / beside)

by the window

- Our house is **by the sea**. (= beside the sea)
- Who is that man **by the window**?
- 'Is there a public phone here?' 'Yes, **by the door**.'

D

under

under the table

under a tree

- The cat is **under the table**.
- The girl is standing **under a tree**.
- I'm wearing a jacket **under my coat**.

E

above and **below**

A is **above the line**.
(= higher than the line)

B is **below the line**.
(= lower than the line)

The pictures are **above the shelves**.

The shelves are **below the pictures**.

up/over/through etc. ⇒ UNIT 103 **by** ⇒ UNIT 104

EXERCISES

102.1 Where are the people in the picture? Complete the sentences.

1 Colin is standing behind Frank.
2 Frank is sitting .... Emma.
3 Emma is sitting .... Barbara.
4 Emma is sitting .... Donna and Frank.
5 Donna is sitting .... Emma.
6 Frank is sitting .... Colin.
7 Alan is standing .... Donna.
8 Alan is standing .... left.
9 Barbara is standing .... middle.

A = Alan B = Barbara C = Colin
D = Donna E = Emma F = Frank

102.2 Look at the pictures and complete the sentences.

1 The cat is under the table.
2 There is a big tree .... the house.
3 The plane is flying .... the clouds.
4 She is standing .... the piano.
5 The cinema is .... the right.
6 She's sitting .... the phone.
7 The switch is .... the window.
8 The cupboard is .... the sink.
9 There are some shoes .... the bed.
10 The plant is .... the piano.
11 Paul is sitting .... Fiona.
12 In Britain we drive .... the left.

102.3 Write sentences about the picture. Use the words in brackets (...).

1 (next to) The bank is next to the bookshop.
2 (in front of) The ....
3 (opposite) ....
4 (next to) ....
5 (above) ....
6 (between) ....

UNIT **103**

up over through etc. (prepositions)

to

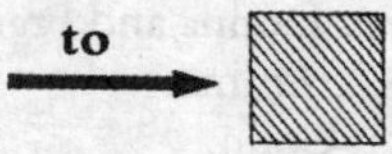

- Jane is going **to** France next week.
- We walked **from** the hotel **to** the station.
- A lot of English words come **from** Latin.

from

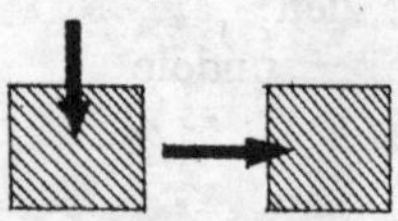

into (in)

- We jumped **into** the water.
- A man came **out of** the house and got **into** a car.
- Why are you looking **out of** the window?
- I took the old batteries **out of** the radio.

We say **put** something **in** ... (*not usually* 'into'):

- I **put** the new batteries **in** the radio.

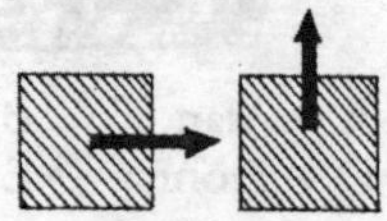

out of

on

- Don't put your feet **on** the table.
- Please take your feet **off** the table.
- I'm going to hang some pictures **on** the wall.
- Be careful! Don't fall **off** your bicycle.
- We got **on** the bus in Princes Street.

off

up

- We walked **up** the hill to the house.
- Be careful! Don't fall **down** the stairs.

down

over

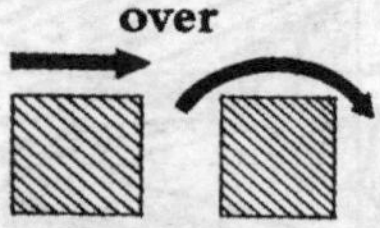

- The plane flew **over** the mountains.
- I jumped **over** the wall into the garden.
- Some people say it is unlucky to walk **under** a ladder.

under

through

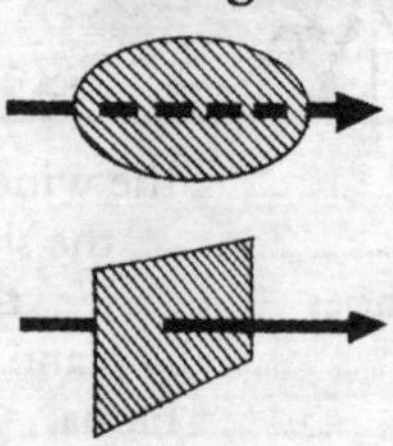

- A bird flew into the room **through** a window.
- The old road goes **through** the village.
- The new road goes **round** the village.
- The bus stop is just **round** the corner.
- I walked **round** the town and took some photographs.

You can also use **around** (= round):

- We walked **around** the town.

round

round the town

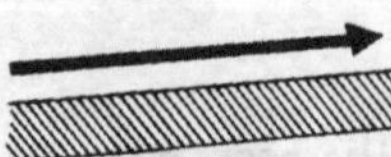

along

- I was walking **along** the road with my dog.
- Let's go for a walk **along** the river.
- The dog swam **across** the river.

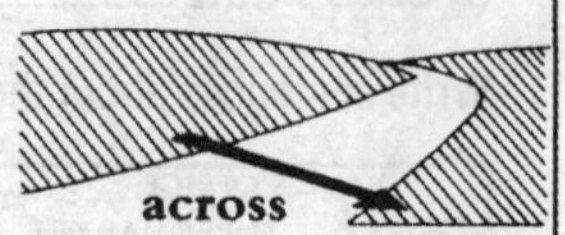

across

past

- They walked **past** me without speaking.
- A: Excuse me, how do I get to the hospital?
- B: Go along this road, **past** the cinema, under the bridge and the hospital is on the left.

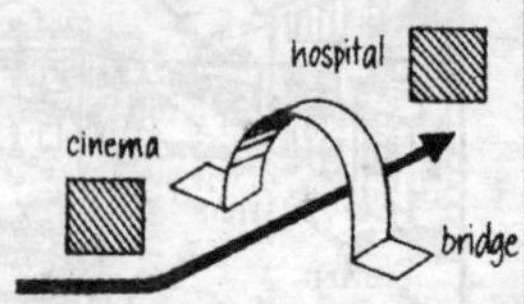

get in/on etc. ⇒ UNIT 55 **in/on** ⇒ UNITS 99-100 **to** ⇒ UNIT 101 **fall off / run away** etc. ⇒ UNIT 107

EXERCISES

103.1 Somebody asks you the way to a place. You say which way to go. Look at the pictures and write sentences beginning **Go ...** .

103.2 Look at the pictures and complete the sentences with a preposition.

1 The dog swam *across* the river.
2 A book fell .... the shelf.
3 A plane flew .... the village.
4 A woman got .... the car.
5 A girl ran .... the road.
6 Suddenly a car came .... the corner.
7 They drove .... the village.
8 They got .... the train.
9 The Moon travels .... the Earth.
10 They got .... the house .... a window.

103.3 Put in a preposition (**over/from/into** etc.).

1 I looked .... the window and watched the people in the street.
2 My house is very near here. It's just .... the corner.
3 Do you know how to put a film .... this camera?
4 How far is it .... here .... the airport?
5 We walked .... the museum for an hour and saw a lot of interesting things.
6 You can put your coat .... the back of the chair.
7 In tennis, you have to hit the ball .... the net.
8 Silvia took a key .... her bag and opened the door.

UNIT 104

on at by with about (prepositions)

A

on holiday	• Jane isn't at work this week. She's **on holiday**.
on television	• We watched the news **on television**.
on the radio	• We listened to the news **on the radio**.
on the phone	• I spoke to Carol **on the phone** last night.
on fire	• The house is **on fire**! Call the fire brigade.
on time (= not late)	• 'Was the train late?' 'No, it was **on time**.'

B

at (the age of) **21** / **at 50 kilometres an hour** / **at 100 degrees** *etc.*:

- Lisa got married **at 21**. (*or* ... **at the age of 21**.)
- The car was travelling **at 50 kilometres an hour** when the accident happened.
- Water boils **at 100 degrees celsius**.

C

by car / **by bus** / **by plane** (*or* **by air**) / **by bike** *etc.*:

- Do you like travelling **by train**?
- Jane usually goes to work **by bike**.

but **on foot**:

- She goes to work **on foot**. (= she walks)

a book **by** ... / a painting **by** ... / a piece of music **by** ... *etc.*:

- Have you read any books **by Charles Dickens**?
- **Who** is that painting **by**? Picasso?

by after the passive (⇒ Unit 21):

- I was bitten **by a dog**.

D

with/without:

- Did you stay at a hotel or **with friends**?
- Wait for me. Please don't go **without me**.
- Do you like your coffee **with** or **without milk**?
- I cut the paper **with a pair of scissors**.

a man **with** a beard / a woman **with** glasses *etc.*:

- Do you know that man **with the beard**?
- I'd like to have a house **with a big garden**.

a man **with** a beard

a woman **with** glasses

E

talk/speak/think/hear/know about ... :

- Some people **talk about their work** all the time.
- I don't **know** much **about cars**.

a book / **a question** / **a programme** (*etc.*) **about** ... :

Did you see **the programme about computers** on TV last night?

by ⇒ UNITS 21, 62, 102   **at/on** ⇒ UNITS 96, 99-100   preposition + **-ing** ⇒ UNIT 105

EXERCISES

104.1 Complete the sentences. Use **on** + one of these:

holiday **the phone** ~~**the radio**~~ **television** **time**

1 We listened to the news on the radio.
2 Please don't be late. Try to be here ....
3 I won't be here next week. I'm going ....
4 'Did you see Linda?' 'No, but I talked to her ....'
5 'What's .... this evening?' 'There's a film at 9 o'clock.'

104.2 Look at the pictures. Complete the sentences with a preposition (**at/by** etc.).

1 I cut the paper with a pair of scissors.
2 She usually goes to work .... car.
3 Who is the woman .... short hair?
4 They are talking .... the weather.
5 The car is .... fire.
6 She's listening to some music .... Mozart.
7 The plane is flying .... 600 miles an hour.
8 They're .... holiday.
9 Do you know the man .... sunglasses?
10 He's reading a book .... grammar .... Vera P. Bull.

104.3 Complete the sentences with a preposition (**at/by/with** etc.).

1 In tennis, you hit the ball .... a racket.
2 It's cold today. Don't go out .... a coat.
3 *Hamlet, Othello* and *Macbeth* are plays .... William Shakespeare.
4 Do you know anything .... computers?
5 My grandmother died .... the age of 98.
6 How long does it take from New York to Los Angeles .... plane?
7 I didn't go to the football match, but I watched it .... television.
8 My house is the one .... the red door on the right.
9 These trains are very fast. They can travel .... very high speeds.
10 I don't use my car very often. I prefer to go .... bike.
11 Can you give me some information .... hotels in this town?
12 I was arrested .... two policemen and taken to the police station.
13 The buses here are very good. They're nearly always .... time.
14 What would you like to drink .... your meal?
15 We travelled from Paris to Moscow .... train.
16 One of the most famous paintings in the world is the *Mona Lisa* .... Leonardo da Vinci.

UNIT 105

afraid of ... good at ... etc. preposition + -ing (good at -ing etc.)

A

afraid of ... / good at ... *etc. (adjective + preposition)*

afraid of ...	• Are you **afraid of** dogs?
angry with somebody **angry about** something	• Why are you **angry with** me? What have I done? • Are you **angry about** last night? (= something that happened last night)
different from ...	• Ann is very **different from** her sister.
fed up with ...	• I'm **fed up with** my job. I want to do something different. (= I've had enough of my job)
full of ...	• The room was **full of people**.
good at ... / **bad at** ...	• Are you **good at** maths? • Tina is very **bad at** writing letters.
interested in ...	• I'm not **interested in** sport.
married to ...	• Sue is **married to** a dentist. (= her husband is a dentist)
nice/kind of somebody to ... (be) **nice/kind to** (somebody)	• It was **kind of** you to help us. Thank you very much. • David is very friendly. He's always very **nice to** me.
sorry about (something) **sorry for** (doing something)	• I'm afraid I can't help you. I'm **sorry about** that. • I'm **sorry for** not phoning you yesterday. (*or* I'm sorry I didn't phone you)

B

preposition + **-ing**

After a preposition (**at/with/for** *etc.*), a verb ends in **-ing**:

I'm not very good **at**	tell**ing**	stories.
Are you fed up **with**	do**ing**	the same thing every day?
I'm sorry **for**	not phon**ing**	you yesterday.
Mark is thinking **of**	buy**ing**	a new car.
Tom left **without**	say**ing**	goodbye. (= he didn't say goodbye)
After	do**ing**	the shopping, they went home.

before/after -ing ⇒ UNIT 98 think about/of ⇒ UNIT 106

EXERCISES

105.1 Look at the pictures and complete the sentences with a preposition (**of/in** etc.).

1 He's afraid of dogs.
2 She's interested .... science.
3 She's married .... a footballer.
4 She's very good .... languages.
5 He's fed up .... the weather.
6 'Can I help you?' 'Oh, that's very kind .... you.'

105.2 Put in the right preposition (**of/in/with** etc.).

1 I'm not interested in sport.
2 I'm not very good .... sport.
3 I like Sarah. She's always very kind .... me.
4 I'm sorry .... your broken window. It was an accident.
5 He's very brave. He isn't afraid .... anything.
6 It was very nice .... Julia to let us stay in her flat.
7 Life today is very different .... life 50 years ago.
8 Are you interested .... politics?
9 Some people are afraid .... spiders.
10 Chris was angry .... what happened.
11 These boxes are very heavy. They are full .... books.
12 I'm sorry .... getting angry .... you yesterday.

105.3 Complete the sentences.

1 I'm not very good at telling stories. (good / tell)
2 I wanted to go to the cinema but Paula wasn't .... (interested / go)
3 Sue isn't very .... up in the morning. (good / get)
4 Let's go! I'm .... (fed up / wait)
5 I'm .... you up in the middle of the night. (sorry / wake)

105.4 Complete the sentences. Use **without -ing**.

1 (Tom left / he didn't say goodbye) Tom left without saying goodbye.
2 (Sue walked past me / she didn't speak) Sue walked ....
3 (Don't do anything / ask me first) Don't ....
4 (I went out / I didn't lock the door) I ....

105.5 Write sentences about yourself. Use the words in brackets (...).

1 (interested) I'm interested in sport.
2 (afraid) I'm ....
3 (not very good) I'm not ....
4 (not interested) ....
5 (fed up) ....

UNIT 106 listen to ... look at ... etc. (verb + preposition)

A

ask (somebody) **for** ...	● A man stopped me and **asked me for** money.
belong to ...	● Does this book **belong to** you? (= Is this your book?)
happen to ...	● I can't find my pen. What's **happened to** it?
listen to ...	● **Listen to** this music. It's beautiful.
speak/talk to somebody **about** something	● Did you **talk to** Paul **about** the problem? ● *(on the phone)* Can I **speak to** Chris, please?
thank somebody **for** ...	● **Thank** you very much **for** your help.
think about ... *or* **think of** ...	● He never **thinks about** (*or* **of**) other people. ● Mark is **thinking of** (*or* **about**) buying a new car.
wait for ...	● Don't go yet. **Wait for** me.
write to somebody *but* **(tele)phone** somebody *(no preposition)*	● I never get letters. Nobody **writes to** me. ● I must **phone** my parents. (*not* 'phone to my parents')

B look at / look for / look after

look at ...

● She's **looking at** her watch.
● **Look at** these flowers! They're beautiful.
● Why are you **looking at** me like that?

look for ...
(= try to find)

● He's lost his key. He's **looking for** it.
● I'm **looking for** Sarah. Have you seen her?

look after ...
(= take care of, keep safe)

● When Barbara is at work, a friend of hers **looks after** her children.
● Don't lose this book. **Look after** it. (= Keep it safe.)

C depend

We say **depend on** ... :
● A: Do you like eating in restaurants?
B: Sometimes. It **depends on** the restaurant. (*not* 'it depends of')

You can say **it depends what/where/how** *(etc.) with or without* **on**:
● A: Do you want to come out with us?
B: It **depends where** you're going. *or* It **depends on where** ...

For word order (It depends where **you're** going.), see Unit 48.

 wait ⇒ UNIT 53 preposition + **-ing** ⇒ UNIT 105

EXERCISES

106.1 Look at the pictures and complete the sentences with a preposition (**to/for** etc.).

1 She's looking at her watch.
2 He's listening .... the radio.
3 They're waiting .... a taxi.
4 Paul is talking .... Jane.
5 They're looking .... a picture.
6 Sue is looking .... Tom.

106.2 Complete the sentences with a preposition (**to/for/about** etc.) if necessary.

1 Thank you very much for your help.
2 This is not my umbrella. It belongs .... a friend of mine.
3 *(on the phone)* Can I speak .... Mr Davis, please?
4 *(on the phone)* Thank you .... phoning. Goodbye.
5 What happened .... Mary last night? Why didn't she come to the party?
6 We're thinking .... going to Australia next year.
7 We asked the waiter .... coffee but he brought us tea.
8 'Do you like reading books?' 'It depends .... the book.'
9 John was talking but nobody was listening .... what he was saying.
10 We waited .... Karen until 2 o'clock but she didn't come.
11 'Are you writing a letter?' 'Yes, I'm writing .... Diane.'
12 Don't forget to phone .... your mother this evening.
13 He's alone all day. He never talks .... anybody.
14 'How much does it cost to stay at this hotel?' 'It depends .... the type of room.'
15 Catherine is thinking .... changing her job.

106.3 Complete these sentences. Use **at/for/after**.

1 I looked .... the newspaper but I didn't read it carefully.
2 When you are ill, you need somebody to look .... you.
3 Excuse me, I'm looking .... Hill Street. Can you tell me where it is?
4 Goodbye! Have a nice holiday and look .... yourself.
5 I'm going to take a photograph of you. Please look .... the camera and smile.
6 Barry is looking .... a job. He wants to work in a hotel.

106.4 Answer these questions with **It depends ...** .

1	Do you want to go out with us?	It depends where you're going.
2	Do you like eating in restaurants?	It depends on the restaurant.
3	Do you enjoy watching TV?	It depends ....
4	Can you do something for me?	It ....
5	Are you going away this weekend?	....
6	Can you lend me some money?	....

UNIT 107

go in fall off run away etc. (phrasal verbs 1)

A *phrasal verb* is a verb (**go/look/be** *etc.*) + **in/out/up/down** *etc.*

in

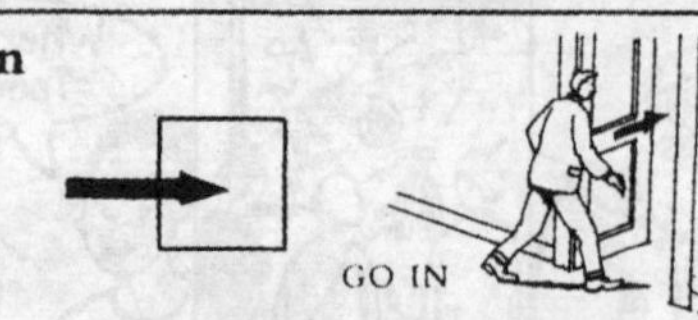

- Ann opened the door of the car and **got in**. (= **into** the car)
- I waited outside the house. I didn't **go in**.

out

- The car stopped and a woman **got out**. (= **out of** the car)
- I went to the window and **looked out**.

on

- The bus arrived and I **got on**.

off

- Be careful! Don't **fall off**.

up

- He **stood up** and left the room.
- I usually **get up** early. (= get out of bed)
- We **looked up** at the stars.

down

- Would you like to **sit down**?
- The picture **fell down**.
- **Lie down** on the floor.

away *or* **off**

- The thief **ran away**. (*or* ... **ran off**)
- Ann got into the car and **drove away**. (*or* ... **drove off**)

be/go away (= in/to another place)
- Ann has **gone away** for a few days.

back

- We went out for dinner and then **went back** to our hotel.
- Go away and don't **come back**!

be back:
- Ann is away. She'll **be back** on Monday.

over

- The wall wasn't very high, so we **climbed over**.
- **Turn over** and look at the next page.

round (*or* **around**)

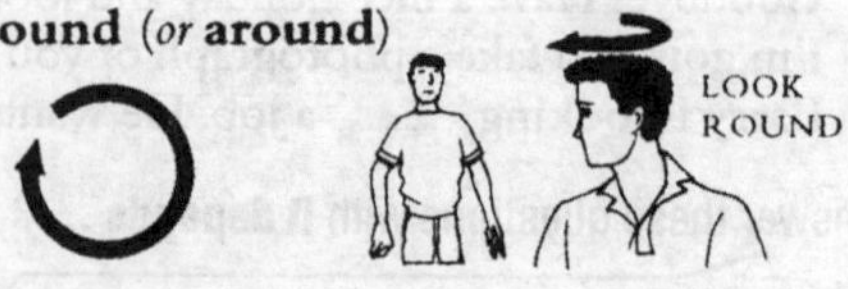

- Somebody shouted my name, so I **looked round** (*or* **around**).
- We went for a long walk. After six miles we **turned round** (*or* **around**) and went back.

get ⇒ UNIT 55 put on / take off etc. (phrasal verbs 2) ⇒ UNIT 108 list of phrasal verbs ⇒ APPENDIX 6

EXERCISES

107.1 Look at the pictures and complete the sentences. Use the verbs in the list + **in/out/up** etc.

got got ~~looked~~ looked rode sat turned went

1 I went to the window and *looked out*.
2 The door was open, so we ....
3 He heard a plane, so he ....
4 She got on her bike and ....
5 I said hello and he ....
6 The bus stopped and she ....
7 There was a free seat, so she ....
8 A car stopped and two men ....

107.2 Complete the sentences. Use **out/away/back** etc.

1 'What happened to the picture on the wall?' 'It fell *down*.'
2 Please don't go .... ! Stay here with me.
3 She heard a noise behind her, so she looked ....
4 I'm going .... now to do some shopping. I'll be .... at 5 o'clock.
5 I'm feeling very tired. I'm going to lie .... on the sofa.
6 When you have read this page, turn .... and read the other side.
7 Jim is from Canada. He lives in London now but he wants to go .... to Canada.
8 We haven't got a key to the house, so we can't get ....
9 I was very tired this morning. I couldn't get ....
10 Ann is going on holiday next month. She's going .... on the 5th and coming .... on the 24th.

107.3 Complete the sentences. Use a verb from the box + **on/off/up** etc. If necessary, put the verb into the correct form. All these phrasal verbs (**wake up** etc.) are in Appendix 6.

break	fall	give	slow	take
carry	get	hold	speak	~~wake~~

\+ **on/off/up/down/over**

1 I went to sleep at 10 o'clock and *woke up* at eight o'clock the next morning.
2 'It's time to go.' '.......... a minute. I'm not ready yet.'
3 The train .... and finally stopped.
4 I like flying but I'm always nervous when the plane ....
5 How was your exam? How did you .... ?
6 It's difficult to hear you. Can you .... a little?
7 This car isn't very good. It has .... many times.
8 When babies try to walk, they sometimes ....
9 I told him to stop but he .... Perhaps he didn't hear me.
10 I tried to find a job but I .... It was impossible.

UNIT 108

put on your shoes put your shoes on (phrasal verbs 2)

A

Sometimes a phrasal verb (**put on / take off** etc.) has an *object*. For example:

verb	*object*	*verb*	*object*
put on	your coat	**take off**	your shoes

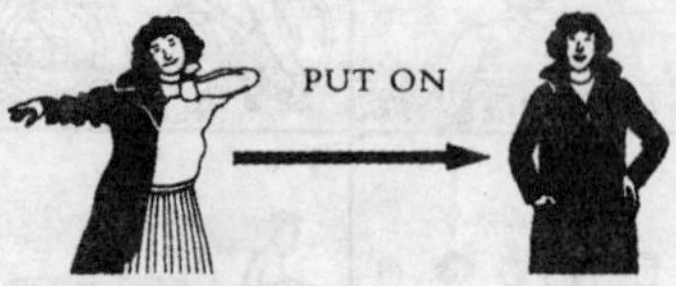

You can say:

put on your coat
or **put** your coat **on**

take off your shoes
or **take** your shoes **off**

but **it/them** *(pronouns)* always go *before* **on/off** *etc.*:

put **it on** (*not* 'put on it')

take **them off** (*not* 'take off them')

- It was cold, so I **put on** my coat. (*or* I **put** my coat **on**)
- Here's your coat. **Put it on.**
- I'm going to **take off** my shoes. (*or* **take** my shoes **off**)
- Your shoes are dirty. **Take them off.**

B

Some more phrasal verbs + *object*:

turn on / turn off (lights, machines, taps etc.):

- It was dark, so I **turned on** the light. (*or* I **turned** the light **on**)
- I don't want to watch this programme. You can **turn it off.**

also **switch on / switch off** (lights, machines etc.):

- I **switched on** the light and **switched off** the television.

pick up / put down:

- Those are my keys on the floor. Can you **pick them up** for me?
- I stopped reading and **put** my book **down.** (*or* **put down** my book)

bring back / take back / give back / put back:

- You can take my umbrella but please **bring it back.**
- I **took** my new sweater **back** to the shop. It was too small for me.
- I've got Diane's keys. I must **give them back** to her.
- I read the letter and then **put it back** in the envelope.

go in / fall off etc. (phrasal verbs 1) ⇒ UNIT 107 more phrasal verbs + object ⇒ APPENDIX 7

EXERCISES

108.1 Look at the pictures. What did these people do?

1 He turned on the light. (OR turned the light on)
2 She ....
3 He ....
4 She ....
5 He ....
6 She ....

108.2 You can write these sentences in three different ways. Complete the table.

1	I turned on the radio.	I turned the radio on.	I turned it on.
2	He put on his jacket.	He	He ....
3	She	She took her glasses off.	....
4	Put down your pens.	....	....
5	They gave back the money.	....	....
6	....	I turned the lights off.	....

108.3 Complete the sentences. Use one of the verbs in the list + **it/them**.

bring **pick** **switch** **take** ~~**turn**~~ **(+ on/off/up/back)**

1 I wanted to watch something on television, so I turned it on .
2 I bought a lamp but it doesn't work. I'm going to .... to the shop.
3 There were some gloves on the floor, so I .... and put them on the table.
4 When I finished working on the computer, I ....
5 Thank you for lending me these books. I won't forget to ....

108.4 Complete the sentences. Choose from the boxes. All these verbs are in Appendix 7.

your cigarette	a glass	*or*	me / it / them	in	up	on	away
a pair of shoes	~~ten houses~~			out	~~down~~	over	round

1 They knocked ten houses down (OR down ten houses) when they built the new road.
2 That music is very loud. Can you turn it down ?
3 I knocked .... and broke it.
4 If you want to know what a word means, you can look .... in a dictionary.
5 I want to keep these magazines. Please don't throw ....
6 Somebody gave me a form and told me to fill ....
7 I tried .... in the shop but I didn't buy them.
8 I visited the school. One of the teachers showed ....
9 'Do you play the piano?' 'No, I started to learn but I gave .... after a month.'
10 You're not allowed to smoke here. Please put ....

UNIT 109

and but or so because

A

and but or so because

We use these words *(conjunctions)* to join two sentences. They make one longer sentence from two shorter sentences:

sentence A The car stopped. — The driver got out. *sentence B*

The car stopped **and** the driver got out.

B

and/but/or

sentence A		*sentence B*
We stayed at home	**and**	(we)* watched television.
My sister is married	**and**	(she)* lives in London.
He doesn't like her	**and**	she doesn't like him.
I bought a newspaper	**but**	I didn't read it.
It's a nice house	**but**	it hasn't got a garden.
Do you want to go out	**or**	are you too tired?

* It is not necessary to repeat 'we' and 'she'.

Study these sentences. We use **and** between the last two things:

- I got home**,** had something to eat**,** sat down in an armchair **and** fell asleep.
- Ann is at work**,** Sue has gone shopping **and** Chris is playing football.

C

so *(the result of something)*

sentence A		*sentence B*
It was very hot,	**so**	I opened the window.
The water wasn't clean,	**so**	we didn't go swimming.
They like films,	**so**	they often go to the cinema.

D

because *(the reason for something)*

sentence A		*sentence B*
I opened the window	**because**	it was very hot.
We didn't go swimming	**because**	the water wasn't clean.
Lisa is hungry	**because**	she didn't have breakfast.

Because is also possible at the beginning:

- **Because the water wasn't clean**, we didn't go swimming.

E

In these examples there is more than one conjunction:

- It was late **and** I was tired, **so** I went to bed.
- I always enjoy visiting London, **but** I wouldn't like to live there **because** it's too big.

when/while/before etc. ⇒ UNIT 110

EXERCISES

109.1 Write sentences. Choose from the boxes and use **and/but/or**.

~~I stayed at home.~~	I didn't have your number.
~~I bought a newspaper.~~	Shall I wait here?
I went to the window.	~~I didn't read it.~~
I wanted to phone you.	I went by bus this morning.
I jumped into the river.	~~I watched television.~~
I usually drive to work.	I swam to the other side.
Do you want me to come with you?	I looked out.

1 *I stayed at home and watched television.*
2 *I bought a newspaper but I didn't read it.*
3 I ....
4 ....
5 ....
6 ....
7 ....

109.2 Look at the pictures and complete the sentences. Use **and/but/so/because**.

1 It was very hot, *so he opened the window.*
2 They didn't play tennis ....
3 They went to the museum ....
4 Bill wasn't hungry, ...
5 Ann was late ....
6 Sue said ....

109.3 Write sentences about what you did yesterday. Use **and/but** etc.

1 (and) *In the evening I stayed at home and studied.*
2 (because) *I went to bed very early because I was tired.*
3 (but) ....
4 (and) ....
5 (so) ....
6 (because) ....

UNIT 110 When ...

A

When I went out, it was raining.

This sentence has two parts:

part A		*part B*
when I went out	+	**it was raining**

You can begin with part A *or* part B:

- **When I went out**, it was raining.
  It was raining when I went out.

We write a comma (,) if part A (**When ...**) is before part B:

- **When** you're tired**,** don't drive.
  Don't drive **when** you're tired.
- Ann was very happy **when** she passed her exam.
  When Ann passed her exam**,** she was very happy.

We do the same in sentences with **before/while/after**:

- Always look both ways **before** you cross the road.
  Before you cross the road**,** always look both ways.
- **While** I was waiting for the bus, it began to rain.
  It began to rain **while** I was waiting for the bus.
- He never played football again **after** he broke his leg.
  After he broke his leg, he never played football again.

B

When I am ... / When I go ... *etc.*

Next week Jill is going to New York. She has a friend, Barbara, who lives in New York but Barbara is also going away – to Mexico. So they won't meet in New York.

Barbara **will be** in Mexico **when** Jill **is** in New York.

The time is *future* (**next week**) but we say:
... **when** Jill **is** in New York. (*not* 'when Jill will be')

We use the *present* (**I am** / **I go** *etc.*) with a *future meaning* after **when**:

- **When** I **get** home this evening, I'm going to have a shower.
  (*not* 'When I will get home')
- I can't talk to you now. I'll talk to you later **when I have** more time.

We do the same after **before/while/after/until**:

- Please close the window **before** you **go** out. (*not* 'before you will go')
- Julia is going to live in our flat **while** we **are** away. (*not* 'while we will be')
- I'll stay here **until** you **come** back. (*not* 'until you will come back')

until ⇒ UNIT 97 **before/while/after** ⇒ UNIT 98 **if and when** ⇒ UNIT 111

EXERCISES

110.1 Make sentences beginning with **when**. Choose from the boxes.

When	+	~~I went out~~ I'm tired I phoned her I go on holiday the programme ended I arrived at the hotel	+	I switched off the TV I always go to the same place there were no rooms ~~it was raining~~ there was no answer I like to watch TV

1 *When I went out, it was raining.*
2 ...
3 ...
4 ...
5 ...
6 ...

110.2 Complete the sentences. Choose from the box.

somebody broke into the house	before they came here	when they heard the news
~~before they crossed the road~~	while they were away	they didn't believe me
they went to live in New Zealand		

1 They looked both ways *before they crossed the road.*
2 They were very surprised ...
3 After they got married, ...
4 The letter arrived ...
5 Where did they live ...?
6 While they were asleep, ...
7 When I told them the news, ...

110.3 Which is right? Choose the correct form.

1 ~~I stay~~ / I'll stay here until you come / ~~you'll come~~ back. I'll stay and you come are right.
2 I'm going to bed when I finish / I'll finish my work.
3 We must do something before it's / it will be too late.
4 Julia is going away soon. I'm / I'll be very sad when she leaves / she'll leave.
5 Don't go out yet. Wait until the rain stops / will stop.
6 We come / We'll come and visit you when we're / we'll be in England again.
7 When I come / I'll come to see you tomorrow, I bring / I'll bring the photographs.
8 I'm going to Paris next week. I hope to see some friends of mine while I'm / I'll be there.
9 'Don't forget to give me your address.' 'OK, I give / I'll give it to you before I go / I'll go.'

110.4 Use your own ideas to complete these sentences.

1 Can you close the window before *you go out* ?
2 What are you going to do when ...?
3 When I have more time, ...
4 I'll wait for you while ...
5 When I start my new job, ...
6 Will you be here when ...?

UNIT 111

If we go ... If you see ... etc.

A

If can be *at the beginning* of a sentence or *in the middle:*

If ... ,	... (**if** *at the beginning*)
If we go by bus,	it will be cheaper.
If you don't hurry,	you'll miss the train.
If you're hungry,	have something to eat.
If the phone rings,	can you answer it, please?

...	**if** ... (**if** *in the middle*)
It will be cheaper	**if** we go by bus.
You'll miss the train	**if** you don't hurry.
I'm going to the concert	**if** I can get a ticket.
Do you mind	**if** I use your phone? (= Is it OK if I use it?)

In conversation, we often use the **if**-part of the sentence alone:

- 'Are you going to the concert?' 'Yes, **if I can get a ticket**.'

B

If you see Ann tomorrow ... *etc.*

After **if**, we use the present (*not* 'will'). We say: **if** you **see ...** (*not* 'if you will see'):

- **If** you **see** Ann tomorrow, can you ask her to phone me?
- **If I'm** late this evening, don't wait for me. (*not* 'if I will be')
- What shall we do **if** it **rains**? (*not* 'if it will rain')
- **If** I **don't feel** well tomorrow, I'll stay at home.

C

if and **when**

If I go out = it is possible that I will go out, but I'm not sure:

- A: Are you going out later?
- B: Perhaps. **If I go out**, I'll close the window.

When I go out = I'm going out (for sure):

- A: Are you going out later?
- B: Yes, I am. **When I go out**, I'll close the window.

- **When** I get home this evening, I'm going to have a shower.
- **If** I'm late this evening, don't wait for me. (*not* 'When I'm late')
- We're going to play tennis **if** it doesn't rain. (*not* 'when it doesn't rain')

when ⇒ UNIT 110 **if I had / if we went** ... etc. ⇒ UNIT 112

EXERCISES

111.1 Make sentences beginning with **if**. Choose from the boxes.

If +	~~you don't hurry~~ you pass the exam you fail the exam you don't want this magazine you want those pictures you're busy now you're hungry you need money	+	we can have lunch now you can have them I can lend you some you'll get a certificate ~~you'll be late~~ I'll throw it away we can talk later you can do it again

1 If you don't hurry, you'll be late.
2 If you pass ....
3 If ....
4 ....
5 ....
6 ....
7 ....
8 ....

111.2 Which is right?

1 If I'm / ~~I'll be~~ late this evening, don't wait for me. I'm is right
2 Will you write to me if I give / I'll give you my address?
3 If there is / will be a fire, the alarm will ring.
4 If I don't see you tomorrow morning, I phone / I'll phone you in the evening.
5 I'm / I'll be surprised if Martin and Julia get / will get married.
6 Do you go / Will you go to the party if they invite / they'll invite you?

111.3 Use your own ideas to complete these sentences.

1 I'm going to the concert if I can get a ticket.
2 If you don't hurry you'll miss the train.
3 I don't want to go swimming if ....
4 If you go to bed early tonight, ...
5 Turn the television off if ....
6 Tina won't pass her exams if ....
7 If I have time tomorrow, ...
8 We can go to the beach tomorrow if ....

111.4 Put in **if** or **when**.

1 If I'm late this evening, don't wait for me.
2 I'm going to do some shopping now. .... I come back, we can have lunch.
3 I'm thinking of going to see Tim. .... I go, will you come with me?
4 .... you don't want to go out tonight, we can stay at home.
5 Do you mind .... I close the window?
6 John is still at school. .... he leaves school, he wants to go to university.
7 Shall we have a picnic tomorrow .... the weather is good?
8 We're going to Madrid next week. We haven't got anywhere to stay – we hope to find a hotel .... we arrive. I don't know what we'll do .... we don't find anywhere.

UNIT
112 If I had ... If we went ... etc.

A

Dan likes fast cars but he doesn't have one.
He doesn't have enough money.

If he **had** the money, he **would buy** a fast car.

Usually **had** is *past*, but in this sentence **had** is *not* past. **If** he **had** the money = if he had the money *now* (but he *doesn't* have it).

IF	I you it they *etc.*	**had/knew/lived/went** (*etc.*) ... , **didn't have/know/go** (*etc.*) ... , **was/were** ... , **could** ... ,	I you it they *etc.*	**would(n't)** **could(n't)**	buy ... be ... have ... go ... *etc.*

You can say:

- **If he had** the money, he would buy a car. (**If** ... *at the beginning*)

or He would buy a car **if he had** the money. (... **if** ... *in the middle*)

I'd / she'd / they'd *etc.* = I **would** / she **would** / they **would** *etc.*:

- I don't know the answer. **If** I **knew** the answer, **I'd tell** you.
- It's raining , so we're not going out. We'**d get** wet **if** we **went** out.
- Jane lives in a city. She likes cities. She **wouldn't be** happy **if** she **lived** in the country.
- **If** you **didn't have** a job, what **would** you **do**? (but you *have* a job)
- I'm sorry I can't help you. **I'd help** you **if I could.** (but I *can't*)
- **If** we **had** a car, we **could travel** more. (but we *haven't* got a car, so we *can't* travel much)

B

If (I) **was/were ...**

You can say: **if** (I/he/she/it) **was** *or* **were** ... :

- It's cold. **If I were** you, **I'd put** your coat on. (*or* If I **was** you ...)
- It's not a very nice place. I **wouldn't go** there **if** I **was** you. (*or* ... if I **were** you)
- It **would be** nice if the weather **were** (*or* **was**) better.

C

Compare:

if I **have** / **if** it **is** *etc.*	**if** I **had** / **if** it **was** *etc.*
• I must go and see Ann. **If** I **have** time, I **will go** today. (= perhaps I'll have time, so perhaps I'll go)	• I must go and see Ann. **If I had** time, I **would go** today. (= I *don't* have time today so I will *not* go)
• I like that jacket. **I'll buy** it **if** it **isn't** too expensive. (= perhaps it will not be too expensive)	• I like that jacket but it's very expensive. **I'd buy** it **if** it **wasn't** so expensive. (= it *is* expensive, so I'm *not* going to buy it)
• **I'll help** you **if I can**. (= perhaps I can help)	• **I'd help** you **if I could** but I can't.

if we go / if I have / if I can etc. ⇒ UNIT 111

EXERCISES

112.1 Complete the sentences.

1 I don't know the answer. If I ..knew.. the answer, I'd tell you.
2 I have a car. I couldn't travel very much if I ..didn't have.. a car.
3 I don't want to go out. If I .... to go out, I'd go.
4 We haven't got a key. If we .... a key, we could get into the house.
5 I'm not hungry. I would have something to eat if I .... hungry.
6 Sue enjoys her work. She wouldn't do it if she .... it.
7 You can't drive. If you .... drive, I would lend you my car.
8 He speaks too fast. I could understand him better if he .... more slowly.
9 I have a lot to do today. If I .... so much to do, we could go out.

112.2 Put the verb in the correct form.

1 If ..he had.. the money, he would buy a fast car. (he/have)
2 Jane likes living in a city. ..She wouldn't be.. happy if she lived in the country. (she/not/be)
3 If I wanted to learn Italian, ... to Italy. (I/go)
4 I haven't told Ann what happened. She'd be angry if .... (she/know)
5 If .... a map, I could show you where I live. (we/have)
6 What would you do if .... a lot of money? (you/win)
7 It's not a very good hotel. .... there if I were you. (I/not/stay)
8 If .... nearer London, we would go there more often. (we/live)
9 It's a pity you have to go now. .... nice if you had more time. (it/be)
10 I'm not going to take the job. I'd take it if .... better. (the salary/be)
11 I don't know anything about cars. If the car broke down, ... what to do. (I/not/know)
12 If you could change one thing in the world, what .... ? (you/change)

112.3 Complete the sentences. Choose from the box and put the verb in the correct form.

we (have) a bigger house	I (watch) it	~~it (be) a bit cheaper~~
we (buy) a bigger house	every day (be) the same	I (be) bored
we (have) some pictures on the wall	the air (be) cleaner	

1 I'd buy that jacket if ..it was a bit cheaper..
2 If there was a good film on TV tonight, ...
3 This room would be nicer if ....
4 If there wasn't so much traffic, ...
5 Life would be boring if ....
6 If I had nothing to do, ...
7 We could invite all our friends to stay if ....
8 If we had more money, ...

112.4 Complete the sentences. Use your own ideas.

1 I'd go to the dentist if ..I had a toothache..
2 If I could go anywhere in the world, ...
3 I wouldn't be very happy if ....
4 I'd buy a house if ....
5 If I saw an accident in the street, ...
6 The world would be a better place if ....

UNIT 113

a person **who** … a thing **that/which** … (relative clauses 1)

A

I met a woman. **She** can speak six languages.
2 sentences

she → who

1 sentence
I met **a woman who** can speak six languages.

Jim was wearing a hat. **It** was too big for him.
2 sentences

it → that *or* **which**

1 sentence
Jim was wearing **a hat that** was too big for him.
or
Jim was wearing **a hat which** was too big for him.

B

who is for people (*not* things):

A thief is **a person**	**who** steals things.	
Do you know **anybody**	**who** can play the piano?	
The man	**who** phoned	didn't give his name.
The people	**who** work in the office	are very friendly.

C

that is for things *or* people:

An aeroplane is **a machine**	**that** flies.	
Emma lives in **a house**	**that** is 500 years old.	
The people	**that** work in the office	are very friendly.

You can use **that** for people, but **who** is more usual.

D

which is for things (*not* people):

An aeroplane is **a machine**	**which** flies. (*not* 'a machine who …')
Emma lives in **a house**	**which** is 500 years old.

Do not use **which** for people:

- Do you remember **the woman who** was playing the piano at the party? (*not* 'the woman which …')

who and **which** in questions ⇒ UNITS 44, 46 **the people we met** (relative clauses 2) ⇒ UNIT 114

EXERCISES

113.1 Choose from the boxes and write sentences: **A … is a person who … .** Use a dictionary if necessary.

~~a thief~~	a dentist
a butcher	a fool
a musician	a genius
a patient	a liar

doesn't tell the truth	is ill in hospital
looks after your teeth	~~steals things~~
is very intelligent	is very stupid
plays a musical instrument	sells meat

1 A thief is a person who steals things.
2 A butcher is a person ....
3 A musician ....
4 ....
5 ....
6 ....
7 ....
8 ....

113.2 Make one sentence from two.

1 (A man phoned. He didn't give his name.)
The man who phoned didn't give his name.
2 (A woman opened the door. She was wearing a yellow dress.)
The woman .... a yellow dress.
3 (Some students took the exam. Most of them passed.)
Most of the students ....
4 (A policeman stopped our car. He wasn't very friendly.)
The ....

113.3 Put in **who** or **which**.

1 I met a woman who can speak six languages.
2 What's the name of the woman .... lives next door?
3 What's the name of the river .... flows through the town?
4 Where is the picture .... was hanging on the wall?
5 Do you know anybody .... wants to buy a car?
6 You always ask questions .... are difficult to answer.
7 I have a friend .... is very good at repairing cars.
8 I think everybody .... went to the party enjoyed it very much.
9 Why does he always wear clothes .... are too small for him?

113.4 Right or wrong? Correct the mistakes.

1 A thief is a person (which) steals things — … a person who steals …
2 An aeroplane is a machine that flies. — OK
3 A coffee maker is a machine who makes coffee. ....
4 Have you seen the money that was on the table? ....
5 I don't like people which never stop talking. ....
6 I know somebody that can help you. ....
7 I know somebody who works in that shop. ....
8 Correct the sentences who are wrong. ....

UNIT **114**

the people **we met** the hotel **you stayed at** (relative clauses 2)

A

The man is carrying a bag.
It's very heavy. } *2 sentences*

The bag (**that**) **he is carrying** is very heavy.
1 sentence

Ann took some photographs.
Have you seen them? } *2 sentences*

Have you seen **the photographs (that) Ann took?**
1 sentence

You can say:

- The bag **that** he is carrying … *or* The bag he is carrying … (*with or without* **that**)
- … the photographs **that** Ann took? *or* … the photographs Ann took?

You do not need **that/who/which** when it is the *object:*

subject	*verb*	*object*	
The man	was carrying	a bag	→ **the bag** (that) **the man was carrying**
Ann	took	some photographs	→ **the photographs** (that) **Ann took**
You	wanted	the book	→ **the book** (that) **you wanted**
We	met	some people	→ **the people** (who) **we met**

- Did you find **the book you wanted**? (*or* … the book **that** you wanted?)
- **The people we met** were very nice. (*or* The people **who** we met …)
- **Everything I said** was true. (*or* Everything **that** I said …)

Note that we say:

- The film **we saw** was very good. (*not* 'The film we saw *it* was …')

B

Sometimes there is a *preposition* (**to/in/at** etc.) after the verb:

Jill **is talking to** a man. → Do you know **the man Jill is talking to**?
We **stayed at** a hotel. → **The hotel we stayed at** was near the station.
I **told** you **about** some books. → These are **the books I told you about.**

Note that we say:

… the books **I told you about** (*not* 'the books I told you about *them*')

You can say: (a place) **where** … :

- **The hotel where** we stayed was near the station. (= The hotel we stayed **at** …)

C

You must use **who/that/which** when it is the *subject* (⇒ Unit 113):

- I met a woman **who can speak** six languages. (**who** is the *subject*)
- Jim was wearing a hat **that was** too big for him. (**that** is the *subject*)

a person who …, a thing that/which … (relative clauses 2) ⇒ UNIT 113

EXERCISES

114.1 Make one sentence from two.

1 (Ann took some photographs. Have you seen them?)
Have you seen the photographs Ann took?

2 (You gave me a pen. I've lost it.)
I've lost the ....

3 (Sue is wearing a jacket. I like it.)
I like the ....

4 (I gave you some flowers. Where are they?)
Where are the .... ?

5 (He told us a story. I didn't believe it.)
I..........

6 (You bought some oranges. How much were they?)
How .... ?

114.2 Make one sentence from two.

1 (I was carrying a bag. It was very heavy.)
The bag I was carrying was very heavy.

2 (You cooked a meal. It was excellent.)
The ....

3 (I'm wearing shoes. They aren't very comfortable.)
The shoes ....

4 (We invited some people to dinner. They didn't come.)
The ....

114.3 Complete the sentences. Use the information in the box.

I looked at a map	they live in a house	you were looking for some keys
I was sitting on a chair	we were waiting for a bus	you spoke to some people
~~you stayed at a hotel~~	Linda is dancing with a man	

1 What's the name of *the hotel you stayed at* ?
2 Who are the people .... ?
3 Did you find the .... ?
4 The .... is too small for them.
5 The .... wasn't very clear.
6 I fell off ....
7 .... was very late.
8 Who is .... ?

114.4 Read the situations and complete the questions. Use ... **where** ... .

1 John stayed at a hotel. You ask him:
Did you like *the hotel where you stayed?*

2 Sue had dinner in a restaurant. You ask her:
What's the name of the restaurant ....

3 Sarah lives in a village. You ask her:
Do you like ....

4 Richard works in a factory. You ask him:
How big ....

Appendix 1 Active and passive

1.1 Present and past:

	active	passive
present simple	We **make** butter from milk. Somebody **cleans** these rooms every day. People never **invite** me to parties. How **do** they **make** butter?	Butter **is made** from milk. These rooms **are cleaned** every day. I **am** never **invited** to parties. How **is** butter **made**?
past simple	Somebody **stole** my car last week. Somebody **stole** my keys yesterday. They **didn't invite** me to the party. When **did** they **build** these houses?	My car **was stolen** last week. My keys **were stolen** yesterday. I **wasn't invited** to the party. When **were** these houses **built**?

present continuous	They **are building** a new airport at the moment. (= it isn't finished) They **are building** some new houses near the river.	A new airport **is being built** at the moment. Some new houses **are being built** near the river.
past continuous	When I was here a few years ago, they **were building** a new airport. (= it wasn't finished at that time)	When I was here a few years ago, a new airport **was being built**.

present perfect	Look! They **have painted** the door. These shirts are clean. Somebody **has washed** them. Somebody **has stolen** my car.	Look! The door **has been painted.** These shirts are clean. They **have been washed**. My car **has been stolen**.
past perfect	Ann said that somebody **had stolen** her car.	Ann said that her car **had been stolen.**

1.2 **Will / can / must / have to** *etc.*

active	passive
Somebody will **clean** the office tomorrow. Somebody must **clean** the office. I think they'll **invite** you to the party. They can't **repair** my watch. You should **wash** this sweater by hand.	The office will **be cleaned** tomorrow. The office must **be cleaned**. I think you'll **be invited** to the party. My watch can't **be repaired**. This sweater should **be washed** by hand.
They are going **to build** a new airport. Somebody has **to wash** these clothes. They had **to take** the injured man to hospital.	A new airport is going **to be built**. These clothes have **to be washed**. The injured man had **to be taken** to hospital.

Appendix 2 List of irregular verbs (⇒ Unit 24)

infinitive	*past simple*	*past participle*
be	**was/were**	**been**
beat	**beat**	**beaten**
become	**became**	**become**
begin	**began**	**begun**
bite	**bit**	**bitten**
blow	**blew**	**blown**
break	**broke**	**broken**
bring	**brought**	**brought**
build	**built**	**built**
buy	**bought**	**bought**
catch	**caught**	**caught**
choose	**chose**	**chosen**
come	**came**	**come**
cost	**cost**	**cost**
cut	**cut**	**cut**
do	**did**	**done**
draw	**drew**	**drawn**
drink	**drank**	**drunk**
drive	**drove**	**driven**
eat	**ate**	**eaten**
fall	**fell**	**fallen**
feel	**felt**	**felt**
fight	**fought**	**fought**
find	**found**	**found**
fly	**flew**	**flown**
forget	**forgot**	**forgotten**
get	**got**	**got**
give	**gave**	**given**
go	**went**	**gone**
grow	**grew**	**grown**
hang	**hung**	**hung**
have	**had**	**had**
hear	**heard**	**heard**
hide	**hid**	**hidden**
hit	**hit**	**hit**
hold	**held**	**held**
hurt	**hurt**	**hurt**
keep	**kept**	**kept**
know	**knew**	**known**
leave	**left**	**left**
lend	**lent**	**lent**

infinitive	*past simple*	*past participle*
let	**let**	**let**
lie	**lay**	**lain**
light	**lit**	**lit**
lose	**lost**	**lost**
make	**made**	**made**
mean	**meant**	**meant**
meet	**met**	**met**
pay	**paid**	**paid**
put	**put**	**put**
read /riːd/*	**read** /red/*	**read** /red/*
ride	**rode**	**ridden**
ring	**rang**	**rung**
rise	**rose**	**risen**
run	**ran**	**run**
say	**said**	**said**
see	**saw**	**seen**
sell	**sold**	**sold**
send	**sent**	**sent**
shine	**shone**	**shone**
shoot	**shot**	**shot**
show	**showed**	**shown**
shut	**shut**	**shut**
sing	**sang**	**sung**
sit	**sat**	**sat**
sleep	**slept**	**slept**
speak	**spoke**	**spoken**
spend	**spent**	**spent**
stand	**stood**	**stood**
steal	**stole**	**stolen**
swim	**swam**	**swum**
take	**took**	**taken**
teach	**taught**	**taught**
tear	**tore**	**torn**
tell	**told**	**told**
think	**thought**	**thought**
throw	**threw**	**thrown**
understand	**understood**	**understood**
wake	**woke**	**woken**
wear	**wore**	**worn**
win	**won**	**won**
write	**wrote**	**written**

* *pronunciation*

The following verbs can be regular (**-ed**) *or* irregular (**-t**):

infinitive	*past simple / past participle*
burn	**burned** *or* **burnt**
dream	**dreamed** *or* **dreamt**

infinitive	*past simple / past participle*
learn	**learned** *or* **learnt**
smell	**smelled** *or* **smelt**

Appendix 3 Irregular verbs in groups

past simple / past participle are the same:

1

cost	→	**cost**
cut	→	**cut**
hit	→	**hit**
hurt	→	**hurt**

let	→	**let**
put	→	**put**
shut	→	**shut**

2

lend	→	**lent**
send	→	**sent**
spend	→	**spent**
build	→	**built**

lose	→	**lost**
shoot	→	**shot**
get	→	**got**
light	→	**lit**
sit	→	**sat**

burn	→	**burnt**
learn	→	**learnt**
smell	→	**smelt**

keep	→	**kept**
sleep	→	**slept**

feel	→	**felt**
leave	→	**left**
meet	→	**met**
dream	→	**dreamt** /dremt/*
mean	→	**meant** /ment/*

3

bring	→	**brought** /brɔːt/*
buy	→	**bought** /bɔːt/*
fight	→	**fought** /fɔːt/*
think	→	**thought** /θɔːt/*
catch	→	**caught** /kɔːt/*
teach	→	**taught** /tɔːt/*

4

sell	→	**sold**
tell	→	**told**

find	→	**found**
have	→	**had**
hear	→	**heard**
hold	→	**held**
read	→	**read** /red/*
say	→	**said** /sed/*

pay	→	**paid**
make	→	**made**

stand	→	**stood**
understand	→	**understood**

* *pronunciation*

past simple / past participle are different:

1

break	→	**broke**	**broken**
choose	→	**chose**	**chosen**
speak	→	**spoke**	**spoken**
steal	→	**stole**	**stolen**
wake	→	**woke**	**woken**

2

drive	→	**drove**	**driven**
ride	→	**rode**	**ridden**
rise	→	**rose**	**risen**
write	→	**wrote**	**written**

beat	→	**beat**	**beaten**
bite	→	**bit**	**bitten**
hide	→	**hid**	**hidden**

3

eat	→	**ate**	**eaten**
fall	→	**fell**	**fallen**
forget	→	**forgot**	**forgotten**
give	→	**gave**	**given**
see	→	**saw**	**seen**
take	→	**took**	**taken**

4

blow	→	**blew**	**blown**
grow	→	**grew**	**grown**
know	→	**knew**	**known**
throw	→	**threw**	**thrown**
fly	→	**flew**	**flown**
draw	→	**drew**	**drawn**
show	→	**showed**	**shown**

5

begin	→	**began**	**begun**
drink	→	**drank**	**drunk**
swim	→	**swam**	**swum**
ring	→	**rang**	**rung**
sing	→	**sang**	**sung**
run	→	**ran**	**run**

6

come	→	**came**	**come**
become	→	**became**	**become**

Appendix 4 Short forms (**he's / I'd / don't** etc.)

4.1 In spoken English we usually pronounce '**I am**' as one word. The short form (**I'm**) is a way of writing this:

I am → **I'm**		• **I'm** feeling tired this morning.
it is → **it's**		• 'Do you like this jacket?' 'Yes, it**'s** very nice.'
they have → **they've**		• 'Where are your friends?' 'They**'ve** gone home.'
etc.		

When we write short forms, we use ' (*an apostrophe*):

I ~~a~~m → I**'m** he ~~i~~s → he**'s** you ~~ha~~ve → you**'ve** she ~~wi~~ll → she**'ll**

4.2 We use these forms with **I/he/she** *etc.*:

am → **'m**	**I'm**						
is → **'s**		**he's**	**she's**	**it's**			
are → **'re**					**we're**	**you're**	**they're**
have → **'ve**	**I've**				**we've**	**you've**	**they've**
has → **'s**		**he's**	**she's**	**it's**			
had → **'d**	**I'd**	**he'd**	**she'd**		**we'd**	**you'd**	**they'd**
will → **'ll**	**I'll**	**he'll**	**she'll**		**we'll**	**you'll**	**they'll**
would → **'d**	**I'd**	**he'd**	**she'd**		**we'd**	**you'd**	**they'd**

- I**'ve** got some new shoes.
- We**'ll** probably go out this evening.
- It's 10 o'clock. You**'re** late again.

's = **is** *or* **has**:

- She**'s** going out this evening. (she**'s** going = she **is** going)
- She**'s** gone out. (she**'s** gone = she **has** gone)

'd = **would** *or* **had**:

- A: What would you like to eat?
  B: I**'d** like a salad, please. (I**'d** like = I **would** like)
- I told the police that I**'d** lost my passport. (I**'d** lost = I **had** lost)

Do *not* use **'m/'s/'d** etc. at the end of a sentence (⇒ Unit 39):

- 'Are you tired?' 'Yes, I **am**.' (*not* 'Yes, I'm.')

4.3 We use short forms with **I/you/he/she** etc. but you can use short forms (especially **'s**) with other words too:

- **Who's** your favourite singer? (= who **is**)
- **What's** the time? (= what **is**)
- **There's** a big tree in the garden. (= there **is**)
- **My sister's** working in London. (= my sister **is** working)
- **Paul's** gone out. (= Paul **has** gone out)
- **What colour's** your car? (= What colour **is** your car?)

4.4 Negative short forms (⇒ Unit 42):

isn't (= is not)	**don't** (= do not)	**can't** (= cannot)
aren't (= are not)	**doesn't** (= does not)	**couldn't** (= could not)
wasn't (= was not)	**didn't** (= did not)	**won't** (= will not)
weren't (= were not)		**wouldn't** (= would not)
hasn't (= has not)		**shouldn't** (= should not)
haven't (= have not)		**mustn't** (= must not)
hadn't (= had not)		**needn't** (= need not)

- We went to her house but she **wasn't** at home.
- 'Where's David?' 'I **don't** know. I **haven't** seen him.'
- You work all the time. You **shouldn't** work so hard.
- I **won't** be here tomorrow. (= I will not)

4.5 **'s** (*apostrophe* + **s**)

's can mean different things:

(1) **'s** = **is** *or* **has** (⇒ section 4.2 of this appendix)

(2) **let's** = let **us** (⇒ Unit 52)
- The weather is nice. **Let's** go out. (= Let **us** go out.)

(3) Ann**'s** camera (= her camera) / my brother**'s** car (= his car) / the manager**'s** office (= his/her office) *etc.* (⇒ Unit 63)

Compare:
- **Ann's** camera was very expensive. (**Ann's** camera = **her** camera)
- **Ann's** a very good photographer. (**Ann's** = Ann **is**)
- **Ann's** got a new camera. (Ann's got = Ann **has** got)

Appendix 5 Spelling

5.1 Words + -s and -es (birds/watches *etc.*)

noun + s (plural) (⇒ Unit 65)
bird → birds   mistake → mistakes   hotel → hotels

verb + s (he/she/it -s) (⇒ Unit 5)
think → thinks   live → lives   remember → remembers

but

+ es after -s / -sh / -ch / -x:
bus → buses   pass → passes   address → addresses
dish → dishes   wash → washes   finish → finishes
watch → watches   teach → teaches   sandwich → sandwiches
box → boxes

also
potato → potatoes   tomato → tomatoes
do → does   go → goes

-f / -fe → -ves:
shelf → shelves   knife → knives   *but* roof → roofs

5.2 Words ending in -y (baby → babies / study → studied *etc.*)

-y → -ies:
study → studies (*not* 'studys')   family → families (*not* 'familys')
story → stories   city → cities   baby → babies
try → tries   marry → marries   fly → flies

-y → -ied (⇒ Unit 11):
study → studied (*not* 'studyed')
try → tried   marry → married   copy → copied

-y → -ier/-iest (⇒ Units 86 and 89):
easy → easier/easiest (*not* 'easyer/easyest')
happy → happier/happiest   lucky → luckier/luckiest
heavy → heavier/heaviest   funny → funnier/funniest

-y → -ily (⇒ Unit 85):
easy → easily (*not* 'easyly')
happy → happily   lucky → luckily   heavy → heavily

y does not change to i if the ending is -ay/-ey/-oy/-uy:
holiday → holidays (*not* 'holidaies')
enjoy → enjoys/enjoyed   stay → stays/stayed   buy → buys   key → keys
but
say → said   pay → paid   (*irregular verbs*)

5.3 -ing

Verbs that end in -e (make/write/drive *etc.*) → **-~~e~~ing**:
make → **making** write → **writing** come → **coming** dance → **dancing**

Verbs that end in -ie → **-ying**:
lie → **lying** die → **dying** tie → **tying**

5.4 stop → stopped, big → bigger *etc.*

Vowels and consonants:

Vowel letters: a e i o u
Consonant letters: b c d f g k l m n p r s t w y

Sometimes a word ends in a *vowel* + a *consonant*. For example: **stop, big, get**.
Before **-ing/-ed/-er/-est**, the consonant at the end (**-p/-g/-t** etc.) is 'doubled' (**-pp-/-gg-/-tt-** *etc.*).
For example:

V = *vowel*
C = *consonant*

	V+C			
stop	ST**O P**	p → **pp**	**stopping**	**stopped**
run	R**U N**	n → **nn**	**running**	
get	G**E T**	t → **tt**	**getting**	
swim	SW**I M**	m → **mm**	**swimming**	
big	B**I G**	g → **gg**	**bigger**	**biggest**
hot	H**O T**	t → **tt**	**hotter**	**hottest**
thin	TH**I N**	n → **nn**	**thinner**	**thinnest**

This does *not* happen
(1) if the word ends in *two* consonant letters (C + C):

	C+C		
help	HE**L P**	**helping**	**helped**
work	WO**R K**	**working**	**worked**
fast	FA**S T**	**faster**	**fastest**

(2) if the word ends in two vowel letters + a consonant letter (V + V + C):

	V+V+C		
need	N**E E D**	**needing**	**needed**
wait	W**A I T**	**waiting**	**waited**
cheap	CH**E A P**	**cheaper**	**cheapest**

(3) in longer words (two syllables or more) if the last part of the word is *not* stressed:

		stress			
	happen	**HAP**-pen		→	**happening/happened** (*not* 'happenned')
	visit	**VIS**-it		→	**visiting/visited**
	remember	re-**MEM**-ber		→	**remembering/remembered**
but	prefer	pre-**FER**	*(stress at the end)*	→	**preferring/preferred**
	begin	be-**GIN**	*(stress at the end)*	→	**beginning**

(4) if the word ends in **-y** or **-w**. (At the end of words, **y** and **w** are not consonants.)
enjoy → **enjoying/enjoyed** snow/**snowing/snowed** few/**fewer/fewest**

Appendix 6 Phrasal verbs (**look out / take off** etc.)

This is a list of some important phrasal verbs (⇒ Unit 107).

out

look out / watch out = be careful:
- **Look out**! There's a car coming!

on

come on = be quick / hurry:
- **Come on**! Everybody is waiting for you.

hold on = wait:
- Can you **hold on** a minute? (= can you wait?)

carry on = continue:
- Don't stop working. **Carry on.** (= continue working)
- A: Excuse me, where is the station, please?
  B: **Carry on** along this road and turn right at the lights. (= Continue along …)

also **go on / walk on / drive on** etc. = continue going etc.:
- Don't stop here. **Drive on.**

get on = manage (in a job, at school, in an exam etc.):
- How are you **getting on** in your new job? (= are you doing OK?)

off

take off = leave the ground *(for planes)*:
- The plane **took off** 20 minutes late but landed on time.

up

wake up = stop sleeping:
- I often **wake up** in the middle of the night.

speak up = speak more loudly:
- I can't hear you. Can you **speak up** a bit?

hurry up = do something more quickly:
- **Hurry up!** We haven't got much time.

wash up = wash the plates etc. after a meal:
- Do you want me to **wash up**? (*or* … to do the washing-up?)

grow up = become an adult:
- What does your son want to do when he **grows up**?

give up = stop trying:
- I know it's difficult but don't give up. (= don't stop trying)

down

slow down = go more slowly:
- You're driving too fast. **Slow down.**

break down = stop working *(for cars/machines etc.)*:
- Sue was very late because her car **broke down**.

over

fall over = lose your balance:
- **I fell over** because my shoes were too big for me.

Appendix 7 Phrasal verbs + object (**fill in** a form / **put out** a fire etc.)

This is a list of some important phrasal verbs + object (⇒ Unit 108).

in

fill in (a form) = complete (a form):
- Can you **fill in this form**, please?

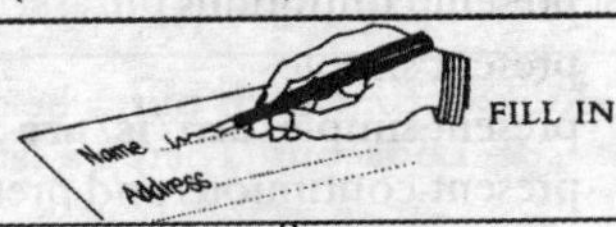

out

put out (a fire / a cigarette):
- The fire brigade arrived and **put the fire out**.

cross out (a mistake / a word etc.):
- If you make a mistake, **cross it out**.

on

try on (clothes) = put on clothes to see if they fit you:
- *(in a shop)* This is a nice jacket. Shall I **try it on**?

up

give up = stop something that you do:
- Tom **gave up smoking** five years ago. (= he stopped smoking)
- 'Are you still learning Italian?' 'No, I **gave it up**.'

ring up = (tele)phone:
- Sue **rang me up** last night. (*also* 'Sue **rang me** last night.' *without* 'up')

look up (a word in a dictionary etc.):
- I didn't know the meaning of the word, so I **looked it up** in a dictionary.

turn up = make louder (TV, radio, music etc.)
- Can you **turn the radio up**? I can't hear it.

down

knock down (a building) = demolish:
- They are going to **knock down** the school and build a new one.

turn down = make more quiet (TV, radio, music etc.):
- The music is too loud. Can you **turn it down**?

away

throw away (rubbish, things you don't want):
- These apples are bad. Shall I **throw them away**?
- Don't **throw away that picture.** I want it.

put away = put something in the place where you usually keep it:
- After they finished playing, the children **put their toys away**.

back

pay somebody **back** (money that you borrowed):
- Thank you for lending me the money. I'll **pay you back** next week.

over

knock over (a cup / a glass / a person etc.):
- Be careful. Don't **knock your cup over**.
- There was an accident at the end of the road. A man was **knocked over** by a car. (*or* A man was **knocked down** by a car.)

round/around

show (somebody) **round/around** = take somebody on a tour of a place:
- We visited a factory last week. The manager **showed us round**.

Additional exercises

List of exercises:

1–2	**am/is/are**	UNITS 1-2
3	present continuous	UNITS 3-4
4	present simple	UNITS 5-7
5–7	present simple, **am/is/are** and **have (got)**	UNITS 1-2, 5-7, 9
8–9	present continuous and present simple	UNITS 3-8
10–13	**was/were** and past simple	UNITS 10-12
14	past simple and past continuous	UNITS 11-14
15	present and past	UNITS 3-14
16–18	present perfect	UNITS 15-18
19–22	present perfect and past simple	UNITS 19-20
23	present, past and present perfect	UNITS 3-20
24–27	passive	UNITS 21-22
28	future	UNITS 26-29
29	past, present and future	UNITS 3-20, 26-29
30	**-ing** and infinitive	UNITS 50-54, 98, 105
31–32	**a** and **the**	UNITS 64, 68-72
33	prepositions	UNITS 96-101, 104

am/is/are

UNITS 1–2

1 **Write sentences for the pictures. Use the words in the boxes + is/isn't/are/aren't.**

~~The windows~~	on the table
~~Ann~~	hungry
Kate	asleep
The children	~~open~~
Bill	full
The books	near the station
The hotel	a doctor
The bus	~~happy~~

1 *The windows are open.*
2 *Ann isn't happy.*
3 Kate ....
4 ....
5 ....
6 ....
7 ....
8 ....

2 Complete the sentences.

1 'Are you hungry?' 'No, but ...I'm... thirsty.'
2 '...How are... your parents?' 'They're very well.'
3 'Is Linda at home?' 'No, ... at work.'
4 '.......................... my keys?' 'In the kitchen.'
5 Where is Pete from? .... American or British?
6 .... hot today. The temperature is 35 degrees.
7 'Are you a teacher?' 'No, ... a student.'
8 '.......................... your umbrella?' 'Green.'
9 Where's your car? .... in the car park?
10 '.......................... tired?' 'No, I'm fine.'
11 '.......................... these oranges?' 'Thirty pence each.'

present continuous (**I'm working / are you working?** etc.)

UNITS 3–4

3 Use the words in brackets to write sentences.

1 A: Where are your parents?
B: ...They're watching TV.... (they/watch/TV)
2 A: Paula is going out.
B: ...Where's she going?... (where/she/go?)
3 A: Where's David?
B: .... (he/have/a bath)
4 A: .... ? (the children/play?)
B: No, they're asleep.
5 A: .... ? (it/rain?)
B: No, not at the moment.
6 A: Where are Sue and Steve?
B: .... (they/come/now)
7 A: .... ? (why/you/stand/here?)
B: .... (I/wait/for somebody)

present simple (**I work / she doesn't work / do you work?** etc.)

UNITS 5–7

4 Complete the sentences. Use the present simple.

1 ...Sue always arrives... at work early. (Sue/always/arrive)
2 ...We don't watch... TV very often. (we/not/watch)
3 How often ...do you wash... your hair? (you/wash)
4 I want to go to the cinema but .... to go. (Chris/not/want)
5 .... to go out this evening? (you/want)
6 .... near here? (Ann/live)
7 .... a lot of people. (Sarah/know)
8 I enjoy travelling but .... very much. (I/not/travel)
9 What time .... in the morning? (you/usually/get up)
10 My parents are usually at home in the evening. .... very often. (they/not/go out)
11 .... work at five o'clock. (Tim/always/finish)
12 A: What .... ? (Jill/do)
B: .... in a hotel. (she/work)

present simple, **am/is/are** and **have (got)**

UNITS 1–2, 5–7, 9

5 Read the questions and Claire's answers. Then write sentences about Claire.

1	Are you married?	No.	1	*She isn't married.*
2	Do you live in London?	Yes.	2	*She lives in London.*
3	Are you a student?	Yes.	3	....
4	Have you got a car?	No.	4	....
5	Do you go out a lot?	Yes.	5	....
6	Have you got a lot of friends?	Yes.	6	....
7	Do you like London?	No.	7	....
8	Do you like dancing?	Yes.	8	....
9	Are you interested in sport?	No.	9	....

6 Complete the questions.

1
What's your name ?
.... married?
Where .... ?
.... any children?
How .... ?

Brian.
Yes, I am.
In Barton Road.
Yes, a daughter.
She's three.

2
.... ?
.... ?
.... your job?
.... a car?
.... to work by car?

I'm 29.
I work in a supermarket.
No, I hate it.
Yes, I have.
No, I usually go by bus.

3
Who is this man?
.... ?
.... ?
.... in London?

That's my brother.
Michael.
He's a travel agent.
No, in Manchester.

7 Make sentences from these words.

1. Sarah often / tennis — *Sarah often plays tennis.*
2. I / a new car — *I've got a new car.*
3. my shoes / dirty — *My shoes are dirty.*
4. Sonia / 32 years old — Sonia ....
5. I / two sisters — ....
6. we often / TV in the evening — ....
7. Ann never / a hat — ....
8. a bicycle / two wheels — ....
9. these flowers / beautiful — ....
10. Mary / German very well — ....

present continuous (**I'm working**) and present simple (**I work**) UNITS 3–8

8 Complete the sentences.

9 Which is right?

1 'Are you speaking / Do you speak English?' 'Yes, a little.' Do you speak is right
2 Sometimes we're going / we go away at weekends.
3 It's a nice day today. The sun is shining / shines.
4 *(You meet Ann in the street.)* Hello, Ann. Where are you going / do you go?
5 How often are you going / do you go on holiday?
6 Emily is a writer. She's writing / She writes books for children.
7 I'm never reading / I never read newspapers.
8 'Where are Michael and Jane?' 'They're watching / They watch TV in the living room.'
9 Helen is in her office. She's talking / She talks to somebody.
10 What time are you usually having / do you usually have dinner?
11 John isn't at home at the moment. He's visiting / He visits some friends.
12 'Would you like some tea?' 'No, thank you. I'm not drinking / I don't drink tea.'

was/were and past simple (**I worked / did you work? etc.**) UNITS 10–12

10 Complete the sentences. Use one word only.

1 I got up early and *had* a shower.
2 Tom was tired last night, so he .... to bed early.
3 I .... this pen on the floor. Is it yours?
4 Kate got married when she .... 23.
5 Helen is learning to drive. She .... her first lesson yesterday.
6 'I've got a new job.' 'Yes, I know. David .... me.'
7 'Where did you buy that book?' 'It was a present. Ann .... it to me.'
8 We .... hungry, so we had something to eat.
9 'Did you enjoy the film?' 'Yes, I .... it was very good.'
10 'Did Mary come to your party?' 'No, we .... her, but she didn't come.'

11 Look at the questions and Kevin's answers.
Write sentences about Kevin when he was a child.

When you were a child …

	Question	Answer		Sentence
1	Were you tall?	No.	1	*He wasn't tall.*
2	Did you like school?	Yes.	2	*He liked school.*
3	Were you good at sport?	Yes.	3	He ....
4	Did you play football?	Yes.	4	....
5	Did you work hard at school?	No.	5	....
6	Did you have a lot of friends?	Yes.	6	....
7	Did you have a bicycle?	No.	7	....
8	Were you a quiet child?	No.	8	....

12 Complete the questions.

	Question	Answer
1	*Did you have* a nice holiday?	Yes, it was great, thanks.
2	*Where did you go* ?	To Amsterdam.
3	.... there?	Five days.
4	.... Amsterdam?	Yes, very much.
5	.... ?	I have friends in Amsterdam, so I stayed with them.
6	.... good?	Yes, it was warm and sunny.
7	.... back?	Yesterday.

13 Put the verb in the right form (positive, negative or question).

1 It was a good party. *I enjoyed* it. (I/enjoy)
2 '*Did you do* the shopping?' (you/do) 'No, I *didn't have* time.' (I/have)
3 'Did you phone Alan?' 'No, I'm afraid ....' (I/forget)
4 I like your new watch. Where .... it? (you/get)
5 I saw Lucy at the party but .... to her. (I/speak)
6 A: .... a nice weekend? (you/have)
B: Yes, I went to stay with some friends of mine.
7 Paul wasn't well yesterday, so .... to work. (he/go)
8 'Is Mary here?' 'Yes, ... five minutes ago.' (she/arrive)
9 Where .... before he came here? (Robert/live)
10 The restaurant wasn't expensive. .... very much. (the meal/cost)

past simple (**I worked**) and past continuous (**I was working**)

14 Look at the pictures and complete the sentences. Use the past simple or past continuous.

1

It was raining (rain) when we went (go) out.

2

When I arrived at the office, Jane and Paul .... (work) at their desks.

3

I .... (open) the window because it was hot.

4

The phone .... (ring) while Sue .... (cook) the dinner.

5

I .... (hear) a noise outside, so I .... (look) out of the window.

6

Tom .... (look) out of the window when the accident .... (happen).

7

Richard had a book in his hand but he .... (not/read) it. He .... (watch) TV.

8

Catherine bought a magazine but she .... (not/read) it. She didn't have time.

9

I .... (finish) my meal, ... (pay) the bill and .... (leave) the restaurant.

10

I .... (see) Kate this morning. I .... (walk) along the street and she .... (wait) for the bus.

present and past

UNITS 3–14

15 Complete the sentences. Use one of these forms:

the present simple (**I work** etc.) the present continuous (**I am working** etc.)
the past simple (**I worked** etc.) the past continuous (**I was working** etc.)

1 You can turn off the television. I 'm not watching (not/watch) it.
2 Last night Jenny fell (fall) asleep while she was reading (read).
3 Listen! Somebody ………………………… (play) the piano.
4 'Have you got my key?' 'No, I ………………………… (give) it back to you.'
5 David is very lazy. He ………………………… (not/like) hard work .
6 Where ………………………… (your parents/go) for their holidays last year?
7 I ………………………… (see) Diane yesterday. She ………………………… (drive) her new car.
8 A: ………………………… (you/watch) television very often?
B: No, I haven't got a television set.
9 A: What ………………………… (you/do) at 6 o'clock last Sunday morning?
B: I was in bed asleep.
10 Andy isn't at home very much. He ………………………… (go) away a lot.
11 I ………………………… (try) to find a job at the moment. It's very difficult.
12 I'm tired this morning. I ………………………… (not/sleep) very well last night.

present perfect (**I have done / she has been** etc.)

UNITS 15–18

16 Look at the pictures and complete the sentences. Use the present perfect.

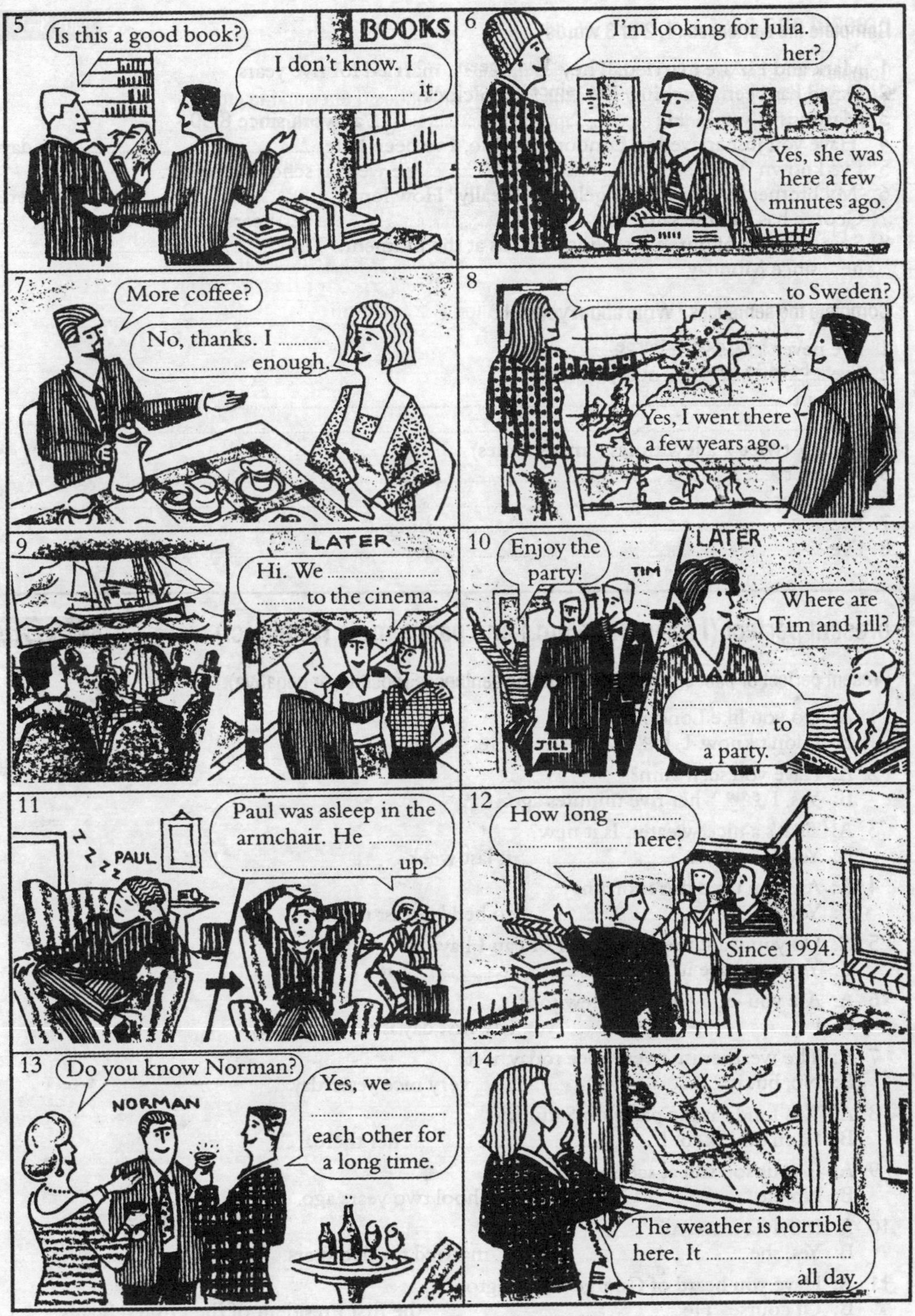
5
Is this a good book?
BOOKS
I don't know. I .... it.
6
I'm looking for Julia. .... her?
Yes, she was here a few minutes ago.
7
More coffee?
No, thanks. I .... enough.
8
.... to Sweden?
Yes, I went there a few years ago.
9
LATER
Hi. We .... to the cinema.
10
Enjoy the party!
TIM
JILL
LATER
Where are Tim and Jill?
.... to a party.
11
PAUL
Paul was asleep in the armchair. He .... up.
12
How long .... here?
Since 1994.
13
Do you know Norman?
NORMAN
Yes, we .... each other for a long time.
14
The weather is horrible here. It .... all day.

17 Complete the sentences (1, 2 or 3 words).

1 Mark and Liz are married. They have been married for five years.
2 David has been watching TV since 5 o'clock.
3 Martin is at work. He .... at work since 8.30.
4 'Have you just arrived in London?' 'No, I've been here .... five days.'
5 I've known Ann .... we were at school together.
6 'My brother lives in Los Angeles.' 'Really? How long .... there?'
7 George has had the same job .... 20 years.
8 Some friends of ours are staying with us at the moment. They .... here since Monday.

18 Complete the sentences. Write about yourself.

1 I've never ridden a horse.
2 I've been to London many times.
3 I've just ....
4 I've ....
(once / twice / a few times / many times)
5 I haven't .... yet.
6 I've never ....
7 I've .... since ....
8 I've .... for ....

---

present perfect (**I have done** etc.) and past simple (**I did** etc.) UNITS 19–20

19 Present perfect or past simple? Complete the sentences (positive or negative).

1 A: Do you like London?
B: I don't know. I haven't been there.

2 A: Have you seen Ann?
B: Yes, I saw her five minutes ago.

3 A: That's a nice sweater. Is it new?
B: Yes, I .... it last week.

4 A: Are you tired this morning?
B: Yes, I .... to bed late last night.

5 A: Do you want the newspaper or can I have it?
B: You can have it. I .... it.

6 A: Are you enjoying your new job?
B: I .... yet. My first day is next Monday.

7 A: The weather isn't very nice today, is it?
B: No, but it .... very nice yesterday.

8 A: Was Linda at the party on Saturday?
B: I don't think so. I .... her there.

9 A: Is your son still at school?
B: No, he .... school two years ago.

10 A: Is Sylvia married?
B: Yes, she .... married for five years.

11 A: Have you heard of George Washington?
B: Of course. He .... the first President of the United States.

20 Make sentences from the words in brackets (...). Use the present perfect or past simple.

1 A: Have you been to Scotland?
B: Yes, I went there last year. (I / go / there / last year)

2 A: Do you like London?
B: I don't know. I've never been there. (I / never / there)

3 A: What time is Paul going out?
B: .... (he / already / go)

4 A: Has Catherine gone home?
B: Yes, ... (she / go / at 4 o'clock)

5 A: New York is my favourite city.
B: Is it? ....? (how many times / you / there?)

6 A: What are you doing this weekend?
B: I don't know. .... (I / not / decide / yet)

7 A: I can't find my address book. Have you seen it?
B: .... (it / on the table / last night)

8 A: Are you hungry?
B: No, ... (I / just / eat)

9 A: Paula and Sue are here.
B: Are they? ....? (what time / they / arrive?)

21 Present perfect or past simple? Complete the sentences.

1 A: Have you been to France?
B: Yes, many times.
A: When .... the last time?
B: Two years ago.

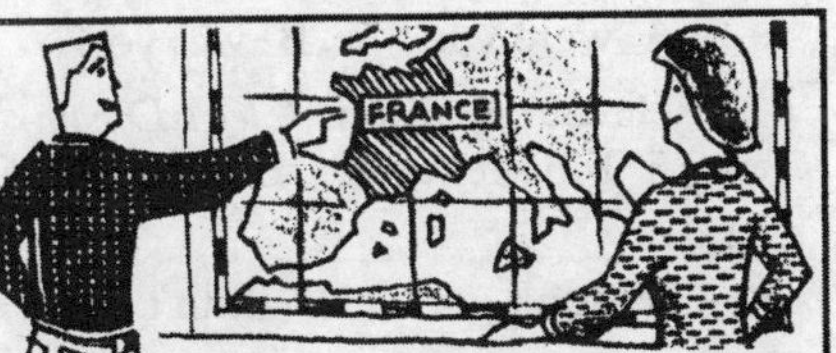

2 A: Is this your car?
B: Yes, it is.
A: How long .... it?
B: It's new. I .... it yesterday.

3 A: Where do you live?
B: In Harold Street.
A: How long .... there?
B: Five years. Before that ....
in Mill Road.
A: How long .... in Mill Road?
B: About three years.

4 A: What do you do?
B: I work in a shop.
A: How long .... there?
B: Nearly two years.
A: What .... before that?
B: I .... a taxi driver.

22 Write sentences about yourself.

1 (yesterday morning) I was late for work yesterday morning.
2 (last night) ....
3 (yesterday afternoon) ....
4 (... days ago) ....
5 (last week) ....
6 (last year) ....

present, past and present perfect

UNITS 3–20

23 Which is right?

1 'Is Sue working ?' 'No, she's on holiday.'
A Does Sue work B Is working Sue C Is Sue working D Does work Sue

2 'Where .... ?' 'In a village near London.'
A lives your uncle B does your uncle live C your uncle lives
D does live your uncle

3 I speak Italian but .... French.
A I speak not B I'm not speaking C I doesn't speak D I don't speak

4 'Where's Tom?' '.......... a shower at the moment.'
A He's having B He have C He has D He has had

5 Why .... angry with me yesterday?
A were you B was you C you were D have you been

6 My favourite film is *Cleo's Dream*. .... it four times.
A I'm seeing B I see C I saw D I've seen

7 I .... out last night. I was too tired.
A don't go B didn't went C didn't go D haven't gone

8 Liz is from Edinburgh. She .... there all her life.
A is living B has lived C lives D lived

9 My friend .... for me when I arrived.
A waited B has waited C was waiting D has been waiting

10 'How long .... English?' 'Six months.'
A do you learn B are you learning C you are learning
D have you been learning

11 Martin is English but he lives in France. He has been there ....
A for three years B since three years C three years ago D during three years

12 'What time .... ?' 'About an hour ago.'
A has Ann phoned B Ann has phoned C did Ann phone D is Ann phoning

13 What .... when you saw her?
A did Sue wear B was Sue wearing C has Sue worn D was wearing Sue

14 'Can you drive?' 'No, ... a car but I want to learn.'
A I never drove B I'm never driving C I've never driven
D I was never driving

15 I saw Lisa at the station when I was going to work this morning but she .... me.
A didn't see B don't see C hasn't seen D didn't saw

passive

UNITS 21–22, APPENDIX 1

24 Complete the sentences.

1

These houses *were built* 20 years ago. Before that there was a cinema here but the building .... (damage) in a fire and had to .... (knock down).

2

This bridge .... (build) in 1925. It .... (use) by hundreds of people every day. At the moment the bridge .... (paint).

3

This street .... (call) Wilton Street. It used to .... (call) James Street but the name .... (change) a few years ago.

4

This is a bicycle factory. Bicycles .... (make) here since 1931. It's the largest bicycle factory in the country – hundreds of bicycles .... (produce) here every year.

25 Complete the sentences.

1 We *were invited* (invite) to the party but we didn't go.
2 The museum is very popular. Every year it .... (visit) by thousands of people.
3 Many buildings .... (damage) in the storm last week.
4 A new road is going to .... (build) next year.
5 'Where's your jacket?' 'It .... (clean). It will be ready tomorrow.'
6 She's famous now, but in a few years her name will .... (forget).
7 'Shall I do the washing-up?' 'No, it .... (already/do).'
8 Milk should .... (keep) in a fridge.
9 .... (you/ever/bite) by a snake?
10 My bag .... (steal) from my car yesterday afternoon.

26 Write a new sentence with the same meaning.

1 Somebody has stolen my keys. — *My keys have been stolen.*
2 Somebody stole my car last week. — My car ....
3 Somebody wants you on the phone. — You ....
4 Somebody has eaten the bananas. — The ....
5 Somebody will repair the machine. — The ....
6 Somebody is watching us. — We ....
7 Somebody has to buy the food. — The ....

27 Active or passive? Complete the sentences.

1 They *are building* (build) a new airport at the moment.
2 These shirts are clean now. They *have been washed* (wash).
3 'How did you fall?' 'Somebody .... (push) me.'
4 'How did you fall?' 'I .... (push).'
5 I can't find my bag. Somebody .... (take) it!
6 My watch is broken. It .... (repair) at the moment.
7 Who .... (invent) the camera?
8 When .... (the camera/invent)?
9 The letter was for me, so why .... (they/send) it to you?
10 The information will .... (send) to you as soon as possible.

future

UNITS 26–29

28 Which is the best alternative?

1 *We're having* a party next Sunday. I hope you can come.
A We have B We're having C We'll have

2 Do you know about Sally? .... her job. She told me last week.
A She leaves B She's going to leave C She'll leave

3 There's a programme on television that I want to watch. .... in five minutes.
A It starts B It's starting C It will start

4 The weather is nice now but I think .... later.
A it rains B it's raining C it will rain

5 'What .... next weekend?' 'Nothing special. Why?'
A do you do B are you doing C will you do

6 'When you see Ann, can you ask her to phone me?' 'OK, ... her.'
A I ask B I'm going to ask C I'll ask

7 'What would you like to drink, tea or coffee?' '............ tea, please.'
A I have B I'm going to have C I'll have

8 Don't take that newspaper away. .... it.
A I read B I'm going to read C I'll read

9 Rachel is ill, so .... to the party tomorrow night.
A she doesn't come B she isn't coming C she won't come

10 I want to meet Sarah at the station. What time ....?
A does her train arrive B is her train going to arrive C is her train arriving

11 'Will you be at home tomorrow evening?' 'No. ....'
A I go out B I'm going out C I'll go out

12 '............ you tomorrow?' 'Yes, OK.'
A Do I phone B Am I going to phone C Shall I phone

past, present and future

UNITS 3–20, 26–29

29 Complete the sentences.

1 A: *Did you go* (you/go) out last night?
B: No, ... (I/stay) at home.
A: What .... (you/do)?
B: .... (I/watch) television.
A: .... (you/go) out tomorrow night?
B: Yes, ... (I/go) to the cinema.
A: Which film .... (you/see)?
B: .... (I/not/know). .... (I/not/decide) yet.

2 A: Are you on holiday here?
B: Yes, we are.
A: How long .... (you/be) here?
B: .... (we/arrive) yesterday.
A: And how long .... (you/stay)?
B: Until the end of next week.
A: And .... (you/like) it here?
B: Yes, ... (we/have) a wonderful time.

3 A: Oh, ... (I/just/remember) – .... (Jill/phone) while you were out.
B: .... (she/always/phone) when I'm not here. .... (she/leave) a message?
A: No, but .... (she/want) you to phone her back as soon as possible.
B: OK, ... (I/phone) her now. .... (you/know) her number?
A: It's in my address book. .... (I/get) it for you.

4 A: .... (I/go) out with Chris and Steve this evening. .... (you/want) to come with us?
B: Yes, where .... (you/go)?
A: To the Italian restaurant in North Street. .... (you/ever/eat) there?
B: Yes, ... (I/be) there two or three times. In fact I .... (go) there last night but I'd love to go again!

5 A: .... (I/lose) my glasses again. .... (you/see) them?
B: .... (you/wear) them when .... (I/come) in.
A: Well, ... (I/not/wear) them now, so where are they?
B: .... (you/look) in the kitchen?
A: No, ... (I/go) and look now

30 Which is correct?

1 Don't forget to switch off the light before you go out.
A switch B to switch C switching

2 It's late. I must .... now.
A go B to go C going

3 I'm sorry but I haven't got time .... to you now.
A for talking B to talk C talking

4 Bill is always in the kitchen. He enjoys ....
A cook B to cook C cooking

5 We've decided .... away for a few days.
A go B to go C going

6 You're making too much noise. Can you please stop .... ?
A shout B to shout C shouting

7 Would you like .... to dinner on Sunday?
A come B to come C coming

8 That bag is too heavy for you. Let me .... you.
A help B to help C helping

9 There's a swimming pool near my house. I go .... every day.
A to swim B to swimming C swimming

10 Did you use a dictionary .... the letter?
A to translate B for translating C for translate

11 I'd love .... a car like yours.
A have B to have C having

12 Could you .... me with this bag, please?
A help B to help C helping

13 I don't mind .... here but I'd prefer to sit by the window.
A sit B to sit C sitting

14 Do you want .... you?
A that I help B me to help C me helping

15 I always read the newspaper before .... work.
A start B to start C starting

16 I wasn't feeling very well but the medicine made me .... better.
A feel B to feel C feeling

17 Shall I phone the restaurant .... a table?
A for reserve B for reserving C to reserve

18 Tom looked at me without .... anything.
A say B saying C to say

31 Complete the sentences.

32 Put in **a/an** or **the** where necessary. If **a/an/the** are not necessary, leave an empty space (–).

1 Who is ...the... best player in your team?
2 I don't watch ...–... television very often.
3 'Is there ...a... bank near here?' 'Yes, at ...the... end of this street.'
4 I can't ride .... horse.
5 .... sky is very clear tonight.
6 Do you live here or are you .... tourist?
7 What did you have for .... lunch?
8 Who was .... first President of .... United States?
9 'What time is it?' 'I don't know. I haven't got .... watch.'
10 I'm sorry but I've forgotten your name. I can never remember .... names.
11 What time is .... next train to London?
12 Kate never writes .... letters. She prefers to phone people.
13 'Where's Sue?' 'She's in .... garden.'
14 Excuse me, I'm looking for .... Majestic Hotel. Is it near here?
15 Gary was ill .... last week, so he didn't go to .... work.
16 Everest is .... highest mountain in .... world.
17 I usually listen to .... radio while I'm having .... breakfast.
18 I like .... sport. My favourite sport is .... basketball.
19 Julia is .... doctor. Her husband is .... art teacher.
20 My apartment is on .... second floor. Turn left at .... top of .... stairs, and it's on .... right.
21 After .... dinner, we watched .... television.
22 Last year we had .... wonderful holiday in .... south of .... France.

prepositions

UNITS 96–101, 104

33 Put in a preposition (**in/for/by** etc.).

1 Helen is studying law ...at... university.
2 What is the longest river .... Europe?
3 Is there anything .... television this evening?
4 We arrived .... the hotel after midnight.
5 'Where's Mike?' 'He's .... holiday.'
6 Tom hasn't got up yet. He's still .... bed.
7 Linda is away. She's been away .... Monday.
8 The next meeting is .... 15 April.
9 I usually go to work .... car.
10 There's too much sugar .... my coffee.
11 Kevin lived in London .... six months. He didn't like it very much.
12 Were there a lot of people .... the party?
13 What are you doing .... the moment? Are you working?
14 I don't know any of the people .... this photograph.
15 The train was very slow. It stopped .... every station.
16 I like this room. I like the pictures .... the walls.
17 'Did you buy that picture?' 'No, it was given to me .... a friend of mine.'
18 I'm going away .... a few days. I'll be back .... Thursday.
19 Silvia has gone .... Italy. She's .... Milan at the moment.
20 Ann left school .... fifteen and got a job .... a shop.

Key to Exercises

UNIT 1

1.1
2 they're
3 it's not / it isn't
4 that's
5 I'm not
6 you're not / you aren't

1.2
2 'm/am	6 are
3 is	7 is ... are
4 are	8 'm/am ... is
5 's/is	

1.3
2 My brother **is** a teacher.
3 This house **isn't / is not** very big.
4 The shops **aren't / are not** open today.
5 My keys **are** in my bag.
6 Jenny **is** 18 years old.
7 You **aren't / are not** very tall.

1.4
Example answers:
1 My name is Robert.
2 I'm from Australia.
3 I'm 25.
4 I'm a computer programmer.
5 I'm married.
6 My favourite colours are black and white.
7 I'm interested in machines.

1.5
2 They're/They are cold.
3 He's/He is hot.
4 He's/He is afraid.
5 They're/They are hungry.
6 She's/She is angry.

1.6
2 **I'm / I am** hungry. *or* **I'm not / I am not** hungry.
3 **It's / It is** warm today. *or* **It isn't / It's not** warm today.
4 **I'm / I am** afraid of dogs. *or* **I'm not / I am not** afraid of dogs.
5 My hands **are** cold. *or* My hands **aren't / are not** cold.
6 Canada **is** a very big country.
7 Diamonds **aren't / are not** cheap.
8 **I'm / I am** interested in football. *or* **I'm not / I am not** interested in football.
9 Rome **isn't / is not** in Spain.

UNIT 2

2.1
2 F	6 E
3 H	7 B
4 C	8 I
5 A	9 D

2.2
3 Is your job interesting?
4 Are the shops open today?
5 Are you interested in sport?
6 Is the post office near here?
7 Are your children at school?
8 Why are you late?

2.3
2 Where is
3 How old are
4 How much are
5 What is
6 Who is
7 What colour are

2.4
2 Are you married or single?
3 Are you American?
4 How old are you?
5 Are you a teacher?
6 Is your wife a lawyer?
7 Where's/Where is she from?
8 What's/What is her name?
9 How old is she?

2.5
2 Yes, I am. *or* No, I'm not.
3 Yes, it is. *or* No, it isn't. / No, it's not.
4 Yes, they are. *or* No, they aren't. / No, they're not.
5 Yes, it is. *or* No, it isn't. / No, it's not.
6 Yes, I am. *or* No, I'm not.

UNIT 3

3.1
2 's/is waiting
3 're/are playing
4 He's/He is lying
5 They're/They are having
6 She's/She is sitting

3.2
2 's/is cooking
3 're/are standing
4 is swimming
5 're/are staying
6 's/is having
7 're/are building
8 'm/am going

3.3
3 She's/She is sitting on the floor.
4 She's not/She isn't reading a book.
5 She's not/She isn't playing the piano.
6 She's/She is laughing.
7 She's/She is wearing a hat.
8 She's not/She isn't writing a letter.

3.4
3 I'm sitting on a chair. *or* I'm not sitting on a chair.
4 I'm eating. *or* I'm not eating.
5 It's raining. *or* It isn't raining. / It's not raining.
6 I'm learning English.
7 I'm listening to music. *or* I'm not listening to music.
8 The sun is shining. *or* The sun isn't shining.
9 I'm wearing shoes. *or* I'm not wearing shoes.
10 I'm not reading a newspaper.

UNIT 4

4.1

2 Are you going now?
3 Is it raining?
4 Are you enjoying the film?
5 Is that clock working?
6 Are you writing a letter?

4.2

2 Where is she going?
3 What are you eating?
4 Why are you crying?
5 What are they looking at?
6 Why is he laughing?

4.3

3 Are you listening to me?
4 Where are your friends going?
5 Are your parents watching television?
6 What is Ann cooking?
7 Why are you looking at me?
8 Is the bus coming?

4.4

2 Yes, I am. *or* No, I'm not.
3 Yes, I am. *or* No, I'm not.
4 Yes, it is. *or* No, it isn't. / No, it's not.
5 Yes, I am. *or* No, I'm not.
6 Yes, I am. *or* No, I'm not.

UNIT 5

5.1

2 thinks
3 flies
4 dances
5 has
6 finishes

5.2

2 live
3 She eats
4 They play
5 They go
6 He sleeps

5.3

2 open
3 closes
4 teaches
5 meet
6 washes
7 costs
8 cost
9 boils
10 like … likes

5.4

2 I often play basketball.
3 Margaret usually works hard.
4 Jenny always wears nice clothes.
5 We always have dinner at 7.30.
6 Tim never watches television.
7 Children usually like chocolate.
8 Julia always enjoys parties.

5.5

Example answers:
2 I usually read in bed.
3 I often get up before 7 o'clock.
4 I never go to work by bus.
5 I usually drink two cups of coffee in the morning.

UNIT 6

6.1

2 Jane doesn't play the piano very well.
3 They don't know my phone number.
4 We don't work very hard.
5 He doesn't have a bath every day.
6 You don't do the same thing every day.

6.2

2 Carol doesn't like classical music.
I like (*or* I don't like) classical music.
3 Bill and Rose don't like boxing.
Carol likes boxing.
I like (*or* I don't like) boxing.
4 Bill and Rose like horror films.
Carol doesn't like horror films.
I like (*or* I don't like) horror films.

6.3

2-5 *You can use:*
I never… (go/ride *etc.*) *or*
I often… *or*
I don't…very often.

6.4

2 doesn't use
3 don't go
4 doesn't wear
5 don't know
6 doesn't cost
7 don't see

6.5

3 don't know
4 doesn't talk
5 drinks
6 don't believe
7 like
8 doesn't eat

UNIT 7

7.1

2 Do you play tennis?
3 Does Ann play tennis?
4 Do your friends live near here?
5 Does your brother speak English?
6 Do you do exercises every morning?
7 Does Paul often go away?
8 Do you want to be famous?
9 Does Linda work hard?

7.2

3 How often do you watch TV?
4 What do you want for dinner?
5 Do you like football?
6 Does your brother like football?
7 What do you do in the evenings?
8 Where does your sister work?
9 Do you often go to the cinema?
10 What does this word mean?
11 Does it often snow here?
12 What time do you usually go to bed?
13 How much does it cost to phone New York?
14 What do you usually have for breakfast?

7.3

2 Do you enjoy / Do you like
3 do you start
4 Do you work
5 do you go
6 does he do
7 does he teach
8 Does he enjoy / Does he like

7.4

2 Yes, I do. *or* No, I don't.
3 Yes, I do. *or* No, I don't.
4 Yes, it does. *or* No, it doesn't.
5 Yes, I do. *or* No, I don't.

UNIT 8

8.1

2 No, she isn't.
Yes, she does.
She's playing the piano.
3 Yes, he does.
Yes, he is.
He's cleaning a window.
4 No, they aren't.
Yes, they do.
They teach.

8.2

2 don't
3 are
4 does
5 's/is … don't
6 do
7 does
8 doesn't

8.3

4 is singing
5 She wants
6 do you read
7 you're/you are sitting
8 I don't understand
9 I'm going … Are you coming
10 does your father
11 I'm not listening
12 He's / He is cooking
13 doesn't usually drive … usually walks
14 doesn't like … She prefers

UNIT 9

9.1

2 he's got
3 they've got
4 she hasn't got
5 it's got
6 I haven't got

9.2

2 Have you got a passport? *or* Do you have …?
3 Has your father got a car? *or* Does your father have …?
4 Has Carol got many friends? *or* Does Carol have …?
5 Have you got any brothers or sisters? *or* Do you have …?
6 How much money have we got? *or* … do we have?
7 What kind of car has Julia got? *or* … does Julia have?

9.3

2 Tina hasn't got a bicycle. / Tina doesn't have a bicycle.
I've got a bicycle. / I have a bicycle. *or* I haven't got a bicycle. / I don't have a bicycle.
3 Tina has got long hair. / Tina has long hair.
I've got long hair. / I have long hair. *or* I haven't got long hair. / I don't have long hair.
4 Tina has got two sisters and two brothers. / Tina has two….
(example answer) I've got two brothers and one sister.

9.4

3 's got / has got
4 haven't got
5 've got / have got
6 haven't got
7 hasn't got

9.5

3 have got four wheels (*or* have four wheels)
4 's got / has got a lot of friends (*or* has a lot of friends)
5 've got / have got a toothache. (*or* have a toothache)
6 hasn't got a key (*or* doesn't have a key)
7 has got six legs (*or* has six legs)
8 haven't got much time (*or* don't have much time)

UNIT 10

10.1

2 Carol and Jack were at/in the cinema.
3 Sue was at the station.
4 Mr and Mrs Hall were in/at a restaurant.
5 Ben was on the beach / on a beach / at the seaside.
6 *(example answer)* I was at work.

10.2

2 is … was
3 am
4 was
5 were
6 are
7 Was
8 was
9 are … were

10.3

2 wasn't … was
3 was … were
4 Were … was … wasn't
5 were
6 weren't … were

10.4

2 Was your exam difficult?
3 Where were Ann and Chris last week?
4 How much was your new camera?
5 Why were you angry yesterday?
6 Was the weather nice last week?

UNIT 11

11.1

2 opened
3 started … finished
4 wanted
5 happened
6 rained
7 enjoyed … stayed
8 died

11.2

2 saw
3 played
4 paid
5 visited
6 bought
7 went
8 thought
9 copied
10 knew
11 put
12 spoke

11.3

2 got
3 had
4 left
5 drove
6 arrived
7 parked
8 went
9 had
10 went
11 waited
12 departed
13 arrived
14 took

11.4

2 lost her keys
3 met her friends
4 bought two newspapers
5 went to the cinema
6 ate an orange
7 had a shower
8 came (to see us)

11.5

Example answers:
2 I got up late yesterday.
3 I met some friends at lunchtime.
4 I played volleyball.
5 I wrote a letter.
6 I lost my keys.

UNIT 12

12.1

2 didn't work
3 didn't go
4 didn't have
5 didn't do

12.2

2 Did you enjoy the party?
3 Did you have a good holiday?
4 Did you finish work early?
5 Did you sleep well last night?

12.3

2 I got up before 7 o'clock. *or* I didn't get up before 7 o'clock.
3 I had a shower. *or* I didn't have a shower.
4 I bought a magazine. *or* I didn't buy a magazine.
5 I ate meat. *or* I didn't eat meat.
6 I went to bed before 10.30. *or* I didn't go to bed before 10.30.

12.4

2 did you arrive
3 Did you win
4 did you go
5 did it cost
6 Did you go to bed late
7 Did you have a nice time
8 did it happen / did that happen

12.5

2 bought
3 Did it rain
4 didn't stay
5 opened
6 didn't have
7 did you do

UNIT 13

13.1

2 Carol and Jack were at/in the cinema. They were watching a film.
3 Tom was in his car. He was driving.
4 Catherine was at the station. She was waiting for a train.
5 Mr and Mrs Hall were in the park. They were walking.
6 I was in a café. I was having a drink with some friends.

13.2

2 she was swimming / she was having a swim.
3 she was reading a/the newspaper.
4 she was cooking (lunch).
5 she was having breakfast.
6 she was listening to music/… listening to the radio.

13.3

2 What were you doing
3 Was it raining
4 Why was Ann driving so fast
5 Was Tim wearing a suit

13.4

2 He was carrying a bag.
3 He wasn't going to the dentist.
4 He was eating an ice-cream.
5 He wasn't carrying an umbrella.
6 He wasn't going home.
7 He was wearing a hat.
8 He wasn't riding a bicycle.

UNIT 14

14.1

1 happened … was painting … fell
2 arrived … got … were waiting
3 was walking … met … was going … was carrying… stopped

14.2

2 was studying
3 did the post arrive … came … was having
4 didn't go
5 were you driving … stopped … wasn't driving
6 Did your team win … didn't play
7 did you break the window … were playing … kicked … hit
8 Did you see … was wearing
9 were you doing
10 lost … did you get … climbed

UNIT 15

15.1

2 She has closed the door.
3 They have gone to bed.
4 It has stopped raining.
5 He has had a bath.
6 The picture has fallen down.

15.2

2 've bought / have bought
3 's gone / has gone
4 Have you seen
5 has broken
6 've told / have told
7 has taken
8 has she gone
9 've forgotten / have forgotten
10 's invited / has invited
11 Have you decided
12 haven't seen

UNIT 16

16.1

2 He's/He has just got up.
3 They've/They have just bought a car.
4 The race has just started.

16.2

2 they've/they have already seen it.
3 I've/I have already phoned him.
4 He's/He has already gone (away).
5 I've/I have already read it.
6 She's/She has already started (it).

16.3

2 The bus has just gone.
3 The bus hasn't gone yet.
4 He hasn't opened it yet.
5 They've/They have just finished their dinner.
6 It hasn't stopped raining yet.

16.4

2 Have you met your new neighbours yet?
3 Have you written the letter yet?
4 Has he/Tom sold his car yet?

UNIT 17

17.1

3 Have you ever been to Australia?
4 Have you ever lost your passport?
5 Have you ever flown in a helicopter?
6 Have you ever eaten Chinese food?
7 Have you ever been to New York?
8 Have you ever driven a bus?
9 Have you ever broken your leg?

17.2

Helen:
2 Helen has never been to Australia.
3 Helen/She has eaten Chinese food a few times.
4 Helen/She has never driven a bus.

You (example answers):
5 I've / I have never been to New York.
6 I've / I have played tennis many times.
7 I've / I have never flown in a helicopter.
8 I've / I have been late for work a few times.

17.3

2–6
She has done a lot of interesting things.
She has travelled all over the world. *or* She has been all over the world.
She has been married three times.
She has written ten books.
She has met a lot of interesting people.

17.4

2 gone
3 been ... been
4 been
5 gone
6 been
7 been
8 gone

UNIT 18

18.1

3 have been
4 has been
5 have lived / have been living
6 has worked / has been working
7 has had
8 have been learning

18.2

2 How long have they been there / in Brazil?
3 How long have you known her?
4 How long has she been learning Italian?
5 How long has he lived in Canada? / How long has he been living ...?
6 How long have you been a teacher?
7 How long has it been raining?

18.3

2 She has lived in Wales all her life.
3 They have been on holiday since Sunday.
4 The sun has been shining all day.
5 She has been waiting for ten minutes.
6 He has had a beard since he was 20.

18.4

2 know
3 have known
4 have you been
5 works
6 has been
7 have you lived
8 I've had
9 is ... has been

UNIT 19

19.1

3 for
4 since
5 since
6 for
7 for
8 for ... since

19.2

Example answers:
2 A year ago.
3 A few days ago.
4 Two hours ago.
5 Six months ago.

19.3

3 for 20 years
4 20 years ago
5 ten minutes ago
6 an hour ago
7 for six months
8 for a long time
9 a few days ago

19.4

2 been here since Tuesday.
3 raining for an hour.
4 known Sue for two years.
5 had my/a camera since 1989.
6 been married for six months.
7 been studying medicine (at university) for three years.
8 played / been playing the piano since he was seven years old.

19.5

Example answers:
1 I've lived in ... all my life.
2 I've been in the same job for ten years.
3 I've been learning English for six months.
4 I've known Chris for a long time.
5 I've had a headache since I got up this morning.

UNIT 20

20.1

2 I started (it) last week.
3 they arrived at 5 o'clock.
4 she went (away) on Friday.
5 I wore them yesterday.

20.2

3 WRONG – I finished
4 RIGHT
5 WRONG – did you finish
6 RIGHT
7 WRONG – Jim's grandmother died
8 WRONG – Where were you

20.3

3 played
4 did you go
5 Have you ever met
6 wasn't
7 've/have just washed

8 washed
9 's/has visited
10 hasn't come

20.4

1 Did you have
was
2 Have you seen
went
haven't seen
3 has worked / has been working
was
worked
didn't enjoy
4 've/have seen
've/have never spoken
Have you ever spoken
met

UNIT 21

21.1

3 Glass is made from sand.
4 Stamps are sold in a post office.
5 This room isn't used very often.
6 Are we allowed to park here?
7 How is this word pronounced?
9 The house was painted last month.
10 Three people were injured in the accident.
11 My bicycle was stolen a few days ago.
12 When was this bridge built?
13 Were you invited to the party last week?
14 How were these windows broken?
15 I wasn't woken up by the noise.

21.2

2 Football **is played** in most …
3 Why **was the letter sent** to …?
4 … where cars **are repaired**.
5 Where **were** you born?
6 How many languages **are spoken** …
7 … but nothing **was** stolen.
8 When **was** the bicycle **invented**?

21.3

3 is made
4 were damaged
5 was given
6 are shown
7 were invited
8 was made
9 was stolen … was found

21.4

2 Sally was born in Birmingham.
3 Her parents were born in Ireland.
4 I was born in …
5 My mother was born in …

UNIT 22

22.1

2 A bridge is being built.
3 The windows are being cleaned.
4 The grass is being cut.

22.2

3 The window **has been** broken.
4 The roof **is being** repaired.
5 The car **has been** damaged.
6 The houses **are being** knocked down.
7 The trees **have been** cut down.
8 They **have been** invited to a party.

22.3

3 has been repaired
4 was repaired
5 are made
6 were they built
7 Is the computer being used (*or* Is anybody using the computer)
8 are they called
9 were blown
10 was damaged … hasn't been repaired

UNIT 23

23.1

3 are
4 Does
5 Do
6 Is
7 do
8 Is
9 does
10 Are

23.2

2 don't
3 'm/am not
4 isn't
5 don't
6 doesn't
7 'm/am not
8 aren't

23.3

2 Did
3 were
4 was
5 Has
6 did
7 were
8 Has
9 did
10 have

23.4

2 was
3 Have
4 are
5 were
6 've/have
7 is
8 was
9 has

23.5

3 eaten
4 enjoying
5 damaged
6 use
7 gone away
8 understand
9 listening
10 pronounced
11 open

UNIT 24

24.1

3 got
4 brought
5 paid
6 enjoyed
7 bought
8 sat
9 left
10 happened
11 heard
12 put
13 caught
14 watched
15 understood

24.2

2 began begun
3 ate eaten
4 drank drunk
5 drove driven
6 ran run
7 spoke spoken
8 wrote written
9 came come
10 knew known
11 took taken
12 went gone
13 gave given
14 threw thrown
15 forgot forgotten

24.3

3 slept
4 saw
5 rained
6 lost … seen
7 stolen
8 went
9 finished
10 built

11 learnt/learned
12 ridden
13 known
14 fell ... hurt

24.4

2 told
3 won
4 met
5 woken up
6 swam
7 thought
8 spoken
9 cost
10 driven
11 sold
12 flew

UNIT 25

25.1

2 He used to play football.
3 She used to be a taxi driver.
4 They used to live in the country.
5 He used to wear glasses.
6 This building used to be a hotel.

25.2

2–6
She used to play volleyball.
She used to go out most evenings. / She used to go out in the evenings.
She used to play the guitar.
She used to read a lot. / She used to like reading.
She used to go away two or three times a year. / She used to travel a lot.

25.3

3 used to have
4 used to be
5 go
6 used to eat
7 watches
8 used to live
9 get
10 did you use to play

UNIT 26

26.1

2 Richard is going to the cinema.
3 Barbara is meeting Dave.
4 Denise is having lunch with Ken.
5 Tom and Sue are going to a party.

26.2

2 Are you working next week?
3 What are you doing tomorrow evening?
4 What time are your friends arriving?
5 When is Liz going on holiday?

26.3

Example answers:
3 I'm going away at the weekend.
4 I'm playing basketball tomorrow.
5 I'm meeting a friend this evening.
6 I'm going to the cinema on Thursday evening.

26.4

3 She's getting
4 are going ... are they going
5 finishes
6 I'm not going
7 I'm going ... We're meeting
8 are you getting ... leaves
9 does the film begin
10 are you doing ... I'm working

UNIT 27

27.1

2 I'm going to buy a newspaper.
3 We're going to play football.
4 I'm going to have a bath.

27.2

3 'm/am going to walk
4 's/is going to stay
5 'm/am going to eat
6 're/are going to give
7 's/is going to lie down
8 Are you going to watch
9 is Rachel going to do

27.3

2 The shelf is going to fall (down).
3 The car is going to turn (left).
4 He's/He is going to kick the ball.

27.4

Example answers:
1 I'm going to phone Ann this evening.
2 I'm going to get up early tomorrow.
3 I'm going to buy some new clothes tomorrow.

UNIT 28

28.1

2 she'll be
3 she was
4 she'll be
5 she's
6 she was
7 she'll be

28.2

Example answers:
2 I'll be at home.
3 I'll probably be in bed.
4 I'll be at work.
5 I don't know where I'll be.

28.3

2 'll/will
3 won't
4 won't
5 'll/will
6 'll/will
7 won't

28.4

3 I think we'll win the game.
4 I don't think I'll be here tomorrow.
5 I think Sue will like her present.
6 I don't think they'll get married.
7 I don't think you'll enjoy the film.

28.5

2 are you doing
3 They're going
4 she'll lend
5 I'm going
6 will phone
7 He's working
8 Will

UNIT 29

29.1

2 I'll send
3 I'll eat
4 I'll sit
5 I'll do
6 I'll stay
7 I'll show

29.2

2 I think I'll have
3 I don't think I'll play
4 I don't think I'll buy

29.3

2 I'll do
3 I watch
4 I'll go
5 is going to buy
6 I'll give
7 Are you doing ... I'm going

29.4

2 Shall I turn off the television?
3 Shall I make some sandwiches?
4 Shall I turn on the light?

29.5

2 where shall we go?
3 what shall we buy?
4 who shall we invite?

UNIT 30

30.1

2 I might see you tomorrow.
3 Ann might forget to phone.
4 It might snow today.
5 I might be late tonight.
6 Mary might not be here.
7 I might not have time to meet you.

30.2

2 I might go away.
3 I might see her on Monday.
4 I might have fish.
5 I might get/take a taxi. *or* ... go by taxi.
6 I might buy a new car.

30.3

3 He might get up early.
4 He isn't / He's not working tomorrow.
5 He might be at home tomorrow morning.
6 He might watch television.
7 He's going out in the afternoon.
8 He might go shopping.

30.4

Example answers:
1 I might read a newspaper.
2 I might go for a drink with some friends.
3 I might have an egg for breakfast.

UNIT 31

31.1

2 Can you ski?
3 Can you play chess?
4 Can you run ten kilometres?
5 Can you drive?
6 Can you ride a horse?
7 I can/can't swim.
8 I can/can't ski.
9 I can/can't play chess.
10 I can/can't run ten kilometres.
11 I can/can't drive.
12 I can/can't ride a horse.

31.2

2 can see
3 can't hear
4 can't find
5 can speak

31.3

2 couldn't eat
3 can't decide
4 couldn't find
5 can't go
6 couldn't go

31.4

2 Can/Could you pass the salt, (please)?
3 Can/Could you turn off the radio, (please)?
4 Can/Could I have tomato soup, (please)?
5 Can/Could you give me your phone number, (please)?
6 Can/Could I borrow your pen, (please)? *or* Can/Could you lend me...?

UNIT 32

32.1

2 must meet
3 must wash
4 must learn
5 must go
6 must win
7 must be

32.2

2 I must
3 I had to
4 I must
5 I had to
6 I had to
7 I must

32.3

2 needn't hurry
3 mustn't lose
4 needn't wait
5 mustn't forget
6 needn't write

32.4

2 C
3 A
4 E
5 B

32.5

3 needn't
4 had to
5 must
6 mustn't
7 must
8 had to
9 needn't

UNIT 33

33.1

2 You should go
3 You should clean
4 you should visit
5 you should wear
6 You should take

33.2

2 He shouldn't eat so much.
3 She shouldn't work so hard.
4 He shouldn't drive so fast.

33.3

2 Do you think I should learn (to drive)?
3 Do you think I should get another job?
4 Do you think I should invite Gary (to the party)?

33.4

3 I think you should sell it.
4 I think she should have a holiday.
5 I don't think they should get married.
6 I don't think you should go to work.
7 I think he should go to the doctor.
8 I don't think we should stay there.

33.5

Example answers:
2 I think everybody should have enough food.
3 I think people should drive carefully.
4 I don't think the police should carry guns.
5 I think I should do more exercise.

UNIT 34

34.1

2 have to do
3 has to read
4 have to speak
5 has to travel

34.2

2 have to go
3 had to buy
4 have to change
5 had to answer

34.3

2 did he have to wait
3 does she have to go
4 did you have to pay
5 do you have to do

34.4

2 doesn't have to wait.
3 didn't have to get up early.
4 doesn't have to work (so) hard.
5 don't have to leave now.

34.5

3 have to pay
4 had to borrow
5 must stop *or* have to stop
6 has to meet
7 must tell *or* have to tell

34.6

2 I have to go to work every day.
3 I have to write a letter tomorrow.
4 I had to go to the dentist yesterday.

UNIT 35

35.1

2 Would you like an apple?
3 Would you like some coffee? / … a cup of coffee?
4 Would you like some cheese? / … a piece of cheese?
5 Would you like a sandwich?
6 Would you like some cake? / … a piece of cake?

35.2

2 Would you like to play tennis tomorrow?
3 Would you like to see my holiday photographs?
4 Would you like to go to a concert next week?
5 Would you like to borrow my umbrella?

35.3

2 Do you like
3 Would you like
4 would you like
5 Would you like
6 I like
7 would you like
8 Would you like
9 Do you like
10 I'd like

UNIT 36

36.1

3 There's / There is a hospital.
4 There isn't a swimming pool.
5 There are two cinemas.
6 There isn't a university.
7 There aren't any big hotels.

36.2

Example answers:
3 There is a university in …
4 There are a lot of big shops.
5 There isn't an airport.
6 There aren't many factories.

36.3

2 There's / There is
3 is there
4 There are
5 are there
6 there isn't
7 Is there
8 Are there
9 There's / There is … There aren't

36.4

2–6
There are nine planets in the solar system.
There are fifteen players in a rugby team.
There are twenty-six letters in the English alphabet.
There are thirty days in September.
There are fifty states in the USA.

36.5

2 It's
3 There's
4 There's … Is it
5 Is there … there's
6 It's
7 Is there

UNIT 37

37.1

2 There was a carpet
3 There were three pictures
4 There was a small table
5 There were some flowers
6 There were some books
7 There was an armchair
8 There was a sofa

37.2

3 There was
4 Was there
5 there weren't
6 There wasn't
7 Were there
8 There wasn't
9 There was
10 there weren't

37.3

2 There are
3 There was
4 There's / There is
5 There's been / There has been
6 there was
7 there will be
8 there were … there are
9 There have been
10 there will be (*or* there are)

UNIT 38

38.1

2 It's cold.
3 It's windy.
4 It's sunny/fine. *or* It's a nice day.
5 It's snowing.
6 It's cloudy.

38.2

2 It's / It is
3 Is it
4 is it … it's / it is
5 It's / It is
6 Is it
7 is it
8 It's / It is
9 It's / It is

38.3

2 How far is it from the hotel to the beach?
3 How far is it from New York to Washington?
4 How far is it from your house to the airport?

38.4

3 It	6 it
4 There	7 There
5 It	8 It

38.5

2 It's nice to see you again.
3 It's impossible to work in this office.
4 It's easy to make friends.
5 It's interesting to visit different places.
6 It's dangerous to go out alone

UNIT 39

39.1

2 is	5 will
3 can	6 was
4 has	

39.2

2 'm not	5 isn't
3 weren't	6 hasn't
4 haven't	

39.3

3 doesn't	6 does
4 do	7 don't
5 did	8 didn't

39.4

Example answers:

2 I like sport but my sister doesn't.
3 I don't eat meat but Jenny does.
4 I'm American but my husband isn't.
5 I haven't been to Japan but Jenny has.

39.5

2 wasn't	7 has
3 are	8 do
4 has	9 hasn't
5 can't	10 will
6 did	11 might

39.6

2 Yes, I have. *or* No, I haven't.
3 Yes, I do. *or* No, I don't.
4 Yes, it is. *or* No, it isn't.
5 Yes, I am. *or* No, I'm not.
6 Yes, I do. *or* No, I don't.
7 Yes, I will. *or* No, I won't.
8 Yes, I have. *or* No, I haven't.
9 Yes, I did. *or* No, I didn't.
10 Yes, I was. *or* No, I wasn't.

UNIT 40

40.1

2 Do you?	5 Do I?
3 Didn't you?	6 Did she?
4 Doesn't she?	

40.2

3 Have you?	8 Aren't you?
4 Can't she?	9 Did you?
5 Were you?	10 Does she?
6 Didn't you?	11 Won't you?
7 Is there?	12 Isn't it?

40.3

2 aren't they
3 wasn't she
4 haven't you
5 don't you
6 doesn't he
7 won't you

40.4

2 are you	6 didn't she
3 isn't she	7 was it
4 can't you	8 doesn't she
5 do you	9 will you

UNIT 41

41.1

2 either	5 either
3 too	6 either
4 too	7 too

41.2

2 So am I.	9 Neither have I.
3 So have I.	10 Neither am I.
4 So do I.	11 Neither do I.
5 So will I.	
6 So was I.	
7 Neither can I.	
8 Neither did I.	

41.3

1 So am I.
2 So can I. *or* I can't.
3 Neither am I. *or* I am.
4 So do I. *or* I don't.
5 Neither do I. *or* I do.
6 So did I. *or* I didn't.
7 Neither have I. *or* I have.
8 Neither do I. *or* I do.
9 So am I. *or* I'm not.
10 Neither have I. *or* I have.
11 Neither did I. *or* I did.
12 So do I. *or* I don't.

UNIT 42

42.1

2 They aren't / They're not married.
3 I haven't had dinner.
4 It isn't cold today.
5 We won't be late.
6 You shouldn't go.

42.2

2 I don't like cheese.
3 They didn't understand.
4 He doesn't live here.
5 Don't go away!
6 I didn't do the shopping.

42.3

2 They haven't arrived.
3 I didn't go to the bank.
4 He doesn't speak German.
5 We weren't angry.
6 He won't be pleased.
7 Don't phone me tonight.
8 It didn't rain yesterday.
9 I couldn't hear them.
10 I don't believe you.

42.4

2 'm not / am not
3 can't
4 doesn't
5 isn't / 's not
6 don't … haven't
7 Don't
8 didn't
9 haven't
10 won't
11 didn't
12 weren't

42.5

3 He wasn't born in London.
4 He doesn't like London.
5 He'd like to live in the country.
6 He can drive.
7 He hasn't got a car.
8 He doesn't read newspapers.
9 He isn't interested in politics.
10 He watches TV most evenings.
11 He didn't watch TV last night.
12 He went out last night.

UNIT 43

43.1

3 Were you late this morning?
4 Has Ann got a key?
5 Will you be here tomorrow?
6 Is Paul going out this evening?
7 Do you like your job?
8 Does Linda live near here?
9 Did you enjoy your holiday?
10 Did you have a shower this morning?

43.2

2 Do you use it a lot?
3 Did you use it yesterday?
4 Do you enjoy driving?
5 Are you a good driver?
6 Have you ever had an accident?

43.3

3 What are the children doing?
4 How is cheese made?
5 Is your sister coming to the party?
6 Why don't you tell the truth?
7 Have your guests arrived yet?
8 What time does your train leave?
9 Was your car damaged in the accident?
10 Why didn't Ann go to work?

43.4

3 What are you reading?
4 What time did she go (to bed)?
5 When are they going?
6 Where did you meet him?
7 Where has she gone?
8 Why can't you come (to the party)?
9 How much do you need?
10 Why doesn't she like you?
11 How often does it rain?
12 When did you do the shopping?

UNIT 44

44.1

2 What fell off the shelf?
3 Who wants to see me?
4 Who took your umbrella?
5 What made you ill?
6 Who is/Who's coming?

44.2

3 Who did you phone?
4 What happened last night?
5 Who knows the answer?
6 Who did the washing-up?
7 What did Jill do?
8 What woke you up?
9 Who saw the accident?
10 Who did you see?
11 Who has got / Who's got your pen?
12 What does this word mean?

44.3

2 Who phoned you ?
What did she want?
3 Who did you ask?
What did he say?
4 Who got married?
Who told you?
5 Who did you meet?
What did she tell you?
6 Who won?
What did you do (after the game)?
7 Who gave you a book?
What did Catherine give you?

UNIT 45

45.1

2 What are you looking for?
3 Who did you go to the cinema with?
4 What/Who was the film about?
5 Who did you give the money to?
6 Who was the book written by?

45.2

2 What are they looking at?
3 Who is he writing to?
4 What are they talking about?
5 What is she listening to?
6 Which bus are they waiting for?

45.3

2 Which hotel did you stay at?
3 Which (football) team does he play for?
4 Which school did you go to?

45.4

2 What is the food like?
3 What are the people like?
4 What is the weather like?

45.5

2 What was the film like?
3 What were the lessons like?
4 What was the hotel like?

UNIT 46

46.1

3 What colour is it?
4 What time did you get up?
5 What type of music do you like?
6 What kind of car do you want (to buy)?

46.2

2 Which coat
3 Which film
4 Which bus

46.3

3 Which
4 What
5 Which
6 What
7 Which
8 Who
9 What
10 Which
11 What

46.4

2 How far
3 How old
4 How often
5 How deep
6 How long

46.5

2 How heavy is this box?
3 How old are you?
4 How much did you spend?
5 How often do you watch TV?
6 How far is it from Paris to Moscow?

UNIT 47

47.1

2 How long does it take by car from Rome to Milan?
3 How long does it take by train from Paris to Geneva?
4 How long does it take by bus from the city centre to the airport?

47.2

Example answers:
2 It takes … hours to fly from … to New York.
3 It takes … years to study to be a doctor in …
4 It takes … to walk from my home to the nearest shop.
5 It takes … to get from my home to the nearest airport.

47.3

2 How long did it take you to walk to the station?
3 How long did it take him to clean the windows?
4 How long did it take you to learn to ski?
5 How long did it take them to repair the car?

47.4

2 It took us 20 minutes to walk home. / … to get home.
3 It took me six months to learn to drive.
4 It took Mark/him two hours to drive to London. / … to get to London.
5 It took Linda a long time to find a job. / … to get a job.
6 It took me … to …

UNIT 48

48.1

2 I don't know where she is.
3 I don't know how old it is.
4 I don t know when he'll be here.
5 I don't know why he was angry.
6 I don't know how long she has lived here.

48.2

2 where Susan works
3 what Peter said
4 why he went home early
5 what time the film begins
6 how the accident happened

48.3

2 are you
3 they are
4 the museum is
5 do you want
6 elephants eat

48.4

2 Do you know if/whether they are married?
3 Do you know if/whether Sue knows Bill?
4 Do you know if/whether George will be here tomorrow?
5 Do you know if/whether he passed his exam?

48.5

2 Do you know where Paula is?
3 Do you know if/whether she is working today? / … she's working today?
4 Do you know what time she starts work?
5 Do you know if/whether the shops are open tomorrow?
6 Do you know where Sarah and Tim live?
7 Do you know if/whether they went to Ann's party?

48.6

Example answers:
2 Do you know what time the bus leaves?
3 Excuse me, can you tell me where the station is?
4 I don't know what I'm going to do this evening.
5 Do you know if Tom is working today?

UNIT 49

49.1

2 She said (that) she was very busy.
3 She said (that) she couldn't go to the party.
4 He said (that) he had to go out.
5 He said (that) he was learning Russian.
6 She said (that) she didn't feel very well.
7 They said (that) they would be home late. / … they'd be …
8 She said (that) she had just come back from holiday. / … she'd just come back …
9 She said (that) she was going to buy a computer.
10 They said (that) they hadn't got a key. / They said (that) they didn't have a key.

49.2

2 She said (that) she wasn't hungry.
3 he said (that) he needed it.
4 she said (that) she didn't want to go.
5 She said (that) I could have it.
6 He said (that) he would send me a postcard. / … he'd send …
7 Linda said (that) he had gone home. / … he'd gone home.
8 He said (that) he wanted to watch TV.
9 She said (that) she was going to the cinema.

49.3

3 said	7 said
4 told	8 told
5 tell	9 tell
6 say	10 say

UNIT 50

50.1

3 phone
4 phone Paul
5 to phone Paul
6 to phone Paul
7 phone Paul
8 to phone Paul
9 phone Paul
10 phone Paul

50.2

3 get
4 going
5 watch
6 flying
7 listening
8 eat
9 waiting
10 wear
11 doing … staying

50.3

4 to go	13 having
5 rain	14 to have
6 to leave	15 hear
7 help	16 go
8 studying	17 listening
9 to go	18 to make
10 wearing	19 to know … tell
11 to stay	20 use
12 have	

UNIT 51

51.1

3 to see
4 to swim
5 cleaning
6 to go
7 visiting
8 going
9 to be
10 waiting
11 to do
12 to speak
13 to ask
14 crying / to cry
15 to work … talking

51.2

3 reading
4 to see
5 to send
6 walking
7 to lose
8 to help
9 to go
10 watching / to watch
11 to wait
12 raining

51.3

2 going/to go to museums.
3 writing/to write letters.
4 to go (there)
5 travelling by train
6 going to … to eat at

51.4

Example answers:
1 I enjoy cooking.
2 I don't like driving.
3 If it's a nice day tomorrow, I'd like to have a picnic by the lake.
4 When I'm on holiday, I like to do very little.
5 I don't mind travelling alone but I prefer to travel with somebody.
6 I wouldn't like to live in a big city.

UNIT 52

52.1

2 I want you to listen carefully.
3 I don't want you to be angry.
4 Do you want me to wait for you?
5 I don't want you to phone me tonight.
6 I want you to meet Sarah.

52.2

2 A woman told me to turn left after the bridge.
3 I advised him to go to the doctor.
4 She asked me to help her.
5 I told Tom to come back in ten minutes.
6 Paul let me use his phone.
7 I told her not to phone before 8 o'clock.
8 Ann's mother taught her to play the piano.

52.3

2 to repeat
3 wait
4 to arrive
5 to get
6 go
7 borrow
8 to tell
9 to make (*or* to get)
10 think

UNIT 53

53.1

2–4
I went to the café to meet a friend.
I went to the post office to get some stamps.
I went to the supermarket to buy some food.

53.2

2 to read the newspaper.
3 to open this door
4 to get some fresh air
5 to wake him up
6 to see who it was

53.3

Example answers:
2 to talk to you now.
3 to tell her about the party.
4 to do some shopping.
5 to buy a car.

53.4

2 to	7 to
3 to	8 to
4 for	9 for
5 to	10 to … for
6 for	

53.5

2 for the film to begin.
3 for it to arrive.
4 for you to tell me.

UNIT 54

54.1

3 to
4 to
5 – (*no preposition*)
6 for
7 to
8 on … to
9 for
10 on
11 to
12 – (*no preposition*)
13 on
14 for
15 on

54.2

2 went fishing.
3 goes swimming
4 going skiing.
5 go shopping.
6 went jogging

54.3

2 to the bank
3 shopping
4 to sleep
5 home
6 skiing
7 riding
8 for a walk
9 on holiday … to Portugal

UNIT 55

55.1

2 get your jacket
3 get a doctor
4 get a taxi
5 get the job
6 get some milk
7 get a ticket
8 gets a good salary

55.2

2 getting dark
3 getting married
4 getting ready
5 getting late

55.3

2 get wet
3 got married
4 get angry
5 got lost
6 get old
7 got better
8 get nervous

55.4

2 got to Bristol at 11.45.
3 I left the party at 11.15 and got home at midnight.
4 *(Example answer)* I left home at 8.30 and got to the airport at 10 o'clock.

55.5

2 got off
3 got out of
4 got on

UNIT 56

56.1

2 do
3 make
4 made
5 did
6 do
7 done
8 make
9 making
10 do
11 doing

56.2

2 They're/They are doing (their) homework.
3 He's/He is doing the shopping. *or* He is shopping.
4 She's/She is making a jacket.
5 They're/They are doing an exam/examination. (*or* … taking an exam.)
6 She's/She is doing exercises.
7 She's/She is making a phone-call. *or* She's/She is phoning somebody.
8 He's/He is making the/his bed.
9 She's/She is doing the washing-up. *or* She is washing up. / She is doing the dishes. / She is washing the dishes.
10 He's/He is making a (shopping) list.
11 They're/They are making a film.
12 He's/He is taking a photograph.

56.3

2 make
3 do
4 done
5 made
6 doing
7 did
8 do
9 making
10 made
11 make … do

UNIT 57

57.1

3 He hasn't got / He doesn't have
4 George had
5 Have you got / Do you have
6 we didn't have
7 She hasn't got / She doesn't have
8 Did you have

57.2

2 She's/She is having a cup of tea.
3 He's/He is having a rest.
4 They're/They are having a nice time.
5 They're/They are having dinner.
6 He's/He is having a bath.

57.3

2 Have a nice/good journey!
3 Did you have a nice/good weekend?
4 Did you have a nice/good game (of tennis)?
5 Have a nice/good meal!

57.4

2 have something to eat
3 had a glass of water
4 have a walk
5 had an accident
6 have a look

UNIT 58

58.1

2 him
3 them
4 her
5 him
6 them
7 her

58.2

2 I … them
3 he … her
4 they … us
5 we … him
6 she … them
7 they … me
8 she … you

58.3

2 I like him.
3 I don't like it.
4 Do you like it?
5 I don't like her.
6 Do you like them?

58.4

2 him
3 them
4 they
5 us
6 She
7 them
8 me
9 her
10 He … it

58.5

2 Can you give it to him?
3 Can you give them to her?
4 Can you give it to me?
5 Can you give it to them?
6 Can you give them to us?

UNIT 59

59.1
2 her hands
3 our hands
4 his hands
5 their hands
6 your hands

59.2
2 They live with their parents.
3 We live with our parents.
4 Julia lives with her parents.
5 I live with my parents.
6 John lives with his parents.
7 Do you live with your parents?
8 Most children live with their parents.

59.3
2 their
3 his
4 his
5 her
6 their
7 her
8 their

59.4
2 his
3 Their
4 our
5 her
6 my
7 your
8 her
9 their
10 my
11 Its
12 His ... his

59.5
2 my key
3 Her husband
4 your coat
5 their homework
6 his name
7 Our house

UNIT 60

60.1
2 mine
3 ours
4 hers
5 theirs
6 yours
7 mine
8 his

60.2
2 yours
3 my ... Mine
4 Yours ... mine
5 her
6 My ... hers
7 their
8 Ours

60.3
3 of hers
4 friends of ours
5 friend of mine
6 friend of his
7 friends of yours

60.4
2 Whose camera is this?
It's hers.
3 Whose gloves are these?
They're mine.
4 Whose hat is this?
It's his.
5 Whose money is this?
It's yours.
6 Whose books are these?
They're ours.

UNIT 61

61.1
2 Yes, I know her but I can't remember her name.
3 Yes, I know them but I can't remember their names.
4 Yes, I know you but I can't remember your name.

61.2
2 to stay with him at his house
3 to stay with them at their house
4 to stay with me at my house
5 to stay with her at her house
6 to stay with you at your house?

61.3
2 I gave her my address and she gave me hers.
3 He gave me his address and I gave him mine.
4 We gave them our address and they gave us theirs.
5 She gave him her address and he gave her his.
6 You gave us your address and we gave you ours.
7 They gave you their address and you gave them yours.

61.4
2 them
3 him
4 our
5 yours
6 us
7 her
8 their
9 mine

UNIT 62

62.1
2 myself
3 herself
4 themselves
5 myself
6 himself
7 yourself
8 yourselves

62.2
2 When I saw him, he was by himself.
3 Don't go out by yourself.
4 I went to the cinema by myself.
5 My sister lives by herself.
6 Many people live by themselves.

62.3
2 They can't see each other.
3 They often write to each other.
4 They don't know each other.
5 They're / They are sitting next to each other.
6 They gave each other presents/a present.

62.4
3 each other
4 yourselves
5 us
6 ourselves
7 each other
8 each other
9 them
10 themselves

UNIT 63

63.1
3 Mary is Brian's wife.
4 James is Julia's brother.
5 James is Daniel's uncle.
6 Julia is Paul's wife.
7 Mary is Daniel's grandmother.
8 Julia is James's sister.
9 Paul is Julia's husband.
10 Paul is Daniel's father.
11 Daniel is James's nephew.

63.2
2 Andy's
3 David's
4 Jane's
5 Diane's
6 Alice's

63.3
3 OK
4 Bill's phone number

5 My brother's job
6 OK
7 OK
8 Paula's favourite colour
9 your mother's birthday
10 My parents' house
11 OK
12 OK
13 Silvia's party
14 OK

UNIT 64

64.1

2 a
3 a
4 an
5 a
6 an
7 a
8 an
9 an

64.2

2 a vegetable
3 a game
4 a tool
5 a mountain
6 a planet
7 a fruit
8 a river
9 a flower
10 a musical instrument

64.3

2 He's a shop assistant.
3 She's a photographer.
4 She's a taxi driver.
5 He's an electrician.
6 She's a nurse.
7 He's a private detective.
8 I'm a/an …

64.4

2–8
Tom never wears **a** hat.
I can't ride **a** bicycle.
My brother is **an** artist.
Barbara works in **a** bookshop.
Ann wants to learn **a** foreign language.
Jim lives in **an** old house.
This evening I'm going to **a** party.

UNIT 65

65.1

2 boats
3 women
4 cities
5 umbrellas
6 addresses
7 knives
8 sandwiches
9 families
10 feet
11 holidays
12 potatoes

65.2

2 teeth
3 people
4 children
5 fish
6 leaves

65.3

3 … with a lot of beautiful tree**s**.
4 … with two **men**.
5 OK
6 … three child**ren**.
7 Most of my friends **are** student**s**.
8 He put on his pyjama**s** …
9 OK
10 Do you know many **people** …
11 I like your trousers. Where did you get **them**?
12 … full of tourist**s**.
13 OK
14 **These** scissors **aren't** …

65.4

2 are
3 don't
4 watch
5 were
6 live
7 Do
8 are
9 them
10 some

UNIT 66

66.1

3 a jug
4 milk
5 toothpaste
6 a toothbrush
7 an egg
8 money
9 a wallet
10 sand
11 a bucket
12 an envelope

66.2

3 … **a** hat.
4 … **a** job?
5 OK
6 … **an** apple …
7 … **a** party …
8 … **a** wonderful thing.
9 … **an** island.
10 … **a** key.
11 OK
12 … **a** good idea.
13 … **a** car?
14 … **a** cup of coffee?
15 OK
16 … **an** umbrella.

66.3

2 a piece of wood
3 a glass of water
4 a bar of chocolate
5 a cup of tea
6 a piece of paper
7 a bowl of soup
8 a loaf of bread
9 a jar of honey

UNIT 67

67.1

2 I bought a newspaper (*or* a paper), some flowers (*or* a bunch of flowers) and a pen.
3 I bought some stamps, some postcards and some bread (*or* a loaf of bread).
4 I bought some toothpaste, some soap (*or* a bar of soap) and a comb.

67.2

2 Would you like some coffee? (*or* … a cup of coffee?)
3 Would you like a biscuit?
4 Would you like some bread? (*or* … a piece of bread? / a slice of bread?)
5 Would you like a chocolate?
6 Would you like some chocolate? (*or* … a piece of chocolate?)

67.3

2 some … some
3 some
4 a … some
5 an … some
6 a … a … some
7 some
8 some
9 some … a

67.4

2 eyes
3 hair
4 information
5 chairs
6 furniture
7 job
8 lovely weather

UNIT 68

68.1

3 a
4 the
5 an
6 the … the
7 a … a
8 a … a
9 … **a** student … **a** journalist … **a** flat near **the** college … **The** flat is …
10 … two children, **a** boy and **a** girl. **The** boy is seven years old and **the** girl is three … in **a** factory … hasn't got **a** job …

68.2

2 **the** airport
3 **a** cup
4 **a** nice picture
5 **the** radio
6 **the** floor

68.3

2 … send me **a** postcard.
3 What is **the** name of …
4 … **a** very big country.
5 What is **the** largest …
6 … **the** colour of **the** carpet.
7 … **a** headache.
8 … **an** old house near **the** station.
9 … **the** name of **the** director of **the** film …

UNIT 69

69.1

3 … **the** second floor.
4 … **the** moon?
5 … **the** best hotel in this town?
6 OK
7 … **the** city centre.
8 … **the** end of May.
9 OK
10 … **the** first time I met her.
11 OK
12 What's **the** biggest city in **the** world?
13 OK
14 My dictionary is on **the** top shelf on **the** right.
15 We live in **the** country about five miles from **the** nearest village.

69.2

2 the same time
3 the same age
4 the same colour
5 the same problem

69.3

2 **the** guitar
3 breakfast
4 **the** radio
5 television/TV
6 **the** sea

69.4

2 **the** name
3 **The** sky
4 television
5 **the** police
6 **the** capital
7 lunch
8 **the** middle

UNIT 70

70.1

2 **the** cinema
3 hospital
4 **the** airport
5 home
6 prison

70.2

3 school
4 **the** station
5 home
6 bed
7 **the** post office

70.3

2 **the** cinema
3 go to bed
4 go to prison
5 go to **the** dentist
6 go to university/college
7 go to hospital / are taken to hospital

70.4

3 **the** doctor
4 OK
5 OK
6 OK
7 **the** bank
8 OK
9 OK
10 **the** city centre
11 **the** station
12 OK
13 OK
14 OK
15 **the** theatre

UNIT 71

71.1

Example answers:
2 I don't like dogs.
3 I don't mind museums.
4 I love big cities.
5 I like basketball.
6 I love TV quiz shows.
7 I don't like loud music.
8 I hate computer games.

71.2

Example answers:
2 I'm not interested in politics.
3 I'm interested in sport.
4 I don't know much about art.
5 I don't know anything about astronomy.
6 I know a little about economics.

71.3

3 friends
4 parties
5 **The** shops
6 **the** milk
7 milk
8 football
9 computers
10 **The** water
11 cold water
12 **the** salt
13 **the** people
14 Vegetables
15 **the** children
16 **the** words
17 photographs
18 **the** photographs
19 English … international business
20 Money … happiness

UNIT 72

72.1

3 Sweden
4 **The** Amazon
5 Asia
6 **The** Pacific

7 **The** Rhine
8 Kenya
9 **The** United States
10 **The** Andes
11 Tokyo
12 **The** Alps
13 **The** Red Sea
14 Malta
15 **The** Bahamas

72.2

3 OK
4 **the** Philippines
5 **the** south of France
6 **the** Regal Cinema
7 OK
8 **the** Museum of Modern Art
9 OK
10 Belgium is smaller than **the** Netherlands.
11 **the** Mississippi … **the** Nile
12 **the** National Gallery
13 **the** Park Hotel in Hudson Road
14 OK
15 **The** Rocky Mountains are in North America.
16 OK
17 **The** Panama Canal joins **the** Atlantic Ocean and **the** Pacific Ocean.
18 **the** United States
19 **the** west of Ireland
20 OK

UNIT 73

73.1

2 that house
3 these postcards
4 those birds
5 this seat
6 These plates

73.2

2 Is that your umbrella?
3 Is this your book?
4 Are those your books?
5 Is that your bicycle?
6 Are these your keys?
7 Are those your keys?
8 Is this your watch?
9 Are those your glasses?
10 Are these your gloves?

73.3

2 that's	6 this is
3 This is	7 That's
4 That's	8 that's
5 that	

UNIT 74

74.1

2 I don't need one.
3 I'm going to buy one.
4 I haven't got one.
5 I've just had one.
6 there's one in Mill Road.

74.2

2 a new one
3 a better one
4 an old one
5 a big one
6 a different one

74.3

2 Which ones?
The green ones.
3 Which one?
The one with a/the red door.
4 Which one?
The black one.
5 Which ones?
The ones on the wall.
6 Which ones?
The ones on the top shelf.
7 Which one?
The tall one with long hair.
8 Which ones?
The yellow ones.
9 Which one?
The one with a moustache and glasses.
10 Which ones?
The ones you took on the beach last week.

UNIT 75

75.1

2 some	8 some
3 any	9 some
4 any	10 any … any
5 any	11 some … any
6 some	12 some
7 any	

75.2

2 some letters
3 any photographs
4 any foreign languages
5 some friends
6 some milk
7 any batteries
8 some fresh air
9 some cheese
10 any help

75.3

3 I've got some / I have some
4 I haven't got any / I haven't any / I don't have any
5 I didn't buy any
6 I bought some

75.4

2 something
3 anything
4 anything
5 Somebody/Someone
6 anything
7 anybody/anyone
8 something
9 anything
10 anybody/anyone

UNIT 76

76.1

2 There are no shops near here.
3 Carol has got no free time.
4 There is no light in this room.
6 There isn't any tea in the pot.
7 There aren't any buses today.
8 Tom hasn't got any brothers or sisters.

76.2

2 any	8 no
3 any	9 any
4 no	10 no
5 any	11 None
6 no	12 any
7 any	

76.3

2 no money
3 any questions
4 no friends
5 no difference
6 any furniture
7 no answer

8 any heating
9 any photographs ... no film

76.4

Example answers:
2 Three.
3 Two cups.
4 None.
5 None.

UNIT 77

77.1

2 There's nobody in the office.
3 I've got nothing to do.
4 There's nothing on TV.
5 There was no-one at home.
6 We found nothing.

77.2

2 There wasn't anybody on the bus.
3 I haven't got anything to read.
4 I haven't got anyone to help me.
5 She didn't hear anything.
6 We haven't got anything for dinner.

77.3

3a Nothing.
4a Nobody./No-one.
5a Nobody./No-one.
6a Nothing.
7a Nothing.
8a Nobody./No-one.

3b I don't want anything.
4b I didn't meet anybody/anyone.
5b Nobody/No-one knows the answer.
6b I didn't buy anything.
7b Nothing happened.
8b Nobody/No-one was late.

77.4

3 anything
4 Nobody/No-one
5 Nothing
6 anything
7 anybody/anyone
8 nothing
9 anything
10 anything
11 nobody/no-one
12 anything
13 Nothing
14 Nobody/No-one ... anybody/anyone

UNIT 78

78.1

2 something
3 somewhere
4 somebody/someone

78.2

2a Nowhere.
3a Nothing.
4a Nobody./No-one.
2b I'm not going anywhere.
3b I don't want anything.
4b I'm not looking for anybody/anyone.

78.3

3 anything
4 anything
5 somebody/someone
6 something
7 anybody/anyone ... nobody/no-one
8 anything
9 Nobody/No-one
10 anybody/anyone
11 Nothing
12 anywhere
13 somewhere
14 anything
15 anybody/anyone

78.4

2 anything to eat
3 nothing to do
4 anywhere to sit
5 something to drink
6 nowhere to stay
7 something to read
8 somewhere to play

UNIT 79

79.1

2 Every day
3 every time
4 Every room
5 every word

79.2

2 every day
3 all day
4 every day
5 all day
6 every day
7 all day

79.3

2 every
3 all
4 all
5 Every
6 all
7 every
8 all
9 every

79.4

2 everything
3 Everybody/Everyone
4 everything
5 everywhere
6 Everybody/Everyone
7 everywhere
8 Everything

79.5

2 is
3 has
4 likes
5 has
6 was
7 makes

UNIT 80

80.1

3 Some
4 Most of
5 most
6 any of
7 all *or* all of
8 None of
9 any of
10 Most
11 most of
12 Some
13 All *or* All of
14 some of
15 most of

80.2

2 All of them.
3 Some of them.
4 None of them.
5 Most of them.
6 None of it.

80.3

3 Some people ...
4 Some of **the** questions ... *or* Some questions ...
5 OK
6 All insects ...
7 OK (*or* ... all **of** these books)
8 Most of **the** students ... *or* Most students ...
9 OK
10 ... most of **the** night

UNIT 81

81.1

3 Both	9 Neither
4 Neither	10 either of
5 Neither	11 Both
6 both	12 neither of
7 Either	13 Both
8 neither of	14 either of

81.2

2 Both windows are open.
3 Neither man is wearing a hat.
4 Both men have (got) cameras. *or* … are carrying cameras.
5 Both buses go to the airport. *or* … are going to the airport.
6 Neither answer is right.

81.3

3 Both of them are students.
4 Neither of them has (got) a car.
5 Both of them live in London.
6 Both of them like cooking.
7 Neither of them can play the piano.
8 Both of them read newspapers.
9 Neither of them is interested in sport.

UNIT 82

82.1

2 many	8 many
3 much	9 How many
4 many	10 How much
5 many	11 How much
6 much	12 How many
7 much	

82.2

2 much time
3 many countries
4 many people
5 much luggage
6 many times

82.3

2 a lot of interesting things
3 a lot of accidents
4 a lot of fun
5 a lot of traffic

82.4

3 a lot of snow
4 OK
5 a lot of money
6 OK
7 OK
8 a lot

82.5

3 She plays tennis a lot.
4 He doesn't use his car much. (*or* … a lot.)
5 He doesn't go out much. (*or* … a lot.)
6 She travels a lot.

UNIT 83

83.1

2 a few	5 a little
3 a little	6 a few
4 a few	

83.2

2 a little milk
3 A few days
4 a little Russian
5 a few friends
6 a few times
7 a few chairs
8 a little fresh air

83.3

2 very little coffee
3 very little rain
4 very few hotels
5 very little time
6 Very few people
7 very little work

83.4

2 A few	5 few
3 a little	6 a little
4 little	7 little

83.5

2 … a little luck
3 … a few things
4 OK
5 … a few questions
6 … few people

UNIT 84

84.1

2 I like that green jacket.
3 Do you like classical music?
4 I had a wonderful holiday.
5 We went to a Chinese restaurant.

84.2

2 black clouds
3 long holiday
4 hot water
5 fresh air
6 sharp knife
7 dangerous job

84.3

2 It looks new.
3 I feel ill.
4 You look surprised.
5 They smell nice.
6 It tastes horrible.

84.4

2 It doesn't look new.
3 You don't sound American.
4 I don't feel cold.
5 They don't look heavy.
6 It doesn't taste good.

UNIT 85

85.1

2 badly	5 fast
3 quietly	6 dangerously
4 angrily	

85.2

2 Come quickly
3 work hard
4 sleep well
5 win easily
6 Think carefully
7 know her very well
8 explain things very clearly/well

85.3

2 angry	7 suddenly
3 slowly	8 quiet
4 slow	9 badly
5 careful	10 nice *(See Unit 84.)*
6 hard	

85.4

2 well	5 well
3 good	6 good … good
4 well	

UNIT 86

86.1

2 bigger
3 slower
4 more expensive
5 higher
6 more dangerous

86.2

2 stronger
3 happier
4 more modern
5 more important
6 better
7 larger
8 more serious
9 prettier
10 more crowded

86.3

2 hotter/warmer
3 more expensive
4 worse
5 further
6 more difficult *or* harder

86.4

3 taller
4 harder
5 more comfortable
6 better
7 nicer
8 heavier
9 more interested
10 warmer
11 better
12 bigger
13 more beautiful
14 sharper
15 more polite

UNIT 87

87.1

3 Liz is taller than Ben.
4 Liz starts work earlier than Ben.
5 Ben works harder than Liz.
6 Ben has got more money than Liz.
7 Liz is a better driver than Ben.
8 Ben is more patient than Liz.
9 Ben is a better dancer than Liz. / Ben dances better than Liz.
10 Liz is more intelligent than Ben.
11 Liz speaks French better than Ben. / Liz speaks better French than Ben. / Liz's French is better than Ben's.
12 Ben goes to the cinema more than Liz. / … more often than Liz.

87.2

2 You're older than her. / … than she is.
3 You work harder than me. / … than I do.
4 You watch TV more than him. / … than he does.
5 You're a better cook than me. / … than I am. *or* You cook better than me. / … than I do.
6 You know more people than us. / … than we do.
7 You've got more money than them. / … than they have.
8 You can run faster than me. / … than I can.
9 You've been here longer than her. / … than she has.
10 You got up earlier than them. / … than they did.
11 You were more surprised than him. / … than he was.

87.3

2 Jack's mother is much younger than his father.
3 My camera cost a bit more than yours. / … than your camera. *or* My camera was a bit more expensive than …
4 I feel much better today than yesterday. / … than I did yesterday. / … than I felt yesterday.
5 It's a bit warmer today than yesterday. / … than it was yesterday.
6 Ann is a much better tennis player than me / than I am. *or* Ann is much better at tennis than me / than I am. *or* Ann plays tennis much better than me / than I do.

UNIT 88

88.1

2 A is longer than B but not as long as C.
3 C is heavier than A but not as heavy as B.
4 A is older than C but not as old as B.
5 B has got more money than C but not as much as A. *or* … but less (money) than A.
6 C works harder than A but not as hard as B.

88.2

2 Your room isn't as big as mine. / … as my room.
3 I didn't get up as early as you. / … as you did.
4 They didn't play as well as us. / … as we did.
5 You haven't been here as long as me. / … as I have.
6 He isn't as nervous as her. / … as she is.

88.3

2 as
3 than
4 than
5 as
6 than
7 as
8 than

88.4

2 Julia lives in the same street as Caroline.
3 Julia got up at the same time as Andrew.
4 Andrew's car is the same colour as Caroline's.

UNIT 89

89.1

2 C is longer than A.
D is the longest.
B is the shortest.
3 D is younger than C.
B is the youngest.
C is the oldest.
4 D is more expensive than A.
C is the most expensive.
A is the cheapest.
5 A is better than C.
A is the best.
D is the worst.

89.2

2 the happiest day
3 the best film
4 the most popular singer
5 the worst mistake
6 the prettiest village
7 the coldest day
8 the most boring person

89.3

2 Everest is the highest mountain in the world.
3–6
Alaska is the largest state in the USA.
Brazil is the largest country in South America.
Jupiter is the largest planet in the solar system.
The Nile is the longest river in Africa. / … in the world.

UNIT 90

90.1

2 enough chairs
3 enough paint
4 enough wind

90.2

2 The car isn't big enough.
3 His legs aren't long enough.
4 He isn't strong enough.

90.3

3 old enough
4 enough time
5 big enough
6 eat enough
7 enough fruit
8 tired enough
9 practise enough

90.4

2 sharp enough to cut
3 warm enough to have
4 enough bread to make
5 well enough to win
6 enough time to read

UNIT 91

91.1

2 too heavy
3 too low
4 too fast
5 too big
6 too crowded

91.2

3 enough
4 too many
5 too
6 enough
7 too much
8 enough
9 too
10 too many
11 too much

91.3

3 It's too far.
4 It's too expensive.
5 It isn't / It's not big enough.
6 It was too difficult.
7 It isn't good enough.
8 I'm too busy.
9 It was too long.

91.4

2 too early to go to bed.
3 too young to get married.
4 too dangerous to go out at night.
5 too late to phone Ann (now).
6 too surprised to say anything.

UNIT 92

92.1

3 I like this picture very much.
4 Tom started his new job last week.
5 OK
6 Jane bought a present for her friend. *or* Jane bought her friend a present.
7 I drink three cups of coffee every day.
8 OK
9 I borrowed fifty pounds from my brother.

92.2

2 I wrote two letters this morning.
3 Paul passed the exam easily.
4 Ann doesn't speak French very well.
5 I did a lot of work yesterday.
6 Do you know London well?
7 We enjoyed the party very much.
8 I explained the problem carefully.
9 We met some friends at the airport.
10 Did you buy that jacket in England?
11 We do the same thing every day.
12 I don't like football very much.

92.3

2 I arrived at the hotel early.
3 Julia goes to Italy every year.
4 We have lived here since 1988.
5 Sue was born in London in 1960.
6 Paul didn't go to work yesterday.
7 Ann went to the bank yesterday afternoon.
8 I had my breakfast in bed this morning.
9 Barbara is going to university in October.
10 I saw a beautiful bird in the garden this morning.
11 My parents have been to the United States many times.
12 I left my umbrella in the restaurant last night.
13 Are you going to the cinema tomorrow evening?
14 I took the children to school this morning.

UNIT 93

93.1

2 He always gets up early.
3 He's / He is never late for work.
4 He sometimes gets angry.
5 He often goes swimming.
6 He's / He is usually at home in the evenings.

93.2

2 Susan is always polite.
3 I usually finish work at 5 o'clock.
4 Jill has just started a new job.
5 I rarely go to bed before midnight.
6 The bus isn't usually late.
7 I don't often eat fish.
8 I will never forget what you said.
9 Have you ever lost your passport?
10 Do you still work in the same place?

11 They always stay in the same hotel.
12 Diane doesn't usually work on Saturdays.
13 Is Tina already here?
14 What do you usually have for breakfast?
15 I can never remember his name.

93.3

2 Yes, and I also speak French.
3 Yes, and I'm also hungry.
4 Yes, and I've also been to Ireland.
5 Yes, and I also bought some books.

93.4

1 They both play football.
They're/They are both students.
They've both got cars./They both have cars.
2 They are/They're all married.
They were all born in England.
They all live in New York.

UNIT 94

94.1

2 Do you still live in Clare Street?
3 Are you still a student?
4 Have you still got a motor-bike? / Do you still have ...
5 Do you still go to the cinema a lot?
6 Do you still want to be a teacher?

94.2

2 He was looking for a job.
He's/He is still looking (for a job).
He hasn't found a job yet.
3 She was asleep/sleeping. *or* She was in bed.
She's/She is still asleep/sleeping. *or* ... still in bed.
She hasn't woken up yet. / She hasn't got up yet. / She isn't awake yet. / She isn't up yet.
4 They were having dinner. / They were eating.
They're / They are still having dinner. / ... still eating.
They haven't finished (dinner) yet. / They haven't finished eating yet.

94.3

2 Is Ann here yet? *or* Has Ann arrived/come yet?
3 Have you got your (exam) results yet? / Have you had your... / Have you received your...
4 Have you decided where to go yet? / Do you know where you're going yet?

94.4

3 She's/She has already gone/left.
4 I've already got one. / I already have one.
5 I've/I have already paid (it).
6 he already knows.

UNIT 95

95.1

2 He gave it to Gary.
3 He gave them to Sarah.
4 He gave it to his sister.
5 He gave them to Robert.
6 He gave it to a neighbour.

95.2

2 I gave Joanna a plant.
3 I gave Richard some gloves / a pair of gloves.
4 I gave Diane some chocolates / a box of chocolates.
5 I gave Rachel some flowers / a bunch of flowers.
6 I gave Kevin a pen.

95.3

2 Can you lend me an umbrella?
3 Can you give me your address?
4 Can you lend me ten pounds?
5 Can you send me some information?
6 Can you show me the letter?
7 Can you get me some stamps?

95.4

2 lend you some money
3 send the letter to me
4 buy you a present
5 pass me the sugar
6 give it to her
7 the policeman my identity card

UNIT 96

96.1

3 at	11 at
4 on	12 in
5 in	13 on
6 in	14 on
7 on	15 at
8 on	16 at
9 at	17 at
10 on	18 in

96.2

2 on	11 at
3 at	12 on
4 in	13 in
5 in	14 at
6 in	15 in
7 on	16 on
8 on	17 in
9 in	18 at
10 at	19 at

96.3

2 on Friday
3 on Monday
4 at 4 o'clock on Thursday / on Thursday at 4 o'clock
5 on Saturday evening
6 at 2.30 on Tuesday (afternoon) / on Tuesday (afternoon) at 2.30

96.4

2 I'll phone you in three days.
3 My exam is in two weeks.
4 Tom will be here in half an hour. / ... in 30 minutes.

96.5

3 in
4 – *(no preposition)*
5 – *(no preposition)*
6 in
7 at
8 – *(no preposition)*
9 – *(no preposition)*
10 on
11 in
12 at

UNIT 97

97.1

2 Alex lived in Canada **until** 1990.
3 Alex has lived in England **since** 1990.
4 Alice lived in France **until** 1991.
5 Alice has lived in Switzerland **since** 1991.
6 Carol worked in a hotel **from** 1990 **to** 1993.
7 Carol has worked in a restaurant **since** 1993.
8 Gerry was a teacher **from** 1983 **to** 1989.
9 Gerry has been a salesman **since** 1989.
11 Alex has lived in England for ...... years.
12 Alice has lived in Switzerland for ...... years.
13 Carol worked in a hotel for three years.
14 Carol has worked in a restaurant for ...... years.
15 Gerry was a teacher for six years.
16 Gerry has been a salesman for ...... years.

97.2

2 until
3 for
4 since
5 Until
6 for
7 for
8 until
9 since
10 until
11 for
12 until
13 Since
14 for

UNIT 98

98.1

2 after lunch
3 before the end
4 during the course
5 before they went to Australia
6 during the night
7 while you are waiting
8 after the concert

98.2

3 while
4 for
5 while
6 during
7 while
8 for
9 during
10 while

98.3

2 eating
3 answering
4 having/taking
5 finishing/doing
6 going/travelling

98.4

2 John worked in a bookshop for two years after leaving school.
3 Before going to sleep, I read a few pages of my book.
4 After walking for three hours, we were very tired.
5 Let's have a cup of coffee before going out.

UNIT 99

99.1

2 **In** the box.
3 **On** the box.
4 **On** the wall.
5 **At** the bus stop.
6 **In** the field.
7 **On** the balcony.
8 **In** the pool.
9 **At** the window.
10 **On** the ceiling.
11 **On** the table.
12 **At** the table.

99.2

2 in
3 on
4 in
5 on
6 at
7 in
8 in
9 at
10 at
11 in
12 at
13 on
14 at
15 **on** the wall **in** the living room

UNIT 100

100.1

2 **At** the airport.
3 **In** bed.
4 **On** a ship.
5 **In** the sky.
6 **At** a party.
7 **At** the doctor's.
8 **On** the second floor.
9 **At** work.
10 **On** a plane.
11 **In** a taxi.
12 **At** a wedding.

100.2

2 in
3 in
4 at
5 at
6 in
7 at
8 at
9 in
10 in
11 on
12 on
13 at
14 in
15 on

UNIT 101

101.1

2 to
3 in
4 to
5 in
6 to
7 to
8 in

101.2

3 to
4 to
5 **at home ... to work**
6 at
7 – *(no preposition)*
8 to
9 at
10 **at a restaurant ... to the hotel**

101.3

2 to
3 to
4 in
5 to
6 to
7 at
8 to
9 to
10 at
11 at
12 **to Mary's house ... at home**
13 – *(no preposition)*
14 study **at** ... go **to**

101.4
1 to
2 – *(no preposition)*
3 at
4 in
5 to
6 – *(no preposition)*

101.5
Example answers:
2 to work.
3 at work.
4 to Canada.
5 to parties.
6 at a friend's house.

UNIT 102

102.1
2 next to / beside / by
3 in front of
4 between
5 next to / beside / by
6 in front of
7 behind
8 **on the left**
9 **in the middle**

102.2
2 behind
3 above
4 in front of
5 on
6 by / next to / beside
7 below / under
8 above
9 under
10 by / next to / beside
11 opposite
12 on

102.3
2 The fountain is in front of the theatre.
3 The bank/bookshop is opposite the theatre. *or* Paul's office is opposite the theatre. *or* The theatre is opposite ...
4 The bank/bookshop/supermarket is next to ...
5 Paul's office is above the bookshop.
6 The bookshop is between the bank and the supermarket.

UNIT 103

103.1
2 Go under the bridge.
3 Go up the hill.
4 Go down the steps.
5 Go along this street.
6 Go into the hotel.
7 Go past the hotel.
8 Go out of the hotel.
9 Go over the bridge.
10 Go through the park.

103.2
2 off
3 over
4 out of
5 across
6 round/around
7 through
8 on
9 round/around
10 **into** the house **through** a window

103.3
1 out of
2 round/around
3 in
4 **from** here **to** the airport
5 round/around
6 on/over
7 over
8 out of

UNIT 104

104.1
2 on time
3 on holiday
4 on the phone
5 on television

104.2
2 by
3 with
4 about
5 on
6 by
7 at
8 on
9 with
10 **about** grammar **by** Vera P. Bull

104.3
1 with
2 without
3 by
4 about
5 at
6 by
7 on
8 with
9 at
10 by
11 about
12 by
13 on
14 with
15 by
16 by

UNIT 105

105.1
2 in
3 to
4 at
5 with
6 of

105.2
2 at
3 to
4 about
5 of
6 of
7 from
8 in
9 of
10 about
11 of
12 **for** getting angry **with** you

105.3
2 interested in going
3 good at getting
4 fed up with waiting
5 sorry for waking

105.4
2 Sue walked past me without speaking.
3 Don't do anything without asking me first.
4 I went out without locking the door.

105.5
Example answers:
2 I'm afraid of the dark.
3 I'm not very good at drawing.
4 I'm not interested in cars.
5 I'm fed up with living in London.

UNIT 106

106.1
2 to
3 for
4 to
5 at
6 for

106.2
2 to
3 to
4 for
5 to
6 of/about
7 for
8 on
9 to
10 for
11 to
12 – *(no preposition)*
13 to
14 on
15 of/about

106.3
1 at
2 after
3 for
4 after
5 at
6 for

106.4
Example answers:
3 It depends on the programme.
4 It depends (on) what it is.
5 It depends on the weather.
6 It depends (on) how much you want.

UNIT 107

107.1
2 went in
3 looked up
4 rode off
5 turned round/around *or* looked round/around
6 got off
7 sat down
8 got out

107.2
2 away/out
3 round/around
4 going **out** … be **back**
5 down
6 over
7 back
8 in
9 up
10 going **away** … coming **back**

107.3
2 Hold on
3 slowed down
4 takes off
5 get on
6 speak up
7 broken down
8 fall over / fall down
9 carried on
10 gave up

UNIT 108

108.1
2 She took off her hat. *or* She took her hat off.
3 He put down his bag. *or* He put his bag down.
4 She picked up the magazine. *or* She picked the magazine up.
5 He put on his sunglasses. *or* He put his sunglasses on.
6 She turned off the tap. *or* She turned the tap off.

108.2
2 He put his jacket on. He put it on.
3 She took off her glasses. She took them off.
4 Put your pens down. Put them down.
5 They gave the money back. They gave it back.
6 I turned off the lights. I turned them off.

108.3
2 take it back
3 picked them up
4 switched it off
5 bring them back

108.4
3 I knocked over a glass / I knocked a glass over
4 look it up
5 throw them away
6 fill it in
7 tried on a pair of shoes / tried a pair of shoes on
8 showed me round (*or* around)
9 gave it up *or* gave up (*without* it)
10 put out your cigarette / put your cigarette out

UNIT 109

109.1
3 I went to the window and (I) looked out.
4 I wanted to phone you but I didn't have your number.
5 I jumped into the river and (I) swam to the other side.
6 I usually drive to work but I went by bus this morning.
7 Do you want me to come with you or shall I wait here?

109.2
Example answers:
2 because it was raining. / because the weather was bad.
3 but it was closed.
4 so he didn't eat anything. / so he didn't want anything to eat.
5 because there was a lot of traffic. / because the traffic was bad.
6 Sue said goodbye, got into her car and drove off/away.

109.3
Example answers:
3 I went to the cinema **but** the film wasn't very good.
4 I went to a café **and** met some friends of mine.
5 There was a film on television, **so** I watched it.
6 I got up in the middle of the night **because** I couldn't sleep.

UNIT 110

110.1
2 When I'm tired, I like to watch TV.
3 When I phoned her, there was no answer.
4 When I go on holiday, I always go to the same place.
5 When the programme ended, I switched off the TV.
6 When I arrived at the hotel, there were no rooms.

110.2

2 when they heard the news
3 they went to live in New Zealand
4 while they were away
5 before they came here
6 somebody broke into the house
7 they didn't believe me

110.3

2 I finish
3 it's
4 I'll be … she leaves
5 stops
6 We'll come … we're
7 I come … I'll bring
8 I'm
9 I'll give … I go

110.4

Example answers:
2 you finish your work?
3 I'll write some letters.
4 you get ready.
5 I won't have much free time.
6 I come back?

UNIT 111

111.1

2 If you pass the exam, you'll get a certificate.
3 If you fail the exam, you can do it again.
4 If you don't want this magazine, I'll throw it away.
5 If you want those pictures, you can have them.
6 If you're busy now, we can talk later.
7 If you're hungry, we can have lunch now.
8 If you need money, I can lend you some.

111.2

2 I give
3 is
4 I'll phone
5 I'll be … get
6 Will you go … they invite

111.3

Example answers:
3 … the water is dirty.
4 … you'll feel better in the morning.
5 … you're not watching it.
6 … she doesn't study.
7 … I'll go and see Chris.
8 … the weather is good.

111.4

2 When
3 If
4 If
5 if
6 When
7 if
8 when … if

UNIT 112

112.1

3 wanted
4 had
5 was/were
6 didn't enjoy
7 could
8 spoke
9 didn't have

112.2

3 I'd go / I would go
4 she knew
5 we had
6 you won
7 I wouldn't stay
8 we lived
9 It would be
10 the salary was/were
11 I wouldn't know
12 would you change

112.3

2 I'd watch it / I would watch it
3 we had some pictures on the wall
4 the air would be cleaner
5 every day was/were the same
6 I'd be bored / I would be bored
7 we had a bigger house / we bought a bigger house
8 we would/could buy a bigger house

112.4

Example answers:
2 I'd go to Antarctica
3 I didn't have any friends
4 I had enough money
5 I'd call the police
6 there were no guns

UNIT 113

113.1

2 A butcher is a person who sells meat.
3 A musician is a person who plays a musical instrument.
4 A patient is a person who is ill in hospital.
5 A dentist is a person who looks after your teeth.
6 A fool is a person who is very stupid.
7 A genius is a person who is very intelligent.
8 A liar is a person who doesn't tell the truth.

113.2

2 The woman who opened the door was wearing a yellow dress.
3 Most of the students who took the exam passed (it).
4 The policeman who stopped our car wasn't very friendly.

113.3

2 who
3 which
4 which
5 who
6 which
7 who
8 who
9 which

that *is also correct in all these sentences.*

113.4

3 … a machine **that/which** makes coffee.
4 OK (**which** *is also correct*)
5 … people **who/that** never stop talking.
6 OK (**who** *is also correct*)
7 OK (**that** *is also correct*)
8 … the sentences **that/which** are wrong.

UNIT 114

114.1

2 I've lost the pen you gave me.
3 I like the jacket Sue is wearing.
4 Where are the flowers I gave you?
5 I didn't believe the story he told us.
6 How much were the oranges you bought?

114.2

2 The meal you cooked was excellent.
3 The shoes I'm wearing aren't very comfortable.
4 The people we invited to dinner didn't come.

114.3

2 Who are the people you spoke to?
3 Did you find the keys you were looking for?
4 The house they live in is too small for them.
5 The map I looked at wasn't very clear.
6 I fell off the chair I was sitting on.
7 The bus we were waiting for was very late.
8 Who is the man Linda is dancing with?

114.4

2 What's the name of the restaurant where you had dinner?
3 Do you like the village where you live?
4 How big is the factory where you work?

Key to Additional exercises

1

3 Kate is a doctor.
4 The children are asleep.
5 Bill isn't hungry.
6 The books aren't on the table.
7 The hotel is near the station.
8 The bus isn't full.

2

3 she's/she is
4 Where are
5 Is he
6 It's/It is
7 I'm/I am *or*
No, I'm not. I'm a student.
8 What colour is
9 Is it
10 Are you
11 How much are

3

3 He's/He is having a bath.
4 Are the children playing?
5 Is it raining?
6 They're/They are coming now.
7 Why are you standing here?
I'm/I am waiting for somebody.

4

4 Chris doesn't want
5 Do you want
6 Does Ann live
7 Sarah knows
8 I don't travel
9 do you usually get up
10 They don't go out
11 Tim always finishes
12 does Jill do … She works

5

3 She's/She is a student.
4 She hasn't got a car.
5 She goes out a lot.
6 She's got / She has got a lot of friends.
7 She doesn't like London.
8 She likes dancing.
9 She isn't / She's not interested in sport.

6

1 Are you married?
Where do you live?
Have you got / Do you have any children?
How old is she?
2 How old are you?
What do you do? / Where do you work? / What's your job?
Do you like/enjoy your job?
Have you got / Do you have a car?
Do you (usually) go to work by car?
3 What's his name? / What's he called?
What does he do? / What's his job?
Does he live/work in London?

7

4 Sonia is 32 years old.
5 I've got / I have two sisters.
6 We often watch TV in the evening.
7 Ann never wears a hat.
8 A bicycle has got two wheels.
9 These flowers are beautiful.
10 Mary speaks German very well.

8

3 are you cooking?
4 plays
5 I'm going
6 It's raining
7 I don't watch
8 we're looking
9 do you pronounce

9

2 we go
3 is shining
4 are you going
5 do you go
6 She writes
7 I never read
8 They're watching
9 She's talking
10 do you usually have
11 He's visiting
12 I don't drink

10

2 went
3 found
4 was
5 had
6 told
7 gave
8 were
9 thought
10 invited

11

3 He was good at sport.
4 He played football.
5 He didn't work hard at school.
6 He had a lot of friends.
7 He didn't have a bicycle.
8 He wasn't a quiet child.

12

3 How long were you there? / How long did you stay there?
4 Did you like/enjoy Amsterdam?
5 Where did you stay?
6 Was the weather good?
7 When did you get/come back?

13

3 I forgot
4 did you get
5 I didn't speak
6 Did you have
7 he didn't go
8 she arrived
9 did Robert live
10 The meal didn't cost

14

2 were working
3 opened
4 rang … was cooking
5 heard … looked
6 was looking … happened
7 wasn't reading … was watching
8 didn't read
9 finished … paid … left
10 saw … was walking … was waiting

15

3 is playing
4 gave
5 doesn't like
6 did your parents go
7 saw … was driving
8 Do you watch
9 were you doing
10 goes
11 'm/am trying
12 didn't sleep

16

3 it's/it has just finished/ended.
4 I've/I have found them.
5 I haven't read it.
6 Have you seen her?
7 I've/I have had enough.
8 Have you (ever) been to Sweden?
9 We've/We have (just) been to the cinema.
10 They've/They have gone to a party.
11 He's/He has just woken up.
12 How long have you lived here? *or* … have you been living here?
13 We've/We have known each other for a long time.
14 It's/It has been raining all day. *or* It has rained all day. *or* It has been horrible/bad all day.

17

3 has been
4 for
5 since
6 has he lived / has he been / has he been living
7 for
8 have been

18

Example answers:
3 I've just started this exercise.
4 I've met Julia a few times.
5 I haven't had dinner yet.
6 I've never been to Australia.
7 I've lived here since I was born.
8 I've lived here for three years.

19

3 bought
4 went
5 've/have read *or* 've/have finished with
6 haven't started (it) *or* haven't begun
7 was
8 didn't see
9 left
10 's/has been
11 was

20

3 He's/He has already gone.
4 she went at 4 o'clock.
5 How many times have you been there?
6 I haven't decided yet.
7 It was on the table last night.
8 I've just eaten.
9 What time did they arrive?

21

1 When was the last time? *or* When did you go the last time?
2 How long have you had it? I bought it yesterday.
3 How long have you lived / have you been / have you been living there? Before that we lived in Mill Road. How long did you live in Mill Road?
4 How long have you worked / have you been working there? What did you do before that? I was a taxi driver. *or* I worked as a taxi driver.

22

Example answers:
2 I didn't go out last night.
3 I was at work yesterday afternoon.
4 I went to a party a few days ago.
5 It was my birthday last week.
6 I went to America last year.

23

2 B
3 D
4 A
5 A
6 D
7 C
8 B
9 C
10 D
11 A
12 C
13 B
14 C
15 A

24

1 was damaged … be knocked down
2 was built … is used … is being painted
3 is called … be called … was changed
4 have been made … are produced

25

2 is visited
3 were damaged
4 be built
5 is being cleaned
6 be forgotten
7 has already been done
8 be kept
9 Have you ever been bitten
10 was stolen

26

2 My car was stolen last week.
3 You're/You are wanted on the phone.
4 The bananas have been eaten.
5 The machine will be repaired.
6 We're/We are being watched.
7 The food has to be bought.

27

3 pushed
4 was pushed
5 has taken
6 is being repaired
7 invented
8 was the camera invented
9 did they send / have they sent
10 be sent

28

2 B
3 A
4 C
5 B
6 C
7 C
8 B
9 B
10 A
11 B
12 C

29

1 I stayed
did you do
I watched
Are you going
I'm going
are you going to see
I don't know. I haven't decided
2 have you been
We arrived
are you staying / are you going to stay
do you like
we're having
3 I've just remembered – Jill phoned
She always phones … Did she leav
she wants
I'll phone … Do you know
I'll get
4 I'm going … Do you want
are you going
Have you ever eaten
I've been … I went
5 I've lost … Have you seen
You were wearing … I came
I'm not wearing
Have you looked / Did you look
I'll go

30

2 A
3 B
4 C
5 B
6 C
7 B
8 A
9 C
10 A
11 B
12 A
13 C
14 B
15 C
16 A
17 C
18 B

31

2 a car
3 the fridge
4 a teacher
5 school
6 the cinema
7 a taxi
8 the piano
9 computers
10 the same

32

4 **a** horse
5 **The** sky
6 **a** tourist
7 for lunch (-)
8 **the** first President of **the** United States
9 **a** watch
10 remember names (-)
11 **the** next train
12 writes letters (-)
13 **the** garden
14 **the** Majestic Hotel
15 ill last week (-) … to work (-)
16 **the** highest mountain in **the** world
17 to **the** radio … having breakfast (-)
18 like sport (-) … is basketball (-)
19 **a** doctor … **an** art teacher
20 **the** second floor … **the** top of **the** stairs … on **the** right
21 After dinner (-) … watched television (-)
22 **a** wonderful holiday in **the** south of France (-)

33

2 in
3 on
4 at
5 on
6 in
7 since
8 on
9 by
10 in
11 for
12 at
13 at
14 in
15 at
16 on
17 by
18 for … on
19 to … in
20 at … in

Index

The numbers are unit numbers (not page numbers).

The numbers are unit numbers (not page numbers).

The numbers are unit numbers (not page numbers)

The numbers are unit numbers (not page numbers).

The numbers are unit numbers (not page numbers).